T0261253

RESEARCH HANDBOOK ON PUBLIC MANAGEMENT AND ARTIFICIAL INTELLIGENCE

ELGAR HANDBOOKS IN PUBLIC ADMINISTRATION AND MANAGEMENT

This series provides a comprehensive overview of recent research in all matters relating to public administration and management, serving as a definitive guide to the field. Covering a wide range of research areas including national and international methods of public administration, theories of public administration and management, and technological developments in public administration and management, the series produces influential works of lasting significance. Each *Handbook* will consist of original contributions by preeminent authors, selected by an esteemed editor internationally recognized as a leading scholar within the field. Taking an international approach, these *Handbooks* serve as an essential reference point for all students of public administration and management, emphasizing both the expansion of current debates, and an indication of the likely research agendas for the future.

For a full list of Edward Elgar published titles, including the titles in this series, visit our website at www.e-elgar.com.

Research Handbook on Public Management and Artificial Intelligence

Edited by

Yannis Charalabidis

Professor of Digital Governance, Department of Information and Communication Systems Engineering, University of the Aegean, Greece

Rony Medaglia

Professor with special responsibilities in Digitalization and the UN Sustainable Development Goals, Department of Digitalization, Copenhagen Business School, Denmark

Colin van Noordt

PhD Researcher, Ragnar Nurkse Department of Innovation and Governance, Tallinn TalTech, Estonia

ELGAR HANDBOOKS IN PUBLIC ADMINISTRATION AND MANAGEMENT

Edward Elgar
PUBLISHING

Cheltenham, UK • Northampton, MA, USA

© Yannis Charalabidis, Rony Medaglia and Colin van Noordt 2024
Chapter 12 © European Union
Cover image: Michael Dziedzic on Unsplash.

With the exception of any material published open access under a Creative Commons
licence (see www.elgaronline.com), all rights are reserved and no part of this publication
may be reproduced, stored in a retrieval system or transmitted in any form or by any means,
electronic, mechanical or photocopying, recording, or otherwise without the prior permission
of the publisher.

Chapter 12 is available for free as Open Access from the individual product page at www.
elgaronline.com under a Creative Commons Attribution NonCommercial-NoDerivatives 4.0
International (https://creativecommons.org/licenses/by-nc-nd/4.0/) license.

Published by
Edward Elgar Publishing Limited
The Lypiatts
15 Lansdown Road
Cheltenham
Glos GL50 2JA
UK

Edward Elgar Publishing, Inc.
William Pratt House
9 Dewey Court
Northampton
Massachusetts 01060
USA

A catalogue record for this book
is available from the British Library

Library of Congress Control Number: 2023951222

This book is available electronically in the **Elgar**online
Political Science and Public Policy subject collection
http://dx.doi.org/10.4337/9781802207347

MIX
Paper | Supporting
responsible forestry
FSC
www.fsc.org   FSC® C013604

ISBN 978 1 80220 733 0 (cased)
ISBN 978 1 80220 734 7 (eBook)

Printed and bound by CPI Group (UK) Ltd, Croydon, CR0 4YY

Contents

Advisory board and reviewers

EDITORIAL ADVISORY BOARD

Naomi Aoki, University of Tokyo, Japan
J. Ramon Gil-Garcia, University at Albany, State University of New York, USA
Marko Grobelnik, Josef Stefan Institute, Slovenia
Atreyi Kankanhalli, National University of Singapore, Singapore
Robert Krimmer, Tartu, Estonia
Ines Mergel, University of Konstanz, Germany
Gianluca Misuraca, Universidad Politecnica de Madrid, Spain
Panos Panagiotopoulos, Queen Mary University of London, United Kingdom
Dimitris Sarantis, United Nations University, Portugal

ADDITIONAL REVIEWERS

Agneta Ranerup, University of Gothenburg, Sweden
Aleksandrs Cepilovs, eu-Lisa, Estonia
Joep Crompvoets, KU Leuven, Belgium

Contributors

EDITORS

Yannis Charalabidis is a Professor of Digital Governance at the Department of Information and Communication Systems Engineering, University of the Aegean, based in Samos, Greece. He is the founding director of the Digital Governance Research Centre, coordinating policy making, research and application projects for governments and enterprises worldwide. He is heading the MSc on Digital Innovation and Entrepreneurship, in collaboration with the National Technical University of Athens. He has more than 25 years of experience in designing, implementing and managing complex information systems, 10 of which as general manager in SingularLogic Group, leading company expansion in Greece and Europe. He has published more than 10 books and 300 papers in international journals and conferences, and actively participates in international scientific and policy making bodies. Yannis has been teaching as an invited professor at UC Berkeley, TU Delft, Stevens Institute NY, State University NY, University of Washington, City University Hong Kong, Swinburne University Melbourne and Wollongong University in Australia. In 2018, he was included in the '100 most influential people in Digital Government', by Apolitical Group. In 2022, he was ranked as the 6th most prolific author in Digital Government, among 10,000 authors of the domain, by the Washington University survey.

Rony Medaglia is a Professor with Special Responsibilities on Digitalisation and the UN Sustainable Development Goals at the Copenhagen Business School, Department of Digitalization, in Denmark. His research focuses on digitalisation in the public sector, from the perspectives of digital service provision, citizen engagement and sustainability. His research is published in international journals such as *Government Information Quarterly*, the *Journal of Information Technology*, the *Information Systems Journal*, and the *International Journal of Information Management*, and he has received the Danish Society for Education and Business (DSEB) Education Award (2019) for his teaching of digitalisation. He is currently the President of the Special Interest Group on e-Government of the Association for Information Systems (AIS) and has conducted research and teaching on government digitalisation in a global context, including numerous bi-lateral research collaborations with universities in China, funded by the Sino-Danish Center for Education and Research (SDC), and is working as an expert for the European Commission.

Colin van Noordt recently completed his PhD at the Ragnar Nurkse Department of Innovation and Governance at Tallinn University of Technology (TalTech), in Estonia. His thesis focuses on the public value created using Artificial Intelligence technologies within public services and the requirements to do so effectively. In combination with doing his PhD, Colin was working as an External Expert for the AI Watch team of the European Commission, contributing to the research activities on the use of AI within public services. Since September 2023, Colin took a position at the Dutch Court of Audit as a Researcher to research and audit the use of algorithms and cloud services within the Dutch government. Before, he was Program Director for AI at Digital Nation where he led the AI strategy activities and advising on AI capacity building, involvement in several activities regarding the AI4GOV Master, the Dutch government, UNESCO and the European Commission. In addition, Colin was Research Assistant to the InTouch.AI.EU project which aims to promote the EU vision on sustainable and trustworthy AI internationally. Colin graduated magna cum laude the Master of Science in Public Sector Innovation and eGovernance from the Erasmus Mundus joint programme organised by the University of Leuven, the University of Münster and TalTech. Before he earned a bachelor's in public administration from the University of Leiden.

CONTRIBUTORS

Dr. Patricia Gomes Rêgo de Almeida is Coordinator of Innovation and Digital Strategy at the Brazilian Chamber of Deputies. She has a Masters degree in Electrical Engineering from the Federal University of Rio Grande do Norte and a PhD in Business Administration from the University of Brasilia, where she researched Artificial Intelligence governance and regulation. She has been involved in many projects related to Artificial Intelligence governance, digital transformation and the digital parliament. Patricia also coordinates the innovation hub on open data of the Inter-Parliamentary Union.

Naomi Aoki (PhD, Public Administration) is an academic specialising in public administration and management. She is currently an Associate Professor in the Graduate School of Public Policy at the University of Tokyo, Japan, and was formerly an Assistant Professor at the National University of Singapore. One of her research interests is examining the societal implications of the use of Artificial Intelligence in the public sector.

Matthias Döring is Associate Professor in Public Administration at the Department of Political Science and Public Management at the University of Southern Denmark. His research focuses on citizen-state interactions, street-level bureaucracy, service management, and digitalisation.

David Duenas-Cid is an Associate Professor at Kozminski University (Poland). Awarded with a Marie Skłodowska-Curie Widening Fellowship (2022–23), his recent research is related to the development of trust and distrust in the implementation of internet voting. He serves as a General Chair at the E-Vote-ID conference, President of the Thematic Group in Digital Sociology at the International Sociological Association, and Program Chair at the Annual International Conference on Digital Government Research (2023 and 2024).

Ouh Eng Lieh obtained his PhD in Computer Science (Software Engineering) from the National University of Singapore. He was involved in several large-scale information technology industry projects for a decade at international software companies before joining academia as an educator. His research areas are software reuse, software architecture design, design thinking and software analytics.

Dr. Fotios Fitsilis is a parliamentary practitioner and researcher focusing on e-governance. He has been working in the Hellenic Parliament since 2007, where he heads the Department of Scientific Documentation and Supervision in the Scientific Service. In 2017, he co-founded the Hellenic OCR Team, a scientific initiative for the processing and analysis of parliamentary institutions and their data. Fotios has authored dozens of popular science essays on the interface of science and technology with society and over 50 scientific publications, including five books.

Sarah Giest is a Professor of Public Policy with a focus on Innovation and Sustainability at the Institute of Public Administration, Leiden University. In the larger context of government innovation, her research focuses on the adoption of data- and AI-driven technologies in public sector institutions and their effect on decision-making. In the past, Sarah has collaborated with Dutch local and national governments as well as supervised PhDs on this topic.

J. Ramon Gil-Garcia is a Full Professor of Public Administration and Policy and the Director of the Center for Technology in Government, University at Albany, State University of New York (SUNY). Currently, he is also a professor at the Business School at Universidad de las Américas Puebla in Mexico. Dr. Gil-Garcia is the author or co-author of articles in prestigious international journals in Public Administration, Information Systems, and Digital Government and some of his publications are among the most cited in the field of digital government research worldwide.

Antti Hahto has worked both in research and industry, establishing new data science business and practical utilisation of AI technologies. He has specialised in several Big Science projects, such as ITER fusion power plant and particle accelerators. He worked as a tech lead in Finland's national Artificial Intelligence program and is currently data analytics lead for Finland's largest private employer.

Gerhard Hammerschmid is Professor of Public and Financial Management and Director of the Centre for Digital Governance at the Hertie School in Berlin. His research focuses on public management reform, comparative public administration, public sector performance management and how digitalisation is affecting government. He contributed to various EU-funded research projects on public sector innovation and digital government transformation and his research has been published in journals such as *PAR*, *GIQ*, *Public Administration*, *Governance* and *IRAS*.

Teresa M. Harrison is a Research Professor in the Department of Communication and Professor Emerita at the University at Albany. She is also a Faculty Fellow at the Center for Technology in Government. Her research interests focus on communication, technology and government, with special emphasis on the relationship between computer-mediated phenomena and democratic processes and practices.

Lisa Hohensinn is an Assistant Professor in the Institute for Public Management and Governance, WU Vienna University of Economics and Business, Austria. She has been a visiting scholar at Stanford University, Suffolk University Boston, and University of Mannheim. Her research interests include public innovation management, digital transformation and accounting innovation.

Alex Ingrams is an Assistant Professor in the Institute of Public Administration, Leiden University, and a member of the Hague Centre of Digital Governance. His research interests focus on the intersection of transparency policy with technological change and administrative reforms. He teaches in the Institute of Public Administration and the Leiden Institute of Advanced Computer Science. He also coordinates a bachelor specialisation in digitalisation, data and governance.

Petri Kettunen, Docent, University Researcher, received his D.Sc. (Tech.) degree in 2009 from Helsinki University of Technology following an extensive industrial career mainly in telecom business. Since 2010 he has been at the University of Helsinki, Department of Computer Science. His current research interests include agile software enterprises, continuous innovation of software-intensive products and services, sustainability in software engineering and future software development organisations.

Bram Klievink is Professor and Chair of Digitalisation and Public Policy at the Public Administration Institute at Leiden University. He has a multi-disciplinary background with degrees in information technology, political science, and technology and public administration. His research focuses on understanding the complexities of digital technologies in public policy and policy implementation.

Aleksi Kopponen has been a Special Advisor of Digitalisation in the Ministry of Finance, Finland since 2015 and a PhD Student in Aalto University School of Business, Finland. He has led a national human-centric digital transformation in public governance operations. His research interests include public governance digital transformation, specifically the digital twin paradigm. In 2023, Aleksi started as a Director of Transformation in the City of Tampere, Finland, pushing human-centric operations in practice.

Oliver Krancher is an Associate Professor in the Business IT Department of the IT University of Copenhagen, Denmark. He received his PhD from the University of Bern. His research interests revolve around IS sourcing, IS development and the management of Artificial Intelligence. He has published in leading information systems and software engineering journals, including the *Journal of Management Information Systems*, the *Journal of the Association for Information Systems*, the *European Journal of Information Systems*, *Empirical Software Engineering*, and *Information & Software Technology*. He is a co-founder of the Association for Information System's (AIS) Special Interest Group on Advances in Sourcing and has served as a special issue editor at the *Journal of Information Technology* and as a Track Chair at various conferences.

Alvina Lee is a third-year Doctorate of Engineering student at SMU School of Computing and Information Systems, supervised by Professor Venky Shanakraraman, Professor Ouh Eng Lieh and Professor Hady W. Lauw. Her research focuses on digital government and recommender systems to enhance service delivery. She currently works in the Business Technology Group of a Singapore Government Agency and has received multiple government awards in recognition of her contribution to the public sector.

Luis Felipe Luna-Reyes is a Professor in the Department of Public Administration and Policy and a Fellow of the National Academy of Public Administration. He is also a Faculty Fellow at the Center for Technology in Government, a Research Fellow at the Universidad de las Americas, Puebla and a member of the Mexican National Research System. His research is at the intersection of Public Administration, Information Systems and Systems Sciences.

Muiris MacCarthaigh is Professor of Politics and Public Policy at Queens University Belfast. His research engages with a variety of debates within and between political science, public sector governance and public policy, including the growing role of technology and AI in government. He is involved in a number of Doctoral Training Programmes connecting the social and computer sciences.

Marina Manzoni has MAs in Economics and Humanities (foreign languages and social studies). She joined the European Commission in 1991 where she has been working as Innovation Officer for Digital Technologies and Applications addressing societal challenges in support to businesses, citizens and the public sector – notably in the areas of eBusiness, eInclusion and eGoverment. She moved to the Digital Economy Unit of the Joint Research Center (JRC) of the European Commission in 2015, where she is contributing to the development of research and innovation policies in the area of Digital Transformation and Governance of the Public Sector, including Citizen Science and Artificial Intelligence applied to Public Services.

Keegan McBride is a Departmental Research Lecturer in AI, Government and Policy, and Course Director of the Social Science of the Internet MSc program at the Oxford Internet Institute. He is an expert on the topic of digital government and has published research in leading journals and conferences on topics such as Artificial Intelligence in the public sector, open government data, government digitalisation and government interoperability and data exchange systems. In his research he aims to develop an understanding about the future trajectory of the state in the digital age by exploring the complex and co-evolutionary relationships between technology, society and the state.

Prof. Dr. Ines Mergel is Full Professor of Digital Governance and Public Administration at the University of Konstanz, Germany. She is an elected fellow of the National Academy of Public Administration (NAPA) and a Schmidt Futures Innovation Fellow. Her research focuses on the social affordances of agile governance in the public sector. She is the co-founder of 'Teaching Public Service in the Digital Age', an initiative to bring digital competences into public administrations.

Tommi Mikkonen is a Professor of Software Engineering at University of Jyväskylä, Finland. He received his PhD in software engineering from Tampere University of Technology in 1999. He has authored more than 300 scientific articles and supervised more than 500 theses of different degrees. His interests include software architectures, software engineering and public sector software.

Gianluca Misuraca is Founder and Vice President for International Relations and Technology Diplomacy of Inspiring Futures (IF), a global advisory consultancy in Strategic Foresight, Social Innovation and Digital Governance headquartered in Lausanne and Seville. He is also an advisor to several international organisations and development institutions worldwide. Among his key assignments he is currently leading the 'International Outreach for Human-centric Artificial Intelligence' (InTouchAI.eu) initiative funded by the European Commission's External Action Service for Foreign Policy Instruments. As part of his academic roles, Gianluca is the Executive Director of the Master in Artificial Intelligence in public services (AI4GOV) led by the Universidad Politécnica de Madrid, a Senior Research Associate at the Department of Design of Politecnico di Milano and a Research Fellow at the Department of eGovernance and Administration of Danube University Krems in Austria. Furthermore, he is a Special Advisor on Democracy in the Digital Age for Re-Imagine Europa (RIE).

Oliver Müller is Professor of Management Information Systems and Data Analytics at Paderborn University. He holds a BSc, MSc and PhD. in Information Systems from the University of Münster's School of Business and Economics. His research interests focus on how (big) data and algorithms can support human judgment and decision making. This includes the design and use of machine learning solutions for supporting human judgment and decision making as well as studying the acceptance and implications of algorithmic/data-driven decision making in organisations. His research has been published in the *Journal of Management Information Systems (JMIS), Journal of the Association of Information Systems (JAIS), European Journal of Information Systems (EJIS), Organizational Research Methods (ORM), European Journal of Operational Research (EJOR), Decision Support Systems (DSS)*, and various others.

Per Rådberg Nagbøl is a Postdoc at the IT University of Copenhagen in collaboration with the Danish Business Authority. He holds a PhD from the IT University of Copenhagen. His research is within Information Systems, focusing on managing Artificial Intelligence. He uses Action Design Research to design systems and procedures for quality assurance and evaluation of Artificial Intelligence, focusing on accurate, transparent and responsible use in the public sector. His work is published in leading Information Systems journals such as the *Journal of the Association for Information Systems* and *MIS Quarterly Executive*. He received the Vinton G. Cerf Award for the Best Student Authored Paper at the 16th International Conference on Design Science Research in Information Systems and Technology (DESRIST, 2021).

Francesco Niglia, PhD is a researcher and director of the 'Responsible Research and Innovation Unit' at the Link Campus University in Rome. Francesco has actively been engaged in the modelling of innovation ecosystems and ethical and sustainable technologies and through different fields of application. Public services, socio-economic environments and social innovation constitute the main contributions in the research of innovation dynamics. He holds a PhD in Complex Systems Engineering at the Innovation Engineering Department of Università del Salento. His current research focuses on Application of Responsible Innovation paradigm into digital domains, the Ethics of Innovation, Territorial Innovation and Sustainability, Artificial Intelligence and Big Data applied to social-oriented services.

Deepak P. is Senior Lecturer of Computer Science at Queens University Belfast. An AI researcher by background, his current research focuses on fairness and ethics within AI algorithms, with an emphasis on using a politically and philosophically informed perspective. He is involved in several interdisciplinary research projects that cut across computing and social sciences.

Theodoros Papadopoulos obtained his BSc in Computer Science from Athens University of Economics and Business, and MSc in Web Technologies from Harokopio University of Athens. His Master thesis focused on Brain-Computer interfaces using machine learning to detect intentions and classify ECG signals. He is currently a PhD candidate in the Department of Information and Communications Systems Engineering at the University of the Aegean, researching Machine Learning and Artificial Intelligence focusing on Natural Language Models. He has been working in ICT since 1998, having acquired and practiced software development, business and systems analysis, consulting, research, architectural and management skills, as well as experience in technical management of European and National research projects. He is responsible for a series of digital initiatives of the Greek Government, and he has been a National Representative in various European Working Groups and committees.

Aleksandra Przegalińska is a Senior Associate Researcher at Harvard University and Associate Professor and vice-president of Kozminski University, responsible for International

Relations and ESR. Aleksandra received her PhD in the philosophy of Artificial Intelligence at the Institute of Philosophy of the University of Warsaw. Aleksandra is the head of the Human-Machine Interaction Research Center at Kozminski University (www.humanrace .edu.pl) and the leader of the AI in Management Program. Until recently, she conducted post-doctoral research at the Center for Collective Intelligence at the Massachusetts Institute of Technology in Boston. She graduated from The New School for Social Research in New York. In 2021, Aleksandra joined the American Institute for Economic Research as Visiting Research Fellow. She is interested in the future of work seen through the lens of emerging technologies, as well as in natural language processing, humanoid Artificial Intelligence, social robots and wearable technologies.

Matti Rossi is a Professor of Information Systems at Aalto University School of Business. He is a past president of the Association for Information Systems and AIS Fellow. He has been the principal investigator in several major research projects funded by the technological development center of Finland and Academy of Finland. He was the winner of the 2013 Millennium Distinction Award of Technology Academy of Finland for open source and data research.

Bartosz Rzycki is a student of computer science and Artificial Intelligence at IE University in Madrid. Also working as a data scientist in Deep.BI where he is responsible for creating machine learning models to increase user engagement, content performance and monetisation for publishers. Selected by the Association of Harvard University Professors and Alumni in Poland as a laureate of a nationwide competition for high-achieving students and industry professionals, in 2022 he was selected by The Nova as one of the 111 best students in Spain and among the 10 best in computer science.

Rodrigo Sandoval-Almazan (PhD) is an Associate Professor at the Political Sciences and Social Sciences Department in the Autonomous University of the State of Mexico. He is National Research Level II on the Mexican National Research Science Ministry. Member of the Mexican Academy of Science since 2018, Dr. Sandoval-Almazan is the author or co-author of articles in scholarly journals in this field. His research interests include Artificial Intelligence in government, social media platforms for government, metrics for digital government and open government.

Sven Schade, PhD is a Scientific Officer at the European Commission's scientific and knowledge management service, the Joint Research Centre (JRC), with a background in geospatial information science and knowledge engineering. His research interests cover digital transformation of public governance, multi-disciplinary interoperability and public participation in science for policy – always with a view to improve inclusive and sustainable transitions. Sven is leading the scientific research of the JRC's Digital Economy Unit, focusing on digital governance and public service innovation in support of EU policies.

Venky Shankararaman is a Professor of Information Systems (Education) and Vice Provost (Education) at Singapore Management University (SMU). He holds a PhD in Engineering from the University of Strathclyde, Glasgow, UK. His current areas of specialisation include business process management and analytics, digital transformation, enterprise architecture and integration and technology enhanced learning.

Stanley Simoes is a Marie Skłodowska-Curie Early Stage Researcher and PhD student at the School of Electronics, Electrical Engineering and Computer Science at Queen's University Belfast. His research interests lie in the field of fair AI, particularly in unsupervised learning.

Luca Tangi, PhD is a Researcher and Scientific Project Officer at the Joint Research Centre (JRC) of the European Commission. Since 2021, he has been collaborating within the AI Watch and Innovative Public Service initiatives, conducting research on the development, uptake and impact of emerging technologies and in particular Artificial Intelligence in the public sector. He holds a PhD at the Department of Management, Economics and Industrial Engineering of Politecnico di Milano. His doctoral work focused on understanding how ICTs are affecting public service delivery and transforming the way public administrations are structured and organised.

Melvin Tay is a PhD student in the Graduate School of Public Policy at the University of Tokyo. Among his current research interests is investigating the impact of emerging technologies on public trust in government and national security. He holds a Master of Social Sciences degree in Political Economy and a Bachelor of Social Sciences degree (with first-class honours) in Political Science and Philosophy from the National University of Singapore.

Peter Ulrich joined the European Commission's Joint Research Centre (JRC) in 2020 as Scientific Project Officer to research the role of digital technologies in innovating public services and fostering interoperability. He currently has the role of Briefing Coordinator of the organisation. Before joining the JRC, Peter worked in research development and at an international city network, where he advised local governments on questions of governance and social innovation. He holds degrees in European Studies, Urban Studies, and Public Administration from Maastricht University, Vrije Universiteit Brussel and the Hertie School of Governance respectively.

David Valle-Cruz, PhD, is an Assistant Professor at the Universidad Autónoma del Estado de México. He is a member of the National Research System and the i-Lab México. David is a Computer Engineer and a Computer Scientist; he holds a PhD in Economics and Management. His articles have been published in leading journals, including *Government Information Quarterly*, *Cognitive Computation*, *Information Polity* and the *International Journal of Public Sector Management* (among others). His research interests are related to applied Artificial Intelligence, data science and emerging technologies.

Tero Villman is a futures researcher and a foresight practitioner at the Finland Futures Research Center at the University of Turku, Finland. His research interests include strategic foresight, visionary leadership and shared visions, and transformations, transitions and disruptions.

Masaru Yarime is an Associate Professor in the Division of Public Policy at the Hong Kong University of Science and Technology. He has appointments as Visiting Associate Professor in the Graduate School of Public Policy at the University of Tokyo and is Honorary Associate Professor at the Department of Science, Technology, Engineering and Public Policy at University College London. His research interests center on science, technology and innovation policy for sustainability, particularly the policy implications of data-driven innovations such as AI, the Internet of Things and smart cities.

Foreword

The main goal for governments all around the world is the realisation of public values, by drawing on the appropriate people, processes, systems, and information. Such public values relate to what administrations of all levels contribute to society with the proper corresponding transparency, responsiveness, inclusion, safety, and social security, in line with the agreed international principles of the United Nations' 2030 Agenda for Sustainable Development and its Goals (SDGs).

Pursuing these goals, all sorts and types of public sector organisations try to utilise information and communication technologies, towards the model of digital government, this task requiring the building of the right capabilities and competencies, but also significant transformations for a more holistic digital governance framework.

Lately, digital governance and digital transformation have been highly impacted by the emergence of Artificial Intelligence (AI), as a new powerful tool that promises a new world of increased connectivity, enhanced human-machine collaboration, and more efficient and intelligent data-driven systems for data management, decision support, strategic planning, and forecasting, towards new, unprecedented levels of productivity and overall quality.

Despite these positive opportunities, this emergence of Artificial Intelligence, especially within the public management sphere, poses new questions on how we can build, in parallel to the technological developments, a proper set of rules to regulate its growth and applications, preventing possible misconducts. AI's potential to exacerbate social inequalities, enable mass surveillance, and displace jobs highlights the need for responsible AI development that respects human rights and ensures inclusive benefits.

This book is dedicated to analysing the various aspects and challenges of Artificial Intelligence applications in public management. Its chapters present the foundations, the core strategies, latest research advancements, and practical findings to increase our knowledge of the domain. The authors drive us through theoretical models, principles, methodologies, architectures, and technical frameworks, contributing to a multi-faceted view of this thrilling domain.

We are only at the start of this journey, to carefully reap the benefits of this human invention, for the overall social good.

I congratulate the editors and authors on the excellent work done and hope the present volume to be of use for researchers and practitioners of digital governance and Artificial Intelligence, to harness AI's potential while minimising its risks, working towards a future where AI can significantly contribute to achieving the UN SDGs.

Enjoy reading!

Vincenzo AQUARO
Chief of Digital Government Branch-DPIDG
Department of Economic and Social Affairs
United Nations

Acknowledgments

This book is the result of the collective work of several scholars and researchers. But it is also a product of openness and collaboration among more than one hundred scientists, industry experts and practitioners in the field of Artificial Intelligence and Public Management.

We are also highly grateful to all friends and colleagues involved in guidance, stimulation of the community, the review process and the book finalisation.

We would like to thank Vincenzo Aquaro for his warm foreword in this book.

Special thanks also go to the publisher's team and particularly to Daniel Mather for his professional guidance, support and feedback – decisive for keeping this project on time and of quality.

Finally, a big hug for our family members and close collaborators, for their love and support.

The Editors

Introduction to the *Research Handbook on Public Management and Artificial Intelligence*

Yannis Charalabidis, Rony Medaglia and Colin van Noordt

PUBLIC MANAGEMENT AND ARTIFICIAL INTELLIGENCE: THE BEGINNING OF A NEW JOURNEY?

The public debate on Artificial Intelligence (AI) is not new: the very concept of AI is now more than 50 years old. Over the decades, investments in designing and developing systems that are able to carry out tasks by displaying intelligent, humanlike behaviour, have featured both enthusiastic booms ('AI springs') and severe disillusionments ('AI winters'). Nevertheless, the current convergence of an unprecedented explosion of big data, global connectivity, and maturity of digital infrastructures, seems to have finally brought the potential of AI applications to the interest of a mainstream audience, in both the corporate and the public management worlds.

The application of Artificial Intelligence in a public management context features a wide range of highly relevant potential. This potential includes tackling classic challenges of managing government bureaucracies, such as reducing costs and improving accuracy. The ability of Artificial Intelligence applications, such as Machine Learning, to quickly and accurately identify patterns in large swathes of data, can for example greatly reduce the costs and time necessary for public agencies to process citizen applications of welfare benefits. Moreover, the increased accuracy of AI-supported decision-making can also potentially reduce the biases or corruption that may taint the judgement of policy-makers and bureaucrats. In addition to these classic goals of public management, AI applications also feature the potential to support the development of altogether new public services and new forms of citizen engagement.

The swift diffusion of AI applications is also accompanied by growing concerns about their downsides, and about the new challenges that public managers have to face to mitigate their potential negative effects. On the one hand, the growing complexity of Machine Learning algorithms can make AI-supported outputs inscrutable, challenging the possibility to explain decisions to citizenry, to correct mistakes, and to hold administrations accountable. Since many AI applications feature the capability to autonomously self-direct by processing data with little to no supervision by a human, decisions can potentially become opaque, as they are products of a technological 'black box'. On the other hand, since AI applications are ultimately only as good as the data they are trained on (according to the principle of 'garbage in, garbage out'), delegating decisions to them can worsen societal inequalities and injustices. Input data is, in fact, necessarily a representation of a social reality that includes biases against minorities and disadvantaged groups, and such biases are not only replicated, but potentially amplified by AI applications that are very good at identifying and replicating patterns, but not at compensating them according to principles of fairness and justice.

The uncertainty on the future of AI in public management, in a continuum between utopian and dystopian views, calls for the building of a solid body of research-based knowledge. In the past few years, a first phase of quick increase of attention of the research community on the phenomenon of AI in public management has resulted in the mushrooming of governance principles, position pieces, and speculative contributions, partly due to the lack of a sufficient number of empirical cases to draw data from.

This first phase is now being followed by the first appearance of an increasing number of empirical studies on AI in public management. This stems from the collection of data on real-life cases, and draws on lessons learned from newly drafted regulation, implemented projects, and actual citizen use of novel AI-enabled public services.

OBJECTIVE OF THIS HANDBOOK

The aim of this handbook is to provide an overview of the potentials, challenges, and governance principles of Artificial Intelligence in public management that is based on the state-of-the-art research in this topic area, in a global perspective.

While a solid research foundation represents the starting point of this handbook, the intended audience includes not only researchers in academia, but also public managers, policy-makers, and citizens, both as users and as co-creators of AI-enabled services. As AI is expected to touch upon all of the complex web of relations that stem from the ecosystems that comprise of public actors, businesses, and citizens, this handbook aims to provide an overview of opportunities and challenges that are relevant for each of these stakeholders.

To achieve this goal, we have solicited contributions from a wide variety of experts from across the globe, both in the practice and in the academic world, expecting them to share their cutting-edge research on AI in public management.

As a result, the approach taken in this handbook is necessarily multidisciplinary, drawing on a variety of knowledge perspectives in dialogue with each other, including public administration, general management, information systems, sociology, and computer science.

ORGANISATION OF THE HANDBOOK

The handbook consists of 15 chapters, and is organised in three parts, corresponding to three foci of research.

Part I focuses on research on adoption and implementation of AI in public management. This part includes contributions that focus on establishing key elements of the public management of AI: theory development, driving factors, obstacles, and challenges of diffusion and adoption, organisational and individual impacts, and evaluation models.

Part II focuses on research on examples and case studies of AI in public management. This part includes contributions that draw on the presentation of specific cases, initiatives, and projects of AI in the public sector. Chapters included in this part focus on country-, region-, or sector-specific applications; strategies, policies, and regulations; comparative studies; and case typologies.

Part III focuses on forward-looking research on AI in public management. This part draws on the previous two parts to outline future trends and directions in the evolution of AI adoption and use in the public sector. Chapters included in this part focus on future strategy; policy trends; technological evolution; and new research agendas.

Part I Adoption and Implementation of AI in Public Management

This first part of this handbook focuses on the adoption and implementation of AI in public management, and comprises six chapters.

In Chapter 1, *Artificial Intelligence algorithms and applications in the public sector: A systematic literature review based on the PRISMA approach*, David Valle-Cruz, J. Ramon Gil-Garcia, and Rodrigo Sandoval-Almazan systematically analyse published research on AI in the public sector with two objectives: to identify what are currently the most studied AI algorithms and applications; and highlight the consequences of implementing intelligent algorithms in the public sector. Their findings show that Machine Learning is the dominant technique analysed in research on AI in the public sector. Moreover, this chapter identifies key potential benefits outlined in the research literature, including improved automation, efficiency, and decision support, but also risks related to discrimination against some racial groups, and increases in inequities, due to the fact that AI technologies may not be available to the most vulnerable groups with the greatest needs.

In Chapter 2, *A trifold research synthesis on AI-induced service automation*, Matthias Döring and Lisa Hohensinn also carry out a systematic literature review, with a specific focus on understanding the effects of new automation techniques on the role of key stakeholders of public service delivery: citizens as consumers of public services, and public sector organisations and their employees as service producers. The authors identify seven major research gaps related to intermediate and long-term outcomes of AI in the public sector, the role of citizens and of public employees, and the importance of context. Based on these gaps, the chapter proposes a conceptual model to guide future research.

In Chapter 3, *AI in the public sector: Fundamental operational questions and how to address them*, Muiris MacCarthaigh, Stanley Simoes, and Deepak Padmanabhan set out to identify key challenges arising from the use of AI in the public sector, drawing on practice-based findings. Using cases from three policy areas – public health, policing, and immigration – the authors highlight the relevance of challenges of explicability, accountability, and fundamental rights, and propose some recommendations on how to tackle them.

In Chapter 4, *Towards a systematic understanding of the challenges of public procurement of Artificial Intelligence in the public sector*, Keegan McBride, Colin van Noordt, Gianluca Misuraca, and Gerhard Hammerschmid focus on understanding challenges experienced by public managers in procuring AI for public services. Drawing on documental analysis and interviews with public managers in four European countries, the authors identify 14 key challenges related to the procurement process, to data, to the AI models, and to organisational capacity. Based on an overview of these challenges, they also identify 22 potential strategies on how to tackle them.

In Chapter 5, *Enhancing citizen service management through AI-enabled systems – A proposed AI readiness framework for public sector*, Alvina Lee, Venky Shankararaman, and Ouh Eng Lieh draw on a survey approach in order to map criteria that can be used to assess the readiness of public organisations to implement AI-enabled services. The authors identify 14 sub-criteria of assessment, categorised into the three contexts of technology, organisation, and the environment.

In Chapter 6, *Measuring user-centricity in AI-enabled European public services: A proposal for enabling maturity models*, Francesco Niglia and Luca Tangi propose a framework to measure user-centricity supported by AI-powered functionalities. The authors devise a list of single AI-enabled functionalities for public services that are measurable and enable the definition of a maturity model. The framework is also tested on a small sample of public services.

Part II Examples and Case Studies of AI in Public Management

The second part of this handbook provides examples and case studies of AI in public management, and comprises five chapters.

In Chapter 7, *Application of Artificial Intelligence by Poland's public administration*, Bartosz Rzycki, David Duenas-Cid, and Aleksandra Przegalińska present three cases of AI-driven solutions created and implemented by or with the support of Poland's central public administration. They analyse the dynamics among stakeholders in AI-driven innovation in the public sector, and highlight the potential and limitations of the current scenario in Poland.

In Chapter 8, *The effect of algorithmic tools on public value considerations in participatory processes: The case of regulations.gov*, Sarah Giest, Alex Ingrams, and Bram Klievink analyse the use of algorithmic tools in regulations.gov, a platform in the United States that enables public access to rulemaking procedures and allows for citizen participation in the process. The authors investigate how algorithmic tools that engage with public input affect public values in decision-making processes, and find that the participatory process and the use of algorithmic tools bring their own set of uncertainties and values, and that there needs to be evolving strategies for making value trade-offs at both the organisational and the individual levels. These strategies are needed to deal with competing values and to avoid having too many salient values that lead to paralysis in public institutions.

In Chapter 9, *Artificial Intelligence and its regulation in representative institutions*, Fotios Fitsilis and Patricia Gomes Rêgo de Almeida focus on the adoption of AI systems in parliamentary institutions. The authors compile a list of 39 AI applications used in the parliamentary institutions of eight countries, plus the European Parliament, and discuss their design approaches and functional characteristics. The chapter also highlights implementation factors and limitations in employing AI systems into parliaments, and emphasises the role of parliaments as regulatory actors. In the final part of the chapter, the authors try to anticipate upcoming scenarios in the evolution of representative institutions.

In Chapter 10, *Personalised public services powered by AI: The citizen digital twin approach*, Aleksi Kopponen, Antti Hahto, Tero Villman, Petri Kettunen, Tommi Mikkonen, and Matti Rossi discuss the characteristics of an AI-augmented public service developed by the government in Finland. The service is conceptualised as a Citizen Digital Twin, and consists of a scaffolding model that provides personalised service recommendations based on data collected about a person's holistic situation. Drawing on an example of a possible use of this service, the authors discuss its benefits and possible ethical implications.

In Chapter 11, *Towards a systems view of enterprise data governance for Artificial Intelligence in Government: Implications from algorithmic jobseeker profiling applications*, Luis Luna-Reyes and Teresa Harrison investigate the use case of algorithmic jobseeker profiling in Austria and Poland. The authors analyse the goals of profiling, the kinds of data that are used, how algorithms using this data are deployed, and the stakeholders affected, while outlining the significant risks and challenges of these applications.

Part III Forward-looking Research on AI in Public Management

The third and last part of the handbook focuses on forward-looking research on AI in public management, and comprises four chapters.

In Chapter 12, *Taking stock and looking ahead – Developing a science for policy research agenda on the use and uptake of AI in public sector organisations in the EU*, Luca Tangi, Peter Ulrich, Sven Schade, and Marina Manzoni propose an agenda for science for policy research on AI in the public sector in Europe. Drawing on the findings from the mapping of 686 cases carried out by the European Commission's Joint Research Center, the authors outline existing challenges for the uptake of AI in the public sector in Europe. With the aim of tackling these challenges, the authors propose a science for policy research agenda driven by the overarching principles of trustworthiness and human-centricity, and consisting of three pillars concerning policy approach, management and governance, and enabling innovation.

In Chapter 13, titled *Analysis of driving public values of AI initiatives in government in Europe*, Colin van Noordt, Gianluca Misuraca, and Ines Mergel focus on AI initiatives in government using the lens of public value. The authors analyse 549 cases of use of AI for public services in Europe to understand to what extent they contribute to the public values of professionalism, efficiency, service, and engagement. Their findings show that public administrations are predominantly implementing AI in pursuit of efficiency-related objectives. The authors argue that such prevalent focus on efficiency reveals potential risks of public value destruction when public administrations deploy AI technologies.

In Chapter 14, *Challenges and design principles for the evaluation of productive AI systems in the public sector*, Per Nagbøl, Oliver Krancher, and Oliver Müller focus on the evaluation of AI systems, for which there is still scarce research. Using an Action Design Research (ADR) approach, the authors built, implemented, and evaluated an infrastructure for evaluating productive AI systems in the Danish Business Authority. The study illustrates that key challenges of an evaluation infrastructure reside in tedious work, resource availability, maintaining an overview, ensuring sufficient priority, and timing of evaluations.

In Chapter 15, *Trustworthy Public-Sector AI: Research Progress and Future Agendas*, Naomi Aoki, Melvin Tay, and Masaru Yarime provide a contribution to shape future research on the role of trust in the development of AI in the public sector. The authors conduct a systematic review of literature on trustworthy AI in the public sector, highlighting the dearth of studies in this topic area. Based on this review, the chapter proposes an agenda for future empirical research on the role of trust in AI in the public sector.

CONCLUSIONS

The diversity in approaches, cases, and methodologies showcased in this handbook is a rich representation of both the strengths and the challenges that the swiftly developing area of AI in public management features at this crucial stage.

The growing body of research from numerous disciplinary perspectives is strong evidence that the phenomenon of AI in the public sector is here to stay, be it as a utopian or dystopian – or, more likely, somewhere between the two – anticipation of the consequences it is expected to have in the future.

In putting together this handbook, diversity and a certain level of fragmentation has represented, on the one hand, a challenge, due to the need to link different types of discourses in an overall narrative. When dealing with a socio-technical phenomenon such as the one of AI in public management, there is the need for a strong effort to combine technical, policy, and managerial discourses, and to reconcile research foci on individual, organisational, and policy impacts. On the other hand, such diversity represented not only the attractive feature, but also what we consider the key strength of research on the phenomenon of AI in public management. With the combination of research and practice perspectives, scholars are forced out of ivory tower speculations, while practitioners are provided with tools to elevate their experiences at a higher level of abstraction and generalisability.

It is with the awareness of both these strengths and these weaknesses that we present this handbook. We see it as the starter of a conversation that is destined to continue growing, both in scope, and in relevance.

PART I

ADOPTION AND IMPLEMENTATION OF AI IN PUBLIC MANAGEMENT

1. Artificial intelligence algorithms and applications in the public sector: a systematic literature review based on the PRISMA approach

David Valle-Cruz, J. Ramon Gil-Garcia and Rodrigo Sandoval-Almazan

INTRODUCTION

For some, the world has started the era of the fourth industrial revolution. Emerging technologies such as nanotechnology, biotechnology, quantum computing, and artificial intelligence are changing the status quo through innovative and sophisticated applications (Chakraborty et al., 2022; Philbeck and Davis, 2018). Artificial intelligence (AI) algorithms and applications are increasingly shaping the structures, policies, and processes of organisations worldwide (Makridakis, 2017; Valle-Cruz, Criado, et al., 2020; Zuiderwijk et al., 2021). The public sector is no exception. Governments have adopted these tools and techniques to boost transparency, improve decision-making, increase efficiency, produce high-quality services, perform repetitive tasks, and analyse data, as well as to avoid risks in activities that are potentially dangerous or harmful to human beings (Janssen, Brous, et al., 2020; Medaglia et al., 2021; Sun and Medaglia, 2019; Valle-Cruz et al., 2021; Wirtz et al., 2019). Artificial intelligence applications could include a software core based on various intelligent algorithms (artificial intelligence algorithms) and a physical-mechanical operation that works through cognitive machines. As a consequence, the promise of artificial intelligence consists of massive automation, efficiency, error reduction, alternative and creative ways to solve problems, assistance in decision-making based on data analysis, and the generation of public value (Criado and Gil-Garcia, 2019; Medaglia et al., 2021).

Despite the potential benefits promised by artificial intelligence applications and algorithms, their realisation in the public sector still needs to be clarified and better understood. In fact, some artificial intelligence techniques are so complex that it is difficult to understand how they obtain specific results. All this spawns distrust when using them in government contexts, especially for decision support (Valle-Cruz, Gil-Garcia, et al., 2020; Wirtz et al., 2020). There is also an urgent need for increased explainability of some artificial intelligence applications and tools. This situation arises from the opacity in the coding and the sometimes-unexpected results of artificial intelligence algorithms. In addition, despite a better understanding of artificial intelligence algorithms, there is no guarantee that errors in decision-making will be avoided (Janssen, Hartog, et al., 2020; Zhang et al., 2022). Likewise, there are several unintended consequences related to the use or misuse of artificial intelligence, including accidents and/or bad results that cannot be explained (Janssen, Hartog, et al., 2020; Righetti et al., 2019). In this regard, there is a growing number of empirical and conceptual studies on artificial intelligence in the public sector (de Bruijn et al., 2021; Dwivedi et al., 2021; Valle-Cruz et al., 2022; Wirtz et al., 2019). However, current studies do not elaborate on how specific artificial intelligence applications and algorithms are used in the public sector and, therefore, there is a need for additional studies. There is still much to learn about how artificial intelligence techniques positively or negatively affect the public sector. This chapter is guided by two interrelated research questions: (1) Which are the AI algorithms and applications in the public sector that are most studied in the scientific literature? (2) What are some of the positive and negative consequences from implementing intelligent algorithms and cognitive machines in the public sector? Overall, the use of artificial intelligence techniques in government has not been well explored, and it is worthy of analysis (Valle-Cruz, Gil-Garcia, et al., 2020). This chapter aims to answer these research questions and contribute to our current knowledge through a systematic literature review based on the Preferred Reporting Items for Systematic Reviews and Meta-Analysis (PRISMA) (Page et al., 2021; PRISMA, 2015). The authors analyse existing literature available at the Web of Science, Scopus, and Science Direct related to artificial intelligence algorithms and applications in government settings. The authors begin with a logical search limited to scientific articles in the social sciences, public policy, and public administration and follow the PRISMA methodology.

This chapter lists several artificial intelligence techniques and applications used in the public sector and also provides practical lessons. The chapter starts with an introduction, followed by a description of the PRISMA methodology applied to the Web of Science, Scopus, and Science Direct papers. Section three offers an in-depth look at the systematic literature review, while section four analyses the main results of the literature review. The chapter concludes with a few remarks and suggests ideas for future research on artificial intelligence algorithms and applications in the public sector.

LITERATURE REVIEW BASED ON PRISMA

In order to systematically identify and select scientific literature related to the research topic, we used the Preferred Reporting Items for Systematic Reviews and Meta-Analyses (PRISMA) (Page et al., 2021; PRISMA, 2015). The method ensures that all relevant literature on a topic is captured and provides transparency and traceability about the literature search. The authors decided to search for documents on Web of Science, Scopus, and Science Direct because they are platforms that contain influential and relevant peer-reviewed research on the topic of interest. The literature review was conducted in March 2022. The general selection criteria were English language and scientific and academic journal articles in government, public sector, public administration, public policy, and international relations.

To identify articles relevant to the general topic of this research, the authors searched all abstracts and titles for a syntactic relationship between search terms, for example, between 'artificial intelligence' and 'applications', or 'artificial intelligence' and 'algorithms', or 'artificial intelligence' and 'techniques'. In this logical search, artificial intelligence techniques and algorithms were considered interchangeably. For instance, an artificial neural network is a kind of algorithm used for a prediction and classification task using artificial intelligence. A genetic algorithm is an artificial intelligence technique used for optimisation. In contrast, artificial intelligence applications in the public sector use these techniques or algorithms for certain purposes such as predictive policing, decision support, disaster management, and the provision of public services, among others (Androutsopoulou et al., 2019; Valle-Cruz et al., 2022; Wang and Ma, 2022; Wirtz et al., 2019).

We performed the following logical search: ('Artificial Intelligence' OR 'AI') AND ('Applications' OR 'Algorithms') AND ('Government' OR 'Public Sector' OR 'Public Administration' OR 'Public Policy')

At this stage, we identified 512 documents: 143 in Science Direct, 224 in Web of Science, and 145 in Scopus; 205 duplicate documents were removed before the screening process. In the screening stage, 213 documents were excluded since the title or the abstract was unrelated to artificial intelligence applications and algorithms in the public sector. At this stage, we reviewed 94 documents. Of these, 69 were excluded because the applications or algorithms mentioned in the full text were used exclusively in cases from the private sector or because the application or algorithm applied to the public sector was not identified when reviewing the document.

Finally, the authors included 25 scientific articles related to artificial intelligence algorithms and applications in the public sector (Figure 1.1).

OVERALL TRENDS

This section analyses the 25 articles from the systematic literature review on artificial intelligence algorithms and applications in the public sector. As overall trends, this section presents the evolution of the annual scientific production, journals containing the analysed publications, artificial intelligence algorithms used in government, artificial intelligence applications for government, and artificial intelligence applications in the public sector that should be further researched according to our analysis of the existing literature.

Annual Scientific Production

The systematic literature review identified 25 papers on artificial intelligence algorithms and applications in the public sector. The findings are consistent with the boom of artificial intelligence studies in the public sector (de Sousa et al., 2019; Medaglia et al., 2021; Wirtz et al., 2019). Since the end of the first decade of the 21st century, studies in this area have increased. Figure 1.2 shows the growing trend in the studies; 2021 has 12 papers. The use and implementation of artificial intelligence in the public sector has become widespread, with endeavours spanning predictive analytics, decision support, policy-making assistance, video surveillance, and intelligent transportation systems, to name a few. There is also a growing interest in researching the effects of artificial intelligence on individuals, organisations, and society. Our research in March 2022 showed a clear positive trend, with more studies conducted each year. The low number of documents identified in 2022 is explained because the logical search was conducted in March 2022.

Concerning this type of study, we identify 111 authors in the 25 papers of the systematic literature review. Janssen collaborates on three papers, Gil-Garcia and Medaglia in two each. Furthermore, 108 other authors collaborate on one paper, and the average number of authors per paper is 4.44.

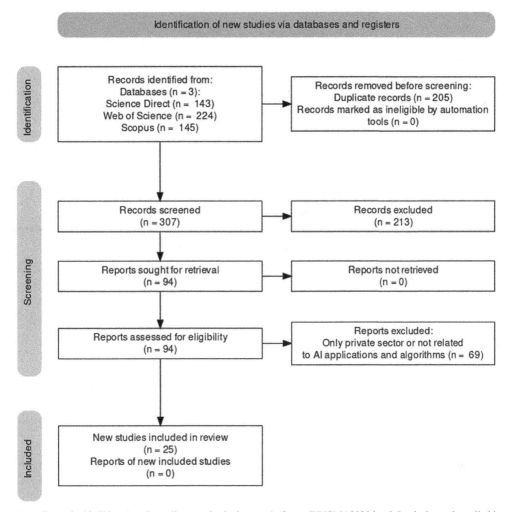

Note: Created with Shiny App: https://www.eshackathon.org/software/PRISMA2020.html. Logical search applied in March 2022.

Figure 1.1   *PRISMA flow diagram for artificial intelligence algorithms and applications in the public sector*

Journals in the Literature Review

The papers are published in 19 journals, predominantly *Government Information Quarterly*, with five publications, *Social Science Computer Review* and *Technological Forecasting and Social Change*, with two articles each. Table 1.1 shows the journals identified in the literature review.

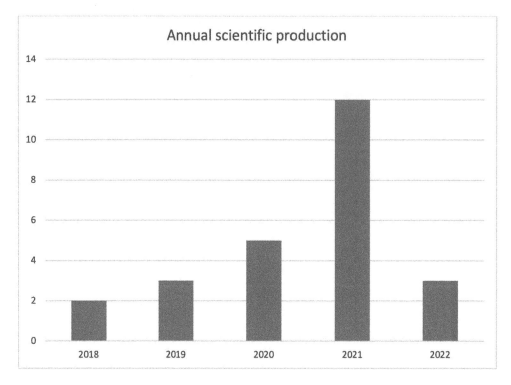

Figure 1.2   *Annual scientific production on applications and algorithms in the public sector*

Artificial Intelligence Algorithms Used in Government

In the selected papers, the authors identified 27 artificial intelligence techniques with potential for application in the public sector. Machine learning is the most recurrent technique in the analysed studies (frequency = 12). Although it is directly related to machine learning, artificial neural networks are the second most frequent technique (frequency = 5), together with fuzzy logic (frequency = 5) and natural language processing (frequency = 5) (see Table 1.2). This classification is based on how the authors identify the different artificial intelligence techniques in their respective papers. However, from the point of view of other scholars, some of these techniques (for example, genetic algorithms, random forest, and support vector machine) are included in broader concepts such as machine learning.

The artificial intelligence techniques that are the most frequently mentioned have some interesting similarities and differences. Both machine learning and artificial neural networks have the potential to analyse trends, identify patterns, and generate predictions. It may be why they are the most widely used techniques in the public sector. Fuzzy logic, for instance, gradually identifies fractions of actual values between 0 and 1. It allows the generation of intelligent systems with non-binary heuristics, which has the potential to simulate some subjectivity in artificial intelligence applications. There are other techniques for designing optimisation models, such as genetic algorithms and ant colony optimisation. Natural language processing is a widely used technique for chatbot implementation and can potentially facilitate

Table 1.1　　*Journals containing publications on artificial intelligence algorithms and applications in the public sector*

Sources	Articles
Government Information Quarterly	5
Social Science Computer Review	2
Technological Forecasting and Social Change	2
Asia Pacific Journal of Public Administration	1
Crime Science	1
Energy Reports	1
Expert Systems with Applications	1
International Journal of Information Management	1
International Journal of Public Administration	1
JEDEM – eJournal of Democracy and Open Government	1
Journal of Information Communication and Ethics in Society	1
New Technology Work and Employment	1
Policy and Society	1
Public Administration Review	1
Socio-Economic Planning Sciences	1
Technology in Society	1
Telematics and Informatics	1
Transforming Government: People, Process and Policy	1
Transportation Engineering	1

Source: Authors' own elaboration.

human-machine interaction and government-to-citizen interaction. Robotics makes it possible to perform repetitive or dangerous physical activities for human beings; a clear example is the sanitisation and dispensing of medicines in hospitals. On the margins of what some authors argue in their papers, some techniques that could not be considered artificial intelligence techniques but areas that apply or support artificial intelligence algorithms are chatbots, augmented reality, data mining technologies, sensors, and serious games.

Artificial Intelligence Applications for Government

Artificial intelligence techniques have several potential uses in the public sector. Perhaps the three main ones will be the internal efficiency of organisations, assistance in data-driven decision-making, and improving public services. In this regard, we identified 10 applications of artificial intelligence in the public sector: (1) Disaster management, (2) Healthcare policy and programs, (3) Public safety and crime prediction, (4) Sustainability and climate change, (5) Smart cities and intelligent transportation, (6) Employment and workplace substitution, (7) Better provision of public services, (8) Public policy and politics, (9) AI-based decision-making, (10) The internal efficiency of public administration. However, using artificial intelligence in the public sector generates challenges that require attention in artificial intelligence governance, explainability, legal frameworks, and AI-based public policies. The above applications will be discussed in the next section.

Table 1.2   *Frequency of occurrence of artificial intelligence techniques in the literature review*

Artificial intelligence technique	Frequency
Machine learning	12
Artificial neural networks	5
Fuzzy logic	5
Natural language processing	5
Genetic algorithms	4
Robotics	4
Chatbots	3
Cognitive mapping	2
Deep learning	2
Expert systems	2
Pattern recognition	2
Random forest	2
Support vector machine	2
Ant colony optimiser	1
Augmented reality	1
Autonomous agents	1
Case-based reasoning	1
Cognitive intelligence	1
Data mining technologies	1
Explainable artificial intelligence	1
Multi-agent systems	1
Predictive analytics	1
Rule-based systems	1
Sensors	1
Serious games	1
Simulated annealing	1
Virtual reality	1

Source: Authors' own elaboration.

Government Artificial Intelligence Topics for Research

The potential and consequences of artificial intelligence in the public sector are a relatively recent topic on the agenda of governments and scientific research. There are some potential benefits and implications of artificial intelligence adoption regarding different topics on the government agenda. Some of these topics are related to business intelligence models, deep learning, data-driven decision-making, crime prediction, and policymaking (de Bruijn et al., 2021; Khan et al., 2021; Valle-Cruz et al., 2022).

Explainable artificial intelligence attempts to counteract the opaque, black-box approaches that often cannot explain where a decision comes from or how it is justified, especially in applications for system risk identification, immigration control, and crime prediction. The more complex artificial intelligence models become, the more accurate they are, but the explainability of how they work can be lost. Explainable, data-driven decisions are often not perceived as objective by the public (de Bruijn et al., 2021).

Artificial intelligence applications related to natural environments and disaster management are a growing research area. In this regard, Kankanamge et al. (2021) argue that it is necessary to understand the functionality and importance of artificial intelligence utilisation to manage and monitor environmental conditions and weather patterns. It is also essential to reduce unnecessary pollution generation and manage the supply of renewable energy through intelligent grid systems (Ahmad et al., 2022).

Furthermore, Loukis et al. (2020) argue a lack of research related to the exploitation of artificial intelligence for the support and enhancement of the higher-level functions of government, especially the strategic ones regarding policymaking. In this regard, AI-based decision support could affect government processes and public policy. It is a topic that needs further research, as there is mistrust in using artificial intelligence applications, bias and discrimination in data and algorithms (Janssen, Hartog, et al., 2020; Valle-Cruz et al., 2022).

Artificial intelligence could empower smart cities and the transportation industry, benefitting governments and society. Some applications have a role in autonomous vehicles, traffic management, route optimisation, logistics, and robotics (Iyer, 2021; Upchurch, 2018). Regarding all these ideas and according to the findings of the systematic literature review, the artificial intelligence techniques applied to the public sector that should be further studied in the near future are:

1. AI-based business intelligence for government
2. AI and data-driven models
3. AI applications concerning the natural and built environments
4. AI for crime prediction
5. AI for policymaking
6. AI for supporting higher level functions
7. Applications for government efficiency
8. Augmented reality and autonomous agents for public services
9. Big data collection and integration for decision-making
10. Data-learning AI development customised for different industries
11. Deep learning and deep neural networks for government
12. Detecting racial bias in algorithms
13. Explainable Artificial Intelligence and interpretable machine learning
14. Intelligent transportation systems
15. Optimisation technology development
16. Prediction and prognosis technology development
17. Predictive analytics
18. Robotics in the public sector

THEMATIC ANALYSIS

Despite the increasing number of conceptual studies and frameworks proposed about the use of artificial intelligence in the public sector, there is still a gap in empirical studies and understanding individual applications in specific contexts. AI-based algorithms and applications could have significant benefits and unexpected outcomes for public organisations and society at large. The unprecedented increase in computing power and data availability has significantly altered organisations' strategies and scope in terms of decisions built on the use of technologies and analytics (de Bruijn et al., 2021; Valle-Cruz et al., 2022).

This section is divided into two parts. The first part covers four main research themes related to artificial intelligence in government settings: artificial intelligence governance, biases and discrimination, explainability, and other challenges. The second part outlines potential applications of artificial intelligence in the public sector, as revealed by this systematic literature review.

General Topics in Current Research about Artificial Intelligence in Government

Artificial intelligence governance

Governance is a recurring topic in studying artificial intelligence (AI) in the public sector. According to Pi (2021), government machine-learning applications need more theoretical and empirical studies and a clear governance framework. The author argues that the public sector plays a dual role: as regulators of AI, governments are obliged to protect citizens from the detrimental impact of algorithms, while as users of AI, governments face pressure to increase their efficiency and respond to the demands of a rapidly evolving society.

Several challenges arise in this context, including issues related to (a) fairness, bias, and discrimination; (b) explainability, transparency, and accountability; and (c) institutional change. To address these challenges, some potential solutions include the design of a user-centered explainable AI, using algorithmic impact assessments, and transforming towards an AI-powered culture.

The rapid evolution of artificial intelligence and the intensifying adoption of artificial intelligence in autonomous vehicles, lethal weapon systems, and robotics raises severe challenges for governments as they must manage the scale and speed of the occurring sociotechnical transitions (Iyer, 2021; Pi, 2021). Implementing artificial intelligence applications in the public sector poses some threats and challenges regarding artificial intelligence governance related to bias and discrimination (Wang and Ma, 2022).

Biases and discrimination

Nevertheless, online economics has not solved the problem of racial bias in its applications. While algorithms are procedures that facilitate automated decision-making, or a sequence of precise instructions, bias is a byproduct of these calculations, which disadvantages historically disadvantaged groups (Galaz et al., 2021; Pi, 2021). In this regard, Lee (2018) argues that algorithmic biases explicitly and implicitly disadvantage racial groups and lead to forms of discrimination. The author posits the need for greater workplace diversity within high-tech industries and public policies that can detect or reduce the likelihood of racial bias in the design and execution of algorithms. Findings suggest that explicit racial bias in algorithms can be mitigated by existing laws, including governing housing, employment, and credit granting. Implicit or unconscious biases are more difficult to correct given the lack of more diverse workplaces and public policies that take a bias detection and mitigation approach.

This document discusses the potential consequences of implementing artificial intelligence applications in the public sector, specifically the growth of digital divides and inequalities. Those who lack access to technology may be further disadvantaged, exacerbating existing inequalities and the deprivation of vulnerable groups (Galaz et al., 2021).

Explainability

De Bruijn et al. (2021) analysed strategies for explainable artificial intelligence (XAI) in three case studies. They found that the context can create strong incentives to challenge and distrust the explanation of artificial intelligence, leading to solid societal resistance. The authors argue that explaining the working and functionality of an algorithm to the public, which might at first sight appear to be a simple problem for the public sector, is often much more complicated. Some of these complex situations include (a) lack of technical knowledge among the public, (b) contested explanations, (c) explanations that may change over time or differ from case to case, (d) various data sources and algorithms being used, (e) algorithms that perform differently from their explanation, and (f) ambiguous problems that can be approached in different ways. Additionally, the sociopolitical context in which XAI is employed can create strong incentives to distrust artificial intelligence explanations, regardless of quality. This is particularly true in situations of high levels of politicisation and where the impact of decisions is high.

Other challenges

Some aspects, such as bias and discrimination, raise challenges in designing, implementing, and using artificial intelligence applications in government. Regarding this idea, Dwivedi et al. (2021) classify artificial intelligence challenges into seven categories: (a) ethical, (b) political, (c) legal and policy, (d) organisational and managerial, (e) data and technological, (f) social, and (g) economic. The authors identified specific artificial intelligence techniques for decision-making, application, and data and information management in their study. In addition, they argue that the trajectory toward the rise of artificial intelligence applications has the potential to change many aspects of human life and impact society. Artificial intelligence can bring numerous benefits, but there is also a significant risk that sectors of society will be excluded from the application of the technology.

Also, Medaglia et al. (2021) argue that artificial intelligence research in public administration is transitioning to what promises to be a pivotal stage. After an initial stage characterised by mapping the risks and benefits of artificial intelligence, a systematic analysis of the benefits and challenges of designing, managing, adapting, and implementing artificial intelligence in government is underway. This research highlights several areas of analysis governance of artificial intelligence, trustworthy artificial intelligence, impact assessment methodologies, and data governance.

Research and policy initiatives focused on artificial intelligence in government are developing rapidly and becoming increasingly relevant worldwide. In this regard, some governments are adopting intelligent technological changes, profoundly impacting the structure of public administration. In this regard, Vogl et al. (2020) analysed the scope and nature of changes in public administration caused by artificial intelligence, focusing on autonomous agents and predictive analytics. The results suggest that local authorities are beginning to adopt innovative technologies. These technologies are having an unforeseen impact on how public administrators and computational algorithms are imbricated in the delivery of public services. This imbrication is described as algorithmic bureaucracy providing a framework to explore how these technologies transform the sociotechnical relationship between workers and their tools and how work is organised in the public sector.

To realise benefits in the delivery of public services, managers of public organisations have significantly increased the adoption of artificial intelligence systems. However, empirical studies on artificial intelligence are still scarce, and it is necessary to systematise the progress of this technology in the public sector, its applications, and its results. De Sousa et al. (2019) examine research about artificial intelligence applied to the public sector, identifying more significant activity in India and the United States. Public services, economic affairs, and environmental protection are the government functions with the most AI-related studies. In addition, the artificial neural network (ANN) technique is the most recurrent in the studies investigated, providing positive results in several areas of application.

Advances in artificial intelligence have attracted the attention of researchers and practitioners. They have opened beneficial opportunities for the use of artificial intelligence in the public sector. In this regard, Wirtz et al. (2019) argued that artificial intelligence applications and challenges have been studied mainly in an isolated and fragmented manner. Their study analyses and compiles relevant insights from the scientific literature to provide an integrative overview of artificial intelligence applications and related challenges. Their findings identified ten areas where artificial intelligence can be applied in the public sector: (1) AI-based knowledge management software, (2) AI process automation systems, (3) virtual agents, (4) predictive analytics and data visualisation, (5) identity analytics, (6) cognitive robotics and autonomous systems, (7) recommendation systems, (8) speech analytics, (9) intelligent digital assistants, and (10) cognitive security analytics and threat intelligence.

Potential Applications of Artificial Intelligence in the Public Sector

Sustainability and climate change

One area in which artificial intelligence has the potential to generate benefits for society is sustainability. Galaz et al. (2021) analysed technocracy in government in an opaque environment with high degrees of automation. The authors discovered that the most rapid development of artificial intelligence and associated technologies in the sustainability domain is occurring in agriculture, with significant investments in China and the United States. The rapid adoption of artificial intelligence by some countries and the lag of others may result in algorithmic biases, distributional effects, and vulnerabilities, all of which can be addressed through artificial intelligence principles and standards. However, this must be complemented by governance mechanisms capable of explicitly integrating sustainability dimensions.

It is difficult to assess the extent to which the risks identified are intrinsic to artificial intelligence and associated technologies or whether they arise because of 'pacing problems' created by new uses of artificial intelligence technologies in various social and environmental contexts, given that both the development and use of these technologies are nascent.

Public policy and politics

Artificial intelligence has the potential to outperform human decision-making in specific domains. It is especially the case when advanced strategic reasoning and analysis of large amounts of data are needed to solve complex problems, which is the case in policy analysis. In this regard, Loukis et al. (2020) proposed a public sector data analysis methodology based on artificial intelligence applications to support policy formulation for managing economic crises leading to economic downturns.

The proposed methodology allows for identifying the characteristics of organisations and their external environment that positively or negatively affects their resilience to economic downturns. All this provides a better understanding of which type of organisations are most affected by the crisis, helping to design public policies for their support. In addition, it sheds light on the practices, resources, and capabilities that enable organisations to improve their ability to cope with the economic crisis. According to the authors, this perspective can be beneficial for designing more effective public policies to reduce the negative impacts of economic crises and thus mitigate their negative consequences for society, such as unemployment, poverty, and social exclusion.

Technology policy in artificial intelligence plays a crucial role in directing its applications toward broadly relevant endpoints and contributes to the critical governance of innovations by governments, industry, and society. Yang and Huang (2022) analysed AI-related policies in China and identified four stages of their evolution based on the frequency of policy issuance, policy trends, and temporal nodes. In their analysis, they found patterns and characteristics of the policy process and anticipated some trends, proposing a quantitative mapping that could be useful for AI policy in China and elsewhere in the world.

Smart cities and intelligent transportation

Artificial intelligence has gained ground worldwide over the last two decades, thanks to the massive volume of data generated through the Internet. Recently, the algorithmic processing of this data has been enormously beneficial to governments and businesses. The robust growth of machine learning algorithms, supported by various technologies such as the Internet of Things, robotic process automation, computer vision, and natural language processing, has enabled the growth of artificial intelligence towards the fourth industrial revolution and the creation of smart cities.

In this regard, Iyer (2021) analysed the issues affecting intelligent transportation systems. Some of the subsystems considered are related to traffic management, public transportation, safety management, manufacturing, and logistics of intelligent transportation systems in which the advantages of artificial intelligence are used. The author argues that artificial intelligence applications raise numerous ethical, social, economic, and legal issues. AI-based applications, being data-driven, raise the issue of cybersecurity and data privacy. An example where artificial intelligence applications are faced with life-or-dead situations is in autonomous vehicles. For this reason, it is essential to grasp how an artificial intelligence algorithm in a fully automated vehicle would make decisions compared to humans. Lack of clear policies, resistance to adopting new technologies, and failure to establish ethical regulations have made artificial intelligence solutions quite elusive for many organisations.

Artificial intelligence is beginning to play an essential role in the energy market. Ahmad et al. (2022) analysed the importance of artificial intelligence in energy systems, finding that the main drivers are fuzzy logic systems, artificial neural networks, genetic algorithms, and expert systems. The energy industry has started using artificial intelligence to connect smart meters, smart grids, and Internet of Things devices in developed countries. These artificial intelligence technologies will lead to improved efficiency, energy management, transparency, and the use of renewable energy. Artificial intelligence can provide businesses and citizens with utilities based on renewable and affordable electricity from alternative sources safely and securely while providing the opportunity to use self-generated energy more efficiently.

Lee and Lim (2021) analysed 660 journal articles and 3,901 news articles through text mining with unsupervised machine learning algorithms to understand Industry 4.0 from multiple disciplinary perspectives. They classify and describe a five-level hierarchy based on their results: (1) infrastructure development for connectivity, (2) artificial intelligence development for data-driven decision-making, (3) system and process optimisation, (4) industrial innovation, and (5) social advancement.

Disaster management

Artificial intelligence has increasingly been used in disaster management activities in recent years. The public engages with artificial intelligence in various ways, with crowdsourcing applications developed for disaster management to manage data collection tasks through social media platforms and increase disaster awareness through vital gaming applications. In this regard, Kankanamge et al. (2021) analysed the public perception of artificial intelligence for disaster management, with the results: (a) younger generations are more appreciative of the opportunities created by AI-driven applications for disaster management, (b) people with higher education have a better understanding of the benefits of artificial intelligence in pre-and post-disaster management, and also (c) administrative and security workers in the public sector, who play a crucial role in disaster management, value artificial intelligence support in disaster management more. The study advocates that the relevant authorities consider public perceptions in their efforts to integrate artificial intelligence into disaster management; however, this perspective can be extended to other public services.

Healthcare policy and programs

During the global public health emergency caused by COVID-19, medical experts began working around the clock to find new technologies to mitigate the COVID-19 pandemic. Recent studies have shown that artificial intelligence has been successfully employed in the healthcare sector for various programs and procedures. In this regard, Khan et al. (2021) provide a comprehensive review of the state-of-the-art applications of artificial intelligence to combat the COVID-19 pandemic. The authors identified that the application of artificial intelligence includes screening and diagnosis, drug repurposing, and prediction and prognosis. It was found that the convolutional neural network (CNN) and its modified models were primarily used to predict the COVID-19 pandemic. In contrast, in the case of machine learning, support vector machine, K-means, linear regression, and random forest were mainly used to combat the COVID-19 pandemic.

Employment and workforce substitution

One topic that has been debated for decades because of the adoption of technologies is employment. In this regard, Upchurch (2018) analysed the long-term debates about technological uniqueness and the sociotechnical and economic limitations of applying robotics and artificial intelligence. The author found that predictions about the end of human labour because of replacement by robots and artificial intelligence lack sufficient analysis and evidence covering technical, social, and economic effects.

Upchurch (2018) argues that '… many of the "end of work" hypotheses, Keynes, through Toffler, Gorz, and Mason [proposed], are based on increased productivity resulting from computerisation, information technology, digitisation, or robotics/artificial intelligence'. However, apart from the 'Golden Age' of the 1950s and 1960s, productivity seems to be decreasing rather than improving as new technologies are incorporated. The reasons for the failure are complex and belie any deterministic approach. First, while new technologies can alter modes of production, their transformative potential is limited by the dialectic of use and non-use, conditioned by factors beyond mere technical innovation.

The authors suggest that job displacement will always be a reason to invest in robots or artificial intelligence. However, the benefits are short-lived, as congestion and other effects subsume the initial impact of the investment. More importantly, robots are still machines and are 'dead' labour that merely passes on current value rather than creates new value.

Public employees play a vital role in adopting and using new technologies in public administration. Their attitude and readiness to use them are relevant to generating sustainable and meaningful digital transformation. Ahn and Chen (2021) explore how the perception of government employees shapes the willingness to support the use of artificial intelligence applications in government, finding that the willingness to implement and employ artificial intelligence technologies in public administration depends on perceptions about new technologies, long-term perspective on the role of artificial intelligence technologies in society, and familiarity with and experience in using some artificial intelligence applications in the past.

The authors found that the perception that artificial intelligence improves work efficiency and effectiveness and a positive, long-term perspective on the future of artificial intelligence concerning human work, the perception of the ultimate harm or benefit of the technology, and their eventual ability to make ethical and moral judgments influenced the willingness to support artificial intelligence technologies in management. A substantial proportion of public employees in the survey responded that they had experienced using some artificial intelligence applications in their work, and this familiarity strongly influences their support for artificial intelligence.

Public safety and crime prediction

Caldwell et al. (2020) conducted a study to identify potential applications of artificial intelligence and related technologies in crime perpetration, identifying some threats. Among those with the most significant social impact are AI-generated fake content and the abuse of driverless vehicle technology to commit terrorist attacks.

Wang and Ma (2022) apply machine learning algorithms to research the prevention of crimes that endanger public health to improve the effectiveness of crime prevention. The authors establish a crime behaviour prediction model based on support vector machines and random forests and use the model to analyse its performance. The results show that this crime prediction model based on a support vector machine and random forest can indeed predict the incidence of crime. The trend of their predicted data is consistent with the actual data. Their findings show that the prediction model established by the artificial intelligence algorithm can effectively predict crime behaviours that endanger public health and provide reliable data for prevention.

Better provision of public services

Androutsopoulou et al. (2019) proposed an architecture for exploiting chatbots in the public sector to improve communication between the government and citizens. The approach is based on natural language processing, machine learning, and data mining technologies, and leverages existing data to develop a new digital communication channel. The main contribution of this work is the integration of toolsets and services to meet the diverse requirements related to communication between citizens and government. The study highlights the potential use of chatbots in the public sector.

Artificial intelligence generates a lot of buzz and excitement about the possibilities it offers governments to deliver better services and interact with citizens, especially in complex policy and service areas (Henman, 2020; Pi, 2021). At the same time, the prospects for artificial intelligence in public administration are also generating considerable concern about its possibilities for accountability, control, and impact on social relations. New technologies, as always, present both positive and negative alternatives. The challenge is to shape and use artificial intelligence to enhance and protect social and economic goals (Loukis et al., 2020; Upchurch, 2018; Valle-Cruz et al., 2022).

Henman (2020) studied how artificial intelligence is used in the public sector for automated decision-making, expressly using chatbots to provide information, advice, and public safety. In his analysis, he identified four challenges to the deployment of artificial intelligence in public administration: accuracy, bias and discrimination; legality, due process and administrative justice; responsibility, accountability, transparency, and explainability; and power, compliance, and control. The authors argue that ethical, legal, and social challenges are not unique to artificial intelligence but are exacerbated by artificial intelligence applications in the public sector.

The use of artificial intelligence applications (and non-AI algorithms) to automate current human activities or do things that were not possible before (for example, making decisions in human service delivery) is where new ethical, legal, and social challenges are emerging. On this continuum of technology adoption (from personal computers to artificial intelligence), insights, experiences, and responses from the past can be leveraged in the deployment of algorithms in government, and learnings from the use of artificial intelligence can be transferred from one place to another.

Internal efficiency of government agencies

Taeihagh (2021) analyses artificial intelligence and describes why more attention should be paid to artificial intelligence governance, arguing that new applications on it offer opportunities to increase economic efficiency and quality of life but also generate unexpected and unintended consequences and pose new forms of risk that must be addressed. To enhance the benefits of artificial intelligence and minimise adverse risks, governments worldwide must better understand the scope and depth of the risks posed and develop regulatory and governance processes and structures to address these challenges. Perhaps the efficiency of public administration will be the immediate application of artificial intelligence from a deterministic point of view; however, in government organisations, all this is more complex.

Artificial intelligence-based decision-making

Artificial intelligence has become an essential tool for governments around the world. However, it is not clear how artificial intelligence can improve decision-making. In this regard, Valle-Cruz, Fernandez-Cortez, and Gil-Garcia (2022) analysed the potential of artificial intelligence techniques in the allocation of public budgets by employing an intelligent budget machine, finding that the advantages of implementing this type of technology as decision support in the assignment of public spending arise from the ability to process large amounts of data and find patterns that are not easy to detect, which include multiple nonlinear relationships. The authors also argue that the perspective supported by artificial intelligence applications has the potential to generate creative ways for decision-making but that it is difficult to include in an artificial intelligence model all the complexity inherent in the phenomena and problems faced by the public sector.

Furthermore, Janssen, Hartog, et al. (2020) argue that artificial intelligence algorithms are increasingly used to support government decision-making. However, they are often opaque to decision-makers and lack clear explanations of their decisions. For this reason, they compare decision-making in three situations: humans making decisions (1) without any algorithm support, (2) supported by business rules, and (3) supported by machine learning. In their study, they found that algorithms help decision-makers make better decisions. The results suggest that explainable artificial intelligence combined with experience helps them detect incorrect suggestions made by algorithms. The findings imply that algorithms should be adopted with caution and that selecting suitable algorithms to support decisions and training decision-makers are critical factors in increasing accountability and transparency.

CONCLUDING REMARKS

This chapter explored AI applications and algorithms in the public sector through a systematic literature review in the Web of Science, Scopus, and Science Direct. The findings showed an increase in studies on artificial intelligence in the public sector, which include a variety of artificial intelligence algorithms and applications used by government organisations. Our study contributes to existing research by identifying and elaborating on specific AI applications and algorithms in the public sector and the potential consequences of implementing some of these emerging technologies.

The first research question asks about the most common artificial intelligence techniques used in the public sector. The findings show a clear dominance of machine learning, which generates mathematical and algorithmic models based on data, and has the potential to support decision-making, improve efficiency, and enable mass automation. However, intelligent automation is not expected to totally replace the government workforce in the short term. Additionally, despite machine learning being only one AI technique, some studies use the terms 'artificial intelligence' and 'machine learning' interchangeably, which contributes to its dominance and high visibility in the field.

Our second research question is: what are the consequences of implementing intelligent algorithms and cognitive machines in the public sector? We found similar conclusions to those of de Sousa et al. (2019), Medaglia et al. (2021), and Wirtz et al. (2019). On one hand, implementing AI in the public sector could lead to automation, efficiency, and improved decision support. More specifically, AI has the potential to revolutionise the public sector regarding sustainability and climate change. It could monitor and potentially predict environmental changes, analyse large data sets to identify climate and weather patterns, and develop models for energy efficiency and resource optimisation. As another specific example, AI can also aid in disaster management by providing real-time information and assisting in recovery efforts. Furthermore, AI can improve government operations by automating processes, improving decision-making, detecting fraud and corruption, and enhancing tax compliance and adherence to regulations. These benefits could lead to increased efficiency and better public services. The possibilities from using AI are virtually endless, and the public sector could greatly benefit from its implementation. Therefore, overall, AI has the potential to revolutionise the public sector, resulting in more effective outcomes and improved services.

However, artificial intelligence applications in the public sector also present significant challenges such as algorithmic biases, which may lead to discrimination against racial minorities, such as Blacks and Latinos. Additionally, access to advanced AI technologies may not be available to the most vulnerable groups with the greatest needs, increasing inequities. Machine learning techniques rely heavily on statistical models and algorithms that allow machines to learn and improve on experience without being explicitly programmed. Applications of AI can automate various tasks such as fraud detection, recommendation systems, and natural language processing. However, data-driven AI algorithms trained on partial or incomplete data may yield systematic biases. For instance, facial recognition technology experiences lower accuracy rates for Black and Latino people, leading to possible discrimination against people of colour. Such challenges may lead to unintended negative consequences, particularly in policies and programs related to social welfare, criminal justice, and healthcare.

Today, AI research in public administration heavily focuses on governance and transparency. Policies, regulations, and ethical considerations are important to guide the development and deployment of AI in the public sector. Therefore, AI algorithms' decision-making processes must be understood to ensure transparency, accountability, and ethical considerations. In addition, governments' adoption of AI technologies can have economic and social implications. For example, the automation of jobs may negatively impact specific sectors, potentially damaging the economy and the wellbeing of society. AI implementation should prioritise responsible and ethical AI standards to address biases, ensure transparency and accountability, and promote equity and inclusion. Additional research in AI governance and explainability can be valuable in guiding policy decisions about to what extent AI should be used in certain government programs and functions.

REFERENCES

Ahmad, T., Zhu, H., Zhang, D., Tariq, R., Bassam, A., Ullah, F., AlGhamdi, A. S., and Alshamrani, S. S. (2022). Energetics systems and artificial intelligence: Applications of industry 4.0. *Energy Reports*, 8, 334–361.

Ahn, M. J., and Chen, Y.-C. (2021). Digital transformation toward AI-augmented public administration: The perception of government employees and the willingness to use AI in government. *Government Information Quarterly*, 39(2), 101664.

Androutsopoulou, A., Karacapilidis, N., Loukis, E., and Charalabidis, Y. (2019). Transforming the communication between citizens and government through AI-guided chatbots. *Government Information Quarterly*, 36(2), 358–367. https://doi.org/10.1016/j.giq.2018.10.001.

Caldwell, M., Andrews, J. T. A., Tanay, T., and Griffin, L. D. (2020). AI-enabled future crime. *Crime Science*, 9(1), 1–13.

Chakraborty, U., Banerjee, A., Saha, J. K., Sarkar, N., and Chakraborty, C. (2022). *Artificial Intelligence and the Fourth Industrial Revolution*. Jenny Stanford Publishing Pte. Ltd.

Criado, J. I., and Gil-Garcia, J. R. (2019). Creating public value through smart technologies and strategies: From digital services to artificial intelligence and beyond. *International Journal of Public Sector Management*, 32(5), 438–450. https://doi.org/10.1108/IJPSM-07-2019-0178.

de Bruijn, H., Warnier, M., and Janssen, M. (2021). The perils and pitfalls of explainable AI: Strategies for explaining algorithmic decision-making. *Government Information Quarterly*, 39(2), 101666.

de Sousa, W. G., de Melo, E. R. P., Bermejo, P. H. D. S., Farias, R. A. S., and Gomes, A. O. (2019). How and where is artificial intelligence in the public sector going? A literature review and research agenda. *Government Information Quarterly*, 36(4), 101392.

Dwivedi, Y. K., Hughes, L., Ismagilova, E., Aarts, G., Coombs, C., Crick, T., Duan, Y., Dwivedi, R., Edwards, J., Eirug, A., Galanos, V., Ilavarasan, P. V., Janssen, M., Jones, P., Kar, A. K., Kizgin, H., Kronemann, B., Lal, B., Lucini, B., … Williams, M. D. (2021). Artificial Intelligence (AI): Multidisciplinary perspectives on emerging challenges, opportunities, and agenda for research, practice and policy. *International Journal of Information Management*, 57(April 2021), 0–1. https://doi.org/10.1016/j.ijinfomgt.2019.08.002.

Galaz, V., Centeno, M. A., Callahan, P. W., Causevic, A., Patterson, T., Brass, I., Baum, S., Farber, D., Fischer, J., and Garcia, D. (2021). Artificial intelligence, systemic risks, and sustainability. *Technology in Society*, 67(November 2021), 101741.

Henman, P. (2020). Improving public services using artificial intelligence: possibilities, pitfalls, governance. *Asia Pacific Journal of Public Administration*, 42(4), 209–221.

Iyer, L. S. (2021). AI enabled applications towards intelligent transportation. *Transportation Engineering*, 5(September 2021), 100083.

Janssen, M., Brous, P., Estevez, E., Barbosa, L. S., and Janowski, T. (2020). Data governance: Organizing data for trustworthy Artificial Intelligence. *Government Information Quarterly*, 37(3), 101493.

Janssen, M., Hartog, M., Matheus, R., Yi Ding, A., and Kuk, G. (2020). Will algorithms blind people? The effect of explainable AI and decision-makers' experience on AI-supported decision-making in government. *Social Science Computer Review*, 40(2), 0894439320980118.

Kankanamge, N., Yigitcanlar, T., and Goonetilleke, A. (2021). Public perceptions on artificial intelligence driven disaster management: Evidence from Sydney, Melbourne and Brisbane. *Telematics and Informatics*, 65(December 2021), 101729.

Khan, M., Mehran, M. T., Haq, Z. U., Ullah, Z., Naqvi, S. R., Ihsan, M., and Abbass, H. (2021). Applications of artificial intelligence in COVID-19 pandemic: A comprehensive review. *Expert Systems with Applications*, 185(December 2021), 115695.

Lee, C., and Lim, C. (2021). From technological development to social advance: A review of Industry 4.0 through machine learning. *Technological Forecasting and Social Change*, 167(June 2021), 120653.

Lee, N. T. (2018). Detecting racial bias in algorithms and machine learning. *Journal of Information, Communication and Ethics in Society*, 16(3), 252–260.

Loukis, E. N., Maragoudakis, M., and Kyriakou, N. (2020). Artificial intelligence-based public sector data analytics for economic crisis policymaking. *Transforming Government: People, Process and Policy*, 14(4), 639–662.

Makridakis, S. (2017). The forthcoming Artificial Intelligence (AI) revolution: Its impact on society and firms. *Futures*, 90, 46–60.

Medaglia, R., Gil-Garcia, J. R., and Pardo, T. A. (2021). Artificial intelligence in government: Taking stock and moving forward. *Social Science Computer Review*, 08944393211034087.

Page, M. J., McKenzie, J. E., Bossuyt, P. M., Boutron, I., Hoffmann, T. C., Mulrow, C. D., Shamseer, L., Tetzlaff, J. M., Akl, E. A., Brennan, S. E., and others. (2021). The PRISMA 2020 statement: An updated guideline for reporting systematic reviews. *Systematic Reviews*, 10(1), 1–11.

Philbeck, T., and Davis, N. (2018). The fourth industrial revolution. *Journal of International Affairs*, 72(1), 17–22.

Pi, Y. (2021). Machine learning in governments: Benefits, challenges and future directions. *JeDEM-EJournal of EDemocracy and Open Government*, 13(1), 203–219.

PRISMA. (2015). Welcome to the Preferred Reporting Items for Systematic Reviews and Meta-Analyses (PRISMA) website! PRISMA Ottawa, ON, Canada.

Righetti, L., Madhavan, R., and Chatila, R. (2019). Unintended consequences of biased robotic and artificial intelligence systems [ethical, legal, and societal issues]. *IEEE Robotics & Automation Magazine*, 26(3), 11–13.

Sun, T. Q., and Medaglia, R. (2019). Mapping the challenges of Artificial Intelligence in the public sector: Evidence from public healthcare. *Government Information Quarterly*, 36(2), 368–383. https://doi.org/10.1016/j.giq.2018.09.008.

Taeihagh, A. (2021). Governance of artificial intelligence. *Policy and Society*, 40(2), 1–21.

Upchurch, M. (2018). Robots and AI at work: The prospects for singularity. *New Technology, Work and Employment*, 33(3), 205–218.

Valle-Cruz, D., Criado, J. I., Sandoval-Almazán, R., and Ruvalcaba-Gomez, E. A. (2020). Assessing the public policy-cycle framework in the age of artificial intelligence: From agenda-setting to policy evaluation. *Government Information Quarterly*, 37(4), 101509.

Valle-Cruz, D., Fernandez-Cortez, V., and Gil-Garcia, J. R. (2022). From E-budgeting to smart budgeting: Exploring the potential of artificial intelligence in government decision-making for resource

allocation. *Government Information Quarterly*, 39(2). https://doi.org/https://doi.org/10.1016/j.giq
.2021.101644.

Valle-Cruz, D., Fernandez-Cortez, V., López-Chau, A., and Sandoval-Almazán, R. (2021). Does Twitter
affect stock market decisions? Financial sentiment analysis during pandemics: A comparative study
of the H1N1 and the COVID-19 periods. *Cognitive Computation*, 1–16.

Valle-Cruz, D., Gil-Garcia, J. R., and Fernandez-Cortez, V. (2020). Towards smarter public budgeting?
Understanding the potential of artificial intelligence techniques to support decision making in government. *The 21st Annual International Conference on Digital Government Research*, 232–242.

Vogl, T. M., Seidelin, C., Ganesh, B., and Bright, J. (2020). Smart technology and the emergence of algorithmic bureaucracy: Artificial intelligence in UK local authorities. *Public Administration Review*,
80(6), 946–961.

Wang, H., and Ma, S. (2022). Preventing crimes against public health with artificial intelligence and
machine learning capabilities. *Socio-Economic Planning Sciences*, 80(March 2022), 101043.

Wirtz, B. W., Weyerer, J. C., and Geyer, C. (2019). Artificial intelligence and the public sector–
applications and challenges. *International Journal of Public Administration*, 42(7), 596–615.

Wirtz, B. W., Weyerer, J. C., and Sturm, B. J. (2020). The dark sides of artificial intelligence: An
integrated AI governance framework for public administration. *International Journal of Public
Administration*, 43(9), 818–829.

Yang, C., and Huang, C. (2022). Quantitative mapping of the evolution of AI policy distribution, targets
and focuses over three decades in China. *Technological Forecasting and Social Change*, 174(January
2022), 121188.

Zhang, C. A., Cho, S., and Vasarhelyi, M. (2022). Explainable Artificial Intelligence (XAI) in auditing.
International Journal of Accounting Information Systems, 46(September 2022), 100572.

Zuiderwijk, A., Chen, Y.-C., and Salem, F. (2021). Implications of the use of artificial intelligence in
public governance: A systematic literature review and a research agenda. *Government Information
Quarterly*, 101577.

2. A trifold research synthesis on AI-induced service automation

Matthias Döring and Lisa Hohensinn

INTRODUCTION

'So, when we talk about the effects of automation on the pleasure of the job, we have to look not merely at the jobs that were automated, but also at the changing complexion of jobs in society as a whole' (Simon, 1981, p. 72). When Herbert Simon addressed his audience with his thoughts on the effects of automation through digitalisation forty years ago, he may have been one of the few scholars who had the potential of today's algorithms, big data, and artificial intelligence in mind. Still, the automation technology that service providers in both the public and private sectors face yields far-reaching potentials and challenges alike.

In recent years, the importance of digitalisation and service automation has increased significantly in various fields of the public sector (Desouza et al., 2020; Lindgren et al., 2019). Modern technology is leveraged to innovate government processes and to stimulate operational capacity, government effectiveness, and public service quality (Sun and Medaglia, 2019; B. W. Wirtz et al., 2020). For example, artificial intelligence (AI), face recognition, and service robots are used to communicate with citizens more efficiently, identify potential criminal activities, or support humans in caring for older people. While early stages of digitalisation have provided useful tools to support otherwise traditional and analogue service provision, new emerging technologies trigger a substantial paradigm shift in (automated) service provision.

Due to its enormous implications and relevance for governments, citizens, and other stakeholders, the research interest in service automation has experienced a boost in recent years. Whereas the digitalisation and automation of services are extensively examined in terms of their technical nature, social scientists have only started to investigate the 'human side' of digitalisation in service provision. In more specific terms, different disciplines deal with the interaction between new automation techniques and the individual being, and how service automation affects policies, trust, and societal outcomes at large.

First, in our literature review, we aim to show that these topics are covered by three distinct fields of research: digital government, service management, and public administration research. While there is a growing overlap and collaboration between these fields, they can be seen as distinct research streams. For example, all three research streams have common subjects, especially frontline employees (Breit et al., 2020; Christ-Brendemühl and Schaarschmidt, 2019; Lam et al., 2017; Løberg, 2021). However, the theoretical and methodological approaches differ quite substantially. For example, due to its multidisciplinary nature, the research field of digital government is considered a distinct field of study with its own academic community and journal outlets, although recently there have been efforts to connect with traditional public administration research (Gil-Garcia et al., 2018). In this chapter, we provide a more comprehensive picture of the state of research, which contributes to the recent systematic literature review by Zuiderwijk, Chen, and Salem (2021) on the implications for the use of AI in public governance.

Second, given the large number and heterogeneity of research approaches, this chapter aims at providing a substantial research agenda based on an overview of scholarly knowledge on (public) service automation. By structuring these insights, we compare three research fields and outline research gaps that should guide future scholars in better understanding how AI-induced technology affects citizen-government interaction. These two goals are complementary because paying attention to research in related research fields will provide us with additional insights and boundary conditions but will also highlight our knowledge gaps. Practitioners may benefit from this synthesis, as it provides a realistic picture of 'what we know and what we do not know' providing realistic expectations regarding the usability and effectiveness of AI-induced technologies.

In the following, we elaborate on three specific topics that are at the centre of recent discussions about automating citizen-government interactions: the effects on citizens, employees, and the management of frontline organisations and interactions. Within these categories, we compare insights from the three research fields to indicate overlaps and additions. The studies on which we build our literature synthesis have been collected by using appropriate search terms (for example, 'artificial intelligence', 'automation', or 'robotisation'), including respective multiple variations in the leading journals within the three research fields. For developing the research gaps for future research, we included empirical studies (qualitative, quantitative, or experimental) that were published before early 2021.

'GETTING TO GRIPS' WITH AI-INDUCED TECHNOLOGY

While being exposed daily to numerous examples of automated services via robotisation, AI, or algorithm-based decisions, most citizens are not aware of such technologies in their service consumption (for example, while using Google Maps). Still, customers value the efficiency of automated processes and accuracy of suggestion systems when looking for new products or services. While these new technologies have already penetrated a broad range of business-to-consumer markets (Guha et al., 2021), they are also increasingly employed in knowledge-intensive business-to-business markets that provide professional services (Pemer, 2021). In the public sector, such applications are not as ubiquitous for various reasons, such as demanding legal standards, a lack of investments in innovative technology for administrative procedures, a resistant organisational culture, or a lack of political leadership (De Vries et al., 2016). Furthermore, applications are associated with challenges, such as data security and privacy, trust in and fairness of AI, ethical criteria and principles, and democratic responsiveness and accountability (Harrison and Luna-Reyes, 2020; König and Wenzelburger, 2020; B. W. Wirtz et al., 2020).

Research on the application of mentioned technologies by the private sector might further elucidate valuable implications for public sector organisations. These tools range from the use of service robots and algorithm-based decision-making to the application of AI. In the public sector, automation is often a decision support technology, intended to support public employees' decision-making processes. It rarely replaces human work, as street-level bureaucrats' decision-making cannot be fully automated but rather depends on human judgement (de Boer and Raaphorst, 2021).

As the term 'AI' tends to be used very loosely due to a lack of common definition and conceptualisation, in this chapter, we refer to Kaplan and Haenlein (2019, p. 17) who define AI as 'a system's ability to interpret external data correctly, to learn from such data, and to use those learnings to achieve specific goals and tasks through flexible adaptation'. The authors refer to different stages of AI: artificial narrow intelligence is applied for specific tasks in specific areas (for example, image detection); artificial general intelligence goes beyond human intelligence in several areas; artificial super intelligence outperforms humans in all areas due to its capacity of 'scientific creativity, social skills, and general wisdom' (Kaplan and Haenlein, 2019, p. 16).

Davenport et al. (2020) add an analytical framework to approaching AI, with the main categories: level of intelligence and type of task that is fulfilled by a specific application. For the former, they differentiate between the mere automation of task and context awareness, which is considered to be much more challenging. This context awareness requires algorithms to 'learn how to learn', which many would regard as the border between simple algorithms (broader definition) and actual artificial intelligence (narrow definition). For the latter, Davenport et al. (2020) differentiate between numeric and non-numeric data processing. Non-numeric data encompasses, for example, text, voice, and face recognition, making analyses much more complex than a statistical analysis of already quantified data. In this framework, algorithm-based decision-making would relate to rather specific applications of automated numeric data processing that provides little context awareness. Huang and Rust (2021) elaborate on a differentiated conceptualisation of AI by focusing on three criteria: the degree of learning capabilities, adaptivity, and connectivity. Accordingly, AI has the capacity for self-learning, meaning that it learns from experiences and adapts to new circumstances without additional programming intervention. Furthermore, AI is connected to other databases and applications to collect additional data and facilitate learning.

In this context, robotisation refers to the use of 'system-based autonomous and adaptable interfaces that interact, communicate and deliver service to an organisation's customers' (J. Wirtz et al., 2018, p. 909). However, concurrent (service) robots have inbuilt AI applications, making them adaptable in a service encounter setting (McLeay et al., 2021). Mende et al. (2019) provide an overview of studies investigating the use of service robots in various fields such as retail, hospitality, and dining. However, these studies also cover core areas of the public sector, such as health and education.

Public sector organisations utilise modern technology not only to design internal processes more efficiently, but also to enhance citizen-government interaction (Androutsopoulou et al., 2019). Leveraging digitalisation and automated processes might be useful for different purposes in public encounters, such as exchanging information, providing public services, and the government's monitoring of citizens' behaviour (Lindgren et al., 2019). On the one hand, new technology enables us to change the communication channel to make interactions more efficient for both citizens and public officials. On the other hand, automated systems and AI-supported decision-making open up new perspectives and possibilities for citizen-government encounters, as the initiation, duration, and scope of digital encounters greatly differ from traditional public encounters (Lindgren et al., 2019). In the following, we concentrate on the focal stakeholders involved in a citizen-government interaction and provide an overview of empirical studies in the field of digital government, service management, and public administration research.

HOW CITIZENS PERCEIVE AND BENEFIT FROM AI-INDUCED TECHNOLOGIES

Being at the receiving end of (semi-)automated services, customers are the focal stakeholders when assessing the success of digitalisation efforts. Potentially, they might benefit from fast, efficient, and failure-free services. However, due to the complexity of service delivery, scholars have been hesitant to see automation in the form of robotisation, AI support, or algorithm-based decision-making as the overall solution for improvements (Dwivedi et al., 2021; van Noordt and Misuraca, 2020).

Various studies have investigated the citizen's perspective in service automation and digitalisation, focusing on potential risks and challenges in applying AI. For example, Janssen et al. (2020) choose an empirical approach to compare decision-making in different situations and shed light on citizens' reservations about AI with respect to their limited understanding of AI decisions. Accordingly, survey participants had to assess the correctness of humans making decisions without the support of algorithms, business rules, or machine learning. Findings show that algorithms combined with experiences supported participants in making correct decisions, but participants were not able to identify all wrong decisions made by an algorithm, pointing to the limited understanding of algorithms.

With the 'black-box problem' of AI (Castelvecchi, 2016) in mind, McClure (2018) studies society's fears of new technologies, such as AI-assisted decisions. Accordingly, 'technophobes', such as those who are afraid of new technologies relevant to work, have a higher likelihood of anxiety-related mental health concerns, and socio-demographic characteristics such as education, ethnicity, and gender are related to fear of and apprehension about robots and AI. Furthermore, individuals with anxieties about technologies are more likely to fear unemployment and financial insecurity. Moreover, Larsson (2021) draws on a Norwegian case of child benefits to understand the actual inclusivity of automated systems by applying Schaffer and Huang's theory of access to digital services (Schaffer and Huang, 1975), and concludes that digitalisation can reinforce social inequalities.

However, Miller and Keiser (2021) find evidence that algorithmic decision-making tools may be perceived as a chance to inhibit existing discrimination. They show that minority groups tend to perceive decisions as fairer if they are made by such tools compared to human actors. In a similar vein, Ranerup and Henriksen (2019) conduct a qualitative, interpretive case study and question the ethical, democratic, and professional values of robotic process automation. The case describes the adoption of automated decision-making related to social assistance, and several qualitative interviews with municipal stakeholders are conducted to learn about value positions and experiences with respect to the model adopted. Their findings highlight the potential of automated decision-making for increased accountability, decreased costs, and enhanced efficiency.

To get a clearer picture about the boundary conditions of how AI-induced technologies are perceived, Aoki (2020) tests whether trust in AI chatbots depends on the area of enquiry and the government's intention to use the chatbot. Findings from an online survey experiment among 8,000 individuals living in Japan confirm that citizens' trust in this new type of communication channel depends on the purpose of communication, where trust in terms of waste sorting is highest and general information is lowest.

How Customers Perceive and Benefit from AI-Induced Technologies

While most of these studies have been conducted in a public service setting, this chapter also aims to integrate other research streams into the discussion. As customers determine the success of automated services in the private sector, it is worthwhile taking the vast literature from service management research into consideration as well. In this literature stream, scholars have focused primarily on psychological consequences of automated and robotised services (Longoni et al., 2019; McLeay et al., 2021; Mende et al., 2019). This psychological dimension relates to the design of such services, their support tools (for example, robots), and their effect on customers' acceptance.

Using multiple experimental vignette studies, Longoni et al. (2019) find substantial mistrust among consumers towards AI applications in health services. A main driver underlying this mistrust is based on the assumption that AI will not take into account personal uniqueness. This scepticism also translates to a higher standard being expected from services provided via AI compared to human providers (Davenport et al., 2020, p. 28).

McLeay et al. (2021) use experimental vignette studies to study the effects of different robot types, the extent of robotisation (augmenting vs. substituting) on the service experience and perceived service innovativeness. Overall, they find only an indirect effect on service experience via perceived innovativeness in the context of airline check-in and restaurant services (experience-based services). In cases of complete service substitution through robots, participants reported worse ethical/societal reputation of a fictitious firm. When personnel are supported by robots but not replaced by them, the authors find no effect. However, the acceptance of these robot applications depends on the context, individual characteristics of customers (openness towards innovation), and cognitive evaluations.

In a similar vein, Mende et al. (2019) employ seven experimental vignette studies using videos of different robot types, comparing classic robots to those with humanoid designs. They find that when exposed to humanoid robots, customers show signs of compensatory behaviour due to social discomfort. Thus, customers focus on status-signalling products and less healthy food, depending on the service context. The results imply that humanoid robots might actually evoke a sensation of eeriness and elicit human identity threats (often referred to as the 'uncanny valley hypothesis').

Belanche et al. (2020) examine how robotisation affects customers' assessment and attribution of service performance. Using experimental vignette studies in a hotel context, Belanche et al. find that customers are more likely to attribute service performance (especially service failures) to human employees than to robots. Likewise, the reduced responsibility attributed to robots leads to higher expectations towards the overall organisation. These results show the essential role that human service personnel play in service interactions – not only for the quality of services, but also as a buffer between customers and the service provider in general.

These studies indicate that automation and robotisation are not a panacea for service improvements and that specific design decisions matter significantly. Furthermore, customers react very differently when exposed to such examples. These results are in line with general assessments of mistrust in new technology. Nevertheless, using automated services may reduce complexity in service settings, as Gäthke (2020) shows in a field experiment in which guests of a trade fair were to use either a traditional two-dimensional map or an augmented reality guidance app. User ratings show a clear preference for the guidance app. While the example covers only a single AI capability (that is, image recognition), it provides an intriguing example of complexity reduction in a service setting that can facilitate the core of services without replacing traditional frontline employees.

All in all, the existing research provides a useful starting point for our understanding of how AI-induced technologies are perceived and judged by customers and citizens. However, the outlined overview also emphasises the research gaps that are still theoretically or empirically vague. The following research gaps are based on the entire synthesis. Where applicable, we highlight first evidence from the three fields.

Research Gap 1 (G1): Intermediate Outcomes of Automated Systems among Citizens

Automated service production and provision are assumed to enhance citizen-state interaction, such as by making communication more efficient by using AI chatbots. However, AI or algorithm-based decision-making can only be used effectively in citizen-state encounters when citizens are willing to accept this technology. Hence, questions regarding the technology acceptance of such services remain essential and are insufficiently covered by empirical studies.

Specifically, scholars will need to acknowledge the diversity of such services and types of technology. Acceptance of such services may depend on various aspects, as will be discussed in the following sections. Direct effects, however, are likely dependent on the visibility of new technologies, the extent of use (augmenting vs. substituting), and the specific tasks that such technologies fulfill. As such, simply processing standardised data (for example, processing tax data for tax returns) might be perceived as less invasive than risk assessments of long-term unemployment, which may require additional job training. Future research is recommended to explore whether there is a difference in mixed decision-making, 'where AI algorithms inform human decision-making in the public sector' (Busuioc, 2020, p. 4) and fully automated decision-making, pointing to the importance of human involvement (Aoki, 2020). In addition, perceptions of service automation might depend on the type of AI technique applied. When researching the potential of robotised services, first studies indicate differences in citizens' perceptions regarding mechanoids and humanoids (Belanche et al., 2020). Thus, robotisation may be accompanied by occurring stereotypes and features depicted in the implemented robot models that may affect the use behaviour and acceptance.

Acceptance of such new technologies is also closely related to questions of perceived fairness and reflections on ethical consequences. Prior studies (for example, Nagtegaal, 2021) found evidence for such effects, however, the study field(s) is far from reaching conclusive results. The case of autonomous driving highlights the question of responsibility attribution in dilemma situations where severe damage results from different options (Goodall, 2016). The inclusion of an additional, non-human actor sheds new light on the perceived ethics and responsibility attribution of automated decision-making. Whereas some argue that the AI provider is responsible for the outcomes of human-made machines (De George, 2008; Neri et al., 2020), others question the human control of machines and refer to the 'problem of many hands'(Coeckelbergh, 2020; van de Poel et al., 2012, p. 49). Although the responsibility of AI has been discussed in previous research (B. W. Wirtz et al., 2020), future research is recommended to investigate this issue in different fields of application. An important research avenue would be to advance our understanding of public employees' and service users' understandings of responsibility attribution and who is to blame in cases of error. The ethical dimension of AI-assisted service seems to be particularly significant when personal data is used to provide a service. Future research might ask to what extent citizens trust machines with their personal data.

Additionally, proponents of these new technologies hope that AI may be used to individualise services to a certain extent (within legal bounds), emphasising information about services depending on individual circumstances, background, and needs (Davenport et al., 2020). As administrative burdens in public service encounters are not perceived equally across citizen populations (Heinrich, 2016), such individualisation efforts may provide new approaches to lowering the experienced burden, for example by tailoring communication to individual needs, enhancing engagement, or providing additional reminders. These factors are likely to affect a wide range of customers' intermediate outcomes, such as general social acceptance of automation, the specific use behaviour, or perceived fairness of decision-making processes.

Research Gap 2 (G2): Moderating Effects Based on Citizens' Traits, Socio-Demographic Characteristics, and Competences

In addition to direct effects of technology-related characteristics, it is crucial to incorporate a citizen focus on the use and acceptance of these new technologies. Research on technology acceptance highlights the relevance of openness towards innovation and change (Rogers, 2003) and individual competences to take advantage of new technologies (Bawden, 2008). Consequently, a digital divide (Norris, 2001) may cause severe differences in the use and acceptance of automated services, depending on the respective services and technologies. As a result, digitalised services may pose an additional administrative burden (Peeters and Widlak, 2018) for those who are most vulnerable.

A lack of knowledge about the content and background of algorithmic decision-making tools may, furthermore, stir mistrust and hesitation towards such newly-designed services. However, we lack substantial empirical evidence to address these potential caveats. Both design decisions and individual factors may affect whether AI applications are perceived as service partners or potential threats (Willems et al., 2022). Additional research is needed to investigate the occurrence of 'uncanny valley effects' (Mori, 1970).

Overall, relevant skills and knowledge may also affect whether service automation is actually perceived as a reduction of the administrative burden (Herd and Moynihan, 2019). While automation may potentially reduce lengthy application processes, using and interacting with bots or digital platforms may provide just another burden for those who feel uncomfortable with digital media. Furthermore, such tools may enforce standardisation, inhibiting discretion for individual circumstances (Buffat, 2015; Peeters and Widlak, 2018).

Research Gap 3 (G3): Long-Term Outcomes of Applying Service Automation to Public Service Delivery

This research gap focuses on the ultimate outcomes of applying AI. Although previous research has already provided first evidence for citizens' trust in new types of communication channels, there is a significant research gap in the effect of using AI technology on the efficiency and effectiveness of public service delivery. In addition to tangible outcomes of automation and digitalisation of tasks, we know little about whether citizens perceive a higher service quality when AI is applied. Are citizens more satisfied with AI-assisted service delivery? Does the application of AI technology change citizens' perceptions of government accountability and legitimacy and general attitudes toward the political-administrative system? Finally, the societal consequences of applying AI-induced technology need to be explored to investigate whether certain societal groups are excluded from the digitalised society.

THE ROLE OF FRONTLINE EMPLOYEES

AI-induced technologies aiming for service automation provide yet another challenge for frontline employees (and street-level bureaucrats) similar to previous digitalisation efforts. Buffat (2015) summarises two competing hypotheses of how such technologies affect frontline employees' work. The curtailment hypothesis supposes that digital tools standardise service provision, curtailing discretion at street level. In contrast, the enablement hypothesis assumes that monotonous routine work is removed from employees' workloads, enabling them to focus on challenging cases. While these hypotheses have been formulated in a broader context of digital processing tools, they remain contemporary in the light of the aforementioned new technologies. For example, Young, Bullock, and Lecy (2019) argue for 'artificial discretion' in contrast to human discretion to understand the impact of AI on public administration and point to the possible impediments in terms of equity, manageability, and political feasibility.

Similar to research on the citizen's perspective, both the potentials and challenges of AI systems are discussed in previous research. Sun and Medaglia (2019) aim to investigate challenges for the adoption of AI in the public sector, by drawing on the concept of technological framing, and conduct a case study in public healthcare in China. In terms of organisational and managerial challenges, government policymakers point to organisational resistance to sharing data, a lack of internal knowledge on AI adoption, and the threat of replacement of the human workforce. These observations are confirmed by studies that elaborate on employees' perceptions of these new technologies. Focusing on the antecedents of AI adoption in public sector organisations more generally, Van Noordt and Misuraca (2020) adopt a multiple case study analysis and identify general key factors promoting the adoption of AI systems, including high-quality data for training AI, maintenance of data, and a data-driven service ecosystem.

To improve our understanding of the changing working routines of bureaucratic organisations resulting from applying algorithms, Meijer, Lorenz, and Wessels (2021) use in-depth qualitative research to analyse predictive policing comparatively in Germany and the Netherlands. Findings indicate that dominant norms and organisational culture affected how the systems were employed. In Berlin, the 'algorithmic cage' describes the more hierarchical control and pressure on the police to use the system, whereas in Amsterdam, the 'algorithmic colleague' provides more room for professional judgement, also pointing to the added value of the system.

These results indicate that similar tools may be differently implemented depending on the institutional setting and individual translation of such tools. Hence, using survey experiments, Nagtegaal (2021) analyses the extent to which the use of algorithms for managerial decisions has an effect on public employees' perception of procedural justice, and finds that the suitability of algorithmic decision-making depends on the complexity of the practice. Accordingly, automation works for low-complexity practices, and a public employee is needed for high-complexity practices. Furthermore, Busch, Hendriksen, and Saebo (2018) elucidate public service workers' reactions to digitised discretionary practices. Drawing on a multiple case analysis of two Norwegian organisations, they found that public service workers perceive digitalisation positively when they have the enhancement of professional aspects of their work in mind. Professional discretion is, however, important in terms of high-complexity tasks. Also, with a special focus on discretion, Ranerup and Henriksen (2020) investigate the changes in civil servants' daily lives and practices resulting from the introduction of robotic process automation (RPA). The authors analyse a case from social services in which a robot process automation is responsible for decision-making in processing requests for social assistance, even though the employee is responsible for the final decision. Findings point to the positive effect of digitalisation in social services on employees' discretionary practices with respect to ethical, democratic, and professional values, but also highlight that positive outcomes of applications are mainly handled by the RPA, and applications that are denied are processed by employees, which might have negative effects on discretion.

However, the implementation of AI-induced technologies is not always that straightforward. Focusing on challenges in implementing AI tools and respective organisational routines, Campion et al. (2020) conduct a case study investigating a collaborative project on AI between a university and county councils in England. The findings identify, among other things, resistance to data sharing due to privacy and security concerns, a lack of knowledge in terms of data management, and organisational hierarchy as barriers in adopting AI tools and implementing organisational routines.

On an organisational level, Kattel, Lember, and Tonurist (2020) investigate the role of technology in collaborative innovation. The findings from their Estonian case studies on collaborative innovation indicate the important role of inter-organisational collaboration in stimulating digital government practices. Additionally, digital infrastructure and capabilities are necessary to move towards human-machine networks and positively affect the process and outcomes of collaborative innovation initiatives. Using a case study in a Swedish public organisation, Wihlborg, Larsson, and Hedström (2016) investigate how automated decision-making changes the division of responsibility in public administration. Accordingly, automated systems change the roles and competences of professionals, and the officers' alliance with either the automated system or the client depends on legitimacy and professional competences. The authors conclude that the practice resembles either a form of caring ethics or a formal legal ethical norm.

The Role of Frontline Employees in Private Services

Again, it is worthwhile incorporating studies from the service management literature that are also interested in how frontline employees make use of these new technologies. Pemer (2021) provides an insightful case study in which she compares digitalisation effects between audit and public relation firms as examples of professional services. Her main finding is a conceptual model that describes how new technologies affect professional services, depending on a technology-service intelligence fit, occupational identity, and service climate. She shows that auditing, despite being a rather conservative and regulated industry, experiences strong disruption due to new technologies and increased competition. At an individual service level, professional frontline employees face pressures to adapt to new digital auditing services, new service roles (for example, coordinators rather than service providers), and new human-to-robot interfaces. New auditors are trained to be bilingual to translate between technological solutions and different groups of experts. Similarly, Kronblad (2020) finds disruptive changes in business models and professionals' occupational roles in legal services.

Such new service roles and the expansion of employees' domains of expertise, however, may lead to substantial resistance to change and tensions in the occupational identity, resulting in technology-induced role ambiguity (Christ-Brendemühl and Schaarschmidt, 2019). These studies imply that, independently of the sector affiliation, new technologies cause a severe shift in service professionals' job roles and occupational identities.

A more sceptical perspective on the potential of new technologies concerns the extent of implementation. For example, Lam et al. (2017) elaborate on the potential benefits and costs of big data application in frontline employee-customer interactions. While they identify a significant potential of big data applications, they concede that firms' absorptive capacities may differ substantially, potentially outweighing costs for big data adoption. Hence, AI-induced technologies should not necessarily be considered suitable for all public organisations at all levels. Moreover, the authors argue that big data should be combined with frontline employees' small data and tacit knowledge to have an effective integrated service provision. These implications are supported by Vogl et al. (2020), who conduct a case study in the UK to learn about the extent and nature of changes in local government resulting from adopting autonomous agents and predictive analysis. Their findings shed light on the government's use of chatbots as autonomous agents supporting citizen-government interactions which exemplify the potential transition from street-level to system-level administration. Accordingly, local authorities apply predictive analysis to enhance decision-making. This adoption indicates a transition to system-level bureaucracy, even though the contextual knowledge of street-level workers is inevitable in system design. Similarly, Jarrahi (2018) argues for a pragmatic approach to including AI in organisational decision-making. He implicitly supports Simon's perspective on the role of AI in overcoming the processing bottleneck of human cognitive capacities. Thus, improved processing power caused by AI provides a solution for dealing with both complexity and uncertainty. However, equivocality in decision-making requires a holistic understanding of circumstances and negotiations between various agencies and interest groups – a skill that current AI applications are not able to provide. Hence, the benefits of AI applications 'are likely to materialise only in long-term partnerships with human capabilities' (Jarrahi, 2018, p. 583). Thus, organisations should refrain from blindly relying on and automating organisational decision-making.

These studies point to various avenues for new research highlighting the substantial changes frontline employees may be facing in the next years. However, further research is needed to substantiate the early findings. Hence, we outline two additional research gaps:

Research Gap 4 (G4): Direct Effects of Automation-Based Technologies on the Use and Acceptance of Frontline Employees

The effects of digitalisation on frontline employees – and specifically street-level bureaucrats – are rooted in a long-standing discussion (Buffat, 2015). There is empirical evidence for hypotheses regarding both curtailment and enablement of discretion due to digitally supported service provision (Bruhn and Ekström, 2017; Hansen et al., 2018; Jansson and Erlingsson, 2014). However, most of these studies are based on single-case studies that provide useful theoretical insights but little empirical generalisability. As automation-based technologies constitute a next level of digital tools, the need for empirical evidence becomes even more pronounced. Hence, future studies need to address how AI-based tools, algorithmic decision-making, or robotisation affect the daily work of frontline employees. Do these tools pose a challenge or threat to existing routines, role identities, professional norms, and available discretion?

Research Gap 5 (G5): Frontline Employees' Effects on Citizens' Perception of Service Automation

Depending on the research questions addressed in G4, frontline employees may have a crucial impact on how citizens perceive these new tools. In cases of complex algorithms, such tools may serve as a Kafkaesque, inaccessible black box that is either used as a source of blind legitimacy or as a scapegoat for unfavourable decisions against citizens. Likewise, frontline employees may also serve as guides during the use of automated services. Thus, they may explain underlying decision processes, used data, routines of quality assessment, or address other ethical concerns that users may experience. Hence, while various scholars predict the diminishing role of frontline employees due to automation (Snellen, 1998, 2002), others emphasise the need for different roles during service encounters (Rafaeli et al., 2016). As a result, future studies need to address frontline employees' impact on citizens' perceptions of automated services. Relevant points raised in the literature include the dominant job role or perceived identity of frontline employees who face the implementation of AI-induced technology (for example, Christ-Brendemühl and Schaarschmidt, 2019). Thus, service professionals are more likely to struggle with changing expectations and roles. Caseworkers who previously used tacit knowledge about customers may find that such new technology threatens their potential power in service organisations.

However, AI-induced technology may also augment service provision by offering real-time support during service encounters, for example via verbal or facial recognition procedures (Davenport et al., 2020). Additionally, decision-support systems may increase the frontline employees' capacities to process data, thus strengthening the service quality and desired outcomes. However, data on such tools remain scarce (for a recent exception, see de Boer and Raaphorst, 2021).

In line with Buffat (2015), we argue for the need for better understanding of which employees are more inclined to accept such innovations and new technologies, and whether potential resistance against them is affected by individual traits, organisational culture, professional norms, or other aspects.

Research Gaps 6 And 7 (G6 & G7): Context Factors Moderating the Effects on Intermediate and Long-Term Outcomes

Finally, general context factors need to be addressed. These encompass sectoral, legal, and cultural differences that may affect the perception of these new technologies, their implementation, and their effectiveness in fulfilling service improvements. The sectoral context accounts for differences in the perception of the invasiveness of these new technologies, the need for personalisation in services, as well as associated norms within respective service sectors. While McLeay et al. (2021) provide first-hand evidence for robotisation in experience-based compared to credence-based services, a more thorough investigation of sectoral differences might be necessary. Are citizens more willing to accept automation in policy fields that mainly process people's data and – conversely – less likely to accept automation in policy areas that provide services in a human-to-human interaction? Furthermore, Belanche et al. (2020) question whether the acceptance of AI substituting human workers will differ depending on the skill-level of substituted jobs.

Lastly, cultural differences may influence individuals' roles in society. Societies in which the individual is not perceived as being as relevant as in others might be more positive towards automation of public services (Li et al., 2010; McLeay et al., 2021).

Although the digitalisation of the public sector and service automation are relevant at an international level, and many countries and international public sector organisations are concerned with these issues, previous research has mainly focused on the application of AI technology in a single country setting. However, it would be pertinent to conduct cross-national studies, as comparative analysis would improve our understanding of the roles of cultures and country contexts in the adoption of AI technologies (Meijer et al., 2021).

(FRONTLINE-) MANAGEMENT USING AI-INDUCED TECHNOLOGY

New technologies infused with complex and learning algorithms not only provide opportunities for direct service provision but may also facilitate how such services are managed – an aspect that is often overlooked in public administration research. Similarly, concepts, such as smart city, may benefit from AI-induced technologies due to the potential of smart combinations of data sources and analysis of data patterns (Meijer and Bolívar, 2016).

However, AI and other automation enhancers may also be useful for improving management. Bromuri et al. (2021), for example, develop a deep learning model to automatically assess the stress levels of frontline employees based on speech emotion recognition. This specific example has been applied in a call centre context, however, application in traditional service encounters seems feasible as well. Such tools may augment frontline management to protect their employees, especially in a service context in which employees face strong emotional strain, for example, due to aggressive customers or heavy emotional labour.

Furthermore, the emergence of chatbots can be seen as an opportunity to acquire rich data on customers' experiences. Sidaoui et al. (2020) develop a deep-learning tool that uses sentiment analysis from free-text and closed-ended questions to provide a fine-grained customer satisfaction assessment. Using such chatbots, organisations are able to combine the richness of traditional interviewers with the scalability of satisfaction surveys, thus providing a cost-efficient analysis.

While these studies provide intriguing approaches to how management may change due to AI-induced technology, none of the research streams reviewed in this chapter captures the potential and challenges sufficiently. This is a more general research gap that has been widely neglected so far.

A MODEL FOR AI-INDUCED TECHNOLOGIES

Based on the findings of the review of the current body of knowledge on digitalisation and service automation in the public and private sector, we developed a conceptual model (see Figure 2.1). This integrative model illustrates how AI-induced technology relates to public employees, citizens, and the organisational context. In addition, the short-term and long-term outcomes of adopting AI-induced technology are scrutinised. In addition to the main concepts relevant to research, we identify the presented research gaps that should guide future research to improve our understanding of digital technology and automated systems in the context of public management.

The model highlights that the success of adopting AI-induced technology depends not only on technical terms but also on different government stakeholders and contextual factors. More than that, the interplay between technology and human actors only is assumed to produce positive outcomes for both the government and citizens, which is illustrated by the arrows in Figure 2.1. Shedding light on how the different research areas are connected and depend on each other is not just valuable for advancing theory but also for developing practical implications.

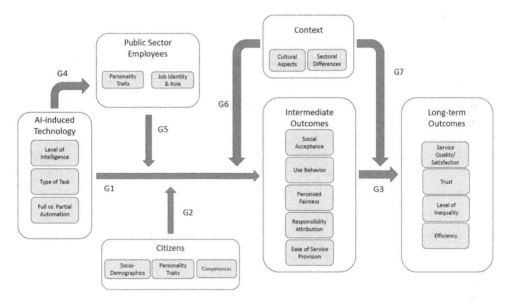

Figure 2.1   *Integrative model of AI-induced technology use and corresponding research gaps*

Generally, our literature review shows that despite the medial omnipresence of terms such as big data, AI, and algorithms, empirical evidence is still rather scant. Although there are some case studies analysing the implementation process of service automation, we know little about possible fields of application in the public sector context. Future research in general is recommended to analyse best practices of applying AI in the public sector and advance our understanding about which policy areas can benefit from service automation. Furthermore, most experimental studies analyse outcomes from automation efforts via vignette studies. Hence, various authors call for field experiments that accompany the roll-out of automation tools (McLeay et al., 2021; Mende et al., 2019). Moreover, new technologies are likely to be perceived with initial reservation and/or euphoria. Thus, longitudinal studies are essential to determine the longevity of found effects (Davenport et al., 2020; McLeay et al., 2021).

CONCLUSION

Focusing on the digitalisation of service delivery and service automation, this chapter explored how AI-induced technology is changing the citizen-government relationship and the roles of key stakeholders involved. Previous research on digital government, service management, and public administration provides empirical evidence on how the interaction with citizens, the roles of public employees, and frontline management are affected by the implementation of AI-induced technology. Focusing on citizens' role, applying modern technology can pose various challenges such as the problem of attributing decision-making to AI, society's fears of AI-assisted decisions, and social inequality resulting from AI decisions. In contrast, previous research has elaborated on the benefits of digitalisation, such as decreased costs, enhanced accountability, and efficacy. Positive effects of applying AI-induced technology might, however, depend on matters of usage, design, and context of the service. Research on the roles of public employees investigates both the potentials and challenges of applying AI. Findings on perceived justice in the use of algorithms for managerial decisions and on the effect of digitalisation on employees' discretionary practices show that the positive effect of applying AI technology largely depends on the type of task. Based on previous research, we develop a research agenda including seven research gaps that should guide future researchers to better understand the effects of AI-induced technology on public service delivery and key stakeholders. These directives for future research not only aim to elucidate the direct effect of applying different types of modern technology but also focus on moderating and contextual factors, illustrating the multifaceted nature of service automation technology.

REFERENCES

Androutsopoulou, A., Karacapilidis, N., Loukis, E., and Charalabidis, Y. (2019). Transforming the communication between citizens and government through AI-guided chatbots. *Government Information Quarterly*, 36(2), 358–367. https://doi.org/10.1016/j.giq.2018.10.001

Aoki, N. (2020). An experimental study of public trust in AI chatbots in the public sector. *Government Information Quarterly*, 37(4), 101490. https://doi.org/10.1016/j.giq.2020.101490

Bawden, D. (2008). Origins and concepts of digital literacy. In *Digital Literacies: Concepts, Policies and Practices* (Vol. 30). Peter Lang.

Belanche, D., Casaló, L. V., Flavián, C., and Schepers, J. (2020). Robots or frontline employees? Exploring customers' attributions of responsibility and stability after service failure or success. *Journal of Service Management*, 31(2), 267–289. https://doi.org/10.1108/JOSM-05-2019-0156

Breit, E., Egeland, C., Løberg, I. B., and Røhnebæk, M. T. (2020). Digital coping: How frontline workers cope with digital service encounters. *Social Policy & Administration*, spol.12664. https://doi.org/10.1111/spol.12664

Bromuri, S., Henkel, A. P., Iren, D., and Urovi, V. (2021). Using AI to predict service agent stress from emotion patterns in service interactions. *Journal of Service Management*, 32(4), 581–611. https://doi.org/10.1108/JOSM-06-2019-0163

Bruhn, A., and Ekström, M. (2017). Towards a multi-level approach on frontline interactions in the public sector: Institutional transformations and the dynamics of real-time interactions. *Social Policy & Administration*, 51(1), 195–215. https://doi.org/10.1111/spol.12193

Buffat, A. (2015). Street-level bureaucracy and e-government. *Public Management Review*, 17(1), 149–161. https://doi.org/10.1080/14719037.2013.771699

Busch, P. A., Henriksen, H. Z., and Sæbø, Ø. (2018). Opportunities and challenges of digitized discretionary practices: A public service worker perspective. *Government Information Quarterly*, 35(4), 547–556. https://doi.org/10.1016/j.giq.2018.09.003

Busuioc, M. (2020). Accountable artificial intelligence: Holding algorithms to account. *Public Administration Review*. https://doi.org/10.1111/puar.13293

Campion, A., Gasco-Hernandez, M., Jankin Mikhaylov, S., and Esteve, M. (2020). Overcoming the challenges of collaboratively adopting artificial intelligence in the public sector. *Social Science Computer Review*, 089443932097995. https://doi.org/10.1177/0894439320979953

Castelvecchi, D. (2016). Can we open the black box of AI? *Nature News*, 538(7623), 20.

Christ-Brendemühl, S., and Schaarschmidt, M. (2019). Frontline backlash: Service employees' deviance from digital processes. *Journal of Services Marketing*, 33(7), 936–945. https://doi.org/10.1108/JSM -03-2019-0125

Coeckelbergh, M. (2020). Artificial intelligence, responsibility attribution, and a relational justification of explainability. *Science and Engineering Ethics*, 26(4), 2051–2068. https://doi.org/10.1007/s11948 -019-00146-8

Davenport, T., Guha, A., Grewal, D., and Bressgott, T. (2020). How artificial intelligence will change the future of marketing. *Journal of the Academy of Marketing Science*, 48(1), 24–42. https://doi.org/ 10.1007/s11747-019-00696-0

de Boer, N., and Raaphorst, N. (2021). Automation and discretion: Explaining the effect of automation on how street-level bureaucrats enforce. *Public Management Review*, 1–21. https://doi.org/10.1080/ 14719037.2021.1937684

De George, R. T. (2008). *The Ethics of Information Technology and Business*. John Wiley & Sons.

De Vries, H., Bekkers, V., and Tummers, L. (2016). Innovation in the public sector: A systematic review and future research agenda: Innovation in the public sector. *Public Administration*, 94(1), 146–166. https://doi.org/10.1111/padm.12209

Desouza, K. C., Dawson, G. S., and Chenok, D. (2020). Designing, developing, and deploying artificial intelligence systems: Lessons from and for the public sector. *Business Horizons*, 63(2), 205–213. https://doi.org/10.1016/j.bushor.2019.11.004

Dwivedi, Y. K., Hughes, L., Ismagilova, E., Aarts, G., Coombs, C., Crick, T., Duan, Y., Dwivedi, R., Edwards, J., Eirug, A., Galanos, V., Ilavarasan, P. V., Janssen, M., Jones, P., Kar, A. K., Kizgin, H., Kronemann, B., Lal, B., Lucini, B., … Williams, M. D. (2021). Artificial Intelligence (AI): Multi-disciplinary perspectives on emerging challenges, opportunities, and agenda for research, practice and policy. *International Journal of Information Management*, 57, 101994. https://doi.org/10 .1016/j.ijinfomgt.2019.08.002

Gäthke, J. (2020). The impact of augmented reality on overall service satisfaction in elaborate services-capes. *Journal of Service Management*, 31(2), 227–246. https://doi.org/10.1108/JOSM-05-2019-0151

Gil-Garcia, J. R., Dawes, S. S., and Pardo, T. A. (2018). Digital government and public management research: Finding the crossroads. *Public Management Review*, 20(5), 633–646. https://doi.org/10 .1080/14719037.2017.1327181

Goodall, N. J. (2016). Away from trolley problems and toward risk management. *Applied Artificial Intelligence*, 30(8), 810–821. https://doi.org/10.1080/08839514.2016.1229922

Guha, A., Grewal, D., Kopalle, P. K., Haenlein, M., Schneider, M. J., Jung, H., Moustafa, R., Hegde, D. R., and Hawkins, G. (2021). How artificial intelligence will affect the future of retailing. *Journal of Retailing*, 97(1), 28–41. https://doi.org/10.1016/j.jretai.2021.01.005

Hansen, H.-T., Lundberg, K., and Syltevik, L. J. (2018). Digitalization, street-level bureaucracy and welfare users' experiences: Digitalization, street-level bureaucracy and welfare users' experiences. *Social Policy & Administration*, 52(1), 67–90. https://doi.org/10.1111/spol.12283

Harrison, T. M., and Luna-Reyes, L. F. (2020). Cultivating trustworthy artificial intelligence in digital government. *Social Science Computer Review*, 089443932098012. https://doi.org/10.1177/ 0894439320980122

Heinrich, C. J. (2016). The bite of administrative burden: A theoretical and empirical investigation. *Journal of Public Administration Research and Theory*, 26(3), 403–420. https://doi.org/10.1093/ jopart/muv034

Herd, P., and Moynihan, D. P. (2019). *Administrative Burden: Policymaking by Other Means*. Russell Sage Foundation. https://ebookcentral.proquest.com/lib/gbv/detail.action?docID=5607528

Huang, M.-H., and Rust, R. T. (2021). Engaged to a robot? The role of AI in service. *Journal of Service Research*, 24(1), 30–41. https://doi.org/10.1177/1094670520902266

Janssen, M., Hartog, M., Matheus, R., Yi Ding, A., and Kuk, G. (2020). Will algorithms blind people? The effect of explainable AI and decision-makers' experience on AI-supported decision-making in government. *Social Science Computer Review*, 089443932098011. https://doi.org/10.1177/0894439320980118

Jansson, G., and Erlingsson, G. Ó. (2014). More e-government, less street-level bureaucracy?: On legitimacy and the human side of public administration. *Journal of Information Technology & Politics*, 11(3), 291–308. https://doi.org/10.1080/19331681.2014.908155

Jarrahi, M. H. (2018). Artificial intelligence and the future of work: Human-AI symbiosis in organizational decision making. *Business Horizons*, 61(4), 577–586. https://doi.org/10.1016/j.bushor.2018.03.007

Kaplan, A., and Haenlein, M. (2019). Siri, Siri, in my hand: Who's the fairest in the land? On the interpretations, illustrations, and implications of artificial intelligence. *Business Horizons*, 62(1), 15–25. https://doi.org/10.1016/j.bushor.2018.08.004

Kattel, R., Lember, V., and Tõnurist, P. (2020). Collaborative innovation and human-machine networks. *Public Management Review*, 22(11), 1652–1673. https://doi.org/10.1080/14719037.2019.1645873

König, P. D., and Wenzelburger, G. (2020). Opportunity for renewal or disruptive force? How artificial intelligence alters democratic politics. *Government Information Quarterly*, 37(3), 101489. https://doi.org/10.1016/j.giq.2020.101489

Kronblad, C. (2020). How digitalization changes our understanding of professional service firms. *Academy of Management Discoveries*, amd.2019.0027. https://doi.org/10.5465/amd.2019.0027

Lam, S. K., Sleep, S., Hennig-Thurau, T., Sridhar, S., and Saboo, A. R. (2017). Leveraging frontline employees' small data and firm-level big data in frontline management: An absorptive capacity perspective. *Journal of Service Research*, 20(1), 12–28. https://doi.org/10.1177/1094670516679271

Li, D., Rau, P. L. P., and Li, Y. (2010). A cross-cultural study: Effect of robot appearance and task. *International Journal of Social Robotics*, 2(2), 175–186. https://doi.org/10.1007/s12369-010-0056-9

Lindgren, I., Madsen, C. Ø., Hofmann, S., and Melin, U. (2019). Close encounters of the digital kind: A research agenda for the digitalization of public services. *Government Information Quarterly*, 36(3), 427–436. https://doi.org/10.1016/j.giq.2019.03.002

Løberg, I. B. (2021). Efficiency through digitalization? How electronic communication between front-line workers and clients can spur a demand for services. *Government Information Quarterly*, 38(2), 101551. https://doi.org/10.1016/j.giq.2020.101551

Longoni, C., Bonezzi, A., and Morewedge, C. K. (2019). Resistance to medical artificial intelligence. *Journal of Consumer Research*, 46(4), 629–650. https://doi.org/10.1093/jcr/ucz013

McClure, P. K. (2018). 'You're fired,' says the robot: The rise of automation in the workplace, technophobes, and fears of unemployment. *Social Science Computer Review*, 36(2), 139–156. https://doi.org/10.1177/0894439317698637

McLeay, F., Osburg, V. S., Yoganathan, V., and Patterson, A. (2021). Replaced by a robot: Service implications in the age of the machine. *Journal of Service Research*, 24(1), 104–121. https://doi.org/10.1177/1094670520933354

Meijer, A., and Bolívar, M. P. R. (2016). Governing the smart city: A review of the literature on smart urban governance. *International Review of Administrative Sciences*, 82(2), 392–408. https://doi.org/10.1177/0020852314564308

Meijer, A., Lorenz, L., and Wessels, M. (2021). Algorithmization of bureaucratic organizations: Using a practice lens to study how context shapes predictive policing systems. *Public Administration Review*, puar.13391. https://doi.org/10.1111/puar.13391

Mende, M., Scott, M. L., van Doorn, J., Grewal, D., and Shanks, I. (2019). Service robots rising: How humanoid robots influence service experiences and elicit compensatory consumer responses. *Journal of Marketing Research*, 56(4), 535–556. https://doi.org/10.1177/0022243718822827

Miller, S. M., and Keiser, L. R. (2021). Representative bureaucracy and attitudes toward automated decision making. *Journal of Public Administration Research and Theory*, 31(1), 150–165. https://doi.org/10.1093/jopart/muaa019

Mori, M. (1970). The uncanny valley. *Energy*, 7(4), 33–35.

Nagtegaal, R. (2021). The impact of using algorithms for managerial decisions on public employees' procedural justice. *Government Information Quarterly*, 38(1), 101536. https://doi.org/10.1016/j.giq.2020.101536

Neri, E., Coppola, F., Miele, V., Bibbolino, C., and Grassi, R. (2020). Artificial intelligence: Who is responsible for the diagnosis? *La Radiologia Medica*, 125(6), 517–521. https://doi.org/10.1007/s11547-020-01135-9

Norris, P. (2001). *Digital Divide: Civic Engagement, Information Poverty, and the Internet World-wide*. Cambridge University Press.

Peeters, R., and Widlak, A. (2018). The digital cage: Administrative exclusion through information architecture – The case of the Dutch civil registry's master data management system. *Government Information Quarterly*, 35(2), 175–183. https://doi.org/10.1016/j.giq.2018.02.003

Pemer, F. (2021). Enacting professional service work in times of digitalization and potential disruption. *Journal of Service Research*, 24(2), 249–268. https://doi.org/10.1177/1094670520916801

Rafaeli, A., Altman, D., Gremler, D. D., Huang, M.-H., Grewal, D., Iyer, B., Parasuraman, A., and Ruyter, K. (2016). The future of frontline research. *Journal of Service Research*, 20(1), 91–99. https://doi.org/10.1177/1094670516679275

Ranerup, A., and Henriksen, H. Z. (2019). Value positions viewed through the lens of automated decision-making: The case of social services. *Government Information Quarterly*, 36(4), 101377. https://doi.org/10.1016/j.giq.2019.05.004

Ranerup, A., and Henriksen, H. Z. (2020). Digital discretion: Unpacking human and technological agency in automated decision making in Sweden's social services. *Social Science Computer Review*, 089443932098043. https://doi.org/10.1177/0894439320980434

Rogers, E. (2003). *Diffusion of Innovations* (5th ed.). Free Press.

Schaffer, B. B., and Huang, W. (1975). Distribution and the theory of access. *Development and Change*, 6(2), 13–36. https://doi.org/10.1111/j.1467-7660.1975.tb00674.x

Sidaoui, K., Jaakkola, M., and Burton, J. (2020). AI feel you: Customer experience assessment via chatbot interviews. *Journal of Service Management*, 31(4), 745–766. https://doi.org/10.1108/JOSM-11-2019-0341

Simon, H. A. (1981). Special feature: Prometheus or Pandora: The influence of automation on society. *Computer*, 14(11), 69–74. https://doi.org/10.1109/C-M.1981.220253

Snellen, I. (1998). Street level bureaucracy in an information age. In I. Snellen and W. van de Donk (eds), *Public Administration in an Information Age: A Handbook* (pp. 497–505). IOS Press.

Snellen, I. (2002). Electronic governance: Implications for citizens, politicians and public servants. *International Review of Administrative Sciences*, 68(2), 183–198. https://doi.org/10.1177/0020852302682002

Sun, T. Q., and Medaglia, R. (2019). Mapping the challenges of Artificial Intelligence in the public sector: Evidence from public healthcare. *Government Information Quarterly*, 36(2), 368–383. https://doi.org/10.1016/j.giq.2018.09.008

van de Poel, I., Nihlén Fahlquist, J., Doorn, N., Zwart, S., and Royakkers, L. (2012). The problem of many hands: Climate change as an example. *Science and Engineering Ethics*, 18(1), 49–67. https://doi.org/10.1007/s11948-011-9276-0

van Noordt, C., and Misuraca, G. (2020). Exploratory insights on artificial intelligence for government in Europe. *Social Science Computer Review*, 089443932098044. https://doi.org/10.1177/0894439320980449

Vogl, T. M., Seidelin, C., Ganesh, B., and Bright, J. (2020). Smart technology and the emergence of algorithmic bureaucracy: Artificial intelligence in UK local authorities. *Public Administration Review*, 80(6), 946–961. https://doi.org/10.1111/puar.13286

Wihlborg, E., Larsson, H., and Hedstrom, K. (2016). 'The Computer Says No!' – A case study on automated decision-making in public authorities. 2016 49th Hawaii International Conference on System Sciences (HICSS), 2903–2912. https://doi.org/10.1109/HICSS.2016.364

Willems, J., Schmidthuber, L., Vogel, D., Ebinger, F., and Vanderelst, D. (2022). Ethics of robotized public services: The role of robot design and its actions. *Government Information Quarterly*, 39(2), 101683. https://doi.org/10.1016/j.giq.2022.101683

Wirtz, B. W., Weyerer, J. C., and Sturm, B. J. (2020). The dark sides of artificial intelligence: An integrated AI governance framework for public administration. *International Journal of Public Administration*, 43(9), 818–829. https://doi.org/10.1080/01900692.2020.1749851

Wirtz, J., Patterson, P. G., Kunz, W. H., Gruber, T., Lu, V. N., Paluch, S., and Martins, A. (2018). Brave new world: Service robots in the frontline. *Journal of Service Management*, 29(5), 907–931. https://doi.org/10.1108/JOSM-04-2018-0119

Young, M. M., Bullock, J. B., and Lecy, J. D. (2019). Artificial discretion as a tool of governance: A framework for understanding the impact of artificial intelligence on public administration. *Perspectives on Public Management and Governance*, gvz014. https://doi.org/10.1093/ppmgov/gvz014

Zuiderwijk, A., Chen, Y.-C., and Salem, F. (2021). Implications of the use of artificial intelligence in public governance: A systematic literature review and a research agenda. *Government Information Quarterly*, 101577. https://doi.org/10.1016/j.giq.2021.101577

3. AI in the public sector: fundamental operational questions and how to address them

Muiris MacCarthaigh, Stanley Simoes[1] and Deepak P.

INTRODUCTION

As the chapters in this volume amply illuminate, Artificial Intelligence (AI) has a rapidly growing influence on the ways in which public services now operate as well as how individuals interact with public sector organisations. Such is the spread of AI in its various manifestations that it challenges national governments and intergovernmental organisations such as the European Union to develop and enforce new regulatory standards with a view to ensuring that AI is trustworthy and free of undue bias. After all, as noted in the EU proposals for 'harmonised rules' on AI, 'the same elements and techniques that power the socio-economic benefits of AI can also bring about new risks or negative consequences for individuals or the society' (European Commission, 2021, p. 1).

The most popular sub-stream of AI, Machine Learning (ML), is increasingly prevalent within the public sector. The founding principle behind ML is that of leveraging past datasets to identify patterns which could assist future problem-solving activities. The historical datasets that ML algorithms work upon are inevitably generated and curated by humans, and thus susceptible to various biases and stereotypes that pervade contemporary society (Henrich et al., 2010; Holstein et al., 2019; Jo and Gebru, 2020). As might be expected, some patterns in such datasets and the decisions they engender may turn out to be unethical or even dubious to the human eye.

The growth and usage of ML, which has been mostly located in the private sector, has not been matched by levels of attention being given to understanding, uncovering, mitigating, or neutralising biases within data and the design of algorithms that work over such data. Adherence to ethical principles within AI (such as unbiased, explainable, and privacy-preserving principles) is widely acknowledged to bring about some trade-offs. In other words, there are costs which are invariably to the detriment of utilitarian metrics (for example, accuracy, efficiency) which are often set aside in order to realise profit motives (Dwork, 2021; Friedler et al., 2019; Kesari, 2022; Kleinberg and Mullainathan, 2019; van der Veer et al., 2021).

The current state-of-the-art of AI therefore, having been nurtured by the private sector, has largely been influenced by algorithmic designs that privilege the financial side of the trade-off. Such matters also pose significant challenges for the public sector which has experienced enormous pressure for quick and effective uptake of the latest algorithms, software and platforms across a diverse range of policy domains. Several important and fundamental questions

[1]   Stanley Simoes was funded by the European Union's Horizon 2020 research and innovation programme under the Marie Skłodowska-Curie grant agreement No 945231; and the Department for the Economy in Northern Ireland.

arise within this context which matter for ensuring safe and effective usage of AI within the public sector.

First, are the tools and techniques to understand and evaluate the biases and stereotypes that are latent within the datasets over which ML algorithms are trained available? Second, when ML decision-making systems are made available without access to the underlying datasets over which they were trained, how is adherence to normative values within decision-making prior to deployment assessed? Third, when such systems are being used on a continuous basis, how can processes be instituted that, in a rational, transparent, and objective manner, help determine whether their stream of decisions are good enough to warrant their continued usage (as opposed to decommissioning or suspending their usage until re-trained on appropriate datasets). Finally, how can effective human-in-the-loop systems be designed which can draw the benefits of ML-based automation whilst also avoiding the harms of biased and unethical ML?

To explore these issues further, in this chapter three specific public sector policy domains are examined: public health, policing, and immigration. Each in its own right has high political salience, with those in positions of political authority being particularly sensitive to public concerns and perceptions about the policy responses to challenges in these domains. Methodologically, they are also the policy domains for which the largest volume of published academic literature (in the English language) is found, albeit concentrated on the more developed parts of the globe arising from the comparatively lower levels of AI usage by governments in the Global South. They are also policy domains within which the potential for significant human costs are high, ranging from incorrect (and potentially fatal) health diagnoses, to incorrect incarceration or punishment in the case of policing, and unfair and life-affecting decisions around immigration and asylum rules with little recourse or accountability opportunity.

Furthermore, the challenges experienced within these policy domains and the potential solutions to them may speak to other domains (such as social welfare, or education) not covered here. And the experiences of certain social cohorts (for example migrants, or minority groups) with ML algorithms are instructive for how such technology will be used elsewhere. Indeed, according to Molnar (2019, p. 306), there is evidence that states deliberate experiment with technology in the domain of migration, as weak state accountability towards migrants makes the migrant population an attractive testing ground for new technologies.

The chapter proceeds to consider each of the three domains in turn, profiling the distinctive challenges arising within the context of AI uptake in each case. Following this, common challenges emerging across the domains are identified and examined. A final section suggests pathways towards addressing these problems.

PUBLIC HEALTH

AI, and especially its sub-streams of ML and big data, have entered healthcare provision in a very significant way over the last two decades. Within the public health system and associated academic research, there have been massive investments towards building capacity as well as the adoption of such technologies. As an example, in 2018 the UK government invested £50 million to establish five AI centres of excellence in digital pathology through the data-focused

Health Data Research UK initiative.[2] There are dedicated centres such as the Oxford Big Data Institute[3] which engage in using AI technologies for the health sector. To better understand these developments, four challenges arising from the use of AI in public health are considered: (1) as a form of delegation of expert oversight in health; (2) disaggregating individual health from population health; (3) new dangers from biased AI in healthcare, and; (4) global equity.

AI as Delegating Expert Oversight

A natural entry point for AI technologies within healthcare practice is through clinical decision support systems (CDSS) (Lysaght et al., 2019). Since the beginning of its use in the 1980s, CDSS have had enormous successes, particularly through their ability to provide consistency and improve accuracy in diagnosis, along with their ability to reduce manual errors.[4] For example, CDSS usage in phone-based patient screening ensures that all pertinent questions are asked, making sure that there is no important piece of patient information omitted. Early versions of CDSS, from their descriptions, were transparent and quite amenable to scrutiny and audit, and often acted as facilitators to help a medical expert. In this perspective, they were simply ensuring conformance to a formal process, and their operation was verifiable. With the advent of AI, CDSS are witnessing an expansion of capabilities in clinical fields such as cardiology (Choi et al., 2020) whereby they are used for a significantly broader range of decisions.

Recent approval of AI applications as 'Software as Medical Devices' is also indicative of the trend in this policy domain (Thomasian et al., 2021). In particular, they are likely to offer recommendations based on medical expert judgement derived from their training datasets through ML algorithms. This switch has most likely already happened via CDSS offering suggestions within various scenarios, even while a medical expert retains overall responsibility for the final choice. The quantum of suggestions would inevitably increase, slowly shifting agency from the medical practitioner to the machine and its ability to determine optimal courses of action. Even if the medical practitioner is able to override the AI's suggestions, it may become increasingly difficult to do so, as illustrated in analogous scenarios within other public sector domains (Eubanks, 2018). Further questions arise when CDSS is sourced from a private sector vendor for usage within healthcare delivery in the public sector. Such a development could be considered an implicit form of privatisation within medical decision-making, with potentially unforeseeable long-term consequences.

Individual vs. Population

The technological structure of the vast majority of AI/ML-based algorithms is to leverage large datasets to learn macro trends within a statistical model, which are then used to perform or facilitate individual-level, or micro, decision-making. Making predictions on public health is far more challenging. By way of example, it is likely to be far more accurate to predict the outcome of an individual COVID-19 patient, than it is to predict when the next pandemic

---

[2]   https:// www .hdruk .ac .uk/ news/ new -centres -of -excellence -in -medical -imaging -and -digital -pathology/
[3]   https://www.bdi.ox.ac.uk/
[4]   https://digitalhealth.folio3.com/blog/clinical-decision-support-system-examples-tools/

might occur. Within the healthcare sector, this has led to AI/ML focusing on enhancing individualised treatments and diagnoses, as noted by Holzmeyer (2021).

This is also echoed within an ethics-focused review on AI for health (Murphy et al., 2021), where the authors note the paucity of work on AI ethics in public and population health. It is also notable that public health is an important concern for healthcare provision in the public sector, since that has significant potential to improve citizen well-being which would translate to a lower overall healthcare resource burden in the longer term. The rapid development, enthusiasm, and uptake of AI technologies shifts the focus towards diagnosis of individuals, and risks undermining efforts towards population health from the overall healthcare budget. This individual versus population dichotomy also manifests as tensions between a downstream or reactive focus vis-à-vis an upstream or proactive focus towards healthcare.

New Dangers of Biased AI

As understood in the 1970s, AI largely comprised expert systems which hold (sometimes massive) rule-sets that codify expert knowledge. This ensures that any form of biased operation can be traced back and corrected, even if with some effort. As an example, the hugely popular AI expert system MYCIN, built in the 1970s, had a set of rules, numbering almost 600, which governed its operation (Shortliffe, 1974). On the other hand, new age AI/ML technologies are built using pipelines where biased operation can be brought about from the data (individual data objects, groups, or combinations) they train on, the design of the algorithms, and even through inappropriate or un-intended usage of such technologies. Often, biased operation is unintentional and arises purely from the urge to use more and more data (O'Neil, 2016).

Some of the biases may be nuanced and subjective (Landers and Behrend, 2022) whereas others could be invisible or latent. For example, when AI is used to flag problematic cases for manual inspection, biases manifesting through false negatives could go unnoticed. As the public sector is expected to adhere to the highest degrees of fairness within its operation, it would naturally require continuous oversight to ensure early detection of biases, following which, steps to remedy those may need to be devised and implemented. This is complementary to calls seeking to ensure that AI design be conducted ethically, through embedded ethics (McLennan et al., 2022) and with a focus on trust and reliance (Kerasidou et al., 2022).

Global Equity

The vast majority of AI is designed and trained on datasets within the Global North. Governments within the Global South often find themselves in a position to have to use such technologies which are ill-suited to their population. As noted by Murphy et al. (2021), there has been very little attention given to ethical considerations that arise within the context of low- and middle-income countries (LMICs). Seemingly reasonable medical assumptions, such as those on the uniformity of cancer cell morphology (McKay et al., 2022), could potentially become problematic, especially in cases where the populations used for training and use are very different. Non-attention to these issues could lead to situations whereby AI misdiagnosis snowballs into a significant issue within the Global South, a new frontier of AI-driven global inequality.

As is often said of AI, the technology is here to stay, having delivered enormous benefits within specific health subdomains such as dermatologist-level classification of skin cancer

(Esteva et al., 2017). The hype around AI has resulted in a situation where there is a huge rush towards developing technologies and leveraging them. Governments across the globe have responded positively by funding AI health research, with significant improvements in patient outcomes.

However, there are also concerns about the dangers of AI in healthcare (Karmakar, 2022). Specific themes of high importance for public health were outlined above, namely the movement of agency away from medical experts, AI technologies undermining upstream population-level health concerns, unapparent biases within AI, and the important implications that AI has for global health equity. This suggests that it may be useful to consider the kind of safeguards that need to be installed to ensure that the benefits of AI are extracted while staying within the bounds of ethical operation. The challenges before us on this path are interdisciplinary. While controlling the shift of agency would require know-how from politics and psychology, AI for population health could pose fresh and hard technical challenges for data scientists. Ensuring bias-free operation within health AI requires unique collaborations, similar to suggestions on embedded ethics (McLennan et al., 2022). Issues of global health equity would therefore sit within the intersection of scholarship across development economics, politics, technology, and health.

POLICING

Policing is another prominent policy domain with high levels of direct public engagement, where automation based on AI tools are in widespread use internationally. Babuta and Oswald (2020, pp. 6–9) suggest that the use of algorithms in policing has expanded significantly in scale and complexity in recent years, arising from three inter-related factors:

1. A significant increase in the volume and complexity of digital data available to police forces, necessitating the use of more sophisticated analysis tools.
2. Public service cutbacks have resulted in a perceived need to better allocate limited resources, and a data-driven assessment of risk and demand is deemed more cost effective.
3. Police services are increasingly expected to adopt preventative rather than reactive postures, with more emphasis on anticipating possible harm before it occurs.

As with health, some of the main uses of algorithmically-based AI has been to automate time-consuming and resource-intensive 'back-office' data analysis tasks such as data matching (for example, licence plate readers) and data consolidation (for example, connecting historic and current crime records). In this mode of use, AI can either assist or replace human police administrative work (Joh, 2018). More challenging questions emerge in respect of the use of AI to assist frontline police work, and especially in respect of 'predictive policing'. Two such challenges are considered here: (1) reinforcing social inequalities, and; (2) distanced decision-making.

Reinforcing Social Inequalities

Profiling suspects and geographical locations for crimes is not necessarily a new activity for policing (Schauer, 2003). However, advanced algorithms and data-mining software facilitate new methods and statistical tools to derive detailed insights, inform operational decision-making, profile citizens or social groups, and make better-informed predictions on issues ranging from crime hotspots to recidivism. There are, however, ongoing questions about the use of AI-enabled algorithms being used to determine bail, to engage in surveillance activities, and to facilitate predictive policing. Gehl Sampath (2021, p. 27) also outlines reasons why smart policing in diverse countries in the Global South are a cause for concern.

In fact the issue of predictive policing algorithms (PPA) is one of the most prominent themes in the analysis of AI in public security (Sheehey, 2019). Such algorithms are increasingly accessible and widely used (for example, PredPol, 2021[5]). In essence, it concerns the use of AI technologies to predict threats in law enforcement in the same manner that such technologies are used to predict natural hazards. Predictive policing includes predictive mapping, which involves the use of statistical information to identify locations which are subject to high incidence of certain crimes (for example, street crime, or burglary), as well as risk assessments of individuals based on personal data.

There have been some successful experiments in Germany and Japan (Egbert and Krasmann, 2020; Ohyama and Amemiya, 2018). In the UK, a number of regional police forces have experimented with predictive policing tools, using algorithms and historic data to model and predict where certain types of crime are likely to occur (Christie, 2021). However there are several critiques surrounding the use of PPAs, including their effects on social inequalities and associated injustices.

The primary argument here is that by using existing data or gathering certain data, PPAs reinforce and amplify inherent disparities, leading to flawed or biased predictions which further embed racist, sectarian, or other patterns of social segregation. This includes claims of racial bias whereby algorithms over-predict the risk of people from some racial groups or from neighbourhoods where postcodes function as a proxy for race. In this respect an interesting element of the Black Lives Matter movement in the US has been a debate about the channelling of resources into PPA at the expense of more traditional in-person community policing (Yen and Hung, 2021).

A case in point are the experiments in Chicago, where the police department used two AI-based profiling systems for different purposes. One was used to develop a Strategic Subjects List (referred to as the 'heat list' by police officers) and another to develop a programme called 'One Summer' designed to identify youth at risk of being involved in gun violence (Asaro, 2019, p. 46). While the former was designed as a pre-crime or threat-risk model to reduce crime, the other was designed to channel at-risk youth towards social services and other resources. Both systems were therefore concerned with profiling particular sets of individuals, but the principles and objectives underlying them were starkly different. Other US-focused work, such as that by Richardson et al. (2019), studied how 'dirty data' was used in predictive policing in 13 US jurisdictions.

There are several international studies pointing to evidence of problems with predictive policing. Marda and Narayan (2020) studied the Crime Mapping, Analytics, and Predictive System (CMAPS) – a smart policing system proposed to be used by the Delhi Police for live spatial hotspot mapping of crime, criminal behaviour patterns, and suspect analysis. Their findings revealed the data collection process was biased and the system had little public accountability. In South America, a study by Akpinar et al. (2021) suggests that predictive

---

[5]   https://www.predpol.com/technology/

policing models trained on victim crime reporting data for Bogotá, Colombia could potentially lead to over-policing in high reporting areas and under-policing in low reporting areas.

Distanced Decision-making

Also noting the spread of AI in policing, Oatley (2022, p. 1) posits that around the world 'there has been a growing use of big data analytical approaches to map and understand crime patterns'. He identifies how police forces can now avail of socio-behavioural data (such as social media), transactional datasets (such as financial data), and CCTV as part of their evidence gathering in respect of traditional crimes (robbery, arson, murder, etc.) but also for a range of cybercrimes including money laundering and identity crimes. AI-based applications are used to facilitate automated facial recognition software and autonomous drones for crowd control measures. In an extreme case, Kodali (2017), Suresh (2021), and Umanadh (2019) all report on the use of a smart policing project in Hyderabad, India, that allowed authorities to reach far into citizens' personal lives, including extraction of banking and other personal data. All told, technological tools can survey and make inferences about whole populations in defined areas in a manner that traditional police departments could not.

However, with machines making recommendations, core decision-making activity shifts from the police to AI algorithms. The logic of this is to reimagine the police service as an implementation mechanism for algorithmic suggestions, rather than engaging in decision-making. This issue arises quite starkly in respect of PPAs, where, as well as, the issues of bias discussed above, there are also concerns about how PPAs are understood, and if they are being correctly interpreted and used by police forces (Harris and Burke, 2021). This mirrors the 'McNamara Fallacy' whereby decisions are made based solely on quantitative observation or metrics, ignoring other sources of evidence.

The usage of predictive policing, whether it is humans or AI making the decision, also challenges basic rights of citizenship. This is so since the individual or group predicted to be suspicious often find themselves having to prove they are innocent under most modalities in which the suspiciousness prediction is operationalised by the police force. This violates the fundamental and well accepted principle of 'presumption of innocence', i.e. a person should be regarded as innocent until proven guilty. People repeatedly subjected to such burden of proof (due to repeated stop-and-search) can experience obvious psychological stress and victimisation, often leading to long-term mental health and allied issues.

As with other elements of the public service using AI, the outsourcing of decision-making to algorithms may improve efficiency and accuracy, but it also reduces transparency and responsibility as police administrators may not understand how machine-based decisions were arrived at. Problems of algorithmic accountability are not confined to informational shortcomings and problems with explaining or justifying algorithmic-based decisions, but also in diagnosing failure and securing redress (Busuioc, 2021). Decisions made within 'black box' models of AI can have serious consequences for individuals in policing contexts. Furthermore, as Babuta and Oswald (2020, p. viii) identify, the use by police forces of advanced algorithms, predictive analytics, and 'data scoring' tools also raise legal and ethical concerns.

IMMIGRATION

Our final policy domain is that of immigration. It concerns the movement of people – immigrants – to a country of which they are not citizens. Upon entry, immigrants become members of the public of the receiving country, requiring access to public resources. To manage the demand on these resources and safeguard internal public order and security, states typically seek to regulate the flow of immigrants. With millions of immigration-related decisions to be made each year and the pressure to adopt new technologies within the public sector, many states are increasingly experimenting with AI technologies and big data analysis to supplement human decision-making. This includes, for example, the creation of biometric passports for citizens of one of the world's newest states, South Sudan, the production of which was contracted out to a private company based in Germany (Markó, 2016).

As in other policy domains, AI-based decision-making systems influence the decision-making of various parties concerned with immigration such as administrative tribunals, immigration officers, border agents, and legal analysts (Molnar, 2019). Big data analysis, on the other hand, can be used to discover previously unknown knowledge about migration such as possible future migration patterns, thus providing social scientists with new insights (Bircan and Korkmaz, 2021). These technologies can shorten the time required for making decisions, thereby improving efficiency and productivity, and even leading to economic savings (Chun, 2008).

As previously pointed out, despite the potential benefits that AI technologies can provide, they are also known to suffer from limitations that can have serious negative societal implications. This is especially true for data-driven AI technologies which are trained on historical data to make decisions. Furthermore, the black box nature of these AI technologies makes it difficult to explain the decisions made, inhibiting public accountability. It is also crucial to highlight that the producers of this data are migrants who do not enjoy the same rights as citizens. The procedural part of the democratic framework (for example, elections, the allocation of voting rights, etc.) is incapable of handling these issues, since the narrow interpretation of democracy as an intra-nation electoral process places no emphasis on accountability to immigrants who are non-nationals at their time of arrival, and for a significant period afterwards, if not their lifetimes. It needs strong adherence to democracy as a set of inclusive values to be able to observe, appreciate, and respond to issues of immigration. It is far from straightforward to effectively embed such values within the operation of AI algorithms.

In fact, the absence of democratic controls may be a reason that countries are looking at testing automated decision-making in the context of immigration (Molnar, 2019). Experimenting with automated decision-making systems on disadvantaged populations such as migrants is routinely justified under the pretext of national security, humanitarianism, and development. Like policing, AI-based technology such as facial recognition, biometric scanners, and predictive processing algorithms are being employed by many states for various tasks, from assessing visa and asylum applications to predicting migratory movements. As with policing, however, similar issues around biased profiling arise.

For example, the European Border Surveillance System (Eurosur) was tested along the EU border to prevent cross-border crimes and ensure the safety of immigrants through a network of surveillance and information exchange systems. Member states collect and share information on events at their borders. However, Tazzioli (2018) argues that by virtue of its very design to identify crimes, this system views immigrants as potential criminals rather than people in need. It is instructive to consider here a few examples of AI systems developed for use in immigration-related tasks, their intended goals, and the issues they suffer from. These are: (1) assessing immigrants' applications; (2) lie detection; (3) asylum seeking.

Assessing Immigrants' Applications

Canada has used AI to identify fraudulent applications for entry permits and to determine if the applicant poses a risk to national security (Keung, 2017). Molnar and Gill (2018) have raised multiple concerns about this system. First, the definition of 'fraud' and 'threat' is not clear, causing the interpretation of these terms to affect the decision-making of the system. It is also not clear what types of data will be collected, who can access the data provided by the applicants, and whether this data can be shared. There are also concerns that the collected data could lead to digital surveillance and thus infringe on the privacy rights of the applicants. In 2017, the US experimented with AI to assess immigrants' applications under the Extreme Vetting project (Glaser, 2017). AI was used to decide whether the applicant would be a threat to national security based on data collected from public sources including social media accounts. The US later acknowledged that this could violate the applicant's privacy and right to identity, and discontinued the complete automation of the vetting process (Duarte, 2018).

Lie Detection

Airports in Hungary, Latvia, and Greece tested an AI-based system called iBorderCtrl that detects if an immigrant seeking entry is making false or contradictory statements. It does so by asking the immigrant questions while recording their reactions using a camera. Based on their responses, the individual may be subject to further checks by border guards. Gallagher and Jona (2019) raised concerns about iBorderCtrl's effectiveness and fairness, with O'Shea et al. (2018) reporting that the system recorded 75 per cent accuracy on a study group, not taking into consideration variables such as ethnicity and gender.

Asylum-seeking

The European Asylum Support Office (EASO) developed a data-driven AI algorithm to predict the pressure on asylum administrations of the European Union's member states up to four weeks in advance based on individual-level decision-making and aggregation (Bircan and Korkmaz, 2021). As part of this, member states such as Finland and the Netherlands, and affiliated state Norway, monitored the social media activity of asylum applicants. This was criticised by the European Data Protection Supervisor (EDPS) as putting individuals' rights and freedoms at significant risk, potentially resulting in personal data being used for other purposes.

Other examples of AI technologies being tested to detect fraudulent and illegal activities include facial recognition in Italy to verify the authenticity of photographs in identification documents (Coluccini, 2021), a fully autonomous and unmanned border surveillance system (ROBORDER) for safeguarding the European borders (Csernatoni, 2018), and facial recognition technology in New Zealand for identifying potential troublemakers (Tan, 2018).

There are also examples of AI being used with the objective of improving the lives of immigrants. For example, the International Organization for Migration uses a system called the Displacement Tracking Matrix that predicts the needs of displaced people using phone records, geotagging, and social media activity. In addition, an autonomous robotic life raft is used off the coast of Greece for rescuing refugees (Franz and Bergquist, 2017).

FUNDAMENTAL OPERATIONAL QUESTIONS ARISING

As the three policy domains discussed above identify, data-driven AI technologies have limitations. When used without careful regulation for making immigration-related decisions, AI can potentially aggravate the already vulnerable conditions of refugees and asylum seekers (Molnar and Gill, 2018). When trained for policing using unreliable data, the predictions of these systems can inherit, reproduce, and reinforce existing biases and negatively influence the decision-making of the humans they are meant to assist (Lepri et al., 2018). And even the most advanced AI in use in healthcare cannot account for the unique medical histories of the population. In this section, pulling the findings from these three policy domains together and drawing on Forti (2021), some of the concerns with the use of AI around explicability, accountability, and fundamental rights are set out.

Explicability

AI techniques are inherently opaque. It is difficult for any human to understand the reasoning behind their outputs (Castelvecchi, 2016). The inability to explain the decisions being made, especially in high-stakes settings such as immigration, are a cause for ethical and legal concern (Robbins, 2019). It is important and appropriate to audit such systems to ensure that decisions are not made based on unjustifiably discriminatory factors. Without an explanation mechanism, these discriminatory tendencies could potentially propagate uncontrollably. The lack of explicability also makes it difficult for police suspects or citizens being offered particular treatments to appeal against them.

Accountability

As noted above, the black box nature of AI makes it difficult for humans to audit AI-based decision-making systems for biases and prevent their propagation (Busuioc, 2021). Further, AI-based systems sourced from the private sector also raise intellectual property issues. Proprietary source code and training data prevents such privately-sourced systems from being publicly scrutinised. For example, immigration offices would have to depend on the private sector to disclose information about their systems, report errors, and take action to rectify them. Another problem is the interpretation of values in AI-based systems. The choice of how values are manifested within these systems can affect the decisions made and thus disadvantage certain individuals.

Fundamental Rights Issues

The risk of citizen and migrant rights such as non-discrimination, privacy, and fairness being violated through the use of AI-based systems is a serious concern. Non-discrimination on sensitive attributes such as sex, race, or religion is a fundamental principle of international human rights law. Yet, in respect of immigration in particular, some AI systems are designed to treat certain social groups as potential security threats rather than human beings (Bircan and Korkmaz, 2021), thus unjustifiably discriminating between them (Blasi Casagran, 2021). Furthermore, as with policing or other forms of cohort selection, such discrimination can be self-perpetuating; when these systems are used to flag migrants for further checks, the new decisions could become part of the training data thus reinforcing the already existing bias.

Privacy breaches as a result of data collection from migrants is a very specific issue of concern (Crisp, 2018). There is often a lack of clarity about who can use these systems, the collected data, and for what purposes. Neither migrants nor migration scholars can monitor how countries or their private partners use this data (Bircan and Korkmaz, 2021). Refoulement is yet another important concern. AI-based systems can be used to identify and intercept individuals at the borders, forcibly returning them to their country of origin where they are at a risk of persecution or even death (Beduschi, 2021). Immigrants tend to not have the same rights as citizens, or the means to defend their rights. If used without scrutiny and adequate protections, AI could greatly limit the ability of immigrants and asylum seekers to defend their own rights (Akhmetova, 2020).

RECOMMENDATIONS

A variety of approaches have been suggested to address the issues of bias and unfair selection and decision-making in algorithms during the process of algorithmic design and development. These include using alternative datasets and adopting statistical methods for detecting and eliminating bias. While helpful, these approaches by themselves are not sufficient. To regulate the use of AI, standards and safeguards need to be established during data collection, algorithmic design, and deployment. To advance this, some of the recommendations put forth by scholars towards addressing the fundamental operational questions that arise with the use of AI-based decision-making in the selected policy domains are presented here.

How Much Automation is Too Much?

An important question is whether automated decision-making systems should even be used for making certain high-stakes decisions such as immigrant detention (Oberhaus, 2018) and refugee determination (Molnar and Gill, 2018). In cases where AI is used, affected individuals should be made aware of which part of the decision-making process is influenced by AI, and their right to redress (Forti, 2021). Furthermore, any algorithmic output should be treated as a form of 'intelligence' rather than the basis for a final decision. The design of processes should be such that it does not induce any form of reluctance on the part of the humans engaged in the process to override AI recommendations when they find it appropriate to do so. AI-based automation is heavily dependent on the availability of data, and thus, it is often the case that deepening of AI-based automation translates to deeper and higher intensity data collection and surveillance (for example, the case of smart policing in Hyderabad, above). Thus, notions of acceptable levels of data collection and surveillance provide another dimension of upper limits for AI-based automation.

Involving Stakeholders

It is essential to involve stakeholders – including scholars (for example, from health and public administration in case of public health) – in discussions related to the use of AI for decision-making. The very concept of stakeholder engagement offers the possibility of greater understanding and ultimately the acceptance of AI in decision-making processes. This would help with the development and use of AI-based systems that are reasonable and ethical (Akhmetova, 2020; Bircan and Korkmaz, 2021). Within the context of public health, significant medical expertise may be necessary to evaluate the role of demographic attributes in medical decision-making, especially in order to ensure an acceptable trade-off between medically sensible decision making and unbiased operation.

Explicability and Accountability

AI systems must have an explanation mechanism that produces clear and understandable explanations for the decisions being made. While clarity and understandability were implicit in rule-based medical expert systems such as MYCIN (referenced earlier), this can no longer be expected implicitly in modern AI-powered CDSSs. This would allow humans to independently review these systems' outputs (Harris and Burke, 2021) and monitor the operation of these systems (Santoni de Sio and van den Hoven, 2018). In this way, the use of any decision produced by AI systems becomes the moral responsibility of the human employing the decision.

This paradigm also comes with an implicit danger of absolving corporate AI vendors from responsibility, so this needs to be accompanied with strong legal safeguards. Nevertheless, explanations for an algorithmic decision would enable humans to accept, question, or discard the decision (Robbins, 2019). An accountability framework must also be in place for regulating AI systems and protecting the rights of the affected community (for example, migrants and refugees in the case of immigration, or disadvantaged racial groups in the case of policing). Having independent third parties assess the reliability of AI-based decision-making systems would also contribute positively towards accountability (Forti, 2021).

Safeguarding Fundamental Rights

Protecting existing safeguards against human rights violations by means of AI-based systems is vital to ensure that such systems do not exacerbate discriminatory trends (Forti, 2021), a particular concern within domains of policing and immigration in the contemporary world. Molnar (2019) argues that more specific regulation is necessary to prevent AI from infringing on affected individuals' human rights in high-stakes settings. The '10 steps to protect Human Rights' published by the Council of Europe's Commissioner for Human Rights in 2019, including such issues as impact assessment, independent oversight, and provision of remedies, provides an excellent framework on which to build national-level safeguards (Council of Europe 2019).

CONCLUSIONS

This chapter has identified and elaborated on the fundamental operational challenges brought about by AI and ML use in the public sector by drawing on three policy domains that involve high levels of direct engagement with individuals, be they citizens or otherwise. Doubtless other policy domains would reveal novel challenges arising but the rapid spread of algorithms and big data in public services continues to raise important questions for social as well as computer scientists. In the case of immigration, for example, the datasets and algorithms are usually not publicly available. This may be attributed to the need to protect the privacy of individuals and intellectual property, but the AI community must develop better tools and techniques to evaluate bias in collaboration with non-AI scholars.

Furthermore, to regulate the use of AI, standards and safeguards need to be established during data collection, algorithmic design, and deployment. AI systems should have an explanation mechanism that produces clear and understandable explanations for the decisions being made. An accountability framework must also be in place. Having independent third parties assessing the reliability of AI-based decision-making systems would also contribute positively towards accountability.

REFERENCES

Akhmetova, R. (2020). *Efficient Discrimination: On How Governments Use Artificial Intelligence in the Immigration Sphere to Create and Fortify 'Invisible Border Walls'* (Working Paper No. 149). University of Oxford. Retrieved November 17, 2022, from https://www.compas.ox.ac.uk/2020/efficient-discrimination-on-how-governments-use-artificial-intelligence-in-the-immigration-sphere-to-create-and-fortify-invisible-border-walls/

Akpinar, N.-J., De-Arteaga, M., and Chouldechova, A. (2021). The effect of differential victim crime reporting on predictive policing systems. *Proceedings of the 2021 ACM Conference on Fairness, Accountability, and Transparency (FAccT '21)*, 838–849. https://doi.org/10.1145/3442188.3445877

Asaro, P. M. (2019). AI ethics in predictive policing: From models of threat to an ethics of care. *IEEE Technology and Society Magazine*, 38(2), 40–53. https://doi.org/10.1109/MTS.2019.2915154

Babuta, A., and Oswald, M. (2020, February 23). *Data Analytics and Algorithms in Policing in England and Wales: Towards a New Policy Framework* (Occasional Paper). Royal United Services Institute for Defence and Security Studies. Retrieved November 17, 2022, from https://rusi.org/explore-our-research/publications/occasional-papers/data-analytics-and-algorithms-policing-england-and-wales-towards-new-policy-framework

Beduschi, A. (2021). International migration management in the age of artificial intelligence. *Migration Studies*, 9(3), 576–596. https://doi.org/10.1093/migration/mnaa003

Bircan, T., and Korkmaz, E. E. (2021). Big data for whose sake? Governing migration through artificial intelligence. *Humanities and Social Sciences Communications*, 8, 241. https://doi.org/10.1057/s41599-021-00910-x

Blasi Casagran, C. (2021). Fundamental rights implications of interconnecting migration and policing databases in the EU. *Human Rights Law Review*, 21(2), 433–457. https://doi.org/10.1093/hrlr/ngaa057

Busuioc, M. (2021). Accountable artificial intelligence: holding algorithms to account. *Public Administration Review*, 81(5), 825–836. https://doi.org/10.1111/puar.13293

Castelvecchi, D. (2016). Can we open the black box of AI? *Nature*, 538(7623), 20–23. https://doi.org/10.1038/538020a

Choi, D.-J., Park, J. J., Ali, T., and Lee, S. (2020). Artificial intelligence for the diagnosis of heart failure. *NPJ Digital Medicine*, 3, 54. https://doi.org/10.1038/s41746-020-0261-3

Christie, L. (2021, April 29). *AI in Policing and Security* (Horizon scanning). Westminster: UK Parliament POST. Retrieved November 17, 2022, from https://post.parliament.uk/ai-in-policing-and -security/

Chun, A. H. W. (2008). An AI framework for the automatic assessment of e-government forms. *AI Magazine*, 29(1), 52–64. https://doi.org/10.1609/aimag.v29i1.2086

Coluccini, R. (2021, January 13). *Lo scontro Viminale-Garante della privacy sul riconoscimento facciale in tempo reale*. Investigative Reporting Project Italy. Retrieved November 17, 2022, from https:// irpimedia.irpi.eu/viminale-garante-privacy-riconoscimento-facciale-in-tempo-reale/

Council of Europe Commissioner for Human Rights (2019). *Unboxing Artificial Intelligence: 10 Steps to Protect Human Rights*. Strasbourg: Council of Europe. Available at: https://rm.coe.int/unboxing -artificial-intelligence-10-steps-to-protect-human-rights-reco/1680946e64

Crisp, J. (2018, March 9). *Beware the Notion that Better Data Lead to Better Outcomes for Refugees and Migrants*. Chatham House. Retrieved November 17, 2022, from https://www.chathamhouse.org/ 2018/03/beware-notion-better-data-lead-better-outcomes-refugees-and-migrants

Csernatoni, R. (2018). Constructing the EU's high-tech borders: FRONTEX and dual-use drones for border management. *European Security*, 27(2), 175–200. https://doi.org/10.1080/09662839.2018 .1481396

Duarte, N. (2018, May 22). *ICE Finds Out It Can't Automate Immigration Vetting. Now What?* (Insights). Center for Democracy & Technology. Retrieved November 18, 2022, from https://cdt.org/ insights/ice-cant-automate-immigration-vetting/

Dwork, C. (2021). Differential privacy in distributed environments: an overview and open questions. *Proceedings of the 2021 ACM Symposium on Principles of Distributed Computing (PODC'21)*, 5. https://doi.org/10.1145/3465084.3467482

Egbert, S., and Krasmann, S. (2020). Predictive policing: not yet, but soon preemptive? *Policing and Society*, 30(8), 905–919. https://doi.org/10.1080/10439463.2019.1611821

Esteva, A., Kuprel, B., Novoa, R. A., Ko, J., Swetter, S. M., Blau, H. M., and Thrun, S. (2017). Dermatologist-level classification of skin cancer with deep neural networks. *Nature*, 542(7639), 115–118. https://doi.org/10.1038/nature21056

Eubanks, V. (2018). *Automating Inequality: How High-tech Tools Profile, Police, and Punish the Poor*. St. Martin's Press.

European Commission. (2021). *Proposal for a Regulation of the European Parliament and of the Council: Laying Down Harmonised Rules on Artificial Intelligence (Artificial Intelligence Act) and Amending Certain Union Legislative Acts*. Retrieved November 18, 2022, from https://eur-lex.europa .eu/resource.html?uri=cellar:e0649735-a372-11eb-9585-01aa75ed71a1.0001.02/DOC_1&format= PDF

Forti, M. (2021). AI-driven migration management procedures: fundamental rights issues and regulatory answers. *BioLaw Journal – Rivista di BioDiritto*, (2), 433–451. https://doi.org/10.15168/2284-4503 -833

Franz, J., and Bergquist, C. (2017, May 1). It's a buoy, it's a life raft, it's Emily – the robotic craft that's saving refugees off the coast of Greece. *The World*. Retrieved November 18, 2022, from https:// theworld.org/stories/2017-05-01/it-s-buoy-it-s-life-raft-it-s-emily-robotic-craft-s-saving-refugees- coast-greece

Friedler, S. A., Scheidegger, C., Venkatasubramanian, S., Choudhary, S., Hamilton, E. P., and Roth, D. (2019). A comparative study of fairness-enhancing interventions in machine learning. *Proceedings of the Conference on Fairness, Accountability, and Transparency (FAT* '19)*, 329–338. https://doi.org/ 10.1145/3287560.3287589

Gallagher, R., and Jona, L. (2019, July 26). We tested Europe's new lie detector for travelers – and immediately triggered a false positive. *The Intercept*. Retrieved November 18, 2022, from https:// theintercept.com/2019/07/26/europe-border-control-ai-lie-detector/

Gehl Sampath, P. (2021). Governing Artificial Intelligence in an age of inequality. *Global Policy*, 12(S6), 21–31. https://doi.org/10.1111/1758-5899.12940

Glaser, A. (2017, August 8). ICE wants to use predictive policing technology for its 'extreme vetting' program. *Slate*. Retrieved November 18, 2022, from https://slate.com/technology/2017/08/ice-wants -to-use-predictive-policing-tech-for-extreme-vetting.html

Harris, H., and Burke, A. (2021). Artificial intelligence, policing and ethics – a best practice model for AI enabled policing in Australia. *IEEE 25th International Enterprise Distributed Object Computing Workshop (EDOCW)*, 53–58. https://doi.org/10.1109/EDOCW52865.2021.00032

Henrich, J., Heine, S. J., and Norenzayan, A. (2010). The weirdest people in the world? *Behavioral and Brain Sciences*, 33(2–3), 61–83. https://doi.org/10.1017/S0140525X0999152X

Holstein, K., Wortman Vaughan, J., Daumé, H., Dudik, M., and Wallach, H. (2019). Improving fairness in machine learning systems: what do industry practitioners need? *Proceedings of the 2019 CHI Conference on Human Factors in Computing Systems (CHI '19)*, 1–16. https://doi.org/10.1145/3290605.3300830

Holzmeyer, C. (2021). Beyond 'AI for social good' (AI4SG): social transformations – not tech-fixes – for health equity. *Interdisciplinary Science Reviews*, 46(1–2), 94–125. https://doi.org/10.1080/03080188.2020.1840221

Jo, E. S., and Gebru, T. (2020). Lessons from archives: strategies for collecting sociocultural data in machine learning. *Proceedings of the 2020 Conference on Fairness, Accountability, and Transparency (FAT* '20)*, 306–316. https://doi.org/10.1145/3351095.3372829

Joh, E. E. (2018). Artificial intelligence and policing: first questions. *Seattle University Law Review*, 41(4), 1139–1144. https://digitalcommons.law.seattleu.edu/sulr/vol41/iss4/7/

Karmakar, S. (2022). Artificial Intelligence: the future of medicine, or an over-hyped and dangerous idea? *Irish Journal of Medical Science (1971–)*, 191(5), 1991–1994. https://doi.org/10.1007/s11845-021-02853-3

Kerasidou, C. X., Kerasidou, A., Buscher, M., and Wilkinson, S. (2022). Before and beyond trust: reliance in medical AI. *Journal of Medical Ethics*, 48(11), 852–856. https://doi.org/10.1136/medethics-2020-107095

Kesari, A. (2022). The privacy-fairness-accuracy frontier: a computational law & economics toolkit for making algorithmic tradeoffs. *Proceedings of the 2022 Symposium on Computer Science and Law (CSLAW '22)*, 77–85. https://doi.org/10.1145/3511265.3550437

Keung, N. (2017, January 5). Canadian immigration applications could soon be assessed by computers. *Toronto Star*. Retrieved November 23, 2022, from https://www.thestar.com/news/immigration/2017/01/05/immigration-applications-could-soon-be-assessed-by-computers.html

Kleinberg, J., and Mullainathan, S. (2019). Simplicity creates inequity: implications for fairness, stereotypes, and interpretability. *Proceedings of the 2019 ACM Conference on Economics and Computation (EC '19)*, 807–808. https://doi.org/10.1145/3328526.3329621

Kodali, S. (2017, February 8). *Hyderabad's 'Smart Policing' Project is Simply Mass Surveillance in Disguise*. The WIRE. Retrieved November 28, 2022, from https://thewire.in/government/hyderabad-smart-policing-surveillance

Landers, R. N., and Behrend, T. S. (2022). Auditing the AI auditors: a framework for evaluating fairness and bias in high stakes AI predictive models. *American Psychologist*. https://doi.org/10.1037/amp0000972

Lepri, B., Oliver, N., Letouzé, E., Pentland, A., and Vinck, P. (2018). Fair, transparent, and accountable algorithmic decision-making processes. *Philosophy & Technology*, 31(4), 611–627. https://doi.org/10.1007/s13347-017-0279-x

Lysaght, T., Lim, H. Y., Xafis, V., and Ngiam, K. Y. (2019). AI-assisted decision-making in healthcare. *Asian Bioethics Review*, 11(3), 299–314. https://doi.org/10.1007/s41649-019-00096-0

Marda, V., and Narayan, S. (2020). Data in New Delhi's predictive policing system. *Proceedings of the 2020 Conference on Fairness, Accountability, and Transparency (FAT* '20)*, 317–324. https://doi.org/10.1145/3351095.3372865

Markó, F. D. (2016). 'We are not a failed state, we make the best passports': South Sudan and biometric modernity. *African Studies Review*, 59(2), 113–132. https://doi.org/10.1017/asr.2016.39

McKay, F., Williams, B. J., Prestwich, G., Bansal, D., Hallowell, N., and Treanor, D. (2022). The ethical challenges of artificial intelligence-driven digital pathology. *The Journal of Pathology: Clinical Research*, 8(3), 209–216. https://doi.org/10.1002/cjp2.263

McLennan, S., Fiske, A., Tigard, D., Müller, R., Haddadin, S., and Buyx, A. (2022). Embedded ethics: a proposal for integrating ethics into the development of medical AI. *BMC Medical Ethics*, 23(6). https://doi.org/10.1186/s12910-022-00746-3

Molnar, P. (2019). Technology on the margins: AI and global migration management from a human rights perspective. *Cambridge International Law Journal*, 8(2), 305–330. https://doi.org/10.4337/cilj .2019.02.07

Molnar, P., and Gill, L. (2018, September). *Bots at the Gate: A Human Rights Analysis of Automated Decision-making in Canada's Immigration and Refugee System* (Research Report No. 114). Citizen Lab and International Human Rights Program (Faculty of Law, University of Toronto). Retrieved November 23, 2022, from https://hdl.handle.net/1807/94802

Murphy, K., Di Ruggiero, E., Upshur, R., Willison, D. J., Malhotra, N., Cai, J. C., Malhotra, N., Lui, V., and Gibson, J. (2021). Artificial intelligence for good health: a scoping review of the ethics literature. *BMC Medical Ethics*, 22(14). https://doi.org/10.1186/s12910-021-00577-8

Oatley, G. C. (2022). Themes in data mining, big data, and crime analytics. *WIREs Data Mining and Knowledge Discovery*, 12(2), e1432. https://doi.org/10.1002/widm.1432

Oberhaus, D. (2018, June 26). ICE modified its 'risk assessment' software so it automatically recommends detention. *VICE*. Retrieved November 23, 2022, from https://www.vice.com/en/article/ evk3kw/ice-modified-its-risk-assessment-software-so-it-automatically-recommends-detention

Ohyama, T., and Amemiya, M. (2018). Applying crime prediction techniques to Japan: a comparison between risk terrain modeling and other methods. *European Journal on Criminal Policy and Research*, 24(4), 469–487. https://doi.org/10.1007/s10610-018-9378-1

O'Neil, C. (2016). *Weapons of Math Destruction: How Big Data Increases Inequality and Threatens Democracy*. Crown Books.

O'Shea, J., Crockett, K., Khan, W., Kindynis, P., Antoniades, A., and Boultadakis, G. (2018). Intelligent deception detection through machine based interviewing. *2018 International Joint Conference on Neural Networks (IJCNN '18)*, 1–8. https://doi.org/10.1109/IJCNN.2018.8489392

PredPol. (2021). *Predictive Policing Technology*. Retrieved November 23, 2022, from https://www .predpol.com/technology/

Richardson, R., Schultz, J., and Crawford, K. (2019). Dirty data, bad predictions: how civil rights violations impact police data, predictive policing systems, and justice. *New York University Law Review*, 94, 192–233. https://ssrn.com/abstract=3333423

Robbins, S. (2019). A misdirected principle with a catch: explicability for AI. *Minds and Machines*, 29(4), 495–514. https://doi.org/10.1007/s11023-019-09509-3

Santoni de Sio, F., and van den Hoven, J. (2018). Meaningful human control over autonomous systems: a philosophical account. *Frontiers in Robotics and AI*, 5(15). https://doi.org/10.3389/frobt.2018 .00015

Schauer, F. (2003). *Profiles, Probabilities, and Stereotypes*. Harvard University Press. https://doi.org/10 .4159/9780674043244

Sheehey, B. (2019). Algorithmic paranoia: the temporal governmentality of predictive policing. *Ethics and Information Technology*, 21, 49–58. https://doi.org/10.1007/s10676-018-9489-x

Shortliffe, E. H. (1974). A rule-based computer program for advising physicians regarding antimicrobial therapy selection. *Proceedings of the 1974 Annual ACM Conference – Volume 2 (ACM '74)*, 739. https://doi.org/10.1145/1408800.1408906

Suresh, H. (2021, December 7). Why Hyderabad became India's surveillance capital. *The NEWS Minute*. Retrieved November 28, 2022, from https://www.thenewsminute.com/article/why-hyderabad-became -india-s-surveillance-capital-158466

Tan, L. (2018, April 5). Immigration NZ's data profiling 'illegal' critics say. *NZ Herald*. Retrieved November 23, 2022, from https://www.nzherald.co.nz/nz/immigration-nzs-data-profiling-illegal -critics-say/P5QDBGVDGFSI6I3NV4UHPOSBRA/?cid=1&objectid=12026585

Tazzioli, M. (2018). Spy, track and archive: the temporality of visibility in Eurosur and Jora. *Security Dialogue*, 49(4), 272–288. https://doi.org/10.1177/0967010618769812

Thomasian, N. M., Eickhoff, C., and Adashi, E. Y. (2021). Advancing health equity with artificial intelligence. *Journal of Public Health Policy*, 42(4), 602–611. https://doi.org/10.1057/s41271-021-00319-5

Umanadh, J. (2019, November 7). Telangana govt denies surveillance snooping on citizens. *Deccan Herald*. Retrieved November 28, 2022, from https://www.deccanherald.com/national/south/telangana -govt-denies-surveillance-snooping-on-citizens-774306.html

van der Veer, S. N., Riste, L., Cheraghi-Sohi, S., Phipps, D. L., Tully, M. P., Bozentko, K., Atwood, S., Hubbard, A., Wiper, C., Oswald, M., and Peek, N. (2021). Trading off accuracy and explainability in AI decision-making: findings from 2 citizens' juries. *Journal of the American Medical Informatics Association*, 28(10), 2128–2138. https://doi.org/10.1093/jamia/ocab127

Yen, C.-P., and Hung, T.-W. (2021). Achieving equity with predictive policing algorithms: a social safety net perspective. *Science and Engineering Ethics*, 27(3), 36. https://doi.org/10.1007/s11948-021-00312-x

Young, M. M., Bullock, J. B., and Lecy, J. D. (2019). Artificial discretion as a tool of governance: a framework for understanding the impact of artificial intelligence on public administration. *Perspectives on Public Management and Governance*, 2(4), 301–313. https://doi.org/10.1093/ppmgov/gvz014

4. Towards a systematic understanding on the challenges of public procurement of artificial intelligence in the public sector

Keegan McBride, Colin van Noordt, Gianluca Misuraca and Gerhard Hammerschmid

INTRODUCTION

Artificial Intelligence (AI), can be understood as 'systems designed by humans that, given a complex goal, act in the physical or digital world by perceiving their environment, interpreting the collected structured or unstructured data, reasoning on the knowledge derived from this data and deciding the best action(s) to take (according to pre-defined parameters) to achieve the given goal' (AI HLEG, 2019). AI is studied and applied across sectors, contexts, and domains; it has become ingrained within our societies with its influence likely only to grow as AI technologies improve. The public sector is no exception. In the public sector, it is hoped that the usage of AI can increase governmental effectiveness and efficiency, enable new forms of public services and mechanisms for delivery, assist evidence-based policy making, and play a role in the 'transformation' of the public sector (Berryhill et al., 2019). This is especially true in Europe, where large amounts of effort have been devoted to understanding how AI can be used in the delivery of public services (Misuraca, Van Noordt et al., 2020; van Noordt and Misuraca, 2022) and where one of the most ambitious regulatory approaches to AI is currently being developed (Dempsey et al., 2022). Aiming to understand the impact that AI may have in or on the public sector, scholars of digital government and public administration have devoted a large amount of attention to the issue. However, one area of research that remains under explored is the public sector procurement of AI. This is unfortunate as procurement will likely remain a key method for public sector organisations to develop and implement AI technologies as governments aim to access the AI capacity held within private sector companies. However, procurement is hard, especially when it comes to procuring AI systems. It is for this reason that a report from the House of Lords Select Committee on Artificial Intelligence noted that:

> Most of GovTech is about procurement.... getting procurement rules right is one of the most important parts of driving improvements in technology... [and] that [procurement] is a huge part of driving digital as a whole, including the take-up of AI (House of Lords, 2018).

This raises a clear question of how governments can 'get it right' when procuring AI. One potential way would be through the adoption of well-developed, targeted, and responsible public procurement methods, strategies, and guidelines. While many governments do have large amounts of experience with procurement, including the procurement of digital technologies, procuring AI appears to present new and unique challenges. This represents a clear gap in our knowledge. On the one hand, procuring AI is becoming increasingly important. On the other, there is still limited research on what guidelines and strategies could look like and how they could be enacted to improve the AI procurement process.

This chapter aims to address this gap. It does so by, firstly, exploring what challenges may be encountered during the procurement of AI in the public sector and, secondly, by identifying potential guidelines or strategies that may help to overcome such challenges. The research is guided primarily by the following two research questions:

- What are the key challenges associated with the public procurement of AI?
- What are the commonly occurring strategies, recommendations, and guidelines to overcome such challenges?

To answer these questions, the study is empirically structured as a qualitative, descriptive, exploratory, and comparative multi-case study. The four countries selected for this study were Estonia, the Netherlands, Serbia, and the United Kingdom. These four countries represented the four countries with clearly developed and conceptualised guidelines to better procure AI as well as for overcoming challenges that public sector organisations may encounter during the procurement of AI.

As a result of this research three core contributions are made. First, the chapter helps to conceptualise the concept of procurement of AI in the public sector. Second, the chapter identifies commonly occurring challenges during the process of procuring AI in the public sector. Third, the chapter presents solutions and approaches that have been proposed by public sector organisations for overcoming or preventing these challenges. Taken in totality, these contributions develop a strong foundation for future research on AI in the public sector, particularly research utilising a lens based on procurement or challenges.

To reach these contributions, this chapter proceeds by offering a short conceptual overview on public sector procurement, the use of AI in the public sector, and the challenges of procuring AI in the public sector. Following this, the methodology is presented together with the empirical evidence sources used and the mechanism of data analysis. This is followed by a short overview of each of the selected case countries, the results of the analysis, and a discussion of the findings. The chapter concludes by elucidating on the answers to the research questions, offering future directions for research, and offering initial policy and managerial insights and recommendations.

BACKGROUND LITERATURE

Public Sector Procurement

It can be said that there are at least three primary phases of procurement: feasibility assessment, implementation and organisation of procurement, and monitoring and evaluation of performance (Brown and Potoski, 2003). Within this tri-phasic procurement process, previous research has identified a number of factors that seem to play a role in why a procurement may fail or succeed.

One of the most relevant factors is that of contract-management capacity (Brown and Potoski, 2003); the likelihood that a procurement is successful is highly dependent on how well the organisation is able to manage the process. Second, the identification and formulation of necessary and relevant technical requirements before a procurement takes place (Edler et al., 2006; Georghiou et al., 2014). Third, market knowledge. It must be understood what the current market is actually able to produce; the creation of unrealistic requirements, or an over/underestimation of the current market will lead to potential failure (Edler et al., 2006; Mulligan and Bamberger, 2019). Fourth, Edquist et al. (2000) highlight additional factors that influence whether a procurement is successful: timing, technical competence inside the procuring organisation, and broader organisational competencies. Finally, the organisation must have a high degree of technical knowledge, or, if they do not have this capacity inside their own organisation, must be able to coordinate the attainment of this knowledge (Edler et al., 2006; Edquist et al., 2000).

In the context of AI, this implies that governments must:

- have the ability to successfully manage AI procurement contracts,
- have the relevant technological knowledge and in-house capacities,
- be aware of the current market abilities and relevant state-of-the-art, and
- have an in-depth understanding of their own IT infrastructure, data, and capabilities.

However, as AI expertise in the public sector is scarce (Wirtz et al., 2019), administrations often have to collaborate to get AI capabilities (van Noordt and Misuraca, 2020), and data governance regimes may be lacking (Janssen et al., 2020), so public procurement of AI will likely prove challenging for public sector organisations, especially without additional guidance.

Artificial Intelligence in the Public Sector

Inside the public sector, AI is applied in a wide variety of ways. For example, researchers have explored AI use cases such as: chatbots or virtual assistants (Aoki, 2020; van Noordt and Misuraca, 2019), natural language processing (Agarwal, 2018), food safety (McBride et al., 2019), and automated decision making (Wihlborg et al., 2016). This is not a complete (nor a comprehensive) list, but it does demonstrate that there are a number of different ways that AI is currently being used in the public sector. It is also likely the case that, as AI technology develops, the number of use cases and its influence in, on, and for governments will only grow. What is clear, however, is that (at least currently) AI applications rarely replace governments, but rather augment and improve processes, for example by improving internal efficiency, improving decision making, or improving interactions between governments and citizens.

While research on AI often focuses on 'AI' broadly, data, or algorithms, infrastructure is also a core component for AI. In the above use cases, each one may, individually, be considered 'AI', but each will also utilise different models or algorithms and require different data and infrastructure. As a quick example, a chatbot or NLP service may require large amounts of conversational data to train itself, whereas a computer vision-based service requires large amounts of visual training data. This data is held in different formats, and stored, gathered, and utilised using different technologies. Thus, as the use of AI increases inside the public sector, so too does the amount of infrastructure and technical capacity needed to effectively utilise AI. Due to this mashup of systems, algorithms, services, and infrastructure governments that heavily procure AI run the risk of creating an unmanageable hodgepodge of infrastructure and data.

Challenges of AI Procurement

The purpose of this section is to deal explicitly with the procurement of AI in the public sector, outline the potential challenges, discuss what makes the procurement of AI unique, and to highlight some potential AI procurement best practices that have begun to emerge in the scholarly body of knowledge. This literature is limited to a handful of studies and scholars and is almost entirely based within legal studies; it has not yet widely expanded into the public administration, public management, or broader digital government areas of research.

One of the first challenges that appears during the public procurement of AI is that of data and the legal challenges that may arise as a result of using data in a machine learning service (Janssen et al., 2020). All machine learning algorithms require data to function, the question is, where does this data come from? In case the government is providing the data, they must ensure it is clear where the data can be held. Is it on their own servers, in a cloud, or with the provider? The answer to this will depend on the relevant regulations and legal requirements the procuring organisation is subject to. It is also important to understand how a citizen's data could be removed from the relevant dataset should they request their data be forgotten. If data used in the algorithm is, for example, textual in nature (e.g. emails or chats sent to the government), how is it ensured that any personal information is removed from this data (Harrison and Luna-Reyes, 2020)?

A second challenge, also related to data, is that of data ownership and data sovereignty. If data is collected by a government, but then is used by a private sector company to train an algorithm, can the company sell this trained algorithm to other countries, or can the procuring organisation retain complete ownership over the data? This issue works in the reverse as well, in the case that data is coming from the private sector organisation (Campion et al., 2020).

The potential for bias and discrimination in AI is a third clear challenge. It is apparent that many machine learning algorithms and tools exhibit human bias and discrimination (Caliskan et al., 2017) and these biases can have a real impact if left to their own devices in the public sector. These issues have already materialised when algorithms are used in the public sector for services such as criminal sentencing (Washington, 2018) or predictive policing (Benbouzid, 2019). Furthermore, there needs to be an understanding on who bears responsibility for any potential bias or discriminatory algorithmic decisions. Is it the AI itself? Is it the government? The private sector? Such issues must be covered in either legal regulations, or via the procurement process itself. Some initial initiatives to address these issues have already begun to emerge. For example, both the OECD and the EU have drafted and released guidelines to address ethical creation and use of AI, the Council of Europe has also drafted initial guidelines for procuring AI systems that respect human rights.

A fourth issue associated with public procurement of AI is that of trade secrecy and intellectual property rights, which can affect algorithmic transparency (Brauneis and Goodman, 2018; Mulligan and Bamberger, 2019). For example, a purchased AI solution may be used by different organisations, and, in this case, the provider of the service likely desires to protect their product, algorithm, and the data it uses. This could limit the government from providing this information to any concerned or affected stakeholders.

A fifth issue is that of transparency; one of the best ways to increase transparency appears to be through procurement and regulatory guidelines. As highlighted by Brauneis Goodman, transparency can be increased by placing importance on 'contract language requiring provision and permitting of disclosure of records' therefore 'placing the burden on the contractor to identify and mark specific passages in a document as trade secrets' and subsequently '[linking] disclosure provisions to demands that records be produced to the government' (2018, pp. 164–165).

Finally, it is necessary that the procuring organisation has a clear understanding about how the specific machine learning model works. In their study, Brauneis Goodman (2018) sent record requests to forty-two agencies about six different algorithmic programs in twenty-three states; only one respondent could provide information about the algorithm (Mulligan and Bamberger, 2019). To some extent, this is understandable. If a government organisation is procuring AI they may not have the capability internally to understand the solution. However, it is also imperative that algorithms are developed in an ethical manner, and the only way to ensure this is through the appropriate procurement measures.

METHODOLOGY

Methodologically, this chapter utilises a descriptive and exploratory multi-case study (Yin, 2013) approach to explore the AI procurement guidelines in four European countries: Estonia, the Netherlands, Serbia, and the United Kingdom. For case selection, this study focused on the European context and looked for countries that had made explicit steps at developing, implementing, or trialling guidelines for the procurement of AI in public sector organisations. After this initial review, only the aforementioned four countries had clearly identifiable guidelines related to the procurement of AI in the public sector. Though four countries is not a large sample size, due to the relative newness of the procurement of AI in the public sector, this initial exploration of critical cases is relevant and useful.

Empirically, a number of evidence sources were used to ensure the triangulation of the findings and thereby improve the internal validity of the study. The primary documents analysed during the desk research were the official AI strategies for each country (this exists in three out of four countries: the United Kingdom does not have an official 'AI Strategy', but rather a policy paper) and, in the case of Estonia and the United Kingdom, existing and relevant AI procurement guidelines. Other documents analysed included training seminars recorded and published to YouTube, magazine articles, newspaper articles, and governmental hearings or reports.

The desk research was followed by a total of nine-semi structured interviews (three in Estonia, one in the Netherlands, four in Serbia, and one in the United Kingdom). The nine semi-structured interviews were conducted with the leaders and users of the relevant AI procurement initiatives; interviewees have been anonymised and given a code based on their interview number and the country's guidelines they were involved with. Interviewees were selected due to their direct role in developing their specific country's guidelines for the procurement of AI in the public sector. Though the number of interviewees is low, those interviewed were experts on not only the guidelines, but also the motivation and reasoning behind them.

All conducted interviews were done virtually by the researchers behind this chapter, lasted up to 45 minutes, were transcribed, and then coded and analysed using conventional content analysis (Birks and Mills, 2015; Hsieh and Shannon, 2005). The interview questions all aimed to address different aspects of the AI procurement process, such as: internal organisational capacity, the procurement process, existing guidelines or best practices, AI development strategies, and any encountered barriers to AI adoption. The interviews were conducted after the initial document and textual based desk research and served as a way to get insight about the behind-the-scenes processes associated with the development or ideation of AI procurement guidelines.

As with all research, there is the potential for limitations and weaknesses, thus it must be highlighted that this research offers only a preliminary view of the challenges faced during the public procurement of AI as many of the guidelines studied are still currently under development or in a testing phase. One respondent, NL.PS1, noted that in the Netherlands there were difficulties in assessing the usability of the created guidelines due to a lack of potential cases that they could be validated against. A second potential weakness is similarly related: there is a small bias in the analysed cases as they represent the most developed countries. How other administrations, with less experience, may address similar and/or other public procurement of AI challenges remains unknown; though there is likely to be significant overlap, it is not possible to make a strong statement to this effect, slightly limiting the external applicability of the research.

CASE OVERVIEW

Estonia

Starting in 2016, Estonia began to develop a comprehensive strategic and regulatory approach to the adoption and implementation of AI in the public sector. These efforts were led and coordinated by the Estonian Ministry of Economic Affairs and Communication (MKM). In 2018, a task force was announced that was composed of AI experts, lawyers, and policy makers who were given the responsibility of developing an Estonia AI strategy. This strategy was finished and approved in 2019 and focused on four primary areas: advancing the uptake of AI in the public sector, advancing the uptake of AI in the private sector, developing AI RD and education, and developing a legal environment for the uptake of AI (Riigikantselei and MKM, 2019).

To help address a perceived general lack of knowledge and experience about best practices for AI procurement in the Estonian public sector, the chief data officer has created a number of different guidelines and tools for improving and aiding public sector officials with their procurements (EE.PS1, 2020; EE.PS2, 2020). These include: a questionnaire to decide if AI is the correct technology for a specific project; instruction materials with instructions, recommendations, and best practices for AI projects in the public sector; a reusable structure and template for AI procurements; an overview document for public servants about key terms and concepts in AI; data impact assessments; and a number of training presentations and videos about different AI projects (MKM, 2020; EE.PS1–3, 2020).

The Netherlands

In the Netherlands, Amsterdam has developed AI procurement guidelines to assist with the responsible and democratic use and development of AI technologies within the city (NL.PS1, 2020) and these are being evaluated for use at all administrative levels across the country. The Association of Dutch Municipalities has also made the guidelines available for all municipalities to use. These guidelines consist of nine different articles that describe the various terms and conditions that AI systems should adhere to when they are procured by the municipality. These include transparency requirements, data ownership and governance requirements, AI system quality, risk management and maintenance. The guidelines are still in the testing phase, as the city aims to understand how different stakeholders, such as other municipalities, civil servants, and smaller and bigger companies view and evaluate these guidelines (Amsterdam City, 2020).

The procurement guidelines should be followed whenever a contractor provides an algorithm for decision making, decision support, enforcement, fraud investigations or a system to be used on the staff of the municipality. A key aspect is the requirement for AI to be transparent in three different ways: procedural, technical and explainable (Amsterdam City, 2020). This requires the contractor to document and describe the non-technical, core functioning of the algorithm, the technical quality and operation such as the source code, and explainability of case by case outcomes. At all times decisions with or by AI should be explainable, as per requirement of Dutch public law.

Serbia

The Serbian government has released their strategy regarding the Development of AI in their country for the period 2020–2025. In this document, public procurement has been regarded as an important element to stimulate AI within Serbia. Public procurement is seen in the strategy as a tool to create market opportunities for start-ups and as an opportunity for the public sector to modernise public services (RS.PS1, 2020). The lack of a framework for the use of public procurement for innovative technologies such as AI is regarded as one of the key issues limiting the development of AI adoption in the Serbian public sector (RS.PS1, 2020). Hence, the strategy mentions the need to adopt public procurement regulations, and particularly to regulate issues regarding data ownership and to regulate algorithmic bias (Government of Serbia, 2019). In this respect, it is mentioned that public procurement contracts should include the obligation to assign data to the state and to define the structure, form, and format of the submitted data.

UK

The government of the United Kingdom partnered with the World Economic Forum to draft guidelines for AI procurement in the public sector. These guidelines specifically address challenges that public sector organisations may face during the public procurement of AI based solutions. Public procurement is regarded as the primary mechanism to facilitate the adoption of AI in the government (UK.PS1, 2021), which may be done to improve public sector delivery, reduce costs, improve effectiveness, or reduce administrative burden (Office for AI et al., 2020; World Economic Forum, 2020). In these guidelines, AI is understood as the use of digital technology to create systems that conduct intelligent tasks, but the document itself primarily refers to machine learning. Though the guidelines focus primarily on machine learning, they also acknowledge that there are fundamental differences between different AI-based systems and offer specific guidance for different AI use cases at different stages of readiness. The guidelines provide a number of considerations during various stages of the AI procurement process. These guidelines make it clear that there is a pre-procurement process, which starts by assessing whether or not AI is truly needed and whether or not the relevant data or skillsets exist to develop and evaluate an AI system (Office for AI et al., 2020). Further, the guidelines highlight the need to ensure transparency and explainability of the AI system in the procurement, as this ensures future understanding of the system, and reduces the potential of vendor lock-in. The guidelines also highlight the importance of testing and evaluating AI systems, specifically by using data and impact assessments throughout the entire development process, from ideation through to implementation.

RESULTS AND DISCUSSION

While many governments do have experience with procurement, the research interviewees from all four countries agreed that procuring AI was different, and that because of this there was a clear need for new guidelines. A great example of this comes from UK-PS1 who noted that they saw two reasons why procuring AI was different:

> ... when you procure AI technologies you also, sometimes, make policy decisions. You basically are outsourcing, somewhat, policy decisions and furthermore that, we thought about the public procurement of AI as a policy tool to drive innovation and regulation (UK-PS1, 2021).

The importance of using procurement as a policy tool to drive innovation and regulation has also been mentioned in Serbia and the Netherlands. This brings us to the first important finding of this paper: **there is a conceptual difference between traditional procurements in the public sector and the procurement of AI in the public sector.** While each of the countries selected had guidelines and approaches for AI procurement, the motivational reason behind them slightly differed. For example, in the Netherlands and the UK it was clear that AI procurement emphasis was given to viewing procurement as a policy tool, whereas in Serbia and Estonia AI procurement was emphasised as the means to stimulate and develop the AI ecosystem and private sector. Interestingly, in Estonia, the Netherlands, and the United Kingdom interviewees suggested that the private sector, especially SMEs, were responsive and appreciative of the development of AI procurement guidelines as it helped to improve procurement clarity, relevance, and alignment with the market. On the challenges of procuring AI in the public sector, during this research, 14 key challenges faced during the procurement of AI in the public sector were identified and triangulated.

These challenges can be subdivided into four categories:

- **Procurement Process Challenges:** market knowledge, trade secrecy, service needs, structure
- **Data Challenges:** data availability, data ownership, data governance, data infrastructure
- **AI-Model Challenges:** AI system quality, AI transparency, AI bias
- **Organisational Capacity Challenges:** technical capacity, organisational capacity, individual capacities

To overcome these 14 challenges, a total of 22 potential strategies were identified during this research. These solutions are discussed below through an in-depth overview of the challenges, explanations, solutions, and locations within the procurement process.

While not all challenges or solutions identified were unique to the procurement of AI, more were than were not. In any case, it is useful to provide a systematic overview of all challenges that may be encountered during the procurement of AI in the public sector. Furthermore, it was possible to identify currently proposed solutions for addressing these challenges from the guidelines of the studied countries. This research cannot make a claim on whether or not such solutions work, only that these are what the identified countries dealing with the procurement of AI are currently suggesting in their procurement guidelines.

Procurement Process Challenges

The first group of challenges identified were those specific to the procurement process itself. As a starting point, it must be decided whether AI is actually needed for a specific problem as AI should not be applied just for the sake of using AI. To help public sector organisations overcome this problem, checklists and guidelines have been prepared that allow for an organisation to assess whether an AI-based system should be procured; these checklists exist both in Estonia and the United Kingdom.

A second challenge is having an understanding of the market; this is critical for the success of a procurement. Addressing this issue, EE-PS1 noted during an interview that in Estonia there were problems with procurement from the public sector and the market let them know. However, while there were challenges with the public procurement of AI, 'it's not AI specific, a lot of procurement of anything IT is quite crappy anyways, right. That's a problem in itself' (EE-PS1, 2020). Yet, even so, the interviewee continued on to note that the chief data officer had 'come up with an instruction manual or a guidance paper about how to procure these things' and that since then, they 'hear from the market, [that] it has gotten better' (EE-PS1, 2020). Similar sentiment was offered by UK-PS1, who noted that there 'was a very positive narrative from the private sector' and that the new guidelines 'made it easier for the private sector to reply or participate in procurement' (UK-PS1, 2021) as well as NL-PS1, who stated that companies found the produced guidelines 'quite logical and reasonable' (NL-PS1, 2021).

For trade secrecy challenges, it is important to ensure that government organisations are not stuck in a situation where they are not able to share relevant information about how a specific algorithm or AI-system functions if requested. In the guidelines from the United Kingdom and the Netherlands, specific guidance is given on how to ensure sufficient documentation and transparency of AI systems. An additional way to do this, as highlighted by Brauneis and Goodman (2018), is to place importance on 'contract language requiring provision and permitting of disclosure of records' therefore 'placing the burden on the contractor to identify and mark specific passages in a document as trade secrets' and subsequently '[linking] disclosure provisions to demands that records be produced to the government' (pp. 164–165).

Finally, there is the challenge of procurement structure. In Estonia, the chief data officer has created a standardised template with accompanying questionnaires that can be used by organisations to aid them in the procurement process. Interviewees EE-PS2 and EE-PS3 both noted that this guidance and structure was helpful for their organisations in the procurement process. Such templates and structured documents were not readily apparent in the other studied countries.

An overview of these challenges, and some solutions, can be found in Table 4.1 below:

Table 4.1   Procurement process challenges

Challenge	Explanation	Procurement process stage	Solutions	Source(s)
Procurement Process Challenges				
Market knowledge	There is knowledge about the state-of-the-art and what currently is or is not possible in the market, as well as correct and relevant pricing	Feasibility assessment	1. Engage in market research to understand the state-of-the-art and whether or not a specific project is feasible	Estonia, United Kingdom
Trade secrecy	There is an understanding about who owns the intellectual property of the procured system	Implementation and organisation of procurement	1. Include specific regulations within the procurement on trade secrecy and intellectual property rights 2. Ensure that proper documentation is provided and mandated in procurement documents	The Netherlands, United Kingdom
Service needs	AI is the best solution for the specific problem	Feasibility assessment, monitoring and evaluation of performance	1. Engage in a pre-procurement process to check whether or not AI is the best solution for a specific problem	Estonia, the Netherlands, Serbia, United Kingdom
Structure	There is a clear structure to the AI procurement that enables the suppliers to clearly understand what is needed and what the requirements are	Implementation and organisation of procurement	1. Create standard procurement templates to ensure consistency and validity of AI procurements	Estonia

Data Challenges

The second group of challenges are those related to data, namely its availability, governance, ownership, and infrastructure. In all four of the countries studied, the role of data in AI procurement was given prominence. For example, in Serbia, RS-PS2 noted that there needed to be clear guidelines on how to give data away in an organised way and how such data should be stored, arguing that data infrastructure must be developed before engaging in AI procurement. Additionally, in the Serbian AI strategy, it is noted that 'public procurements and contracts must contain ... the provider's obligation to assign [data] to state authorities' (Government of Serbia, 2019). Thus, when it comes to data governance and data ownership, specific measures may help to ensure that there are proper regulations and governance mechanisms in place for data consumed or generated by AI-systems. Similar arguments existed in all countries studied. Regarding data availability, there are two separate aspects at play. First, whether the data needed for a specific AI-system actually exists. To this end, the United Kingdom guidelines strongly recommended assessing the data quality and availability prior to any tender to understand possible issues of the data available for the procured AI system. In Estonia organisations can engage in deep dive sessions with the chief data officer and private sector experts to explore the organisation's available data and potential AI use cases.

Table 4.2   *Data challenges*

Challenge	Explanation	Procurement process stage	Solutions	Source(s)
		Data Challenges		
Data availability	Making the data required for the AI development available, accessible, or obtainable	Feasibility assessment	1. Conducting a data availability assessment prior to the procurement process 2. Ensuring data access, storage and consent before the procurement	Estonia, United Kingdom
Data ownership	Understanding who owns the data used or created by the AI system	Implementation and organisation of procurement	1. Ensure that the procurement has specific language that data provided by the public administration, or collected in the context of procure-ment, remains with the administration	Estonia, the Netherlands, Serbia, United Kingdom
Data governance	Having the necessary governance and legal mechanisms in place for sharing, collecting, and disseminating data	Feasibility assessment	1. Ensure that the contractor has followed regulations and standards during the collection of their data as well as storage	Estonia, the Netherlands, Serbia, United Kingdom
Data infrastructure	Understanding the necessary infrastructure and its location for a specific AI project (e.g. own premises, in the cloud, with provider)	Feasibility assessment	1. Systematically analyse the current infrastructural capa-bilities of your organisation and make it clear within the procurement	Estonia, Serbia, United Kingdom

The second aspect related to data availability is ensuring that sample data is available and provided during the procurement process. This aspect was highlighted as being important by interviewees from the United Kingdom and Estonia.

AI-Model Challenges

The third grouping of challenges are those related to the AI-model or system itself and concern the quality, transparency, and bias of the system. About transparency and bias of AI-systems, all four countries made explicit commitment to the procurement of transparent, ethical, and unbiased AI. As has been mentioned previously in this chapter, there are several international initiatives that lay out clear guidelines and mechanisms to ensure this, such as the OECD's Principles on Artificial Intelligence of the European Union's Ethics Guidelines for Trustworthy AI. Within the procurement guidelines studied for this chapter, only the United Kingdom and the Netherlands had their own guidelines in place for how this was to be done. Only in Estonia and Serbia were mentions of the international guidelines included. When it comes to ensuring ethical and bias-free AI procurement, several solutions have been suggested. For example, there are checklists, tools, and reviews that should help to check for bias and ethical issues in AI systems. It is also possible to require clear documentation about how the algorithm itself works, how decisions are made, what data are used for making

Table 4.3   AI-model challenges

Challenge	Explanation	Procurement process stage	Solutions	Source(s)
		AI-model Challenges		
AI system quality	The finished system/ model is of high quality and in line with legal regulations over a longer period of time	Implementation and organisation of procurement, monitoring and evaluation of performance	1. Apply risk management strategy to identify and mitigate risks 2. Ensure maintenance (over a period of time) is contractually obligatory	The Netherlands, United Kingdom
AI transparency	The AI system is transparent and explainable, potentially for an audit if deemed necessary	Implementation and organisation of procurement, monitoring and evaluation of performance	1. Including technical, procedural and explainability as mandatory requirements 2. Explainability and interpretability of algorithms as a design criteria 3. Require clear documentation about the functionality of the AI-system, the data used, and how it works (at a minimum)	Estonia, the Netherlands, United Kingdom
AI bias	Potential bias of an AI system is mitigated as much as possible	Implementation and organisation of procurement, monitoring and evaluation of performance	1. Conducting a data assessment to identify and address data bias 2. Measures have to be taken by the contractor to ensure bias is limited. Iterative AI impact assessments at crucial decisions points should be conducted 3. Obligatory documentation on compliance to non-discrimination, equal treatment and proportionality	Estonia, the Netherlands, United Kingdom

such decisions, requiring explainability and interpretability in the technical description of the procurement documents, also requiring contractors to provide and confirm their compatibility with specific guidelines, and utilising iterative assessments of utilised AI systems (Berryhill et al., 2019; Brauneis and Goodman, 2018; Mulligan and Bamberger, 2019).

Organisational Challenges

The final category is that of organisational challenges; these are primarily associated with capacities at the managerial, technical, and individual levels. For AI procurements to be successful, it is important that an organisation develops and maintains the ability to procure AI well. In the case of Serbia, all interviewees noted that there was currently little capacity for procuring AI as there is a general lack of expertise. To counteract this, they have proposed to establish a government-academic collaborative institute to aid the government in future AI procurement. Similarly, in Estonia, the private sector and the chief data officer have worked with different organisations directly to improve understanding of AI, organised educational programs, and provided clear documentation to common questions and problems. Across all countries studied, it was noted that there was a clear need to improve the AI and technological capacity of organisations. This can be done by encouraging participation and availability of AI programs, as well as by making IT experts available across organisations. For example, in the United Kingdom it has been noted that if there is missing capacity:

> you should seek [assistance] from elsewhere in your organization or relevant professional network. And make the consultation and collaboration with appropriate stakeholders a priority (Office for AI et al., 2020).

An overview of these challenges can be found in Table 4.4 below:

Table 4.4   Organisational challenges

Challenge	Explanation	Procurement process stage	Solutions	Source(s)
Organisational capacity challenges				
Technical capacity	The organisation has the necessary technical capacities to implement and procure an AI-based system	Feasibility assessment, implementation and organisation of procurement	1. Encourage participation in and arrange educational courses on AI 2. Consult with governmental experts in other organisations to develop an initial understanding on AI	Estonia, United Kingdom, Serbia
Organisational capacity	The organisation has the necessary organisational capacity to plan and implement an AI-based system	Feasibility assessment, implementation and organisation of procurement	1. Develop clear guidelines that specify the key challenges and risks with public procurement of AI-based systems 2. Provide guidance and best practices for AI procurement, for example by providing templates or sample procurements	Estonia, United Kingdom, the Netherlands, Serbia
Individual capacities	The organisation has employees who possess the necessary capacities to manage, procure, and/ or implement the public procurement of AI-based systems	Feasibility assessment, implementation and organisation of procurement	1. Encourage participation in and arrange educational courses on AI	Estonia

CONCLUSION

This chapter drew on the experiences in drafting guidelines for the procurement of AI in the public sector from Estonia, the Netherlands, Serbia, and the United Kingdom. In doing so, it was possible to make a number of interesting contributions to the current knowledge, both practitioner and academic, on the procurement of AI in the public sector. The first contribution is related to conceptualising the concept of the procurement of AI in the public sector. The second major contribution is related to the elucidation of 14 commonly occurring challenges related to the procurement of AI solutions in the public sector. These challenges were further able to be categorised into procurement process challenges, data challenges, AI-model challenges, and organisational capacity challenges. The third contribution is in identifying commonly occurring proposed solutions in currently existing public sector AI procurement guidelines to overcome these identified challenges. In total, 22 potential strategies have been identified.

This initial work should serve as a strong foundation for any public sector organisation interested in developing their own AI procurement guidelines. For scholars, this work represents one of the first attempts to identify and categorise the challenges and potential solutions for procurement of AI in the public sector. Thus, this chapter is likely to be of interest for those studying procurement and the public sector. While this research has provided a strong foundation on the procurement of AI in the public sector, future research is still needed on the topic. In the course of this research it became clear that there is a wide breadth given between governments about what is considered AI and what is not. Further clarification about this should be sought in future research on the topic of public procurement of AI. Similarly, in this study it became clear that guidelines were just that, guidelines; there was often no obligation to use or implement them. In this way the guidelines may well help procurements to be successful, for example, by providing guidance on how to write procurements better, but does not necessarily guarantee the relevant regulations and safeguards for ethical and unbiased AI are taken into account. While guidelines are apparently important for the public procurement of AI, there are a number of other important and relevant issues that must be explored. These aspects include how AI can be integrated into traditionally existing legacy infrastructural systems, how the legal and regulatory challenges associated with AI can be addressed, how environmental and cultural aspects influence the adoption of AI, and how context influences the ethical implications of AI. Outside of these concerns, there is also a need to further explore how to develop the relevant organisational capacities and culture needed to ensure successful public procurement of AI. In other words, there is a clear need for extensive and comprehensive research within the domain of public administration and management on the subject of public procurement of AI. It is certain that AI is here to stay in the public sector and that procurement will play an increasingly important role in the adoption of AI amongst public sector organisations. In effect, this also raises both the prominence and the need for scholars and experts to conduct research on this emerging area of inquiry. It is critical that scholars and governments alike collaborate and cooperate to make a conscious effort toward generating research and knowledge about the required administrative and organisational capacities needed for the successful public procurement of AI, that procurements can be conducted successfully, that guidelines exist for this process, and that the public procurement of AI is used to generate a positive impact and public value for society.

REFERENCES

Agarwal, P. K. (2018). Public administration challenges in the world of AI and bots. *Public Administration Review*, *78*(6), 917–921.

AI HLEG (2019). A definition of Artificial Intelligence: Main capabilities and scientific disciplines. https://digital-strategy.ec.europa.eu/en/library/definition-artificial-intelligence-main-capabilities-and -scientific-disciplines

Amsterdam City. (2020). Explanatory memorandum to the standard clauses for municipalities for fair use of algorithmic systems.

Aoki, N. (2020). An experimental study of public trust in AI chatbots in the public sector. *Government Information Quarterly*, *37*(4).

Benbouzid, B. (2019). To predict and to manage. Predictive policing in the United States. *Big Data Society*, *6*(1).

Berryhill, J., Kok Heang, K., Clogher, R., and McBride, K. (2019). *Hello, World: Artificial Intelligence and Its Use in the Public Sector* (Vol. 36). OECD Publishing. https://www.oecd-ilibrary.org/ governance/hello-world726fd39d-en

Birks, M., and Mills, J. (2015). *Grounded Theory: A Practical Guide* (2nd ed.). SAGE.

Brauneis, R., and Goodman, E. P. (2018). Algorithmic transparency for the smart city. *Yale Journal of Law and Technology*, *20*(103), 103–176.

Brown, T. L., and Potoski, M. (2003). Contract-management capacity in municipal and county governments. *Public Administration Review*, *63*(2) 153–164.

Caliskan, A., Bryson, J. J., and Narayanan, A. (2017). Semantics derived automatically from language corpora contain human-like biases. *Science*, *356*(6334), 183–186.

Campion, A., Gasco-Hernandez, M., Jankin Mikhaylov, S., and Esteve, M. (2020). Overcoming the challenges of collaboratively adopting artificial intelligence in the public sector. *Social Science Computer Review*, *40*(2), https://doi.org/10.1177/0894439320979953

Dempsey, M., McBride, K., Haataja, M., and Bryson, J. (2022). Transnational digital governance and its impact on artificial intelligence. *The Oxford Handbook of AI Governance*. Oxford University Press.

Edler, J., Ruhland, S., Hafner, S., Rigby, J., Georghiou, L., Hommen, L., Rolfstam, M., Charles, E., Tsipouri, L., and Papadakou, M. (2006). Innovation and public procurement. Review of issues at stake. *Study for the European Commission (no entr/03/24); (2006)*. Fraunhofer Institute for Systems; Innovation Research.

Edquist, C., Hommen, L., and Tsipouri, L. (eds). (2000). *Public Technology Procurement and Innovation* (Vol. 16). Springer US. https://doi. org/10.1007/978-1-4615-4611-5

Georghiou, L., Edler, J., Uyarra, E., and Yeow, J. (2014). Policy instruments for public procurement of innovation: Choice, design and assessment. *Technological Forecasting and Social Change*, *86*, 1–12.

Government of Serbia. (2019). *Strategy for the Development of Artificial Intelligence in the Republic of Serbia for the Period 2020–2025* (tech. rep.). Government of Serbia. https://eur-lex.europa.eu/legal-content/EN/TXT/?uri= COM%3A2018%3A237%3AFIN

Harrison, T. M., and Luna-Reyes, L. F. (2020). Cultivating trustworthy artificial intelligence in digital government. *Social Science Computer Review*, *40*(2), https://doi.org/10.1177/0894439320980122

House of Lords. (2018). *House of Lords Select Committee on Artificial Intelligence AI in the UK: ready, willing and able? Report of Session 2017–19* (tech. rep.). London. https://publications.parliament.uk/ pa/ld201719/ldselect/ldai/100/10002.htm

Hsieh, H.-F., and Shannon, S. E. (2005). Three approaches to qualitative content analysis. *Qualitative Health Research*, *15*(9).

Janssen, M., Brous, P., Estevez, E., Barbosa, L. S., and Janowski, T. (2020). Data governance: Organizing data for trustworthy Artificial Intelligence. *Government Information Quarterly*, *37*(3), 101493 [1–8].

McBride, K., Aavik, G., Toots, M., Kalvet, T., and Krimmer, R. (2019). How does open government data driven co-creation occur? Six factors and a 'perfect storm'; insights from Chicago's food inspection forecasting model. *Government Information Quarterly*, *36*(1), 88–97.

Misuraca, G., Van Noordt, C., et al. (2020). AI watch-artificial intelligence in public services: Overview of the use and impact of AI in public services in the EU. *JRC Working Papers*, (JRC120399).

MKM. (2020). Juhendmaterjalid – Krattide veebileht. Retrieved February 7, 2021, from https://www .kratid.ee/juhendmaterjalid

Mulligan, D. K., and Bamberger, K. A. (2019). Procurement as policy: Administrative process for machine learning. *Berkeley Technology Law Journal*, *34*(3), 773–852.

Office for AI, world economic forum, government digital service, government commercial function, & crown commercial service. (2020). Guidelines for AI procurement. Retrieved February 7, 2021, from https://www.gov.uk/government/publications/guidelines-for-ai-procurement/guidelines-for-ai-procurement

Riigikantselei, and MKM. (2019). Eesti tehisintellekti kasutuselevõtu eksperdirühma aruanne (tech. rep.). Tallinn.

van Noordt, C., and Misuraca, G. (2019). New wine in old bottles: Chatbots in government: Exploring the transformative impact of chatbots in public service delivery. *Lecture Notes in Computer Science (including subseries Lecture Notes in Artificial Intelligence and Lecture Notes in Bioinformatics)*, *11686 LNCS*, 49–59.

van Noordt, C., and Misuraca, G. (2020). Exploratory insights on artificial intelligence for government in Europe. *Social Science Computer Review*, *40*(2), https://doi.org/10.1177/0894439320980449

van Noordt, C., and Misuraca, G. (2022). Artificial intelligence for the public sector: Results of landscaping the use of AI in government across the European Union. *Government Information Quarterly*, *39*(3), https://doi.org/10.1016/j.giq.2022.101714

Washington, A. L. (2018). How to argue with an algorithm: Lessons from the COMPAS-ProPublica debate. *Colorado Technology Law Journal*, *17*(1), 131–160.

Wihlborg, E., Larsson, H., and Hedström, K. (2016). 'The computer says no!' – A case study on automated decision-making in public authorities. *Proceedings of the Annual Hawaii International Conference on System Sciences*, *2016–March*, 2903–2912.

Wirtz, B. W., Weyerer, J. C., and Geyer, C. (2019). Artificial intelligence and the public sector – applications and challenges. *International Journal of Public Administration*, *42*(7), 596–615.

World Economic Forum. (2020). AI procurement in a box: Project overview unlocking public sector AI (tech. rep.). https://www.weforum.org/publications/ai-procurement-in-a-box/project-overview/

Yin, R. K. (2013). *Case Study Research: Design and Methods* (Rev.). Sage publications.

APPENDIX

List of Interviewees

EE.PS1 – Senior government IT advisor.
EE.PS2 – Ministerial Chief Information Officer.
EE.PS3 – Private sector manager involved in organising ministerial data dives.
NL.PS1 – Senior ranking official involved with creation of Amsterdam's AI guidelines.
RS.PS1 – Senior ranking governmental advisor on public sector reform.
RS.PS2 – Official involved in the creation of Serbia's AI strategy.
RS.PS3 – Senior official in Prime Minister's office's IT team.
RS.PS4 – Senior official in Prime Minister's office's IT team.
UK.PS1 – Senior consultant in UK's AI Procurement guidelines team.

5. Enhancing citizen service management through AI-enabled systems – a proposed AI readiness framework for the public sector

Alvina Lee, Venky Shankararaman and Ouh Eng Lieh

INTRODUCTION

Artificial intelligence (AI), as defined by Stone (2018), refers to 'the activity devoted to making machines intelligent, and intelligence is that quality that enables an entity to function appropriately and with foresight in its environment.' To put it simply, AI uses a computer to mimic intelligent human responses with minimal human intervention. Such AI technologies have advanced rapidly in this decade with the drastic increase in data volume and variety and improvements in computing power and storage. With systems like AlphaGo and IBM Watson, AI has demonstrated its capabilities to match up or, in some situations, surpass humans in what was once thought to be uniquely human qualities – strategic thinking and decision making. This has led to the mass adoption of AI technologies, such as recommendation engines used by Amazon and Netflix, inventory management by Samsung (Prabhu and Bhat, 2020), and queue systems by DBS (Palle, 2019). All these adoptions are to serve their customers better and reduce capital costs.

Further, AI has been predicted by many researchers to eventually outperform rule-based recommendation or human activities in the upcoming years (Grace et al., 2018). This is especially so when AI is founded upon the basis that every aspect of learning or any other feature of intelligence can in principle be so precisely described that a machine can be made to simulate it (McCarthy et al., 1955). Hence many are of the belief that AI definitely has the potential to become superior to current rule-based recommendations.

This school of thought is also true of the public sector, whereby citizen service is vital. In utilising government budgets, prudence has to be monitored to ensure the 'best value for money'. In the case of the Singapore Government, a digital blueprint (GovTech, 2020) that encompasses and advocates the use of AI was released as a guiding pole for all ministries and agencies in the nation. To date, 20 ministries have submitted plans on leveraging AI in their operations so that better citizen service management (CSM) and service delivery can be achieved.

So, what do citizens look out for in government services? According to Chen (2010), online transactions with the government and feedback channels are the common activities that citizens will participate in. An example of an online transaction with the government agencies will be the application of government relief, while an example of feedback channels will be like Reach-Singapore, whereby citizens are polled regularly on national initiatives to elicit feedback from the ground. One or more government agencies may be involved in handling these citizen-related activities. Yet, Kubicek and Hagen (2000) showed via research that citizens prefer to have a one-stop portal or channel for all the services across government agencies. Further, citizens are looking out for more one-stop citizen-centric services whereby they can interact with any government agency. The latter will be able to cater with a good understanding of the citizens' interaction with the government. Therefore, with such expectations by citizens regarding the provision of services by the government, the adoption of AI will be on the radar of each government to look into leveraging AI to meet citizens' expectations in the aspect of citizen-centric services.

Hence to leverage AI as part of an agency's digital blueprint, in an attempt to meet citizens' expectations, agencies will be pressed to have a tool to assess their own AI readiness before they take a leap of faith to implement AI as one of their IT enablers.

At this critical juncture, we seek to address the following questions in this chapter:

1. How can we assess the readiness of the government agency to adopt AI-enabled technologies?
2. What are the possible corrective measures if the agency is not ready?

In the context of recommender systems used to respond to citizens' inquiries, these questions are relevant and of value to every government in the world. Without these, it would be hard to determine if government agencies should develop AI systems in this aspect despite challenges in budget and ROI.

This chapter is structured as follows: Section 2 presents a literature review of the AI implementation in other sectors versus the implementation in the public sector. Based on the review, we also discuss why customer service management will require support from AI-enabled technologies and existing frameworks that assess organisations' readiness before adopting AI-enabled technologies. Section 3 describes the use of the Technological-Organisation-Environment (TOE) framework and the detailed components proposed as sub-criteria to assess AI readiness for an agency from the public sector. Finally, the chapter will close with a case study based on a Singapore government agency that had implemented the framework and its sub-criteria to assess readiness before implementing AI-enabled systems to enhance citizen service delivery.

LITERATURE REVIEW

Implementation of AI

AI research began to be cited as early as the 1940s with studies about whether machines could make decisions (Sonak and Sonak, 1985; Abraham, 2002). Later in the 1970s, the concept of applied AI solutions appeared, with research studies done in various areas (Bobrow and Raphael, 1974; Szolovits and Pauker, 1971). Subsequently, more manufacturing and education sectors have developed key areas for their AI implementation.

In the manufacturing sector, prominent research has been carried out in several areas, including inventory monitoring and production schedule. From Rodammer and White's (1988) proposal of an artificial, intelligence-based production scheduler to Li et al.'s (2017) proposal of intelligent manufacturing system architecture and intelligent manufacturing technology systems, it has been proved that AI implementation has come on leaps and bounds in this sector.

In the education sector, Tims (2016) suggested that colleague robots (cobots) or robots working in harmony with teachers or cobots are being applied to teach children routine tasks, including writing and spelling. Whereas in customer service, according to Picard (2008), empathetic AI was implemented to enhance automation in service delivery. She highlighted that emotion plays an essential role in portraying what is considered human behaviour; this implied that including the consideration of emotion will ensure that computers provide better performance in assisting humans and might enhance computers' abilities to make decisions. In recent years, this concept has been accepted by researchers all over the world, hence innovations such as Replika, which supplies artificial people (personal bots) for psychological comfort or well-being (Huet, 2016), and Sophia, the human-like AI from Hanson Robotics that was awarded Saudi citizenship (Retto, 2017). All in all, AI has perpetuated into different sectors, bringing about changes that people have seen the benefits of, and hence many sectors are willing to continue research and adoption.

Governments pick up such benefits that are occurring in the private sectors all around the world, and since the 2010s, the implementation of AI has encompassed several functions of the public sector (Wirtz, Weyerer and Geyer 2019), which include, but are not limited to, public health (Sun and Medaglia, 2018), transport (Kuberka and Singhal, 2020), cybersecurity (Kania, Triolo and Webster, 2018), and even the military (Rasch, Kott and Forbus, 2003). Despite the technological advances in AI, some governments still provide services to citizens without the use of AI, which reflect the limitations or challenges faced in the implementation of AI enhanced systems, such as the prudence in the distribution of budgets across ministries and agencies or the intranet environment that is not conducive to AI implementation. Hence many ministries and agencies instead direct resources to maintain legacy systems (Mehr, Ash and Fellow, 2017). This situation may reduce the confidence and satisfaction of citizens with public services, especially when compared to the level of service that one could get from the private sector.

Despite the limitations and challenges, in Singapore, the push for AI implementation continues. AI capabilities are implemented via AskJamie (Niculescu et al., 2020; Jeffares, 2021), a chatbot developed by GovTech and deployed on all Singapore government agencies' websites, to assist citizens in searching for information. While in the US, the White House Office of Science and Technology Policy released the report on Artificial Intelligence to highlight that the government should aim to fit AI into existing regulatory schemes so as to ensure that it will serve the citizens and form a 'good AI society' (Cath et al., 2018).

It can be concluded that despite limitations, governments around the world still see that AI-enabled technologies are needed for better citizen service delivery in the public sector. The first and most common piece of technology for citizen services will be the implementation of a customer relationship management (CRM) system and chatbot. Such technology is the basis of collating all the interactions that a government body has with their citizens. One such example in Singapore is GatherSG, a lightweight CRM that allows different government agencies to gather feedback from citizens, and this, when coupled with AskJamie, a chatbot, leverages AI to better citizen service by automating responses to citizens' inquiries and allowing feedback to be routed to different agencies within the same platform. On the other hand, New York City has worked with IBM Watson to implement MySurrey App to provide quick answers to citizens' inquiries. Another example is the Mexican government piloting an AI initiative to classify citizens' petitions so as to route them to the correct agency to follow up.

AI-enabled Customer Relationship Management System

Kincaid (2003) defined the customer relationship management system as 'the strategic use of information, processes, technology, and people to manage the customer's relationship with the organisation across the entire customer life cycle.' This emphasised the importance of viewing this system as a comprehensive process of interacting with the citizens of the government. Kennedy (2006) also identified that a customer relationship management system is an effective tool to know the organisation's customers more systematically by 'identifying a company's best customers and maximising their value by satisfying and retaining them.' The same benefits could be extended to the citizens of a nation.

As stated in the previous section on the presence of huge data volume and velocity, the AI integrated CRM system will ensure more benefits can be reaped in citizen service delivery in an effective and calibrated way. Ngai, Xiu and Chau (2009) stated that the application of AI in CRM is an emerging trend in the global economy. However, as Chatterjee, Ghosh and Nguyen (2019) pointed out, there are challenges faced when implementing AI-enabled CRM systems. The first challenge is the presence of subject matter experts in the know-how of customer data. While data can be in abundance, if no one knows how to leverage it, even if there is an effective CRM system, the insights will not be analysed in a manner that the organisation can put to use. The second challenge, as pointed out by Dwivedi et al. (2021), is that the culture of the organisation is a potential barrier to such implementation of AI-enabled CRM systems. If the organisation's employees do not see the value in such technology, benefits from such technological tools cannot be reaped. Finally, the presence of data security and privacy concerns may challenge the implementation and use of AI-enabled CRM systems. The black box characteristics of AI will become increasingly challenging as customers will prefer transparency in such implementation.

The above challenges faced by organisations in the private sector during the implementation of AI-enabled CRM systems are felt in the public sector as well. The explainable element and trusted tech are critical in building up citizens' trust in the government, as Zanzotto (2019) pointed out. Explainable, as defined by Zanzotto (2019), is the ability to explain how the machine made the decision, while trusted tech in this perspective, will then refer to the knowledge life cycle that is clearly and correctly documented in the system to support the explainable aspect of decision making by the machine.

Hence it is only when the existence of trust is present that interactivity between citizens and the AI-enabled systems will increase. This increased interactivity will facilitate governments to understand their citizens better; therefore, during the implementation of AI-enabled CRM systems, especially in the public sector, converting a 'black box' technology to a 'white box' technology must be in the pipeline on top of the other challenges laid out previously.

Hence, a framework for assisting a government agency in assessing their readiness to adopt AI-enabled technologies is essential and of value.

Existing Frameworks in Assessment of AI Readiness

In information systems (IS) research, readiness has always been a topic of discussion (Chatterjee, Ghosh and Nguyen, 2019). Chatterjee, Ghosh and Nguyen (2019) define digital readiness as 'the degree to which an organisation is ready to transform the current organisation digitally.' As AI classifies as digital technology (Agerfalk, 2020), digital readiness can be applied to understand the precursors of AI adoption.

The Technology Acceptance Model (TAM) was first introduced as a framework by Davis (1985) to leverage upon the user acceptance process to assess the successful implementation of IS. However, the limitation of TAM is that it lacks consideration of the business context and environment dimensions, hence it is more suitable for individual use rather than organisational use (Ajibade, 2018). The Technology-Organisations-Environment (TOE) framework was later proposed by Tornatzky et al. (1990) to cover the limitations of TAM, as it analyses a firm from three different dimensions: technology, organisation, and environment. The technological dimension includes all the relevant technologies available within and outside the firm. The organisational dimension describes business characteristics and resources that might influence the adoption process, such as firm size, managerial structure, decision-making, and communication. The environmental dimension refers to the industry's structure, including the firm's competitors, suppliers, customers, and regulatory environment. The versatile nature of the TOE framework was created due to the use of three different dimensions, allowing the flexibility for researchers to apply the framework in their respective domains while studying the possible components that can fall under each dimension that is applicable to the particular business context or industry.

Although the TOE framework is widely used in research due to its versatile nature, the framework has its limitations as it could be affected by the element of bias due to companies' self-assessments. AlSheibani (2018) proposed an enhanced version of the framework by including the components of relative advantage and compatibility of the AI technology with the organisation. Nortje and Grobbelaar (2020) had seven other components, such as employee culture, strategy, security, etc., on top of the TOE framework to assess AI readiness. This is similar to Jöhnk et al. (2021), who proposed an AI readiness framework that incorporated the components of culture and strategy. In the area of AI-enabled CRM systems, Chatterjee et al. (2019) proposed a conceptual readiness framework that took into account integration, auditing, analysis, and regularisation that were not being considered in the frameworks proposed by Nortje and Grobbelaar (2020) and Jöhnk et al. (2021). Yet these components are crucial in the current context, as mentioned in Section 2.2, whereby the explainable element and trusted tech component are essential in AI adoption by organisations, especially government agencies. Further, the component of integration proposed by Chatterjee et al. (2019) is key to an AI readiness framework used by government agencies when citizens are looking for a one-stop portal to complete all their transactions with the government.

In summary, components such as integration, explainable elements, etc., were also not proposed by Stirling et al. (2017), which indicates that the proposed AI readiness index might require modification to meet the current climate that the public sector is in.

PROPOSED AI READINESS FRAMEWORK FOR PUBLIC SECTOR

From the literature review, it is established that the TOE framework, because of its versatile nature, continues to be applicable in today's settings. Hence, the framework that the authors of this chapter propose for implementation in the public sector will be based on TOE. However, the uniqueness of the public sector, such as the presence of highly integrated intranets, robust data governance framework, stringent requirements for security protocols, etc., differentiates the agencies in the public sector from many organisations in the private sector. Hence, the framework applied in the public sector context will have to consider additional sub-criteria under the TOE framework on top of those used in the private sector.

To help identify the sub-criteria that need to be added to the TOE framework in assessing AI readiness in the public sector, a survey protocol was prepared to gather inputs from ICT and operations officers from a government agency based in Singapore.

Methodology

Data collection occurred between May 2020 and October 2021, whereby officers belonging to a government agency that is currently working on the implementation of two projects, i.e., an AI-enabled customer data platform and an AI-enabled customer relationship management system, were surveyed on their future business requirements, experience with current systems and business outcomes for AI-enabled technologies.

The inputs were gathered and organised by significant business functions to form the sub-criteria for the TOE framework. This framework can be further extended to other agencies as it is based on a generic context of citizen service delivery that is a common denominator across the board.

Target participants

A total of 15 officers from 7 different divisions were surveyed based on their knowledge and experience using the agency's existing marketing platform and CRM system. Their years of service with the agency range from 1 year to 20 years. The average number of years of service is 5. Considering their varying work scope, they were able to provide valuable insights into the agency's business landscape and technology landscape from multiple contexts. The work scope of the 7 divisions is indicated in Table 5.1.

Table 5.1   Participants' profile and relevance

Division Name	Specific Work Scope	Relevance
Division 1	Engagement with citizens on their learning and driving life-long learning initiatives	The participants are part of delivering citizen services and hence will often have to handle
Division 2	Engagement with citizens on their upskilling and individual-related initiatives	citizens' inquiries. They have to be aware of what could support their operations better on
Division 3	Engagement with enterprises on the training of their employees	behalf of the organisation.
Division 4	Branding and marketing of the agency at the national level	The participants market the agency's citizen services and will be the responsible party to draft formal reply to citizens for escalated inquiries. They have to be acutely aware of the environmental landscape that the agency is in.
Division 5	Supporting the citizen service delivery by catering to all the inquiries from citizens	The participants are the first point of contact whenever citizens' inquiries come in. They have to be aware of what could support their operations better on behalf of the organisation.

Division Name	Specific Work Scope	Relevance
Division 6	Implementing and maintaining the IT systems for the agency	The participants are generally the implementation team for the AI capability.
Division 7	Supporting the agency in terms of IT infrastructure and aligning the agency's infrastructure with national IT governance	Hence would be better to provide insights on the technological context.

Survey design

A total of 12 open-ended questions were used to survey the participants. The survey questions were grouped according to the three contexts of the TOE framework, as indicated in Table 5.2.

Table 5.2   *List of survey questions under 3 contexts*

Technological Context	Organisational Context	Environmental Context
Have you taken data analytics courses? Please share details of the course, if so.	Can you list down in order of priority what will be the support required to implement AI-enabled CDP and CRM?	What are some of the AI use cases that you know in the market and can be applicable to our agency?
Have you done a data project before to understand the citizens better? Please share details of the project, if so.	What are the current business processes that are not supported by the existing systems and why?	What do you think are the obstacles to implementing AI in the agency?
Have you been involved in projects that deploy analytical models in IT systems?	What AI capability do you think would be required to help you understand the citizens better?	Do you think the agency is comparable to the private sector in terms of technology and why?
How can the current infrastructure or technological systems be adapted to help you do your job better?	Do you think the agency is ready for the implementation of AI and why?	What are the other ways that we could engage citizens more effectively?

Discussion of survey outcomes and translation to sub-criteria for TOE framework

The survey results were collated in the form of qualitative feedback. Each participant had provided their responses based on the open-ended survey questions. From there, stopwords such as 'is, are' etc. are removed. The remaining words were then analysed based on term frequency to identify the possible terms or related concepts when reviewed in accordance with that particular term. For example, 'data' is a term that has appeared many times. Hence it is listed as one of the sub-criteria shared in Section 3.2.1. When going through the detailed feedback that contains the term 'data,' we observed that 10 out of 15 officers related it to data sources to support analytics. Five out of 15 officers mentioned the term 'data' in relation to data analytics training. With that, the term 'data' is translated to a sub-criterion under technological context under the TOE framework.

Technological Context

The technological context covers both the internal and external technology context in the TOE framework. Internal context refers to the existing technology stack that the agency is already using. In contrast, external technology context refers to the technology made available in the market not yet adopted by the agency. The government agency's internal context is an important consideration for readiness assessment for the same reason as a company in the private sector. The reason is that internal context estimates how much an agency or a company can undertake in terms of technology scope and change. Further, the existing technology stack also influences how readily the agency or company will adopt AI; given that sunk costs are in place and being mindful of budget and cost, both a government agency and its technology partner company will need to justify the monetary benefits that adoption of AI can bring about to offset the sunk costs of the existing technology stack if the latter is to be replaced or enhanced.

AI-enabled systems will likely be found in the external context; however, such new technologies are generally provisioned in tiers within this setting. For example, Amazon web services provide different subscription tiers to cater to other organisations in different stages of analytics readiness. Another example is Salesforce CRM, which also offers tiered CRM solutions based on whether the organisation is at the initial phase of dabbling in predictive insights or at the advanced stage with AI built in to provide recommendations in the form of a subsequent call to action. The presence of such tiered technologies available in the external context is an indication to a government agency or a company that the assessment of readiness is dependent on whether many others in the same sector are adopting the corresponding tier of the new technologies.

Proposed sub-criteria under the technological context

From the qualitative data gathered and comparison to existing literature, the results are depicted in Table 5.3 below. In summary, skillset, infrastructure, data, integration and security are the key terms that had been constantly used by the participants as they responded to questions under this context.

Organisational Context

The organisational context refers to the characteristics and resources of the organisation that impact the implementation decision of the new technology. Examples will be product champions and the presence of a cross-functional task force. Suppose the organisation has champions that are well versed or familiar with AI-enabled technologies in the market. In that case, the organisation will likely be made aware of the possibilities of such technologies. Further, an organisation that has many silo workstreams is unlikely to be able to foster AI innovation, as shared by Najdawi and Shaheed (2021). This is probably why companies like Netflix, Facebook, etc., encourage the formation of cross-functional teams to drive innovation, in turn driving the faster adoption of AI.

Proposed sub-criteria under the organisational context

Under the organisational context, participants tend to use terms such as 'management, support, processes, audit, etc.' This highlights that under this context, operations to leverage AI capabilities in the view of the participants that are employees of a government agency, tend to believe that implementation of such capabilities would be smooth with the endorsement of the management, coupled with their business processes being taken care of. Results are depicted in Table 5.4 below.

Environmental Context

The environmental context refers to how the organisation conducts its business, such as industry nature, competitors, regulations, etc. For a private sector, it is likely to be impacted by the

Table 5.3   *Sub-criteria under the technological context*

Sub-criteria under Technological Context	Definition	Assessment if meet criteria
ICT Expertise Terms: AI, training, analytics	ICT expertise is defined as the agency level of specialised ICT knowledge and skills to provide reliable support in using AI-enabled technologies. The agency is likely to have higher readiness if such expertise is available [Lin and Lee, 2005].	The agency can assess the percentage of its ICT officers that had taken up AI and data analytics-related training. Further, the agency can also assess the percentage of its officers in terms of request for retraining in AI and data analytics-related training. The higher the percentage, the more ready the agency is [Wang et al., 2019]. This is because it reflects the willingness of the officers to be trained in this aspect.
ICT Infrastructure Terms: cloud, database	ICT infrastructure in a government agency is defined as the physical technology resources, including server rooms, shared government commercial cloud, and shared private government cloud, which provide the foundation to deploy the AI-enabled technologies. Agency will likely deploy such technology if its infrastructure is sophisticated enough [Kowtha and Choon, 2001]. Currently, taking the Singapore government agency as an example, the shared government commercial cloud will require python or R libraries to be re-packaged and deployed into the environment before deploying AI algorithms. Hence, resources are required for such effort, which translates into the challenges to the agency's readiness.	The agency can assess its readiness by obtaining the number of analytical models deployed within the current ICT infrastructure. If there is none or a low number of such deployments, there are likely challenges to deploying AI-enabled technologies within the existing infrastructure. The agency can also assess its readiness by obtaining the number of officers who are keen to maintain the models deployed within the current ICT infrastructure. The higher the number, the more likely it is able to be maintained in the long run [Düdder et al., 2021].
Data Terms: data	Data in the government agency is defined as the data of the citizens and enterprises that had interactions with the agency, such as transactional data, digital web footprints captured from the front-end sites belonging to the agency, etc. Agency with high volume and high variety of data sources are more likely to adopt AI-enabled technologies [Sharman et al., 2022].	The agency can assess its readiness by doing an environment scan of the current data sources and the volume of data available to the agency.
Security & Privacy Risks Terms: security, privacy	Security and Privacy risks in the government agency are defined as risks associated with data hosting, firewalls, virtualised and shared resources, and data transfer over the internet and intranet to ensure that data privacy cannot be compromised by hacking. Agencies with low security and privacy risks are more likely to be ready to adopt AI-enabled technologies [Subashini and Kavitha, 2011].	The agency can assess its readiness to adopt AI-enabled systems by reviewing its current digital environment regarding security and privacy support.

Sub-criteria under Technological Context	Definition	Assessment if meet criteria
Integration Terms: cross-agency, system integration, single-sign-on	Integration in the government agency is defined as integrating systems within an agency and across agencies, be it via JSON or API. The more integrated the systems are for an agency, the more likely the agency will adopt AI-enabled technologies [Themistocleous and Irani, 2001].	The agency can assess its readiness by reviewing its enterprise architecture blueprint to determine how integrated its systems are within the agency and with the systems of other agencies.
Audit requirements (IT) Terms: audit, tracking	IT audit requirements in the government agency are defined as the log trails captured for every change or adjustment made within the system. The more stringent this is, the longer it takes to deploy AI-enabled technologies [Brundage et al., 2020].	The agency can assess its readiness by reviewing the number of required IT audits per year.

Table 5.4   Sub-criteria under the organisational context

Sub-criteria under Organisational Context	Definition	Assessment if meet criteria
Senior management support Terms: management, forums, approval	Senior management support is defined as the extent to which the management of the government agency will actively support the implementation and management of AI-enabled technologies. This usually comes in the form of approval of budgets, updates required at agency-level forums, and articulation of goals and vision for such technology implementation. The higher the support level, the more likely the agency will implement AI-enabled technologies.	The agency can assess their readiness by knowing the number of approval forums required before procurement of AI-enabled technologies can be achieved. Further, if there is an agency-level forum where the project updates will be reported, the agency is likely ready to embrace this new technology.
Business processes and explainable nature Terms: workflows, operations, processes	Business processes are defined as the operational workflows that a government agency has in place to deliver services to its citizens. The more complex such processes are, the more challenges that the agency will face in translating such processes into the AI-enabled technologies [Clarke, 2019].	The agency can assess its readiness by reviewing the current business processes and derive the percentage of processes that could be translated using AI-enabled technologies with transparency and explainable nature maintained.
Extent of coordination Terms: teamwork, the taskforce	Extent of coordination is defined as the use of different coordination mechanisms while using AI-enabled technologies, such as forming a steering committee to monitor the implementation of such technologies [Pudjianto et al., 2011]. The higher the extent of coordination, the more likely the agency will adopt such technologies [Chatterjee et al., 2019].	The agency can assess its readiness by reviewing the number of cross-functional teams in the agency.
Audit requirements (business) Terms: audit, tracking	Business audit requirements are defined as the audit process of the soundness of the business processes and if measures had been taken to avoid fraud etc. The more stringent this is, the longer it takes to deploy AI-enabled technologies [Brundage et al., 2020].	The agency can assess its readiness by reviewing the steps required in business processes as part of audit requirements. The more steps there are, the more likely the agency is not ready to adopt AI-enabled technologies.

concept of the industry life cycle, as mentioned by Baker (2012). An example is the textile industry, which is at a maturing stage; innovation might not be as clear-cut as a technology industry. However, the industry life cycle concept does not apply to the public sector. It is more susceptible to innovations in other sectors and the dynamics of global issues.

Proposed sub-criteria under the environmental context
Terms such as 'IM8, blueprint, social media,' etc., are being used frequently in the responses of the participants in relation to the survey questions in this context. It reflects that as government officers, there is acute awareness of the existing regulatory frameworks governing the use of AI. Results are depicted in Table 5.5 below.

Table 5.5   Sub-criteria under the environmental context

Sub-criteria under Organisational Context	Definition	Assessment if meet criteria
Regulatory environment Terms: IM8, data classification	Governance refers to the regulatory environment that the government agency has to comply with. With proper and supportive governance, the agency will likely be more ready to implement AI-enabled technologies [Pudjianto et al., 2011].	The agency can assess its readiness by reviewing the AI-enabled technologies that the agency is keen to adopt that are compliant with regulations.
Nation mandate Terms: digital blueprint, IMDA, Govtech	Nation Mandate refers to the overall direction that the nation or country is moving towards. If the whole government is moving towards digitalisation and adoption of AI-enabled technologies, the agency is likely to implement such technologies.	The agency can assess its readiness by reviewing if there is a structured national mandate in place.
Competitive environment Terms: private, new technology, blockchain	Competitive environment is defined as the landscape that the agency is in. If the private sector implements more AI-enabled technologies, this will accelerate the government agency to consider adopting such innovations [Zhu et al., 2003].	The agency can assess its readiness by comparing its current technology stack against the technology products available in the market.
Social approach Terms: social media	The social approach is defined as the social media platforms present in the current environment. The more such platforms exist, the more likely the government agency will consider implementing AI-enabled technologies to reach out to the citizens as an effective way to increase the target base of the organisation [Chatterjee et al., 2019].	The agency can assess its readiness by reviewing the number of social platforms that the government agency is engaging its citizens with. The higher the number of social platforms, the higher the probability that their officers are savvy enough to consider AI-enabled technologies.

CASE STUDY OF AI-ENABLED CUSTOMER DATA PLATFORM – AN APPLICATION OF THE PROPOSED FRAMEWORK

In this section, we describe how the TOE Framework with the various sub-criteria was applied to assess the AI readiness of an agency for the project 'AI-Enabled Customer Data Platform.'

The AI-enabled customer data platform is a system that unifies different data sources, such as cookie data, social media data, etc., for a single individual. With that data, the system can further leverage AI capabilities to recommend content to that individual based on past browsing history or social chatter when the individual landed on the agency's website. This technology empowered the agency to provide personalised and targeted information to the citizens without manual analysis of legacy data to find out possible preference trends and mass disseminate information instead. However, the agency would like to know if their officers are ready for such implementation of AI-enabled systems. Hence this proposed framework was used to assess the AI readiness of the agency.

AI Readiness Assessment

Prior to project implementation, using the above framework, the project team is looking to implement an AI-enabled Customer Data Platform and review the agency's readiness for AI by checking against the sub-criteria as per Table 5.6 below:

Table 5.6   Review under 3 contexts

Technological Context		
Sub-Criteria	What was observed	Assessment
ICT Expertise	80% of the agency's ICT officers had taken and completed the mandate data analytics training, which touches on the application of AI in the public sector.	The higher percentage indicated that the agency is likely to be ready to look into AI-enabled systems.
ICT Infrastructure	Currently, the agency has 60% of its IT applications deployed on the government commercial cloud. Out of the 60%, 100% of the applications involved deploying analytical models, from blockchain technology to fraud detection.	The high percentage indicates that the ICT officers are familiar with analytics-related deployment and will likely face fewer challenges when looking into the deployment of machine learning models in AI-enabled systems.
Data	Currently, the agency has a data lake in place, which helps to consolidate all its data sources in one place to support analytics. Further, considering that the agency manages individual-related initiatives, it has a rich data source with a substantial volume of at least 3 million individuals in Singapore.	The presence of different data sources and high volume is likely to support the data requirements of AI-enabled systems, which generally require a wide variety and volume of data.
Security & Risks	The agency hosted her infrastructure on either the government commercial cloud (a form of national private cloud with substantial penetration tests done regularly) or on-premises. The servers are under lock and key.	Due to the sensitive nature of the agency's data, there are potential risks involved should a data leak incident occur. Considering that an effective AI-enabled system will be best deployed on the public cloud, as mentioned in Section 3.2.1, this poses an issue for the agency when assessing AI readiness.

Technological Context		
Sub-Criteria	**What was observed**	**Assessment**
Integration	While the systems within the agency are fully integrated, these systems are only integrated with two other agencies and no external systems.	It is assessed that integration between systems is a norm for the agency. The presence of the AI-enabled customer data platform will allow the agency to integrate with a centralised web analytics system, i.e., WOGAA (Whole-of-Government Application Analytics – wogaa.sg), to obtain more data. Further, the integration of the platform with other social media platforms will eventually enrich the agency's data sources to better support AI initiatives.
Audit Requirements (IT)	There are strict audit requirements for the agency, and this is conducted twice a year.	It is assessed that given the regular IT audits, the agency is familiar and equipped to know how to take steps to ensure that the AI-enabled customer data platform has logs activated to support such audit activities.
Organisational Context		
Senior Management Support	The leadership group of the agency supported the project as they wanted to streamline the engagement approach and ensure personalised and targeted content was recommended to citizens. Further, a specific forum was set up to track the project closely.	This is a strong indication that there will be support for such AI implementation by the agency.
Business Processes and Explainable Nature	Current business processes to track web data and social media activities are in silos. As a government agency, there might be a need to explain if citizens enquired about the personalised content that surfaced when they landed on the agency's website.	It is assessed that the agency will have to think of alternatives to handle the streamlining of business processes and explain the nature of the personalised outreach.
Extent of Coordination	A cross-functional task force for this project was set up.	Since the task force is cross-functional, it will be easier to implement such projects.
Audit Requirements (Business)	The agency's business processes are audited every five years. There is an existing audit framework within the agency to review its business processes internally.	The agency can ensure that the existing framework reviews the business processes impacted by the project before implementation.
Environmental Context		
Regulatory Environment	There is transparent governance set up by Govtech, the centralised technology arm of the Singapore government, about the implementation of cloud solutions and AI.	The agency is assessed to be compliant with the solutioning of the AI-enabled customer data platform, based on the current Singapore regulatory governance, such as the Instructional Manual (IM8) and Risk Assessment of Software-as-a-service (SaaS) products.

Technological Context		
Sub-Criteria	**What was observed**	**Assessment**
Nation Mandate	There is the overall direction for Singapore to move towards the ideal state of a smart nation.	Implementing an AI-enabled customer data project will propel the agency in the same direction as the smart nation mandate.
Competitive Environment	In recent years, AI-enabled technologies have been implemented in the private sector.	Considering that the agency has partnerships with many companies, including Microsoft and Salesforce in the private sector, to roll out its initiatives, it is aware of the latest developments. It compares its current technology stack against the technology available in the market.
Social Approach	The agency currently owns social media accounts across five different social media platforms. Citizens are active across different platforms.	The multiple numbers of social media platforms that the agency needs to manage to show that it will have a higher AI readiness. It would be familiar with such platforms and require AI-enabled technologies to support citizen engagement across all social media platforms.

Discussion

Out of the 14 sub-criteria under the three contexts, the agency had a fairly high score of 12 for AI readiness, as indicated in table 5.7 below:

Table 5.7   Overall AI readiness score

	Technological Context	**Organisational Context**	**Environmental Context**
Meeting Criteria	5/6	3/4	4/4
Not Meeting Criteria	1/6	1/4	0/4

Although there are three sub-criteria that the project team had assessed that could lead to the agency not being ready for AI-enabled technologies, corrective measures could be taken to address these sub-criteria. Hence the project eventually obtained the budget for the AI-enabled system and awarded the vendor to implement the solution in April 2022. The corrective measures that have been taken are indicated in Table 5.8 below.

The rationale to include corrective measures based on the proposed framework conducted on an actual case study, is to allow other government agencies to consider such measures and not be deterred by the outcomes of the assessment on their own AI readiness.

CONCLUSION

With the pressing need to better serve the citizens by meeting their expectations of service delivery from government agencies, leveraging on AI was one of the key strategies on the radar of each government. In this chapter, we introduced the TOE framework and a survey

Table 5.8   *Corrective measures for sub-criteria*

Sub-criteria	Corrective Measures
Security & Risks	If the agency would like to leverage AI, they will have to take steps to review the data and only allow datasets that have a lower risk to be stored in AI-enabled systems. For this project, the agency had gone with only storing IP addresses, email addresses, and public social media data in the AI-enabled systems.
Business Processes and Explainable Nature	To make sure that the citizens realise that their web data is being used to provide personalised content as they land on the agency's website, a cookie collection clause will prompt for acceptance to allow personalised, targeted content recommendations when the citizens land on the page. If the citizens do not accept it, the personalised content will be removed. In this way, the transparency between the agency and the citizens is maintained. The explainable nature of the AI-enabled customer data platform is also made clear as the citizens will realise that content is recommended based on their agreement to allow the agency to collect their cookie data that helps in providing personalised content as they land on the website of the agency.

approach to propose the sub-criteria under each context in this framework applicable to the public sector. This framework aims to assist government agencies in self-assessing AI readiness before adopting AI-enabled technologies.

We used a case study in Singapore that leveraged this framework to demonstrate how this framework can be implemented to assess AI readiness. We also, via the case study, discussed the corrective measures that the agency could take if it is not ready.

The limitation of this work is that it is still considered exploratory due to insufficient empirical work done in this area for Singapore. However, we are of the belief that it can be further tried and tested in any other government agency that focuses on citizen service delivery to further ascertain this proposed framework. Future work will extend the approach to AI-based projects in contexts other than citizen service delivery across the Singapore government agencies.

REFERENCES

Abraham, T. H. (2002). (Physio) logical circuits: The intellectual origins of the McCulloch–Pitts neural networks. *Journal of the History of the Behavioral Sciences*, 38(1), 3–25.

Ågerfalk, P. J. (2020). Artificial intelligence as digital agency. *European Journal of Information Systems*, 29(1), 1–8.

Ajibade, P. (2018). Technology acceptance model limitations and criticisms: Exploring the practical applications and use in technology-related studies, mixed-method, and qualitative researches. *Library Philosophy & Practice*, 1941.

AlSheibani, S., Cheung, Y., and Messom, C. (2018). Artificial intelligence adoption: AI-readiness at firm-level. In PACIS 2018 Proceedings (p. 37).

Baker, J. (2012). The technology–organization–environment framework. *Information Systems Theory*, 231–245.

Balasubramaniam, N., Kauppinen, M., Hiekkanen, K., and Kujala, S. (2022, March). Transparency and explainability of AI systems: Ethical guidelines in practice. In *International Working Conference on Requirements Engineering: Foundation for Software Quality* (pp. 3–18). Springer, Cham.

Ball, I. (2012). New development: Transparency in the public sector. *Public Money & Management*, 32(1), 35–40.

Bobrow, D. G., and Raphael, B. (1974). New programming languages for artificial intelligence research. *ACM Computing Surveys* (CSUR), 6(3), 153–174.

Brundage, M., Avin, S., Wang, J., Belfield, H., Krueger, G., Hadfield, G., and Anderljung, M. (2020). Toward trustworthy AI development: Mechanisms for supporting verifiable claims. arXiv preprint arXiv:2004.07213.

Cath, C., Wachter, S., Mittelstadt, B., Taddeo, M., and Floridi, L. (2018). Artificial intelligence and the 'good society': The US, EU, and UK approach. *Science and Engineering Ethics*, 24(2), 505–528.

Chatterjee, S., Ghosh, S. K., Chaudhuri, R., and Nguyen, B. (2019). Are CRM systems ready for AI integration? A conceptual framework of organizational readiness for effective AI-CRM integration. The Bottom Line.

Chen, Y. C. (2010). Citizen-centric e-government services: Understanding integrated citizen service information systems. *Social Science Computer Review*, 28(4), 427–442.

Clarke, R. (2019). Principles and business processes for responsible AI. *Computer Law & Security Review*, 35(4), 410–422.

Davis, F. D. (1985). A technology acceptance model for empirically testing new end-user information systems: Theory and results (Doctoral dissertation, Massachusetts Institute of Technology). 12407479.

Düdder, B., Möslein, F., Stürtz, N., Westerlund, M., and Zicari, R. V. (2021). Ethical maintenance of artificial intelligence systems. In *Artificial Intelligence for Sustainable Value Creation* (pp. 151–171). Edward Elgar Publishing.

Dwivedi, Y. K., Hughes, L., Ismagilova, E., Aarts, G., Coombs, C., Crick, T., … and Williams, M. D. (2021). Artificial Intelligence (AI): Multidisciplinary perspectives on emerging challenges, opportunities, and agenda for research, practice and policy. *International Journal of Information Management*, 57, 101994.

Grace, K., Salvatier, J., Dafoe, A., Zhang, B., and Evans, O. (2018). When will AI exceed human performance? Evidence from AI experts. *Journal of Artificial Intelligence Research*, 62, 729–754.

GovTech, Singapore. (2020). Digital Government Blueprint. Government Technology Agency. Retrieved April 30, 2022, from https://www.tech.gov.sg/digital-government-blueprint/

Grosz, B. J., and Stone, P. (2018). A century-long commitment to assessing artificial intelligence and its impact on society. *Communications of the ACM*, 61(12), 68–73.

Huet, Ellen (2016). Pushing the boundaries of AI to talk to the dead, Bloomberg, October 20 (accessed March 21, 2017) [available at https://www.bloomberg.com/news/articles/20161020/pushingth eboundariesofaitotalktothedead].

Jeffares, S. (2021). The non-public encounter: Self-service and the ephemoralisation of public service. In *The Virtual Public Servant* (pp. 125–150). Palgrave Macmillan, Cham.

Jöhnk, J., Weißert, M., and Wyrtki, K. (2021). Ready or not, AI comes—an interview study of organizational AI readiness factors. *Business & Information Systems Engineering*, 63(1), 5–20.

Kania, E., Triolo, P., and Webster, G. (2018). *Translation: Chinese Government Outlines AI Ambitions through 2020*. New America.

Kennedy, A. (2006). Electronic customer relationship management (eCRM): Opportunities and challenges, *Irish Marketing Review*, 18(1/2), 58–69.

Kincaid, J. W. (2003). *Customer Relationship Management: Getting it Right!* Prentice Hall Professional.

Kingsman, N., Kazim, E., Chaudhry, A., Hilliard, A., Koshiyama, A., Polle, R., … and Mohammed, U. (2022). Public sector AI transparency standard: UK government seeks to lead by example. *Discover Artificial Intelligence*, 2(1), 1–9.

Kuberkar, S., and Singhal, T. K. (2020). Factors influencing adoption intention of AI powered chatbot for public transport services within a Smart City. *International Journal of Emerging Technologies in Learning*, 11(3), 948–958.

Kubicek, H., and Hagen, M. (eds) (2000). *One Stop Government in Europe: An Overview*, 11, 1–36.

Li, B. H., Hou, B. C., Yu, W. T., Lu, X. B., and Yang, C. W. (2017). Applications of artificial intelligence in intelligent manufacturing: A review. *Frontiers of Information Technology & Electronic Engineering*, 18(1), 86–96.

McCarthy, J., Minsky, M. L., Rochester, N., and Shannon, C. E. (2006). A proposal for the Dartmouth summer research project on artificial intelligence, August 31, 1955. *AI Magazine*, 27(4), 12–12.

Mehr, H., Ash, H., and Fellow, D. (2017). Artificial intelligence for citizen services and government. Ash Cent. Democr. Gov. Innov. Harvard Kennedy Sch., August, 1–12.

Najdawi, A. (2020, July). Assessing AI readiness across organizations: The case of UAE. In *2020 11th International Conference on Computing, Communication and Networking Technologies (ICCCNT)* (pp. 1–5). IEEE.

Najdawi, A., and Shaheen, A. (2021, February). Which project management methodology is better for AI-transformation and innovation projects? In *2021 International Conference on Innovative Practices in Technology and Management (ICIPTM)* (pp. 205–210). IEEE.

Ngai, E. W., Xiu, L., and Chau, D. C. (2009). Application of data mining techniques in customer relationship management: A literature review and classification. *Expert Systems with Applications*, 36(2), 2592–2602.

Niculescu, A. I., Kukanov, I., and Wadhwa, B. (2020, April). DigiMo-towards developing an emotional intelligent chatbot in Singapore. In *Proceedings of the 2020 Symposium on Emerging Research from Asia and on Asian Contexts and Cultures* (pp. 29–32).

Nielsen, M. M. (2016). E-governance and stage models: Analysis of identified models and selected Eurasian experiences in digitizing citizen service delivery. *Electronic Government, an International Journal*, 12(2), 107–141.

Nortje, M. A., and Grobbelaar, S. S. (2020, June). A framework for the implementation of artificial intelligence in business enterprises: A readiness model. In *2020 IEEE International Conference on Engineering, Technology and Innovation (ICE/ITMC)* (pp. 1–10). IEEE.

Palle, S. (2019). Artificial intelligence using DBS-QOS in banking organizations. *Journal of Scientific Research & Engineering Trends*, 5(1), 2395–566X.

Picard, R. W. (2008). *Toward Machines with Emotional Intelligence*. MIT open access.

Prabhu, S., and Bhat, S. (2020). Application of Artificial Intelligence in Samsung – A case study. *International Journal of Case Studies in Business, IT, and Education* (IJCSBE), 4(2), 280–292.

Pudjianto, B., Zo, H., Ciganek, A. P., and Rho, J. J. (2011). Determinants of e-government assimilation in Indonesia: An empirical investigation using a TOE framework. *Asia Pacific Journal of Information Systems*, 21(1), 49–80.

Rasch, R., Kott, A., and Forbus, K. D. (2003). Incorporating AI into military decision making: An experiment. *IEEE Intelligent Systems*, 18(4), 18–26.

Retto, J. (2017). Sophia, first citizen robot of the world. ResearchGate, URL: https://www. researchgate. net.

Rodammer, F. A., and White, K. P. (1988). A recent survey of production scheduling. *IEEE Transactions on Systems, Man, and Cybernetics*, 18(6), 841–851.

Schlögl, S., Postulka, C., Bernsteiner, R., and Ploder, C. (2019, July). Artificial intelligence tool penetration in business: Adoption, challenges and fears. In *International Conference on Knowledge Management in Organizations* (pp. 259–270). Springer, Cham.

Sharma, H., Soetan, T., Farinloye, T., Mogaji, E., and Noite, M. D. F. (2022). AI adoption in universities in emerging economies: Prospects, challenges and recommendations. In *Re-imagining Educational Futures in Developing Countries* (pp. 159–174). Palgrave Macmillan, Cham.

Sondak, N. E., and Sondak, V. K. (1989, February). Neural networks and artificial intelligence. In *Proceedings of the Twentieth SIGCSE Technical Symposium on Computer Science Education* (pp. 241–245).

Stirling, R., Miller, H., and Martinho-Truswell, E. (2017). Government AI Readiness Index. KOREA, 4, 7–8.

Subashini, S., and Kavitha, V. (2011). A survey on security issues in service delivery models of cloud computing. *Journal of Network and Computer Applications*, 34(1), 1–11.

Sun, T. Q., and Medaglia, R. (2018). *Artificial Intelligence Entering Public Healthcare Ecosystems: Do Policies Matter?* Paper presented at 2017 Pre-ICIS Workshop on e-Government, Seoul, Korea, Republic of.

Szolovits, P., and Pauker, S. G. (1978). Categorical and probabilistic reasoning in medical diagnosis. *Artificial Intelligence*, 11(1–2), 115–144.

Themistocleous, M., and Irani, Z. (2001). Benchmarking the benefits and barriers of application integration. *Benchmarking: An International Journal*, 8(4), 317–331.

Tims, M.J. (2016) Letting artificial intelligence in education out of the box: Educational cobots and smart classrooms. *International Journal of Artificial Intelligence in Education*, 26, 701–712.

Tornatzky, L. G., Fleischer, M., and Chakrabarti, A. K. (1990). *Processes of Technological Innovation.* Lexington Books.

Wang, D., Weisz, J. D., Muller, M., Ram, P., Geyer, W., Dugan, C., ... and Gray, A. (2019). Human-AI collaboration in data science: Exploring data scientists' perceptions of automated AI. *Proceedings of the ACM on Human-Computer Interaction*, 3(CSCW), 1–24.

Wirtz, B. W., Weyerer, J. C., and Geyer, C. (2019). Artificial intelligence and the public sector – applications and challenges. *International Journal of Public Administration*, 42(7), 596–615.

Zanzotto, F. M. (2019). Human-in-the-loop artificial intelligence. *Journal of Artificial Intelligence Research*, 64, 243–252.

6. Measuring user-centricity in AI-enabled European public services: a proposal for enabling maturity models

Francesco Niglia and Luca Tangi

INTRODUCTION

This study aims to present and elaborate on a framework able to evaluate to what extent Artificial Intelligence (AI) based solutions could contribute to enabling the primary user-centricity (UC) principles. Two main steps contribute to this goal. First, the chapter provides a framework measuring the application of UC principles in public services. Second, it applies the framework to AI-based solutions in enabling functionalities and building UC.

The authors ground this research on various reports from the European Commission and other relevant literature. The foci of background studies are the definition of user-centricity, Artificial Intelligence and its taxonomies, existing frameworks for measuring UC implementation in public services, and existing general information about the roles, risks, and opportunities offered by AI-based solutions.

The authors aim to contribute to existing academic literature related to the topics listed above. The first contribution is the definition of a methodology for deepening the understanding of UC principles by disaggregating them into a list of single functionalities. The second is a preliminary list of AI-based solutions to implement each functionality. In addition, the authors include an example of UC measurement by applying a maturity model to a set of AI-enabled public services.

This chapter adopts a simple and linear narrative structure. As the first step, in Section 2, the authors discuss the role of UC for public services, in general, and for AI-enabled ones in more detail. Section 3 highlights the signs of progress and the limitations of existing international initiatives in measuring UC in public services. Section 4 introduces the authors' proposal for a different approach to the same issue as an additional resource. Section 5 provides a clearer insight into the role of AI-based technologies in the proposed framework by linking AI typologies to the principles underlying UC. Section 6 illustrates an example of the deployment of the framework to a sample of AI-based public services. Section 7 opens the debate about some research questions to be further analysed.

WHAT USER-CENTRICITY IS, AND WHY IT IS ESSENTIAL FOR AI-BASED PUBLIC SERVICES

UC is one of the underlying principles of European public services (Pinzon et al., 2019), and the European Commission defines it as 'putting users' needs at the centre when determining which Public Services should be provided and how they should be delivered' (NIFO[1]).

UC is a consolidated approach and holds considerable relevance for public services. Indeed, the concept and the implementation of UC for the public sector have been discussed and formalised by the Member States since 2009 by the 'Malmö Ministerial Declaration on eGovernment' of the European Commission (European Commission, 2009), confirmed in 2017 with the 'Tallinn Declaration on eGovernment' (European Commission, 2017), and renewed in the 'Berlin Declaration on Digital Society and Value-Based Digital Government' (European Commission, 2020a) through the commitment on the implementation of digital means fostering the UC.

As officially described in the Tallinn Declaration, the UC builds on significant priorities toward ensuring high quality, user-centric digital and seamless cross-border public services for citizens and businesses. Its policies leverage the power that digital transformation is expected to strengthen the trust in governments in increasing the transparency, responsiveness, reliability, and integrity of public governance. This declaration provided eight clear 'UC principles for design and delivery of digital public services', constituting specific 'rights' for citizens and business users, who should expect each UC principle to be fulfilled when interacting with public administrations. The UC principles are 1–Digital Interaction; 2–Accessibility, security, availability, and usability; 3–Reduction of the administrative burden; 4–Digital delivery of public services; 5–Citizen engagement; 6–Incentives for digital service use; 7–Protection of personal data and privacy; 8–Redress and complaint mechanisms.

Table 6.3 regroups the description of the eight principles and their policy grounding requirement, while the full description is available (European Commission, 2017).

UC is far from a simple theoretical framework; its application becomes broader concurrently as new technologies are available and policymaking organisations carry out awareness campaigns about its positive impacts.

UC already constitutes one of the pillars for evaluating the quality of public services. As evidence, the last eGovernment Benchmark released by the European Commission, 'Entering a New Digital Government Era' (European Commission, 2021a), underlines how the UC '*excels*' among the four dimensions adopted for their evaluation.

AI and UC are tightly correlated and could mutually benefit when adopted in the public services domain. When focusing on AI, the grounding concept is that it constitutes an enabling set of technologies that 'contribute to better public services in a variety of ways' and 'support Public Administrations' (Tangi et al., 2022). The main objectives of introducing AI in public administrations align with UC goals. They relate to (a) the improvement of processes; (b) enhancing and enabling faster policymaking mechanisms; and (c) improving the participation and experience of citizens and business users when using PS (Misuraca and van Noordt, 2020).

---

[1]   National Interoperability Framework Observatory – Glossary https:// joinup .ec .europa .eu/ collection/nifo-national-interoperability-framework-observatory/glossary/term/user-centricity

Among the many definitions, this chapter considers the definition of AI as provided in the preliminary draft of the AI ACT available at the time of writing (European Commission, 2021e) 'Artificial intelligence system' (AI system) means software that is developed with one or more of the techniques and approaches [...] and can, for a given set of human-defined objectives, generate outputs such as content, predictions, recommendations, or decisions influencing the environments they interact with.' The mentioned techniques and approaches are listed in an annexe of the AI ACT.

By enabling some dynamics and features in services, the successful AI use and value creation for the public sector and society can also comply with the implementation of UC principles (Table 6.1). Moreover, several implementations of AI-based technologies ensure the fulfilment of UC in the public sector by enabling basic functionalities (Table 6.4).

Despite the alignment of the objectives, integrating AI and UC in public services is not an easy task: AI might risk having adverse effects on UC by leveraging unethical aspects such as the violation of individual fundamental rights through a wrong approach to connectivity, opacity, data dependency and autonomy if applied without paying sufficient attention (Union and Renda, 2021).

The claim of the co-existence of potential positive and adverse effects of AI on UC is the first thesis introduced by the authors. These considerations bring us to a double-fold vision of the mutual impact of AI and UC. On the one hand, AI could contribute to improving how we build UC in public services, and on the other hand, the latter could help recognise AI-related risks and contribute to smoothing them. Table 6.1 includes details about this distinction, listing the elements of AI that could either support or worsen the approach to known problems in implementing UC principles. Some notes to Table 6.1 are:

1. The positive role of AI has been retrieved by ISA2 Action 2018 0.1 'Innovative Public Services: Assessment of Technologies and Recommendations and Identification of Interoperability Issues/Risks' with a small author adaptation of the text.
2. The negative role of AI and its related risks is the own authors' elaboration based on the detailed analysis of UC principles' requirements against the possible AI implementations; the latter is discussed in the literature, official EC reports, and case studies analysis (Manzoni et al., 2022; Medaglia et al., 2021).
3. The risk of a jeopardising effect of AI in achieving the eight principles of the Tallinn Declaration is broader than the description provided by the table (as highlighted in AlgorithmWatch Schweiz, 2021; High-Level Expert Group on Artificial Intelligence (HLEG), 2019).

OPPORTUNITIES AND LIMITS OF CURRENT FRAMEWORKS FOR THE MEASUREMENT OF USER-CENTRICITY IN PUBLIC SERVICES

One of this study's contributions is to provide a preliminary solution to overcome the gaps in measuring UC principles. This paragraph constitutes the first step of the discussion about the proposed solution by highlighting the opportunities and the limits of existing official and running frameworks.

Table 6.1   *Expected support and potential risks of AI in user-centricity*

UC principles	How AI contributes to overcoming barriers	AI-related risks
1-Digital interaction	Barriers: Digital divide; difficulties to digitalise some services; collaboration among governmental levels. Role of AI: AI has the potential to overcome the digital divide and give citizens and businesses the option to interact with public administrations digitally.	The continuous implementation of chatbots and natural language processing-based solutions could bring, in some cases, a complete digitalisation of one or more processes of service provision. This aspect goes against the 'possibility by users to choose IF to interact digitally with public services' (*authors' elaboration*).
2-Accessibility, security, availability, and usability	Barriers: Different rules, channels, and principles among Government levels Role of AI: AI holds the potential to make digital PS more accessible (including findable) and secure, and all can use that in a non-discriminatory manner.	Predictive analysis and algorithmic decision-making might create unwanted or unplanned user categories resulting in unbalanced access to services for citizens (Andrus and Villeneuve, 2022).
3-Reduction of the administrative burden	Barriers: Back-office service design not suitable Role of AI: With most implementations, AI can support public administrations' efforts to restructure existing digital processes and services and/or create new and more efficient ones.	*No known harmful effect of AI*
4-Digital delivery of public services	Barriers: Public servants' low skills Role of AI: AI could fully handle online services, including providing any evidence required to obtain a right or fulfil obligations.	*No known harmful effect of AI*
5-Citizen engagement	Barriers: A multidisciplinary approach required Role of AI: AI could support the seamless participation and collection of ideas, comments, and feedback during (even virtual) public debates. AI has the potential to help policymaking in the creation of PS at all governmental levels.	Predictive analysis has the potential to get ahead of citizens' opinions and build a coherent and consistent set of services requirements and features. Due to potential bias, these requirements and features might not correspond to the real users' (citizens) needs and requests (Weyerer and Langer, 2019).
6-Incentives for digital service use	Barriers: Lack of skills to use digital tools and access the internet. Role of AI: AI has the potential to help remove barriers to use digital PS effectively, including benefits such as speed, effectivity, and reduced costs to individuals who can use them.	Rule-based intelligent systems and empowered Knowledge Management might create economic added value and put citizens out of the loop. (Buhmann and Fieseler, 2022).
7-Protection of personal data and privacy	Barriers: Difficulty in designing complex services compliant with GDPR. Role of AI: AI does not have a direct positive impact on this principle. Some implementations of AI could help citizens and authorities recognise early warnings of a data breach or misuse.	Identity recognition-based solutions might increase complexity or make it impossible to perform personal data control (Smith and Miller, 2022).
8-Redress and complaint mechanisms	Barriers: Link complaints with feedback Role of AI: AI can create conditions in the public sector to set up redress mechanisms and complaint procedures that citizens and businesses can have access to online, as well as in other available channels of their choice.	Rule-based systems and algorithm decision-making, if not duly controlled, might start data processing before redressing is claimed, resulting in additional citizens' data storage (Ryan and Stahl, 2021).

Since its preliminary definition, implementing UC principles requires specific user consider-ations (European Commission, 2009). The digitalisation of public services is the way drawn by the EC; indeed, by digitising, governments can also offer services that meet the evolving expectations of citizens and businesses, leading to increased trust in Government (Alzahrani et al., 2017). This aspect would potentially increase the social and economic system's resilience and other positive effects.

Examples of good practices of digitalisation policies supporting or, at least, paving the way to implementing UC processes exist (Molinari et al., 2021). They are being implemented at the European scale: 'In Europe, eight out of ten government services can be completed online (81 per cent)' – source: eGovernment Benchmark 2021 (European Commission, 2021a).

However, despite this increased awareness, UC is not entirely implemented in public services. The reasons for this gap are the difficulties in defining a consolidated use and deployment of user-centric ICTs in public services (Balatsas-Lekkas et al., 2021). Among the problems to solve for the complete achievement of its adoption, we can mention two factors:

1. The UC is not a unique paradigm, and its definition is not uniform. It is a confusing issue for public authorities and stakeholders when approaching it. Among the many definitions, we can mention the following sources:
    a. European Commission: UC is an evolving paradigm even for the EC (European Commission, 2009; European Commission, 2017). This study adopts the last one, 'Tallinn Declaration', as the official definition of the eight funding principles.
    b. The OECD: UC exploits through a six-dimensional approach: 1–Digital by Design; 2–Data-driven public sector; 3–Open by default; 4–User driven; 5–Government as a platform; 6–Proactiveness.
    c. The National Interoperability Framework Observatory (NIFO[2]): UC focuses on the high-level operational features to be implemented. '[...] as far as possible, user needs and requirements should guide the design and development of public services, in accordance with the following expectations: (i) A multi-channel service delivery approach; (ii) A single point of contact should be made available to users; (iii) Users' feedback should be systematically collected, assessed and used to design new public services and to further improve existing ones.'
2. Issues in comparing PA's performances. A high degree of difficulty in comparing the performances of PAs in performing digital government tasks still exists. 'Current monitoring and performance evaluation practices are mainly focused on measuring the performance of specific service areas or agencies. However, the UC government approaches require the development of government-wide, i.e., cross-agency-level performance and impact measurements' (Ozols and Nielsen, 2018). Examples for measuring and exposing performance data are available for the UK (service performance platform), Latvia (Latvijas e-indekss), and Denmark (Digital Scorecard), focusing on customer feedback practices, performance evaluation and monitoring practices, accountability and impact. Benchmarking among Public Authorities' services performances is very difficult due to jeopardised measurement scenarios, different metrics, etc. Open Data exist at the local level and could be better used at the national level if only they were made comparable.

---

[2]   National Interoperability Framework Observatory – Glossary https:// joinup .ec .europa .eu/ collection/nifo-national-interoperability-framework-observatory/glossary/term/user-centricity

Notably, scholars made several attempts to define and measure UC. For example, Verdegem proposed a model for measuring user satisfaction based on a research track concerning the needs and preferences of citizens towards electronic service provision (Verdegem et al., 2009). Bertzen argued using indicators to measure the stages of the lifecycle of an eGovernment service (Bertzen, 2013). Saqib emphasised the need for user-centric e-government to motivate e-government researchers to use this approach to design e-government systems for better user acceptance (Saqib et al., 2018). Finally, other experimental on-field activities aimed at measuring its implementation at a European scale through simple quantitative indicators (Gugliotta et al., 2013).

The difficulties mentioned above still exist, but much work has been done. Tallinn's principles have already started to be translated into operational measures, and metrics are being used to track progress at the European level. Three main existing frameworks for the measurement of the implementation of digital public services and UC are worth analysing: Europe's eGovernment Benchmark (European Commission, 2021a); the Digital Economy and Society Index (European Commission, 2021c), and the Indicators of Citizen-Centric Public Service Delivery (World Bank Group, 2018).

Europe's eGovernment Benchmark proposes and systematically improves a well-assessed methodology to evaluate the acquisition and implementation of digital public services. It considers four top-level key dimensions with 15 sub-indicators (Figure 6.1). The updated methodology for Europe's eGovernment Benchmark (European Commission, 2021b) adopted by CapGemini considers Tallinn's principles by complying with realistic, measurable parameters. Figure 6.1 provides a schematic overview of the critical dimensions and adopted indicators. At the same time, Table 6.5 shows how to relate the 8 UC principles and the 15 indicators of the eGovernment benchmark.

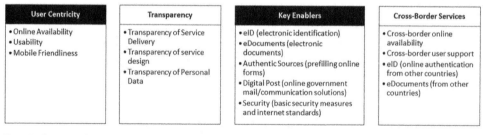

Note: Authors' graphic elaboration on the information provided in Europe's eGovernment Benchmark report 2021 by Capgemini.

Figure 6.1   *Europe's eGovernment performance: top level benchmarks and sub-indicators*

The eGovernment Benchmark method paper 2020–2023 (European Commission, 2021b) clarifies the indicators adopted for measuring the UC 'key dimensions': Online availability, User support, and Mobile friendliness, as follows:

1. Definition of the 'UC' key dimension: the extent to which information and services are available online, supported online and compatible with mobile devices.

2. Definition of indicators:
   a. Online availability: the extent to which informational and transactional services and information concerning these services are provided online and can be reached via a portal website.
   b. User support: the extent to which online support, help features, and feedback mechanisms are available.
   c. Mobile friendliness: the extent to which services are provided through a mobile-friendly interface, an interface that is responsive to the mobile device.

The Digital Economy and Society Index (DESI) represents the official methodological tool for the European Commission to monitor Member States' digital progress. It formally monitors the UC through three indicators that overlap the eGovernment Benchmark. Still, its methodological structure for monitoring the implementation of Digital Public Services (European Commission, 2021d) includes 9 main areas and 24 indicators (Figure 6.2), well-aligned with UC principles and useful for their measurement.

eGovernment users	Pre-filled forms	Digital Public Services for citizens	Digital Public Services for businesses	Open Data	User Centricity	Transparency	Key enablers	Cross-border services
• Digital Interaction with public authorities • Submission of forms to the Public Administrations	• Data already known to the Public Administratio ns • Once-only principle	• Online Availability of service or information concerning service for citizens	• Interoperabili ty and cross-border online availability	• Open Data Policy • Open Data portals • Open Data impacts • Open Data quality	• Online Availability • Usability • Mobile Friendliness	• Transparency of service delivery • Transparency of personal data • Transparency of service design	• Electronic Identification (eID) • eDocuments • Authentic sources • Digital post	• Cross-border online availability • Cross-border user support • Cross-border eID • Cross-border eDocuments:

Note: Authors' graphic elaboration on the information provided in DESI report 2021 by European Commission.

Figure 6.2   *DESI 2021 – Digital public services: indicators and sub-indicators*

The Indicators of Citizen-Centric Public Service Delivery undertake issues dealing with citizen-centric governance indicators, that is, indicators that measure the capacity of public agencies to put the needs of citizens at the centre of their service delivery mechanisms. This framework was prepared in response to a request by the Economic Analysis Unit of the European Commission's Directorate-General for Regional and Urban Policy (DG REGIO) to the World Bank. It identifies four key areas: access, user-centeredness and responsiveness, quality and reliability of service delivery, and public sector integrity. The key areas include 14 indicators, as described in Figure 6.3.

After this brief analysis, when considering adopting these sub-indicators to evaluate the degree of fulfilment of the UC principles, we ought to consider that several gaps exist, as shown in Table 6.2 (*in italic style*). Indeed, when looking at the indicators, they do not cover Tallinn's principles completely. The goal of the table is not to criticise the existing indicators as they are but to analyse those indicators with a novel angle, i.e., in light of the UC principles, to see if and how they are linked with them, even if the indicators are not designed with that specific purpose.

Notably, these frameworks are being refined yearly to answer the continuous adoption of new policy instruments for digital societal and territorial innovation.

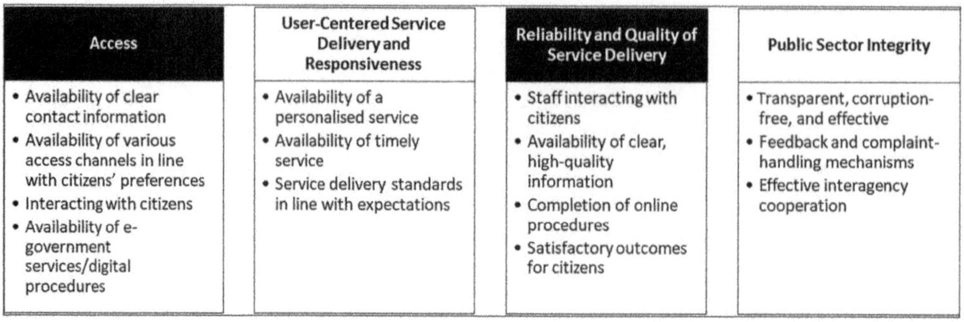

Access	User-Centered Service Delivery and Responsiveness	Reliability and Quality of Service Delivery	Public Sector Integrity
• Availability of clear contact information • Availability of various access channels in line with citizens' preferences • Interacting with citizens • Availability of e-government services/digital procedures	• Availability of a personalised service • Availability of timely service • Service delivery standards in line with expectations	• Staff interacting with citizens • Availability of clear, high-quality information • Completion of online procedures • Satisfactory outcomes for citizens	• Transparent, corruption-free, and effective • Feedback and complaint-handling mechanisms • Effective interagency cooperation

Note: Authors' graphic elaboration on the information provided in Citizen-Centric Public Service Delivery by World Bank Group.

Figure 6.3   Indicators of citizen-centric public service delivery: key areas and indicators

It is possible to appreciate this slight misalignment because the 8 UC principles result from the joint consideration of technological, social, organisational, and legal/ethical aspects, which the previous frameworks do not explicitly include in their scenario analysis.

Table 6.2 includes the authors' elaboration on the 8 UC principles, the relevance of the indicators adopted by the eGovernment benchmark, the DESI 2021, and the Citizens-Centric Public delivery frameworks, and the highlighted gaps.

As a general consideration, the result lacks existing and validated methodologies for measuring the implementation of UC principles in PS in a meaningful way. In particular, with this very preliminary benchmark, the authors highlight the gaps in the measurement of principles 5 (*not considered in the analysed frameworks*), 6 and 8 (*only partially measurable by the existing frameworks*). This output aligns with User Centric Cities' notable initiative, a running project aiming to 'launch a European community of decision-makers that share experience, knowledge and lessons learnt about how to implement user-centricity' ((UCC[3]). The project has analysed five existing frameworks to identify current approaches to the UC assessment of digital public services (Balatsas-Lekkas et al., 2021). Two interesting statements of this report are aligned with the preliminary analysis carried out in the authors' present study:

1. 'The main finding is that currently no instrument or framework includes a user-centricity assessment that is specific to locally offered digital public services.' (ibidem, page 9)
2. 'None of the reviewed instruments and frameworks include measurements that cover exactly the scope of Tallinn Declaration's user-centricity principles. In addition, some principles cover various topics, such as the principle entitled accessibility, security, availability and usability. The adequate measurement of each user-centricity principle, at a local government level may require the development of several metrics.' (ibidem, page 29)

---

[3]   UserCentriCities project, available at https://www.usercentricities.eu/

Table 6.2   *Correlation between the UC principles stated by the Tallinn Declaration and the available indicators in existing frameworks*

UC principles	eGov benchmark indicators	DESI 2021 indicators	Citizen-Centric Public Service Delivery indicators
1-Digital interaction	● Online availability; Digital post; Mobile friendliness	● Digital interaction with P.A. ● Digital post	● Interacting with citizens
2-Accessibility, security, availability, and usability	● Mobile friendliness; eID: Usability	● Usability ● Mobile friendliness	● Availability of timely service
3-Reduction of the administrative burden	● Online availability; Authentic sources; eID; eDocuments; Cross-border services categories	● Online availability of service or services information for citizens	● Availability of clear, high-quality information ● Completion of online procedures
4-Digital delivery of public services	● Online availability; Usability; Mobile friendliness	● Online availability ● Mobile friendliness ● eDocuments	● Availability of various access channels in line with citizens' preferences
5-Citizen engagement	● *Not available*	● *Not available*	● *Not available*
6-Incentives for digital service use	● (*Not covered by the current measurement*)	● *Not available*	● 'Satisfactory outcomes for citizens' and 'Staff interacting with citizens' (*partially covering the UC principle's requirement*)
7-Protection of personal data and privacy	● An operative pilot ran over the last years. *Operative outcomes will soon be released*	● Electronic Identification (eID) ● Authentic sources *Only for users' identification*	● (*Not covered by the current measurement*)
8-Redress and complaint mechanisms	● (*Not directly measured by the benchmark*) Only complaints managed through the Transparency of Public Organisations	● Transparency of service delivery (*partially covering the UC principle's requirement*)	● Feedback and complaint-handling mechanisms (*partially covering the UC principle's requirement*)

A POSSIBLE SOLUTION: A SHIFT FROM NARRATIVE TO A MEASURABLE DEFINITION OF USER-CENTRIC PRINCIPLES

This section completes the description of the main goal by proposing an innovative framework that links the eight principles to a list of enabling functionalities. The authors propose a new measurement methodology based on the concept that the eight UC principles may be disaggregated in single functionalities offered by public services and fulfilled by any solution, particularly AI-based technologies. The single UC functionalities may be better analysed and measured, simplifying the analysis of the services' hindered functioning and enabling the development of maturity or measurement models. Even though not strictly related to AI, this step is necessary to apply a measurable framework to AI-enabled solutions.

The Tallinn Declaration provides a clear vision of policy action lines to build UC in the Member States. These single policies (European Commission, 2017 – Annex: User-centricity principles for design and delivery of digital public services) outline the requirements, including a cost-benefit perspective, the concept of personal data protection or security considerations, and the subsidiarity principle. The narrative defining the eight principles of the Tallinn Declaration provides us with enough information to determine an additional and more detailed layer, which is very helpful to start decreasing the complexity of the principles' implementation. The authors' contribution to the AI domain is the definition of a list of functionalities that exploit the fulfilment of UC through the implementation of AI-based solutions. These functionalities constitute the 'bricks' of the UC itself since they are linked to the policy requirement of each of the eight principles. The list of functionalities constitutes one of the innovative approaches this study discusses. Table 6.3 clarifies how each of the eight principles has been mapped (disaggregated) into functionalities (column 3). Identifying the classes of UC functionalities to be enabled to satisfy the principles at hand is possible. Three main assumptions helped to build the table:

1. The list of the functionalities is in column 3 of the table. The authors elaborated their taxonomy on the text to further discuss this method.
2. All functionalities shall be considered 'enabling factors for the implementation of UC' and are not linked to any specific technology or group of technologies. They are a direct consequence of the definition of the eight principles.
3. The proposed taxonomy for functionalities (in bold) may be extended and enriched to further improve this disaggregation model by including more detailed policy requirements.

Table 6.3   *Mapping of user-centricity principles into single 'functionalities'*

UC principle	Policy requirement for user-centricity principles (European Commission, 2017)	Elicited enabling functionality
1-Digital interaction	To have the option to digitally interact with their administrations.	Access to service
2-Accessibility, security, availability, and usability	That the authenticity of digital public services is secured and can be recognised in a clear and consistent manner.	Authentication (*it refers to making our digital public services secure and properly identifiable*)
	That the principles of universal design have been applied to the setting up of the services and that the websites are simple to read and easy to understand.	Access for all
	That the services are made more accessible (including findable) and secure and can be used by all in a non-discriminatory manner, with appropriate assistance available upon need.	Inclusion for all
3-Reduction of the administrative burden	That public administrations make efforts to reduce the administrative burden on citizens and businesses, namely by optimising and/or creating digital processes and services where relevant and possible.	Simplification of process
	That public administrations make efforts to reduce the administrative burden on citizens and businesses [...] by offering personalised and proactive services.	Anticipation of needs
	Not to be asked to provide the same information to public services more than once, in due respect of data protection rules and regulations.	Once-only principle

UC principle	Policy requirement for user-centricity principles (European Commission, 2017)	Elicited enabling functionality
4-Digital delivery of public services	That public services can as much as possible and appropriately, especially upon request of the user, be fully handled online, including the provision of any evidence required to obtain a right or fulfil obligations.	Improved data collection
	That the status of service delivery can be checked online where relevant.	Monitoring
5-Citizen engagement	That digital means are used to […] involve citizens more in the creation of public services.	Listening to needs Services coding (*it refers to the possibility to develop software (code) for digital services by digitally skilled citizens*)
	That digital means are used to […] empower citizens and businesses to voice their views.	Participation in debates
	That digital means are used to […] allow policy makers to collect new ideas.	Idea feedback collection
	That digital means are used to […] provide better digital public services.	Services improvement
6-Incentives for digital service use	The barriers to use digital public services should be effectively removed, including by extending and promoting […] higher confidence, speed, effectivity.	Improve service efficiency
	The barriers to use digital public services should be effectively removed, including by extending and promoting […] reduced costs to individuals who are able to use them.	Enable incentives
	The barriers to use digital public services should be effectively removed, including by extending and promoting the benefits.	Enable business and benefits
7-Protection of personal data and privacy	That the handling of personal data respects the general data protection regulation and privacy requirements in the EU and national levels.	Secure data collection procedures
	Informing citizens about the use and storage of their personal data and allowing citizens to access and ask for the correction and deletion of personal data, where appropriate.	Data usage and elaboration
8-Redress and complaint mechanisms	That redress mechanisms are available online and that citizens and businesses have access to complaint procedures online, while also in other available channel(s) of their choice.	Redress and autonomy (*freedom to redress and autonomy to use a service*)

Table 6.3 reduces the complexity of the UC study by downgrading it to the analysis of 20 functionalities that different technologies might enable. It would be possible to evaluate each functionality as a single entity or group or weigh their actual implementation by deploying a maturity model that works with easy-to-be-found parameters and empirical or statistical data (Valdés et al., 2011; Tangi et al., 2021).

As a second step, once assigned a 'weighted' score to each functionality, it would be possible to calculate the achievement of each UC principle by re-aggregating the 'score' of single functionalities. Figure 6.4 details the correlation between functionalities' weighted scores and the measurement of UC implementation.

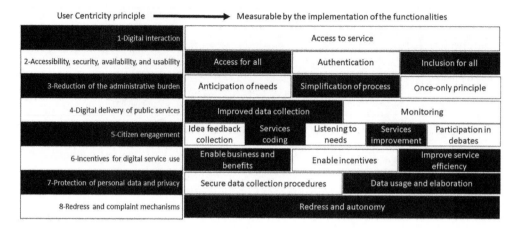

Figure 6.4   Relation between disaggregated UC functionalities and measurement of achievement of UC principles

HOW THE AI FITS INTO THIS METHOD

AI already helps Public Administrations by a) reducing administrative burdens, b) resolving resource allocation problems, c) taking up complex tasks, and many other features (Gianluca Misuraca and van Noordt, 2020; Tangi et al., 2022). AI-enabled UC might be found in several tools and solutions, and many AI technologies can potentially enable it in public services: audio processing, AI-based chatbots, intelligent digital assistants, virtual agents, predictive data analytics, algorithms, and machine learning respond to users' enquiries and provide several advantages to governments (Molinari et al., 2021). Tools and solutions based on AI techniques have been applied in developing targeted, personalised interventions and 'nudges' in healthcare, education, and other social services of general interest (Tangi et al., 2022; Zicari et al., 2021).

The proposed disaggregation method of principles in functionalities fits well with the AI-based solutions for the public sector. On the one hand, it allows the assignment of AI technologies to each functionality; on the other hand, measuring AI-enabled UC supports its fair implementation into public services. However, the impressive growth of AI-based solutions and typologies for the public sector does not allow us to define a closed list fulfilling UC principles.

Given this uncertainty, the authors leverage the 'AI type' classification introduced by the EC-JRC (Misuraca and van Noordt, 2020) and used as official taxonomy by the EU AI-Watch initiative. Six 'AI types' categories characterised by direct interaction with users, citizens and businesses constitute the most suitable set for implementing UC. The following text describes the definitions (source: EC-JRC) and identifies a short rationale about their relevance and contribution to UC (authors' elaboration). The six AI types are:

1. Audio Processing. AI applications of this type can detect and recognise sound, music and other audio inputs, including speech, thus enabling the recognition of voices and transcription of spoken words.

    a.   Relevance: They speed up communication and facilitate the users' listening processes, mainly used for digital services to citizens.

    b.   Targeted principles: UC1, UC5.

2. Chatbots, Intelligent Digital Assistants, Virtual Agents and Recommendation Systems. This AI typology includes virtualised assistants or online 'bots' currently used not only to provide generic advice but also behaviour-related recommendations to users.

    a.   Relevance: They facilitate gathering citizens' feedback and requests and help scout new and improved procedures for enabling collaboration with and between citizens, businesses, and civil society.

    b.   Targeted principles: UC1, UC2, UC3, UC4.

3. Computer Vision and Identity Recognition. AI applications from this category use some form of image, video or facial recognition to gain information on the external environment and/or the identity of specific persons or objects.

    a.   Relevance: They help to reduce the administrative burdens when the identity recognition solutions start being tested in PS.

    b.   Targeted principles: UC4.

4. Machine Learning, Deep Learning. While almost all the other categories of AI use some form of Machine Learning, this residual category refers to AI solutions which are not suitable for the other classifications.

    a.   Relevance: They could include interesting user-centric approaches in services' efficiency improvement by encouraging feedback loops that allow for more user insights and lead to better design and service delivery.

    b.   Targeted principles: UC3, UC5, UC6, UC7.

5. Natural Language Processing, Text Mining and Speech Analytics. AI applications belonging to this type are capable of recognising and analysing speech, written text and communicating back.

    a.   Relevance: These technologies can enhance the communication flow between users and public authorities by leveraging enhanced data access and reuse. AI Semantic matching techniques are used to map and align vocabularies and ontologies and thus can be used to increase interoperability and support the interoperability of services and reduce complexity for users.

    b.   Targeted principles: UC1, UC6, UC8.

6. Predictive Analytics, Simulation and Data Visualisation. These types of AI solutions learn from large datasets to identify patterns in the data that are consequently used to visualise, simulate, or predict new configurations.

    a.   Relevance: These technologies help ensure datasets are effective for public services by strengthening data for PS, and security analytics could support the quality evaluation of user feedback. Moreover, openness and transparency of AI-based algorithms may be fundamental to successfully implementing machine learning and other artificial intelligence applications and maintaining trust.

    b.   Targeted principles: UC3, UC4, UC6, UC7.

The last step of the methodology demonstrates that the framework can map each UC functionality with a list of AI-based solutions to support the fulfilment of UC in public services. This result constitutes the overarching goal of this study.

The authors have performed desk-based research analysis on an available set of AI-based services (Public Sector Tech Watch[4]) belonging to the six AI-type categories explored above. The desk analysis linked the AI-based solutions with the existing UC functionalities empowering the services.

Table 6.4 details the links among principles, functionalities and the preliminary list of AI-based technologies fulfilling them. Notably, this table, even populated by a limited set of existing AI-based solutions, constitutes a relevant result of the present study because it links the conceptual definition of principles with real and existing AI solutions enabling UC. It highlights evidence that UC principles' implementation is measurable by analysing the maturity of AI solutions supporting them. The easy measurement of the AI-based solution maturity and the Technology Readiness Level (TRL) evaluation (EURAXESS[5]) 'supports the conclusion.

The last statement helps answer the authors' primary goal, i.e., the definition of a framework enabling different maturity models to measure the role of AI in fulfilling the eight UC principles.

Table 6.4   Preliminary list of AI-based technologies enabling user-centricity functionalities

UC principle	UC functionality	Enabling AI-based solution
1-Digital interaction	Access to service	Live chat AI
		Concept aggregation (semantic)
		AI automated chat
2-Accessibility, security, availability, and usability	Authentication	Text to image generation
	Access for all	AI automated chat
		Data optimisation
		Speech synthesis and recognition
		Semantic analysis
		Live chat AI
	Inclusion for all	Automated translation
		Natural language processing
		Text-to-speech
3-Reduction of the administrative burden	Simplification of process	AI automated chat
		Data aggregation and matching
		Live chat AI
		Natural language processing
		Profile matching
		Concept aggregation-semantic
	Anticipation of needs	Data forecast
		Data aggregation and matching
		Semantic classification
	Once-only principle	AI automated chat
		Data aggregation and matching

---

4   https://joinup.ec.europa.eu/collection/public-sector-tech-watch
5   'About Technology Readiness Level' https://./cdn1.euraxess.org/career-development/researchers/manual-scientific-entrepreneurship/major-steps/trl

UC principle	UC functionality	Enabling AI-based solution
4-Digital delivery of public services	Improved data collection	Live chat AI
		Data aggregation and matching
	Monitoring	Machine learning
		Face/voice authentication
5-Citizen engagement	Listening to needs	Data aggregation and matching
		Semantic analysis
		Sentiment analysis
		Concept aggregation (semantic)
	Services coding	Semantic analysis
		Concept aggregation (semantic)
	Participation in debates	Speech recognition
		Live chat AI
	Idea feedback collection	Data aggregation and matching
		Semantic analysis
		AI automated chat
	Services improvement	Concept aggregation (semantic)
		Semantic analysis
6-Incentives for digital service use	Improve service efficiency	Data aggregation and matching
		Semantic analysis
		Data deep learning
		AI automated chat
		Concept aggregation (semantic)
		Live chat AI
		Speech recognition
		Data classification
		Machine learning and predictive analysis
		Voice to text mining and analysis
	Enable incentives	Data mining and classification
		Machine learning
		Face/voice authentication
	Enable business and benefits	Data mining and classification
7-Protection of personal data and privacy	Secure data collection procedures	Datasets compliance analysis
		AI *and blockchain*
	Data usage and elaboration	Machine learning and predictive analysis
		Data classification
		Semantic analysis
		Data forecast
8-Redress and complaint mechanisms	Redress and autonomy (*freedom to redress and autonomy to use a service*)	Face/voice authentication
		AI automated chat

AN EXAMPLE OF MEASUREMENT USING THE FRAMEWORK

The authors performed a desk exercise to test, validate, and use the framework idea to provide a preliminary implementation of AI-enabled UC. A maturity model is mandatory if the scope is the measurement of UC principles. Undeniably, a best, fittest, or most effective maturity model does not exist, and its selection is up to each analyst or policymaker. Available data and the scope of measurement rule the definition of the appropriate measurement tool.

The reason lies in the multi-layered definition of public service maturity, which shall consider the simultaneous role of 'four distinct readiness dimensions: technological, societal, organisational and legal' (Bruno et al., 2020a). Therefore, a complete maturity model ought to gather and consider data for weighting assessed technologies (linked to technology readiness level = TRL), societal acceptance (related to societal readiness level = SRL), business processes' readiness (related to organisational readiness level = ORL) and capabilities to operate within the boundaries of the law (related to legal readiness level = LRL). In the majority of cases, these data and information are not available at the same time.

In the desk exercise, the authors adopted a four-level scale maturity model (MM) for public service introduced by the Joint Research Centre (JRC) of the European Commission (Bruno et al., 2020a). The four-level scale identifies four maturity levels and follows the rules:

1 – **NAA (Not At All):** There is no evidence that any AI-based technology has been deployed to support implementing UC functionality in the public service at hand.
2 – **TSE (To Some Extent):** The AI-based technology has been implemented into the analysed public service, and there is some evidence that it addresses the UC functionality assigned. However, there are evident limits in implementing the AI-based service (the case), preventing its potential to support the mentioned functionality.
3 – **TGE (To a Great Extent):** Significant evidence shows that the AI-based technology is mature and adopted by the public administration owner or provider of the public service, though not reaching its full potential in supporting the UC functionality.
4 – **QLS (Quite Likely So):** It is possible to safely state that the AI-based technology is mature, fully operational, and effectively enhancing the UC functionality in the analysed public service. Evidence shows that other public administrations could replicate the AI-based technology in other AI-enabled cases.

These four levels are satisfactorily aligned with the concept and the phases of the 'AI appropriation' by the public sector recently introduced by the JRC: 'By this term [we mean] the union of adoption and implementation, also bearing in mind that individual and group users of a certain technology after it is embedded in an organisational setup make changes to both the technology and the environment, which inevitably feed back into both steps of the singled-out process' (Molinari et al., 2021).

The phases of AI-based technologies appropriation into the public sector go from testing and evaluating technology for its potential use to its permanent adoption through technology enhancement. Levels 2-TSE, 3-TGE, and 4-QLS represent these phases in our model. The additional level 1-NAA identifies the development stage of those technologies that are still not mature enough to fulfil or comply with integrating UC functionalities.

The authors deployed the MM and the framework with a test on 77 services listed in the AI-Watch Database,[6] selected by their coherence with the eligible AI-types. The database consists of AI-enabled PS gathered in more than two years of work by the JRC AI Watch team, and it fairly represents the AI-based landscape of PS in Europe. Given the little available

---

[6]   The AI Watch collection of cases has now migrated into the new observatory named Public Sector Tech Watch https://joinup.ec.europa.eu/collection/public-sector-tech-watch

data and reliable information about the cases, the results of the measurement exercise refer to a comprehensive vision of UC fulfilment based on the sample of 77 services rather than measuring a single service. The authors prefer not to publicly disclose the list of analysed services because the evaluation has been performed with existing information and, due to the experimental character of the framework, the results have not been agreed with the single public authorities delivering the services. This test is ongoing, and the authors are gathering valuable information about the framework's functioning and the implementation status of UC principles into AI-enabled public services.

Table 6.5 clarifies the distribution of the cases addressing each UC functionality and details the scores assigned to each enabling functionality (functionalities not addressed by services have a score = 1). Note that a score of 1 (i.e., no evidence) means there is no evidence of an AI-based solution enabling that functionality; it does not exclude that the specific UC functionality has been implemented by other technical means in the European public services landscape.

Table 6.5   *Representativeness of UC functionalities in the analysed cases and detail of assigned scores*

UC principles	UC functionalities	Cases	Total cases	Overall score	Functionality score
1-Digital interaction	Access to service	13	13	3.33	3.33
2-Accessibility, security, availability, and usability	Access for all	7			2.6
	Authentication	0	7	1.53	1 (*no evidence*)
	Inclusion for all	0			1 (*no evidence*)
3-Reduction of the administrative burden	Anticipation of needs	4			3.66
	Simplification of process	20	24	2.42	2.6
	Once-only digital process	0			1 (*no evidence*)
4-Digital delivery of public services	Improved data collection	1	1	2.50	4
	Monitoring	0			1 (*no evidence*)
	Idea feedback collection	0			1 (*no evidence*)
5-Citizen engagement	Listening to needs	5			2.5
	Participation in debates	2	9	1.90	2.5
	Services coding	0			1 (*no evidence*)
	Services improvement	2			2.5
6-Incentives for digital service use	Enable business and benefits	1			2
	Enable incentives	0	18	1.93	1 (*no evidence*)
	Improve service efficiency	17			2.8
7-Protection of personal data and privacy	Secure data collection procedures	0	5	1.63	1 (*no evidence*)
	Data usage and elaboration	5			2.25
8-Redress and complaint mechanisms	Redress and autonomy	0	0	1.00	1 (*no evidence*)

This desk exercise's first notable result is the possibility of measuring the fulfilment of UC principles through implementing AI-based solutions and technologies. It is a novelty to the authors' best knowledge.

Figure 6.5 provides a preliminary overview of the maturity level of AI-based solutions as an enabler of the principles in public services. The scores relate to the adopted MM (scale of 1 to 4).

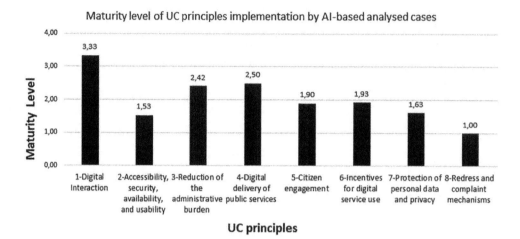

Figure 6.5   *Maturity level of the implementation of UC principles in PS, based on the analysed cases*

The framework is flexible; it allows for using many data sources with different data granularity availability. For example, policymakers and researchers could use other maturity models, such as the ones based on capability (Kim and Grant, 2010), responsiveness (Andersen et al., 2011), and qualitative (Zicari et al., 2021), to name a few.

CONCLUSIONS

This study defines the interrelations between AI deployment in the public sector and improved implementation of UC. The authors' approach targets simplifying the complexity of UC by downgrading it into smaller steps. It leverages matching two main layers of analysis: the inner mechanisms of UC and the role and potentialities of AI technologies in the public sector. The findings relate to these two layers in detail:

1. Performing a refined measurement of UC implementation in the public sector is possible. The study outputs the definition of a framework based on mapping the policy requirements into enabling functionalities. The proposed framework is a new approach. Disaggregating UC principles into functionalities makes this model flexible enough to be usable regardless of the technologies or the solutions one wants to analyse.
2. AI can support UC implementation in the public sector: the study aggregated a preliminary list of AI-based solutions fulfilling this goal (Table 6.4). It constitutes a relevant output because it supports evidence of the AI's role as an enabler of user-centric public services. The availability of AI-based solutions for the public sector is growing, and public administrations will develop and adopt many solutions, improving the implementation of the eight principles. The study proposes a way to measure the maturity of this process.

A preliminary test of the framework on a sample of 77 cases of AI-enabled public services feeds back that AI-based solutions are, to some extent, enabling the UC principles in Europe.

Adopting AI-based UC is still not a mature task, and the challenge related to its complete acquisition by the public sector is to also consider some governance issues that are both economic and structural. The desk exercise highlights evident limits in the acquisition and the implementation phases, preventing UC potentialities. Furthermore, the authors' analysis showed how several existing UC functionalities leverage non-AI-based solutions, although the AI-based ones seem more convenient. This finding strengthens some scholars' considerations about AI maturity in the public sector. For example, AI requires investment and joint consideration to achieve the digital transformation of the public sector (Tangi et al., 2022), from ensuring data access to developing AI models to generating end-user acceptance (Desouza et al., 2020).

From a formal perspective, AI-based solutions or technologies may not necessarily impact all the UC processes. We can say that the lack of AI-based solutions does not represent a functional gap of AI towards UC, but as far as the public sector includes AI-based services, we must understand how to comply with them.

As a final consideration, if well refined, the proposed framework for measuring the UC could help identify needs and spot functional gaps slowing down complete AI acquisition in the public sector.

REFERENCES

AI Watch. https://data.jrc.ec.europa.eu/dataset/7342ea15-fd4f-4184-9603-98bd87d8239a

Alzahrani, L., Al-Karaghouli, W., and Weerakkody, V. (2017). Analysing the critical factors influencing trust in e-government adoption from citizens' perspective: A systematic review and a conceptual framework. *International Business Review*, *26*(1), 164–175.

Andersen, K. N., Medaglia, R., Vatrapu, R., Henriksen, H. Z., and Gauld, R. (2011). The forgotten promise of e-government maturity: Assessing responsiveness in the digital public sector. *Government Information Quarterly*, *28*(4), 439–445.

Andrus, M., and Villeneuve, S. (2022). Demographic-reliant algorithmic fairness: Characterising the risks of demographic data collection in the pursuit of fairness. arXiv preprint arXiv:2205.01038.

Balatsas-Lekkas, A., and Grenman, K. (2021). Baseline survey report: Identifying current approaches to user-centricity assessment of digital public services. European Union. https://www.usercentricities.eu/results/public-deliverables

Berntzen, L. (2013). Citizen-centric eGovernment Services. In *The Sixth International Conference on Advances in Human-oriented and Personalised Mechanisms, Technologies, and Services (CENTRIC)* (pp. 132–136).

Bruno, I., Lobo, G., Covino, B. V., Donarelli, A., Marchetti, V., Panni, A. S., and Molinari, F. (2020, September). Technology readiness revisited: A proposal for extending the scope of impact assessment of European public services. In *Proceedings of the 13th International Conference on Theory and Practice of Electronic Governance* (pp. 369–380).

Bruno, I., Schiavone Panni, A., Marchetti, V., Molinari, F., and Valente Covino, B. (2020). *A Multi-dimensional Framework to Evaluate the Innovation Potential of Digital Public Services: A Step Towards Building an Innovative Public Services Observatory in the EU* (No. JRC121672). Joint Research Centre (Seville site).

Buhmann, A., and Fieseler, C. (2022). Deep learning meets deep democracy: Deliberative governance and responsible innovation in artificial intelligence. *Business Ethics Quarterly*, 1–34.

Desouza, K. C., Dawson, G. S., and Chenok, D. (2020). Designing, developing, and deploying artificial intelligence systems: Lessons from and for the public sector. *Business Horizons*, *63*(2), 205–213.

EURAXESS. About Technology Readiness Level, https://cdn1.euraxess.org/career-development/researchers/manual-scientific-entrepreneurship/major-steps/trl

European Commission. (2009). Ministerial declaration on eGovernment, https://ec.europa.eu/digital-single-market/sites/digital-agenda/files/ministerial-declaration-on-egovernment-malmo.pdf

European Commission. (2017). Ministerial Declaration on eGovernment – the Tallinn Declaration, European Union, https://digital-strategy.ec.europa.eu/en/news/ministerial-declaration-egovernment-tallinn-declaration

European Commission. (2020a). Berlin Declaration on Digital Society and Value-based Digital Government, https://digital-strategy.ec.europa.eu/en/news/berlin-declaration-digital-society-and-value-based-digital-government

European Commission. (2020b). *eGovernment Benchmark 2020: eGovernment that Works for the People*, https://www.capgemini.com/wp-content/uploads/2020/09/eGovernment-Benchmark-2020-Insight-Report.pdf

European Commission, Directorate-General for Communications Networks, Content and Technology. (2021a). *eGovernment Benchmark 2021: Entering a New Digital Government Era: Insight Report*, Publications Office, https://data.europa.eu/doi/10.2759/55088

European Commission, Directorate-General for Communications Networks, Content and Technology. (2021b). *eGovernment Benchmark: Method Paper 2020–2023*, Publications Office. https://data.europa.eu/doi/10.2759/640293

European Commission, Digital Economy and Society Index (DESI). (2021a). Released on 12 November 2021, retrievable at https://digital-strategy.ec.europa.eu/en/policies/desi

European Commission, Digital Economy and Society Index (DESI). (2021b). Methodological Note, retrievable at https://digital-strategy.ec.europa.eu/en/policies/desi

European Commission, Regulation of the European Parliament and of the Council laying down harmonised rules on artificial intelligence (Artificial Intelligence Act) and amending certain Union legislative acts, Brussels, 21.4.2021 COM(2021) 206 final 2021/0106 (COD).

European Commission and CapGemini. (2019). *eGovernment Benchmark 2019: Empowering Europeans through Trusted Digital Public Services. Insight Report*, Publications Office of the European Union, ISBN: 9789276110248

Gugliotta, A., Niglia, F., and Schina, L. (2013, June). An user-centric check of the available e-government services in Europe. In *13th European Conference on eGovernment ECEG 2013* (pp. 230–239). Como, Italy: Department of Theoretical and Applied Sciences, University of Insubria.

Kim, D. Y., and Grant, G. (2010). E-government maturity model using the capability maturity model integration. *Journal of Systems and Information Technology*, 12(3), 230–244.

Manzoni, M., Medaglia, R., Tangi, L., Van Noordt, C., Vaccari, L., and Gattwinkel, D. (2022). AI WatchRoad to the adoption of Artificial Intelligence by the Public Sector: A Handbook for Policymakers, Public Administrations and Relevant Stakeholders, EUR 31054 EN, Publications Office of the European Union, Luxembourg, ISBN 978-92-76-52131-0, doi:10.2760/693531, JRC129100.

Medaglia, R., and Tangi, L. (2022, October). The adoption of Artificial Intelligence in the public sector in Europe: drivers, features, and impacts. In *Proceedings of the 15th International Conference on Theory and Practice of Electronic Governance* (pp. 10–18).

Misuraca, G., and van Noordt, C. (2020). Overview of the use and impact of AI in public services in the EU, EUR 30255 EN. Publications Office of the European Union, Luxembourg. doi, 10, 039619.

Molinari, F., van Noordt, C., Vaccari, L., Pignatelli, F., and Tangi, L. (2021). *AI Watch. Beyond Pilots: Sustainable Implementation of AI in Public Services*, EUR 30868 EN, Publications Office of the European Union, Luxembourg, ISBN 978-92-76-42587-8, doi:10.2760/440212, JRC 126665.

National Interoperability Framework Observatory (NIFO) – Glossary https://joinup.ec.europa.eu/collection/nifo-national-interoperability-framework-observatory/glossary/term/user-centricity

Ozols, G., and Meyerhoff Nielsen, M. (2018). Connected government approach for customer-centric public service delivery: Comparing strategic, governance and technological aspects in Latvia, Denmark and the United Kingdom. https://collections.unu.edu/eserv/UNU:7347/Digital_Transformation_LV_DK_UK.pdf

Pinzon, C., Renard, R., and O'Neil, G. (2019). European Interoperability Framework (EIF) – implementation and governance models, DT4EU – European Commission.

Public Sector Tech Watch. https://joinup.ec.europa.eu/collection/public-sector-tech-watch

Renda, A., Arroyo, J., Fanni, R., Laurer, M., Sipiczki, A., Yeung, T., ... and Milio, S. (2021). Study to support an impact assessment of regulatory requirements for artificial intelligence in Europe. *European Commission: Brussels, Belgium.*

Ryan, M., and Stahl, B. C. (2021). Artificial intelligence ethics guidelines for developers and users: Clarifying their content and normative implications. *Journal of Information, Communication and Ethics in Society, 19*(1), 61–86.

Saqib, M., and Abdus Salam, A. (2018). Towards user centric e-government. In *User Centric E-Government* (pp. 161–165). Springer, Cham.

Smith, M., and Miller, S. (2022). The ethical application of biometric facial recognition technology. *AI & Society, 37*(1), 167–175.

Tangi, L., Soncin, M., Agasisti, T., and Noci, G. (2021). Exploring e-maturity in Italian local governments: Empirical results from a three-step latent class analysis. *International Review of Administrative Sciences*, 00208523211012752.

Tangi, L., Van Noordt, C., Combetto, M., Gattwinkel, D., and Pignatelli, F. (2022). AI Watch. European landscape on the use of Artificial Intelligence by the Public Sector, Publications Office of the European Union, Luxembourg, doi:10.2760/39336, JRC129301.

UserCentriCities (UCC) project, available at https://www.usercentricities.eu/

Valdés, G., Solar, M., Astudillo, H., Iribarren, M., Concha, G., and Visconti, M. (2011). Conception, development and implementation of an e-Government maturity model in public agencies. *Government Information Quarterly, 28*(2), 176–187.

Verdegem, P., and Verleye, G. (2009). User-centered E-Government in practice: A comprehensive model for measuring user satisfaction. *Government Information Quarterly, 26*(3), 487–497.

Weyerer, J.C., and Langer, P.F. (2019, June). Garbage in, garbage out: The vicious cycle of AI-based discrimination in the public sector. In *Proceedings of the 20th Annual International Conference on Digital Government Research* (pp. 509–511).

World Bank Group. (2018). *Indicators of Citizen-Centric Public Service Delivery.* World Bank.

Zicari, R. V., Brodersen, J., Brusseau, J., Düdder, B., Eichhorn, T., Ivanov, T., ... and Westerlund, M. (2021). Z-Inspection®: A process to assess trustworthy AI. *IEEE Transactions on Technology and Society, 2*(2), 83–97.

PART II

EXAMPLES AND CASE STUDIES OF AI IN PUBLIC MANAGEMENT

7. Application of artificial intelligence by Poland's public administration

Bartosz Rzycki, David Duenas-Cid[1] and Aleksandra Przegalińska

INTRODUCTION

This chapter presents an overview and analysis of artificial intelligence (AI)-driven solutions created and implemented by or with the support of the central public administration (PA) in Poland. We focus on GovTech Polska, a special unit within the Chancellery of the Prime Minister that acts as a hub for innovation in central public administration and in designing AI-based tools for other PA units. The development of solutions enabled by emerging technologies, such as AI, blockchain, or the Internet of Things (IoT), and the automation of services are drivers of innovative and sustainable change in organisations. Implementation of such technologies increases organisational flexibility, resilience, and fosters the production of social capital. However, in contrast to business, the PA's implementation of emerging technologies is generally slow and cumbersome. Thus, many civic-centric services lag behind in digitisation and digital transformation.

The type of adoption of emerging technologies also varies. Whereas business tends to take these technologies to scale and explore the newest technological trends, public administration (due to financial and human resource-related constraints) often focuses on pilot projects and is more hesitant to experiment with disruptive technologies.

Among emerging technologies, AI holds a special place. AI is a well-established and broad field of disciplines, including natural language processing, machine vision, machine learning, deep learning, or robotics. The term itself, however, is notoriously hard to define. We have defined AI as follows: 1) as a scientific discipline, where the term is applied to the development of systems endowed with intellectual processes characteristic of humans; and 2) as a field of implementation, where it is understood as the ability of a computer or computer-controlled robot to perform tasks commonly performed by intelligent beings (Dobrev, 2005; Kok et al., 2009).

According to some studies, AI is an umbrella term that encompasses a range of disciplines (Schuett, 2019), like NLP or machine vision. However, other studies underline crucial differences between deep neural network architectures and different machine learning models (Ngiam et al., 2011). According to the second approach, a predictive model based on regression or a simple rule-based chatbot would not necessarily fit within the scope of AI.

[1]   The work of David Duenas-Cid was funded with the project ELECTRUST (EU H2020 MSCA programme, grant agreement no. 101038055) and 'Dynamika (braku) zaufania w kreowaniu systemów głosowania internetowego' (Narodowe Centrum Nauki, OPUS-20 competition, grant agreement no. 2020/39/B/HS5/01661).

According to our hypothesis, AI applications sponsored and/or driven by the public administration in Poland can be classified as fitting under a very broad understanding of AI, covering advanced data analytics, supervised machine learning, and cloud-based solutions. Rarely do they cover applications of neural networks and fail to meet the criteria of narrowly understood AI, conceived as learning neural nets-based architectures.

However, a more modest approach to implementing AI and funding AI-based projects does not mean that the innovation does not occur. A change in the direction of more digital citizen-service is observable. Nevertheless, the question is whether the innovations implemented by the PA in Poland fulfill the condition of being classified as AI-based projects and which stakeholders from public administration are most significant in their development and implementation. Moreover, we are looking at the impact of these projects on PA as a whole. What are the roles played by the different stakeholders while incubating tech-driven innovation? Thus, we propose analysing a set of examples of AI innovation to respond to these questions, describe the field where innovation in AI for PA occurs, and highlight the potentialities and limitations of the current scenario. Moreover, we will examine the dynamics among stakeholders in AI-driven innovation building for PA. Here, we focus on whether we can classify the current scenario of AI-driven innovation as a collaborative strategy or if its shape results from the lack of clear leadership.

CHALLENGES AND ISSUES FOR DEVELOPING AI SYSTEMS IN PUBLIC ADMINISTRATION

Public administration can be understood as 'the part of the economy composed of public enterprise, including military, law enforcement, infrastructure, public transportation, healthcare and the work of elected officials' (Heady, 2001; Rhodes, 2000). Literature on the adoption of technological innovation in and by the public administration is quite vast and well developed. Still, when it comes to artificial intelligence, one can detect a shortage of publications (Campion et al., 2020). As van Noordt and Misuraca (2020, p. 15) state, 'the use of AI in the public sector is still in its infancy; more research is needed to truly understand how systems are adopted by public sector organizations'. The potential of AI-based solutions in PA has raised both expectations and fears (Wang et al., 2020, pp. 1–2). Some researchers portray AI as human beings' best hope to prevent extinction; others describe it as a threat, even predicting that AI will cause Armageddon.

In terms of PA, AI is expected to increase government efficiency, improve the interaction between citizens and governments (Mehr, 2017), and contribute to the redesign of public services, simplifying them and increasing their value for citizens through personalisation (Kuziemski and Misuraca, 2020). As Van Noord and Misuraca (2020) emphasise, AI should support more profound analysis of data, reduce repetitive tasks (Lima and Delen, 2020; Mehr, 2017), and facilitate the achievement of social development goals (Vinuesa et al., 2020).

Indeed, the adoption of AI technologies by PA is not exempt from challenges. Agarwal (2018) lists the following elements to consider when adopting AI: (1) ensuring a smooth transition to digital services including public and private stakeholders; (2) accommodating the transformation of the job market; (3) counteracting the potential decline of revenues derived from the transformation of the job market; (4) protecting consumers from potential biases in AI algorithms and ensuring equal treatment; and (5) ensuring privacy. Like Campion et al.

(2020), Dwivedi et al. (2019) and Sun and Medaglia (2019) summarise seven categories of challenges: (1) social; (2) economic; (3) technological; (4) data related; (5) organisational and managerial; (6) ethical; and (7) political, legal, and policy-related.

Both approaches consider the organisational dimension and how the adoption of AI by the public sector relies on a collaborative process. The central position of PA in the provision of living conditions for the citizenry and the fact that it is often excluded from fundamental and applied research concerning AI (Sousa et al., 2019) makes it of utmost importance to understand how administrations can adopt and implement this technology (Campion et al., 2020). Similarly, the inherent transversal nature of AI brings along the need to create collaborative approaches, gathering different types of stakeholders, from legal experts dealing with the frame where AI is to be inserted (Scherer, 2015; Veale et al., 2018), to IT specialists covering the lack of know-how and technical expertise that characterises PA (Agarwal, 2018; Holdren and Smith, 2016). PA's role, in this situation, is critical for making organisational decisions that will determine the further development of AI (Andrews, 2019). An excess of leadership by the PA can slow down the process and exclude stakeholders. But at the same time, a lack of involvement can entail losing control of the process by outsourcing (Agarwal, 2018) or failing to fulfill the needs and expectations of such developments.

The potential of multi-stakeholder collaboration in public sector innovation has already been analysed and described (Bekkers and Tummers, 2018; de Vries et al., 2016) and, concerning AI use in the public sector, its positive effects (Desouza, 2018; Susar and Aquaro, 2019; van Noordt and Misuraca, 2020) and challenges (Desouza and Jacob, 2017) have been defined. On the positive side, a collaborative strategy can help improve the organisational antecedents (van Noordt and Misuraca, 2020) in which AI is to be implemented, such as increasing the amount of available resources, know-how, skills, or infrastructures. It can also help to enlarge the capacities of the technology allowing its interoperability (Desouza, 2018), potential decentralisation (Montes and Goertzel, 2019), or ensuring that the regulations allow the full development of the projects in which different stakeholders are involved (Cath, 2018). Engaging and activating several partners enables benefitting from their potential and exponentially increasing the reach of the innovation. Amongst the challenges, we can highlight the integration of vast but typically fragmented quantities of data (Desouza and Jacob, 2017), the difficulties for the renovation of new organisational routines (Campion et al., 2020), and the need to create trust among stakeholders (Kankanhalli et al., 2019).

The development of a multi-stakeholder collaborative environment (especially in innovative and cross-cutting technologies) presents itself as a good framework for the development of distributed forms of governance, where the participants renegotiate their traditional roles and adopt different forms of relation to achieve their individual goals while contributing to the general-purpose set up by the leading partner, in this case, the PA. This collaborative governance frame is '[…] a type of governance in which public and private actors work collectively in distinctive ways, using processes, to establish laws and rules for the provision of public goods' (Ansell and Gash, 2008). The adoption of collaborative governance permits the addition of new priorities by participating stakeholders (Carlsson and Sandström, 2008), amongst them sustainability issues or common activities pertaining to peer-production. In the case of sustainable development, AI technologies might have an important impact on the monitoring of environmental protection, creating a better and more efficient holistic energy cycle, or forecasting climate alterations (Sharma et al., 2020).

This perspective involves the adoption of Open Innovation (OI) strategies by all stakeholders in the field, in their search for flexibility and innovativeness (Kankanhalli et al., 2017). Open innovation can be defined as a distributed innovation process based on purposefully managed knowledge flows across organisational boundaries (Chesbrough and Bogers, 2014, p. 17). In AI, OI has been used in the energy sector showing how its use accelerates the implementation of AI by following a natural flow of expert knowledge outside of the company, allowing the implementation of solutions that otherwise would have been out of their reach due to, for example, costs or development complexity (J. J. Yun et al., 2019). Its use replaces the internal learning accumulation by the emergence of new knowledge, allowing for more creative decision-making (J. Yun et al., 2016).

REGULATORY AND STRATEGY CONSIDERATIONS FOR AI DEVELOPMENT

In the Context of European and Global Trends

Poland is an interesting case study. On the one hand Polish policymakers are making a conscious effort to significantly accelerate technology adoption. On the other hand, compared to other EU Member States, Poland is technologically behind its peers which may decrease its future competitiveness.

According to a recent McKinsey (2021) report, Poland 'lags behind European leaders in both the level of cloud adoption and the rate at which adoption is progressing.' The country's level of cloud adoption is 14 times lower than that of the European Frontrunners and 1.5 times lower than the average for Central and Eastern Europe (CEE). The study adds that the 'adoption is progressing at an annual rate of 23 percent, below the 25 percent rate of the European Frontrunners and the 24 percent for Europe's five largest economies.' Even though the report limits itself to measuring cloud solutions adoption, the same can be said of other types of emerging technologies.

Nonetheless, the 2020s has brought an acceleration of the implementation of policies introducing AI solutions to PA. Since 2017, when Canada, Finland, Japan, and the UK created and pioneered some AI strategies, other countries have followed suit. Many of them established special task forces and AI expert groups and created digital strategies feeding the development of AI algorithms. The US National AI Initiative Office coordinates the implementation of a national AI strategy and cooperation among government, industry, and academia. Other countries, like New Zealand, are focusing on the ethical aspects of AI by creating a Data Ethics Advisory Group. Even so, the path to follow in terms of regulating AI is still a subject of debate. In some cases, the interest centres on biases in AI systems, safety (for example, autonomous cars), and data privacy, which pushes for the adoption of strict and binding rules. Yet, as of January 2022 these 'hard laws' are in the minority. The European Commission started working in 2020 on a set of Trustworthy AI regulations and passed three resolutions on intellectual property, civil liability, and AI ethics. In 2021, the European Commission released the first version of the Artificial Intelligence Act, setting rules for AI systems based on their risk. By January 2022, this proposal was being considered by the European Parliament and Member states who are seeking a compromise that would not inhibit the development of AI in the European Union region but ensure its safety and transparency.

These regulatory trends did not bypass Poland. In 2020 the Polish government released its 'Policy for the Development of Artificial Intelligence in Poland 2020' as one of the first parts of its 'Polish Productivity Strategy' and the 'Efficient and Modern State 2030 Strategy' programs. The document is a strategy outline for the growth of AI from the business and science perspectives and includes short-, medium-, and long-term goals set at 2023, 2027, and post-2027 respectively. A special emphasis is put on the role of AI in society, companies, science, education, international cooperation, and the public sector. Yet, the document does not contain specific information on programs that would achieve the government's goals. Despite its lack of detail, this initiative sets the vision for the decade and, in light of the European Parliament's work on AI-specific policies, it is also an introduction to an effort aimed at recognising AI as an indispensable segment of the country's growth. Thus, one can expect more legislative and regulatory documents to follow in the next few years.

However, the document also has limitations. For example, it does not refer to AI activity in defence and national security which may cause serious doubts about how the country handles AI solutions, such as lethal autonomous weapons. This may be particularly important as Poland is a NATO member directly exposed to hybrid and cyber conflicts because of its location on the Eastern flank. Moreover, the document was created without other similar initiatives, such as those by the European Union and UNESCO, in mind. That was because regulations and the vision for AI development within countries is an area of rapid development and Poland was one of the first countries to implement such blueprints. However, once the ground for common regulations in the European Union is established, Polish regulations will most probably need to be modified.

Poland's Strategy for Developing AI

In 2018 Poland accepted the 'Statute on the National Cybersecurity System' as a direct implementation of the EU Network and Information Security directive proposed by the European Commission. The Statute specified the functionality of the national cybersecurity system in order to ensure uninterrupted delivery of key services and digital services as well as the high level of security of ICT. The system includes operators of key and sensitive sectors, such as energy and healthcare, digital service providers, public administration bodies, and telecommunication systems. Moreover, the document specifies the responsibilities within companies, institutions, and the country and sets the blueprint for the reporting of cybersecurity incidents. In addition, new education activities were created to raise awareness in society and the private sector.

Poland is in the initial stages of its development of a collaborative ecosystem for innovation in AI for PA. The country has not created the conditions conducive to economic growth based on new technologies (Prusak, 2017) and lacks programs dedicated to preparing AI for implementation in PA. Nevertheless, recently implemented programs are trying to foster interaction between state-owned companies and private stakeholders to develop AI technologies (Skop et al., 2021), mediated by GovTech Polska. This institution, reporting directly to the prime minister of Poland, aims to provide PA bodies with innovative digital services and helps to centralise the dispersion amongst ministries of programs promoting and facilitating the implementation of new technologies.

A flagship initiative, the GovTech competition platform connects administration with the private technology sector as follows. The administration proposes a set of challenges to be met, and start-ups and small companies apply for the funds offered to Proofs of Concept, followed by full implementations of the proposed solution. At a smaller scale (SMEs and academia), GovTech established the 'E-Pionier' competition providing acceleration services from supervision of product implementation through technology consulting to funding projects. By January 2021, two complete editions had taken place, with 17 challenges solved. The proposed solutions, heavily reliant on the support of PA, transfer the financial costs of innovation to the donors following Mazzucato's (2011) guidelines, reducing risks for private stakeholders and linking the innovation to real problems. In parallel, it forces GovTech Polska to lead the AI innovation field, dealing with the growing network of agents and committing to implement the solutions.

Regarding the private sector, following the Polish Agency for Enterprise Development (Skowrońska and Tarnawa, 2021), 99.8 per cent of the companies in Poland are SMEs, creating a difficult environment for medium-large scale innovation implementation. Previous research has already highlighted the lack of capacity of the Polish SME sector to conduct innovation and its dependence on the institutional system (Lewandowska and Stopa, 2019), and the role of Polish enterprises as innovation adopters, not as creators (Runiewicz-Wardyn, 2013, 2020).

The resulting scenario is characterised by fewer identifiable stakeholders, with public institutions the only ones with the capacity to develop AI for general purposes. The Polish government, aware of this situation, has repeatedly pledged its support for the doctrine proposed by Mazzucato (2011) that the state should lead innovation in technology because the private sector is neither willing nor able to invest in risky sectors. Innovation investments entail risks that scare private investors and vendors due to a lack of certainty on its capacity to generate revenue. The state can cover such uncertainty by acting as a pioneer in innovative sectors. The GovTech Polska initiative fits this scenario, incentivising innovation in technology for governance, leading the innovation of AI, and has already published a 'Strategy on Artificial Intelligence' as a roadmap for its future development.

In general, the ecosystem built by many Polish institutions, especially GovTech and Polish Development Fund, closely follows the strategy of swarm intelligence, creating an environment that fosters innovation in AI. These institutions decided against implementing AI and related technological solutions by outsourcing the product development to software companies with strict guidelines on how the product should work. In contrast, they harnessed the advantages of collective intelligence, defined by Yun et al. (2019) as using the power of many people to solve a difficult problem as a group, by creating programs where open calls for solutions are available to anyone and only problems to be solved are stated. Moreover, crowdsourcing programs in the form of hackathons and more recently 'climathons' (hackathons for climate-friendly technological solutions for Polish cities) involve the participation of public administration institutions. Together, these activities constitute two forms of collective intelligence described by Yun et al. (2019): flow-based (groups working on the same activities and problems) and dialogic (engagement in a dialogue). Furthermore, these activities link AI and collective innovation. This included solutions aiming a better understanding of data about citizens and helping to implement more inclusive decision-making processes (for example, a big data system created by the Ministry of Digitization for investigating the geographical diversity of digital competencies among Polish citizens).

CASE STUDIES

Selection of Case Studies

Given this scenario, we opted for conducting an exploratory study of the Polish situation based on interviews with stakeholders, assuming the capacity of this methodological strategy for the early examination of the topic and opening avenues for further research. An initial overview of the institutional environment leading the development of AI for the Public Sector positioned GovTech Polska as a core actor in the AI development strategy. With that as our pivotal unit, we developed three case studies of related projects, based on companies or institutions that participated in GovTech funding competitions: the Ministry of Digitalization, Orlen, and Ministry of Health. We use the experience of these vendors in their interaction with GovTech Polska to evaluate the process and extract information for mapping the field. This methodological approach is common in the research in AI as seen in the work of Kuziemski and Misuraca (2020), and Van Noord and Misuraca (2020), both using a three-case study to compare international examples of AI adoption by PA, the difference with our proposal being the scale of the cases (international to national).

Following Yin's (2018) case study replication logic, we combined case studies that replicate the type of relation with GovTech Polska with others with contrasting connections with the same unit. For every case study, we conducted in-depth interviews and analysis of secondary data. The interviews were approached inductively, to reveal the underlying elements that connect the practical development of AI projects with the institutional framework and the theoretical background (Thomas, 2006).

Presenting the Case Studies

Hereafter we will present the results of our case studies, including the following information: (1) a description of the vendor providing the service; (2) the recipient of the innovation; (3) an explanation of the motivation of the project; (4) a description of the problem; (5) the solution; (6) the role played by GovTech; (7) advantages and benefits; and (8) problems and limitations of the proposed solution. The information generates a discussion of a map of stakeholders, and follows a similar descriptive purpose to the model proposed by Kuziemski and Misuraca (2020), who focused on goals, drivers, barriers and risks. We focus on specific AI projects.

Datawise[2]
Datawise is a startup that specialises in the analysis, delivery, and integration of data and big data for different clients from big corporations to SMEs. They offer customer segmentation services based on SIM card data, geomarketing, data merging using CRM systems, and data storing and analysis. They use AI in image data extraction and for prognosis-based tasks.

Recipient of the technology: Ministry of Digitization

Motivation: Financial, especially the possibility of obtaining funding in the proof-of-concept stage. The challenge topic relates directly to the services provided by the vendor (for example, geolocation and local context data extraction using big data), and its capacity to adjust those

---

[2]   http://www.datawise.pl/

services to private companies and PA, so the public sector might easily become a potential client.

Description of the problem: The Ministry of Digitization aims to improve the digital skills and competencies of the citizens to increase their capacity to exploit the opportunities provided by the internet. To track and compare the evolution of these skills, a set of indicators is collected by all EU Member States. However, due to budget and time constraints, the statistics cannot scale down and cover Poland's internal geographical disparity, complicating the allocation of resources and projects in the areas and regions of Poland where they would be more needed.

Solution: Datawise proposed merging the available data published by the Ministry of Digitization with big data obtained from mobile network operators. This data registers online behaviours, intensity, and type of websites visited by the customers, allowing its geographical fragmentation. Combining these two datasets reveals the geographical diversity of digital competencies, for example, the percentage of citizens using online banking services. The final solution consisted of a visual map (front end) and a model with data streams on the back end created using big data and statistical algorithms, allowing data to be updated annually.

Role of GovTech: Intermediation. They set up a ready-to-implement infrastructure for the cooperation between companies and beneficiaries – including contracts, negotiations, and formalised contests – which significantly accelerates the process compared with independent management by each administrative unit. GovTech also provides flexible contracts adapted to the characteristics of the technology and industry, including legal foundations, so that companies providing solutions are more willing to participate. This standardisation of the process by which cooperation is initialised constitutes one of Datawise's most significant advantages.

Advantages and benefits:

- Speed of process, professional cooperation, responsiveness
- Reduction of bureaucratic obstacles
- Capacity to use the competition as a self-promotion tool to build credibility among partners and potential clients
- Transparent and well-organised competition
- Access to valuable data
- Financial reward adequate to the complexity of the problem

Problems and limitations:

- Lack of final implementations even though a product has been created
- Lack of expressed reasons for not implementing the product

Veturai[3]

Veturai is a start-up that offers machine learning and big data solutions to various industries, including healthcare and manufacturing. Examples of AI projects include detecting objects and potential risks for autonomous vehicles, algorithmic trading, demand forecasting, and dynamic product pricing. Veturai provides services to private and public units. Some of the services are as follows:

---

3   https://veturai.com/

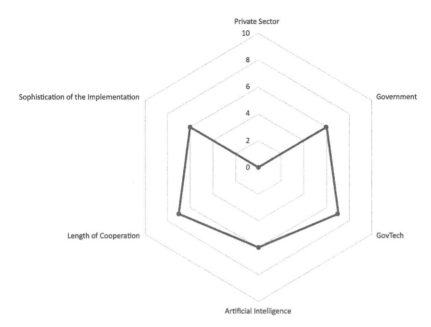

Source: Self-creation, 2022.

Figure 7.1   Ministry of Digitization – assessment on its involvement during collaboration

– detection of overuse and outliers in systems
– satellite imagery analytics
– traffic optimisation and simulation
– adaptive systems for intelligent traffic management
– urban planning
– social media analytics

Recipient of the technology: PKN Orlen.[4] PKN Orlen[5] is a Polish state-owned oil refiner and petrol retailer, with over 2850 fuel stations and 40 petrochemical products marketed to over 60 countries.

Motivation: Financial rewards and networking opportunities. It was an opportunity to create bonds with PA and state-owned companies and to identify their problems. It allows Orlen to trace a strategy of potential uses of AI solutions to respond to these problems. In this way, the company increases the knowledge of future trends and technologies that will be profitable in the medium-term. National and international contracts with PA provide start-ups with a reputation that can facilitate collaboration with other corporations (in this case, with the recipient of the solution, Orlen) and attract new clients.

Description of the problem: The creation of a model for object detection from camera images for security reasons.

[4]   https://www.orlen.pl/pl
[5]   https://www.orlen.pl/en/about-the-company/what-we-do

Solution: Veturai will be responsible for piloting and implementing the automatic vehicle identification mechanism, which will support the transaction handling system through the ORLEN mobile application ('mFlota'). This functionality will simplify and automate the current way of verifying refueled vehicles. The system will be based on scanning specially designed holographic markers placed on the vehicle window. The machine learning algorithms (computer vision techniques) will verify the features of vehicles assigned to fleet cards.

Role of GovTech: Laying the foundation for the future cooperation between the receiver of the technology (PA) and a technological company, including legal procedures, formalised every step of the contests and contracts adjusted to the characteristics of technical cooperation. GovTech's role is finished once the project is submitted. It does not participate in the election of the winners and remains neutral thereafter. Accordingly, the final contract between the start-up (Veturai) and Orlen, including budget details for its implementation, is negotiated without GovTech.

Advantages and benefits:

- Strong emphasis on anonymity during the contest – under no circumstances should the company's name be mentioned (for example, in a presentation or the programming code). Even during in-person meetings, logos, names, or even hardware names should be anonymous. As start-ups admit, they found it one of GovTech's most positive practices.
- Easing risk-taking – since contests and the whole infrastructure was provided by GovTech, the public administration institutions did not feel pressure or a financial burden. Start-up admits that beneficiaries were more willing to take risks than if they organised competition independently.
- Bureaucracy reduction.
- Positive attitude and willingness to cooperate by the beneficiary.
- The fact that GovTech organises the contests makes the system more effective and resilient – no place for mistakes or corruption.

Problems and limitations:

- Lack of standardised procedures during technical dialogues: some companies require non-disclosure agreements before any consultation, while others do not. Some companies need start-ups to bring the prototype in this initial stage. It makes it difficult for technology providers to plan their work and deters them from further involvement.
- Significant delay between winning the contest and signing the contract.
- Limited understanding of technology by the beneficiaries: capabilities, opportunities, and ways of measuring the effectiveness of its implementation.
- Budgetary and legal constraints: budget limits make it difficult to provide long-term solutions. After the successful implementation of a system, some public institutions want to invest in new products supplied by the same start-up/technological company. Still, they face the limitations that GovTech contests involve: the Polish Government Procurement Act limits the amount that a public institution can spend on a project.
- The contest should ensure that all the participants use the same datasets to train machine learning models when submitting the applications.
- Find fairer ways to assess the applications. For example, some companies use expensive hardware to train models, which are not necessarily more effective. Moreover, this hard-

ware would not be used in practice (i.e., in public administration units) to run algorithms, so it does not make any sense to artificially achieve better results to qualify for the next stage. More emphasis should be put on the accuracy of the models and how the product fits its actual environment.

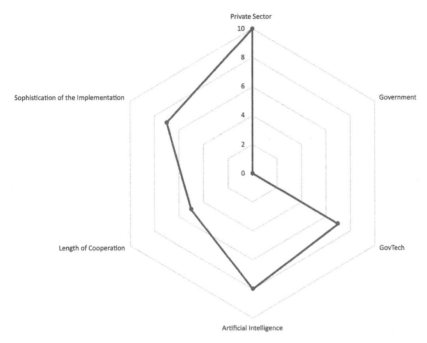

Source: Self-creation, 2022.

Figure 7.2   Orlen – assessment on its involvement during collaboration

Logicai.io[6]

Logicai.io is a young Polish software house focusing on statistical analysis and machine learning technologies. From the advisory role to the actual implementation, the company provides AI services, including data science, reinforcement learning, customer analytics, and computer vision. The company also offers workshops to educate enterprises and AI boot camps for teams and individuals. The company implemented, among others, prediction algorithms, recommendations for search engines, and employee scheduling optimisation for clients such as Alior Bank, Dubai Police Force, Trivago, and Dior.

Recipient of the technology: Ministry of Health

Motivation: Promotion and scope of the contest. As a young company, its participation in competitions helps to promote the company's services in order to compete with more prominent organisations on deep-tech solutions. In addition, the challenge proposed in the contest matches with the services that Logicai provides. Unlike the previous cases, financial reasons

---

6   https://logicai.io/

did not play an important role as the company broke even after calculating all the costs of building a product.

Description of the problem: Financial fraud among the publicly funded health services billing: showing higher rates than the actual costs of the services provided (upcoding and unbundling) by suppliers who want to be paid more than the negotiated amount.

Solution: Logicai proposed an Abuse Detection Module: a set of tools consisting of a web application with ten ML fraud detection algorithms whose task is to spot patterns of potential abuse and an exploratory module that enables browsing through available data to examine the information based on specific parameters set by the user.

Role of GovTech: Laying the foundation for the future cooperation between the recipient of the technology (PA) and a technological company, including legal procedures, formalising every step of the contests, and contracts adjusted to the characteristics of technical cooperation. Yet, GovTech's role is finished once the project is submitted; the entity does not participate in the election of the winners and stays neutral thereafter. Accordingly, the final contract between the start-up and Ministry of Health, including budget details for its implementation, is negotiated without GovTech.

Advantages and benefits:

- Reduction of bureaucracy.
- High responsiveness, organisation, and punctuality of the beneficiary's organisations.
- The open form of the contest is one of the key advantages in the eyes of start-ups, as it allows smaller companies to participate in similar conditions.
- The project's beneficiary is aware of the limitations, advantages, disadvantages, possibilities, and specifications of the implemented technology.
- The competition helped the company build its market position, promote itself, and gain a reputation.

Problems and limitations:

- Limited amount of available data to build a product due to its high sensitivity.
- Reduced budget for the project, meaning that it could not hire additional employees because they struggle with deadlines.
- Financial rewards and other benefits do not outweigh the complexity of the task and are associated with the time necessary to complete.

MAPPING POLAND'S AI ECOSYSTEM

The information collected during the fieldwork allowed us to answer the questions posed in the introduction. When it comes to the roles played by the different stakeholders in the field of AI innovation in Poland, we can enumerate the functions of agents in their area of influence:

- Funding: Entities that directly administer funds or assist in obtaining funds from European Union programs or creating special programs with the funds in the form of grants.
- Research and Education: Entities that contribute to increased knowledge of public administration's employees when it comes to new technologies and their usage.

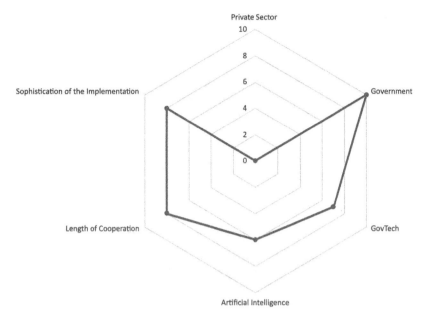

Source: Self-creation, 2022.

Figure 7.3   Ministry of Health – assessment on its involvement during collaboration

- Creation of governmental programs aimed at supporting technical knowledge among society.
- Conducting research that directly or indirectly supports the government.
- Technology Implementation: Public entities that directly implement technologies within public administration.
- Ecosystem Building: Entities focusing on programs that promote innovation within public administration space, such as hackathons.
- Acceleration and Consulting Services: Entities that directly help private companies build and implement new technologies. Consulting can refer to business, funding, and technological space.

Based on these categories and using publicly available information and results of our fieldwork, we can map the organisations within the Polish Innovation Ecosystem. These include public entities controlled by the government and other innovation providers that work with governments (national and regional) and state-owned companies. Some of the entities, such as the National Research Institute, are placed in multiple categories because they create dedicated programs with different purposes. Figure 7.4 depicts how different actors fit into and interact with distinctive fields.

When it comes to AI-driven innovations in public administration in Poland, the landscape became much brighter. Considering Poland's difficulties while joining the EU because of fewer funding opportunities and an underdeveloped business ecosystem, the sector has advanced rapidly. Also, most of the PA programs of the map are in their first or second edition. The tools, methods and market responses are still being carefully tested to detect possibilities

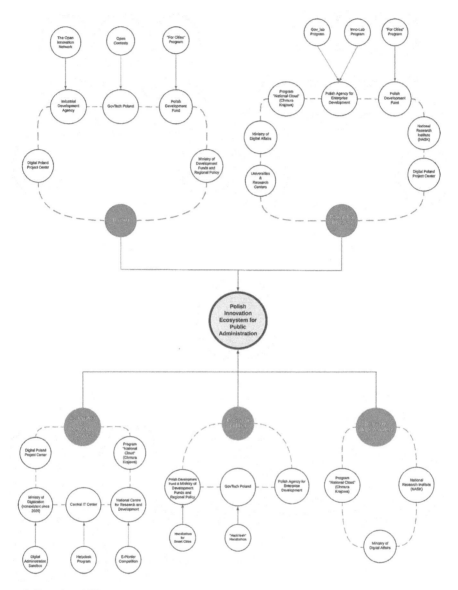

Source: Self-creation, 2022.

Figure 7.4   *Map of Polish innovation ecosystem*

for improvement. So, although the implementation has been far from perfect, it is still a crucial step forward for the country's building of a network of stakeholders and introducing AI.

Still, the focus of innovation in PA is not only on AI. There are many paths to a more effi-cient and effective PA and reducing it to the use of AI would limit the impact of digitisation. Therefore, many programs include multiple technologies aiming to create an ecosystem of digital innovation, in which AI is just a valuable part. The value here lies in the interoperability of the different technologies to ensure the usefulness and capacity of integrating the innovations.

Whereas this scenario seems a logical outcome of the situation described, while analysing how innovation in AI occurs, one can notice how the lack of a clear path of development makes it difficult to meet the expectations of PA. On the one hand, PA lacks the skills and competencies amongst its employees and decision-makers to fully benefit from AI implementation (or to understand the risks associated with certain technologies). In the case studies analysed, it became clear that technology implementation is more effective if the organisation already has the requisite skillset, and the civil servants are trained to cooperate with the private sector. Nevertheless, because PA is dealing with emerging technologies that are still in their infancy, particularly when it comes to their mainstream adoption, PA has a hard time navigating how best to invest in them. Finally, the accelerated transformation of the ecosystem (and the ever-faster innovation pace estimated for the following years) creates an urgent need for a sustainable political environment to ensure the stability of the development plans and the resource availability for fostering innovation. Innovation thrives when long-term vision and clear development plans are in place, and this scenario differs from the frequent institutional and leadership change that Poland has witnessed in recent years.

LIMITATIONS

The main limitation of this study is its introductory nature and innovativeness in the Polish context. The lack of previous studies describing the Polish reality and the innovativeness of the use of AI in PA challenges the creation of a solid theoretical foundation for the research. Even if contradictory, this is, at the same time, its added value: the current piece represents the first attempt at describing the Polish reality and, as such, has great value for the future of the research.

The ecosystem presented should therefore be taken as an introductory map of the institutional agents relevant to the development of AI (especially GovTech Polska) but does not cover all the possible agents at lower administrative levels. In addition, the map represents a fixed photography of a vivid and mutable reality whose validity is limited in time. Still, the data and its interpretation shed light on some of the main properties of the interaction between PA and providers of AI-related innovation.

Further research should consider using a narrower focus on the development and uses of AI frameworks in designated sectors like agriculture or citizen services, or expanding the research sample to find regularities and tendencies for comparison. The further occurrence of GovTech Polska contests will certainly enlarge the availability of data, easing the development of its analysis and adding new sectors to those described in the previous case studies.

CONCLUSIONS

The question we tried to answer is whether the current innovations implemented by the PA in Poland are significant in fulfilling the needs and expectations of the Public Administration itself. Our research aligns with the conclusions raised by Misuraca and Van Noordt (2020), who identify a gap between the transformative potential of AI, its adoption and use.

Automatisation should be one stage in the improvement of public administration, but even though it is not difficult to implement solutions for automating decisions under administrative discretion, 'general clauses or valuation standards' pose a real challenge. Similarly, Etscheid (2019) argues that 'the constant increase of technical possibilities makes the automation of processes more and more attractive for the public administration, but not all administrative processes can be automated from a technical point of view.' From thousands of administrative procedures, decision-makers must select those processes which they consider appropriate for partial or full automation. Taking this into account, we emphasise that even though many of the projects studied here do not fit exactly into a more purist approach to what AI is, and are focused on data analytics, they still affect PA's functioning and greatly contribute to building digital skills and competences across the whole ecosystem. We have also revealed the roles played by the different stakeholders while incubating tech-driven innovation. These roles seem to be robust, exchangeable, and adoptable by different agents. For instance, the funding role may be directed either towards serving the citizens, or internally towards enhancing the technological capabilities of the public administration. Similarly, the roles of a funding institution and the accelerator can be exchangeable.

The Polish ecosystem is still in its infancy and the flexibility of different agents will presumably allow for its rapid growth and complexity. The diversity of actors already present in the current ecosystem depicts the potential for a collaborative environment in which the dialogue between the public and the private interests might contribute to the implementation of AI uses while developing their own goals. Public Administration, in turn, needs to jump into the 'paradox of change' (Tilson et al., 2010), providing a sufficient level of stability (in terms of infrastructures, funds, and applicability of the technology) to ensure the evolution and dynamism of the ecosystem. Finally, in the next years we will experience a significant change of landscape regarding the directions that AI implementation will take in all European Member States, among other elements, because of the upcoming AI Act. This regulation puts great emphasis on trustworthy and transparent AI incubation and enforces reporting whenever black-boxed deep learning systems are implemented in decision-making in various crucial areas, like medical diagnosis or consumer banking. On one hand, this regulation can reshape how AI is being used in PA and redirect attention to simpler machine learning models, but on the other hand it can incentivise PA to use AI more frequently because of higher standards of application.

REFERENCES

Agarwal, P. K. (2018). Public administration challenges in the world of AI and bots. *Public Administration Review*, *78*(6), 917–921. https://doi.org/10.1111/puar.12979

Andrews, L. (2019). Public administration, public leadership and the construction of public value in the age of the algorithm and 'big data.' *Public Administration*, *97*(2), 296–310. https://doi.org/10.1111/padm.12534

Ansell, C., and Gash, A. (2008). Collaborative governance in theory and practice. *Journal of Public Administration Research and Theory*. https://doi.org/10.1093/jopart/mum032

Bekkers, V., and Tummers, L. (2018). Innovation in the public sector: Towards an open and collaborative approach. In *International Review of Administrative Sciences*. https://doi.org/10.1177/0020852318761797

Campion, A., Gasco-Hernandez, M., Jankin Mikhaylov, S., and Esteve, M. (2020). Overcoming the challenges of collaboratively adopting artificial intelligence in the public sector. *Social Science Computer Review*, 1–16. https://doi.org/10.1177/0894439320979953

Carlsson, L., and Sandström, A. (2008). Network governance of the commons. *International Journal of the Commons*, 2(1), 33–54. https://www.jstor.org/stable/26522989

Cath, C. (2018). Governing artificial intelligence: Ethical, legal and technical opportunities and challenges. In *Philosophical Transactions of the Royal Society A: Mathematical, Physical and Engineering Sciences*. https://doi.org/10.1098/rsta.2018.0080

Chesbrough, H., and Bogers, M. (2014). Explicating open innovation: Clarifying an emerging paradigm for understanding innovation. In H. Chesbrough, W. Vanhaverbeke, and J. West (eds), *New Frontiers in Open Innovation* (pp. 3–28). Oxford University Press.

de Vries, H., Bekkers, V., and Tummers, L. (2016). Innovation in the public sector: A systematic review and future research agenda. *Public Administration*, 94(1), 146–166. https://doi.org/10.1111/padm.12209

Desouza, K. C. (2018). Delivering artificial intelligence in government: New IBM Center for the Business of Government Report.

Desouza, K. C., and Jacob, B. (2017). Big Data in the public sector: Lessons for practitioners and scholars. *Administration and Society*, 49(7), 1043–1064. https://doi.org/10.1177/0095399714555751

Dobrev, D. (2005). A definition of artificial intelligence. *Mathematica Balkanica, New Series*, 19, 67–74.

Dwivedi, Y. K., Hughes, L., Ismagilova, E., Aarts, G., Coombs, C., Crick, T., Duan, Y., Dwivedi, R., Edwards, J., Eirug, A., Galanos, V., Ilavarasan, P. V., Janssen, M., Jones, P., Kar, A. K., Kizgin, H., Kronemann, B., Lal, B., Lucini, B., … Williams, M. D. (2019). Artificial Intelligence (AI): Multidisciplinary perspectives on emerging challenges, opportunities, and agenda for research, practice and policy. *International Journal of Information Management*. https://doi.org/10.1016/j.ijinfomgt.2019.08.002

Etscheid, J. (2019). *Artificial Intelligence in Public Administration* (pp. 248–261). https://doi.org/10.1007/978-3-030-27325-5_19

Heady, F. (2001). *Public Administration, a Comparative Perspective*. Marcel Dekker.

Holdren, J., and Smith, M. (2016). *Preparing for the Future of Artificial Intelligence* (p. 58). Executive Office of the President of the United States. https://obamawhitehouse.archives.gov/ sites/default/files/whitehouse_files/microsites/ostp/NSTC/ preparing_for_the_future_of_ai.pdf

Kankanhalli, A., Charalabidis, Y., and Mellouli, S. (2019). IoT and AI for smart government: A research agenda. *Government Information Quarterly*, 36(2), 304–309. https://doi.org/10.1016/j.giq.2019.02.003

Kankanhalli, A., Zuiderwijk, A., and Tayi, G. (2017). Open innovation in the public sector: A research agenda. *Government Information Quarterly*, 34(1), 84–89.

Kok, J. N., Boers, E. J. W., Kosters, W. A., and van der Putten, P. (2009). Artificial Intelligence: Definition, trends, techniques and cases. In J. N. Kok (ed.), *Artificial Intelligence: Encyclopedia of Life Support Systems* (pp. 270–299). Eolss.

Kuziemski, M., and Misuraca, G. (2020). AI governance in the public sector: Three tales from the frontiers of automated decision-making in democratic settings. *Telecommunications Policy*, 44(6), 101976. https://doi.org/10.1016/j.telpol.2020.101976

Lewandowska, A., and Stopa, M. (2019). Do SME's innovation strategies influence their effectiveness of innovation? Some evidence from the case of Podkarpackie as peripheral region in Poland. *Equilibrium*, 14(3), 521–536. https://doi.org/10.24136/eq.2019.025

Lima, M. S. M., and Delen, D. (2020). Predicting and explaining corruption across countries: A machine learning approach. *Government Information Quarterly*, 37(1). https://doi.org/10.1016/j.giq.2019.101407

Mazzucato, M. (2011). *The Entrepreneurial State*. Demos.

McKinsey & Company. (2021). *Cloud 2030: Capturing Poland's Potential for Accelerated Digital Growth*. https://www.mckinsey.com/capabilities/mckinsey-digital/our-insights/cloud-2030-capturing-polands-potential-for-accelerated-digital-growth

Mehr, H. (2017). Artificial intelligence for citizen services and government. *Harvard Ash Center Technology & Democracy*, August, 1–16. https://ash.harvard.edu/files/ash/files/artificial_intelligence_for_citizen_services.pdf

Montes, G. A., and Goertzel, B. (2019). Distributed, decentralized, and democratized artificial intelligence. In *Technological Forecasting and Social Change.* https://doi.org/10.1016/j.techfore.2018.11.010

Ngiam, J., Khosla, A., Kim, M., Nam, J., Lee, H., and Ng, A. (2011). Multimodal deep learning. In L. Getoor and T. Sceffer (eds), *ICML'11: Proceedings of the 28th International Conference on International Conference on Machine Learning* (pp. 689–696). Omnipress.

Prusak, A. (2017). Development of new technologies in the context of the EU funded projects in Poland. In S. Arsovski, D. Tadić, and M. Stefanovic (eds), *2nd International Conference on Quality of Life* (pp. 407–415). University of Kragujevac.

Rhodes, R. A. W. (2000). The governance narrative: Key findings and lessons from the Erc's Whitehall programme. *Public Administration, 78*(2), 345–363. https://doi.org/10.1111/1467-9299.00209

Runiewicz-Wardyn, M. (2013). *Knowledge Flows, Technological Change and Regional Growth in the European Union.* Springer International Publishing. https://doi.org/10.1007/978-3-319-00342-9

Runiewicz-Wardyn, M. (2020). W kierunku otwartych ekosystemów innowacji w Polsce: szanse i wyzwania. *Kwartalnik Nauk o Przedsiębiorstwie, 55*(2), 15–27. https://doi.org/10.33119/KNoP.2020.55.2.2

Scherer, M. U. (2015). Regulating artificial intelligence systems: Risks, challenges, competencies, and strategies. *SSRN Electronic Journal, 29*(2). https://doi.org/10.2139/ssrn.2609777

Schuett, J. (2019). A legal definition of AI. *SSRN Electronic Journal.* https://doi.org/10.2139/ssrn.3453632

Sharma, G. D., Yadav, A., and Chopra, R. (2020). Artificial intelligence and effective governance: A review, critique and research agenda. *Sustainable Futures, 2,* 100004. https://doi.org/10.1016/j.sftr.2019.100004

Skop, M., Orsolya, V., Alishani, A., Arsovski, G., and Izdebski, K. (2021). *alGOVrithms 2.0: The State of Play.* https://opendatakosovo.org/wp-content/uploads/2021/03/ODK_alGOVrithms-2-0_report-2021_1.pdf

Skowrońska, A., and Tarnawa, A. (2021). *Raport o stanie sektora małych i średnich przedsiębiorstw w Polsce.* https://www.parp.gov.pl/component/publications/publication/raport-o-stanie-sektora-malych-i-srednich-przedsiebiorstw-w-polsce-2021

Sousa, W. G., de Melo, E. R. P., de Bermejo, P. H. D. S., Farias, R. A. S., and Gomes, A. O. (2019). How and where is artificial intelligence in the public sector going? A literature review and research agenda. *Government Information Quarterly, 36*(4), 101392. https://doi.org/10.1016/j.giq.2019.07.004

Sun, T. Q., and Medaglia, R. (2019). Mapping the challenges of artificial intelligence in the public sector: Evidence from public healthcare. *Government Information Quarterly.* https://doi.org/10.1016/j.giq.2018.09.008

Susar, D., and Aquaro, V. (2019). Artificial intelligence: Opportunities and challenges for the public sector. *ACM International Conference Proceeding Series, Part F1481*(2017), 418–426. https://doi.org/10.1145/3326365.3326420

Thomas, D. R. (2006). A general inductive approach for analyzing qualitative evaluation data. *American Journal of Evaluation, 27*(2), 237–246. https://doi.org/10.1177/1098214005283748

Tilson, D., Lyytinen, K., and Sørensen, C. (2010). Digital infrastructures: The missing IS research agenda. *Information Systems Research, 21*(4), 748–759. https://doi.org/10.1287/isre.1100.0318

van Noordt, C., and Misuraca, G. (2020). Exploratory insights on artificial intelligence for government in Europe. *Social Science Computer Review,* 089443932098044. https://doi.org/10.1177/0894439320980449

Veale, M., Binns, R., and Edwards, L. (2018). Algorithms that remember: Model inversion attacks and data protection law. *Philosophical Transactions of the Royal Society A: Mathematical, Physical and Engineering Sciences, 376*(2133). https://doi.org/10.1098/rsta.2018.0083

Vinuesa, R., Azizpour, H., Leite, I., Balaam, M., Dignum, V., Domisch, S., Felländer, A., Langhans, S. D., Tegmark, M., and Fuso Nerini, F. (2020). The role of artificial intelligence in achieving the Sustainable Development Goals. In *Nature Communications.* https://doi.org/10.1038/s41467-019-14108-y

Wang, Y., Zhang, N., and Zhao, X. (2020). *Understanding the Determinants in the Different Government AI Adoption Stages: Evidence of Local Government Chatbots in China.* 1–21. https://doi.org/10.1177/0894439320980132

Yin, R. K. (2018). *Case Study Research and Applications: Design and Methods* (6th ed.). SAGE.

Yun, J. J., Jeong, E., Zhao, X., Hahm, S. D., and Kim, K. (2019). Collective intelligence: An emerging world in open innovation. *Sustainability*, *11*(16), 4495. https://doi.org/10.3390/su11164495

Yun, J.J., Lee, D., Ahn, H., Park, K., and Yigitcanlar, T. (2016). Not deep learning but autonomous learning of open innovation for sustainable artificial intelligence. *Sustainability*, *8*(8), 797. https://doi.org/10.3390/su8080797

8. The effect of algorithmic tools on public value considerations in participatory processes: the case of regulations.gov

Sarah Giest, Alex Ingrams and Bram Klievink

INTRODUCTION

Public values governance has become a major subject in contemporary public administration literature (Bryson, Crosby, and Bloomberg, 2014). This focus comes through strongly in recent work on the use of algorithmic decision-making in public organisations because of the far-reaching impacts that algorithms may have on public values such as fairness (Young et al., 2019), accountability (Busuioc, 2020), or efficiency (Young et al., 2019). To tackle the risks of negative impacts on public values, scholars have recommended various approaches including new regulation and codes of conduct, transparency, citizen engagement, and governance reform (for example, Bozeman, 2002; Bryson et al., 2014; O'Flynn, 2007). Given the complexity and urgency around the influence of algorithmic decision making in the public sector, a comprehensive approach is needed to bring about the kinds of changes in organisational behaviour and policy that can adequately control algorithms and bring about the best benefits for public organisations (Ingrams and Klievink, 2022; Giest and Klievink, 2022).

In order to contribute to a more comprehensive lens, in this chapter we study the tension between benefits and costs of algorithmic decision-making, when both are regarded in terms of public values. We use the theoretical notion of Panagiotopoulos, Klievink and Cordella (2019), who look at public value at the point of 'consumption'. This means that ultimately these tensions and the tradeoffs between different public values result in an aggregate public value outcome at the point where the entire process or service meets the public. However, that theory has not yet looked at the specifics of processes in which algorithmic decision-making is used particularly towards advancing public values, whilst seeking to do this in a legitimate way, yet with unavoidable costs to some values.

We study this process of the value tradeoffs of government in the context of public participation, and the use of algorithms in this process. This is a good case of algorithmic decision-making support directed to enable or improve participation values, whilst seeking a balance with value costs. Values like accountability and transparency are simultaneously furthered and hindered by these applications (Ranerup and Henriksen, 2019). Participatory mechanisms are difficult to implement due to practical challenges around aggregating an overwhelming amount of input from citizens, making manual content analysis costly and labour intensive, and around evaluating the outcome (Benouaret et al., 2013; Krippendorff, 2013; Liu, 2016). In fact, some warn that the cost of engaging citizens drains resources from core administrative work (Liu, 2017). To address the flood of information policymakers are faced with, there are some interesting and potentially very effective algorithmic tools for gaining insights from public input that have already been used by governments (for example, Farina et al., 2010; Ingrams et al., 2020; Vydra et al., 2021). However, scholars still have limited understanding of how the insights from these tools should be used and the kinds of challenges they pose for public value management.

We study the case of analytical procedures used in assessing public comments, paying attention to the choices organisations still have to make to process the comments and make policy decisions. We ask how algorithmic tools that engage with public input affect public values in decision-making processes. We look at the case of the eRulemaking initiative 'regulations. gov', which is one of the earliest and most successful examples of digital, public participation in regulatory decision-making. Regulations.gov enables public access to US rulemaking procedures and allows for participation in the process.

We use this case to explore the effects of machine learning tools on value considerations in public decision-making. We rely on a combination of website analysis and interview research. Specifically we look at salient values of transparency, accountability and responsiveness to participation, and how they inform the value creation from public comments.

We observe that ML tools are used relatively rarely and are generally not viewed by agencies as being necessary except in cases of very large quantities of public comments. Further, the comments review process may not lend itself to summarising tools that give a sense of the topics across an entire corpus. Rather, review of public comments is a way of discovering insights into individual comments that can improve regulations. The goal of our exploratory research is to identify practical insights into the aggregate public value of ML-supported public participation procedures with regards to democratic and process legitimacy frameworks, types of analytical tools, troubleshooting, and risk analysis, as well as key protocols and processes.

THEORETICAL BACKGROUND

Algorithmic Decision-making and Public Values

In the last 20 years, algorithmic decision-making tools have expanded rapidly into many areas of business management and operations and are now widespread in organisations. There are many applications including product marketing research, employee evaluation and training, consumer or citizen relations, and research (for example, Boecking, Hall, and Schneider, 2015; Clark et al., 2018; Desmarais et al., 2014). Applications typically involve five steps: (1) source identification and accessing, where the data sources are identified and means of extracting data are built and maintained; (2) data selection and cleaning, where parameters for data analysis are set and data are 'cleaned' in preparation for analysis; (3) model fitting, where specifications are applied to the data and then trained to improve model fit for future applications; (4) visualisation, where the results of the analysis are presented in ways that allow for meaningful empirical and policy information to be inferred; and (5) recommending, where the results of the analysis imply specific decisions.

In the sphere of public participation, technologies have been welcomed by scholars and public officials for their potential to bring decision-makers and the public into closer alignment by enhancing the quality of communication and decreasing transaction costs (Epstein et al., 2014). For example, by using input from citizens in the form of e-petitions or social media data, important knowledge about policy agenda topics or segmentation of policy audiences can be used to support the policymaking process (Dumas et al., 2015; Hagen et al., 2018).

By using the input of citizens to 'receive information and feedback' (Grubmüller et al., 2013, p. 4), IT technologies leverage the knowledge of a dispersed 'crowd' to aid in problem-solving or idea-generation (Prpić et al., 2015). In sum, there is a widely held view among scholars and policymakers that digitalisation of decision-making through production of digital documentation and data, and digital record-keeping offers greater potential to strengthen decision quality and process qualities such as accountability and transparency (Bertot et al., 2010).

But algorithmic decision-making tools also challenge our theoretical and normative assumptions about how public participation influences decision-making processes. Public participation initiatives often receive a high volume of comments, which makes it difficult to manage the review process as well as determine the value of individual input (Liebwald, 2015; Shulman, 2007). A high number of comments might lead to a larger and more fragmented collection of feedback that is difficult for administrators to work through and can come with high administrative costs for managing the process (Dahl, 1994). This further poses a technical challenge and can lead to the risk of black boxing the process. Some go one step further and point towards the challenges of upholding public values that relate to the functioning of democracy, such as legitimacy, equal treatment, accountability, and fairness (Bartneck et al., 2012; van den Berg et al., 2022).

Due to these various challenges to public values from algorithmic decision-making, value trade-offs need to happen (De Graaf and Van der Wal, 2010; Steenhuisen and van Eeten, 2008). But according to Thacher and Rein (2004), trade-offs are not simple because conflicting values may not occur at one time and place and the adoption and operationalisation of values is often done unconsciously rather than through a deliberate institutional plan. For example, speed of decision-making may come at the cost of democratic responsiveness or privacy of input may come at the cost of decision-making transparency. Applying algorithmic tools requires that developers and analysts have a lot of discretion (De Bruijn, 2002; Okwir et al., 2018). This raises the question of who is responsible for making decisions about values – the managers or the technology professionals? Finally, algorithmic decision-making is a sequential activity involving the steps from data generation to interpretation and policy decision-making. This introduces serial dependencies where there are communication challenges between different departments (Arnaboldi et al., 2017; Chen and Hsieh, 2014; Janssen et al., 2017).

Public participation
Public administration theory has given a prominent place to public participation in regulatory law making (for example, Bryer, 2013; Coglianese et al., 2008; Schlosberg, Zavestoski, and Shulman, 2008). Once laws have been passed by legislative bodies, regulations are needed to guide administrators on how the law should be implemented. Political philosophy also suggests that public participation is valuable for public policymaking. According to classic theories of public participation from a range of political scientists and political philosophers such as J. S. Mill, Robert Dahl, John Dewey, and Sherry Arnstein, public participation supports democratic legitimacy, and it also serves a functional purpose as a channel for the public to contribute knowledge and experience in such a way that public policies will become better implemented. Generally speaking, public participation is the involvement of citizens, civil society organisations, businesses, and other organisations. In the context of this research, we specifically focus on public consultation for governmental regulatory decision-making and thus a formal, top-down form of public participation that is led by government (Long and Franklin, 2004). In this context, it is relevant to highlight that there is some evidence that consultation in regu-

latory development has little impact on decision-making (for example, Bryer, 2013) and there are specific examples where the participation design is beset by political manipulation (for example, Lodge and Wegrich, 2015). There is also evidence that the citizens who participate are a rather idiosyncratic group of highly motivated civic influencers and/or groups that have been uniquely galvanised around an issue that affects their economic, political, or social interests (Cleaver, 2005; Cunningham, 1972; Fiorina, 1999; Lodge and Wegrich, 2015). However, scholarship still underlines the importance of finding the right public audiences to support a range of public values such as inclusivity, effectiveness and efficiency (Bryson et al., 2013; van den Berg et al., 2020).

Scholars have also traditionally viewed public participation in government decision-making as an important component of government accountability (Bingham et al., 2005; Dahl 1994; Ingrams, 2019). At the same time, efforts at raising transparency in the public sphere have facilitated the digitalisation of some government processes, which offers a vehicle for public participation through information sharing (Ingrams et al., 2019; Welch, 2012). In general, there is a widely held view among scholars and policymakers that digitalisation of decision-making through production of digital documentation and data and digital record-keeping offers greater potential to strengthen this transparency-accountability link (Bertot et al., 2010).

To address the flood of information policymakers are faced with, there are some interesting and potentially effective algorithmic tools that can support gaining of insights from public input and that have already been used by governments (for example, Ingrams et al., 2020; Vydra et al., 2021). However, scholars still have limited understanding of how analysts should use the insights in ways that are informed by the risks inherent in crowding out or displacement of important public values.

Algorithmic tools

Algorithmic tools have the ability to get through large amounts of data, the speed of work, and a means for handling complex data. ML tools such as Natural Language Processing (NLP) tools in particular enable policymakers to identify and appreciate latent or emergent topics of interest to the public (Hagen et al., 2015). There are a host of other advantages that scholars have discussed. Cost and capacity are known to be barriers to their adoption in the public sector, but it is often taken for granted that, once these barriers are overcome, public agencies will inevitably embark on a determined path to adopt whatever big data technologies they can in the belief that they will thereby become more effective and efficient. We argue in this chapter that public agencies are much more internally fragmented organisationally and behaviorally when it comes to algorithmic decision-making tools (Giest and Klievink, 2022). The kinds of procedural and political impacts of such technologies create uncertainty and put pressure on internal decision-making processes. Further, we argue that the process of adoption of algorithmic decision-making tools is thus characterised by contention and competition between different public value frames.

Public value 'consumption'

While algorithmic decision-making tools such as ML can make detailed insights about data, participation initiatives have always faced problems regarding design and management. This challenge remains especially important for big data tools in public participation. Automated analysis is still in development, and recent research highlights that 'while automated procedures increasingly replace human coders in content analysis procedures, real people are still needed to supplement or feed the machines' (Lind et al., 2017, p. 206). Public participation technologies require users to engage with the human decision-making side of the process in new ways, and the success of their implementation depends heavily on how they are viewed and understood by the users (Farina et al., 2010). Administrators have preconceptions about the composition of the 'crowd' whose opinions must still be factored in by humans and the results of the analysis need to be interpreted and turned into policy (Panagiotopoulos et al., 2017), while technologies present 'differences in information quality and delibera-tiveness of preference formation' (Farina et al., 2012, p. 123). These characteristics of the human-computer interface raise important public value questions about how administrative professionals program data tools, interpret the data, and address challenges such as the trade-offs between citizen preferences and expertise, weighing and prioritising the preferences of different stakeholders, and making their decision-making process transparent. Recalling the theory of Panagiotopoulos, Klievink and Cordella (2019), we use the lens of public value 'consumption' to understand how decision-makers evaluate, consider, and strategise in the realisation of public values through their use of algorithmic decision-making tools. As these tools support some public values at a potential cost to others, it is ultimately a matter of balancing the technology with the intended outcome in terms of public value. This makes the value outcome the aggregate and balanced outcome of the tool's use and value trade-offs in a specific process, in a specific context, and in interplay with other tools or the absence thereof (Panagiotopoulos et al., 2019).

THE CASE OF REGULATIONS.GOV

We identify regulations.gov as an important use case of algorithmic decision-making tools in public participation procedures (Balla, 2015; Bryer, 2013; Ingrams, 2022). Regulations. gov is maintained by the General Services Administration, a central executive agency in the United States government. Our case study of regulations.gov relies on several different types of data collection and analysis. We performed a qualitative website analysis including testing of our own ML models using the regulations.gov Application Programming Interface (API), and carried out interviews with civil servants who were members of the regulatory review teams for seven different executive-level US federal agencies. In the model testing, we extracted thousands of public comments and ran semantic analysis and Latent Dirichlet Analysis (LDA) to find out how well our models performed. To arrange video call interviews, we sent request emails to about 50 such teams who we identified using public information in the US publication, the Federal Register, where information soliciting public submissions on proposed regulations can be found. We focused on the 15 executive federal agencies and their regulator proposals that had received public input in the last five years. These requests resulted in four interviews lasting between 30 minutes and an hour with four different federal agencies that have used ML tools as part of their work of reviewing public comments. We also spoke to teams from three other agencies to understand the general protocols and processes that were used to review public comments. However, we do not focus on the material from the latter interviews as those teams did not have direct experience of working with ML tools, though they were aware of the relevance and potential application of such tools.

Regulations.gov serves as a platform for federal agencies to post information about pro-posed regulations. This is a public participation process that is mandated by the Administrative

Procedures Act (APA), which requires agencies to open up regulations with significant public interest to public review. Public participation in regulatory development thus has a central role to play in government. As such crowdsourcing approaches can attract thousands of public comments, and administrators face the challenge of delivering their legal responsibility to listen and respond to public preferences while overcoming technical challenges of text analysis.

Some proposed regulations that are posted on regulations.gov receive only a handful of public comments. However, volumes of comments in the many thousands are not uncommon. To sort through large numbers of comments, regulators rely on a range of different decision support tools including common types of software packages such as Microsoft Excel and Nvivo, as well as bespoke ML tools provided by IT contractors. Though such automated text analysis tools are used, these complicated decision-making processes are partly embedded in computer programs and the decision-making protocols that surround them. Exploratory analysis of the web platform and interviews with administrators show that administrators are not consistent in their use of tools, preferring to accomplish ad hoc technical goals such as filtering out duplicates and low-quality comments. In-house expertise is normally quite low, meaning that a repertoire of third-party tools is relied on, and details of what tools are being used sometimes remains private and undisclosed. Furthermore, implementation of automated text analysis tools has become a powerful tool of discretion around the question of democratic values versus technical approaches to public participation in regulatory development.

Agencies receive millions of public comments each year across a range of regulations. A rulemaking team typically assigns each person on the team a set number of comments to review, and they respond to them in general groups of topics. Federal agencies sometimes rely on contractors that help them manage a large volume of comments. The number of employees working on reviewing comments varies greatly depending on the case. For larger submissions, agencies often have 20–30 people reading the same comments. The review team creates a shared document where they input all of the issues raised by the comments and organise those issues in a logical manner. Once all the issues raised in the comments are captured in this shared document and organised properly, the team begins to work on how to respond to all of the comments.

In most cases, we found that staff in charge of managing the public comments rely on Microsoft Excel to put all the comments in a spreadsheet and organise and read them that way, sorting columns, deleting duplicates, and filtering out the ones deemed to be unimportant. In other cases where there is a small number of comments, staff read the comments directly on the public facing side of regulations.gov or view the automated emails they receive through the regulations.gov system. Analytics support tools are sourced in a range of different ways: they are outsourced from data analytics companies, provided by or recommended by another federal agency, the Office of the Federal Register (OFR), or commercial and open source software is obtained in-house. OFR has a centralised rule management system that allows proposed rule managers to search, view, redact, download, and process public comments. This system is called the Federal Docket Management System (FDMS). It has two interfaces, the one at regulations.gov is for the public and the other (FDMS.gov) allows the U.S. agencies the ability to process comments received. The U.S. government's e-rulemaking electronic system offers some text analytics tools. The agency platform (FDMS) has some inbuilt tools for filtering out duplicates and a kind of topic-modelling function. The tool works well for its purpose, but it does not help with the work to organise the issues raised by the comments in a logical manner. It simply helps administrators save time reviewing duplicate comments. Another tool provides insights on what issues are being raised by the comments and the percentage of commenters raising these issues.

However, more advanced tools for ad hoc use of systems to capture keywords, phrases, look for special interest groups, professional, academia, and state, federal and tribal governments are provided by contractors, though, for cost reasons, these are not regularly used. Useful services are analyses that point out when comments were unique, and when there were trends outside of what is expected from public preferences towards the regulation. The role of human expertise remains central and financially costly because of the supervision required. During the public comment period agencies may find themselves having to adjust search criteria because the flow of comments takes a turn that was not expected, and topic parameters need to be calibrated.

Departments are given quite a lot of assistance and instruction from the General Services Administration (GSA), which may also check that the agency is giving adequate attention to all the comments. Other tools have been developed but had minimal use. There is a regulatory training group that was set up to examine ways to create a shared database for keeping track of regulations in terms of their topics. These are also seen as being costly and time intensive to set up effectively in the first place. Administrators experience the value trade-off between representation and finding relevant knowledge as a challenge. For example, one interviewee said that 'We are looking to build a record that is based on analysis. A lot of science and data gathering needs to be done before promulgating a rule. Once into the rulemaking, the comments that matter are those that can make those kinds of analytical comments. A comment is not a vote, it is a scientifically informing process.'

Currently, to establish relevance, agencies use a chart that they fill in when they read comments. They look at specific things such as whether they have data or cited a study. Program staff utilise a variety of methods to analyse public submissions. Sometimes they work with dedicated contractors, and at other times they assemble teams across the Service's regional offices to read and respond to the comments received. Filtering out robo-comments is one of the biggest problems in the eyes of staff. 'Robo-comments are a big problem at the moment', according to one respondent. 'We find that detecting those is difficult. The substance of what people are saying is important, but if we are listening to computer-generated input, we won't get the public's message clearly.'

One way to address this issue, is to hire third parties. A company called Textifier produced an ML tool called DiscoverText that has been widely adopted and is targeted at regulations that receive a significant number of public comments as part of mass mail campaigns. This software tool allows Service program staff to quickly review public submissions for substantive comments while ensuring that no comment is overlooked. Special interest groups will also use their legal powers to follow up if their viewpoints have not been included. According to some interview respondents, the teams of analysts and their legal counsels give special attention to the comments from powerful interest groups because they want to avoid the risk that failing to address those comments could result in complaints from those interest groups or, in the worst case scenario, legal action being taken against them. This however potentially favours certain groups over others and challenges the values of transparency and equal participation.

One agency also reported the use of ML tools for topic modelling using natural language processing (NLP) methods. This approach involves managing large amounts of text by discovering semantic patterns according to a predetermined number of topics and associated important words. According to one interviewee, they aimed to 'capture keywords, phrases, look for special interest groups, professional, academia, and state, federal and tribal governments. This company was also asked to point out when comments were unique, and when there were trends outside of what we expected.' Supervised statistical NLP methods discover these patterns through a process referred to as 'training a model' from data that has been manually annotated by human experts who map each document to its predefined categories – the manually annotated data is therefore referred to as training data (Hagen et al., 2015). Topic modelling of this kind has an obvious attraction for analysts if they wish to get insight into the main themes in public comments but there are critical decisions at the level of model programming and inference that reflect public values. Programmers must, for example, decide with the support of statistical programs what number of topics best represents the semantic diversity of the text and to what extent to privilege the most common topics over those that may be more interesting or important content-wise.

Analysts – who are frequently legal specialists – place high value on their APA-enshrined responsibility to give adequate attention to all of the comments they receive. The supporting documentation for the APA, written by the Office of the Federal Registrar (2011), states that, At the end of the process, the agency must base its reasoning and conclusions on the rulemaking record, consisting of the comments, scientific data, expert opinions, and facts accumulated during the pre-rule and proposed rule stages. To move forward with a final rule, the agency must conclude that its proposed solution will help accomplish the goals or solve the problems identified.

Consequently, their written response to the comments should resemble a complete report on the comments, even ones that are deemed to have tangential topic relevance or that present ideas that may be ultimately unfeasible. In this respect, analysts face a trade-off between the democratic responsiveness and effectiveness of their answers, which is attenuated by the inherent logic of algorithmic tools aiming at simplification and reduction of semantic complexity. In this context, policymakers often facilitate case-by-case judgment about how comments should be evaluated and decisions made (what Thacher and Rein (2004) call 'casuistry'). The underlying logic of casuistry is that resolution to conflicts among values are worked out on a case-by-case basis.

We observed three main ways that this process influences the decision regarding what kinds of decision support tools to use:

1. Ignoring algorithmic decision-making tools or minimalising their use in order to focus on manual review and summarisation methods that rely on the capacity for human readers to process the information. This strategy is more common in cases where the number of comments is small. It also generally places more emphasis on the discretion and capacity of the individual analyst to decide how to weigh and incorporate the comments, rather than formalising an algorithmic decision-making system through decision support tools. In practice, this approach may occur very rarely because the acceptance and incorporation of basic decision-making tools such as Microsoft Excel or the FDMS de-duplication tool is widespread.

2. Transforming the comments review process into a process that is based – at least as a first step – on the work of algorithmic decision-making tools. This strategy is more common in cases where the number of comments is large. In the organisation, the strategy takes place through either outsourcing of the review process to data analytics consultants or provision

of special training for use of commercially available ML tools. In practice, this approach may also occur quite infrequently due to a big volume of comments being rare and analysts being cautious about interpreting output based on black box models.

3. Developing a two-level process where human coding and use of basic decision-support tools are used together with algorithmic decision-making tools. This two-level process could be employed in various ways in the organisation: within the same regulatory proposal across different teams of analysts or by the same team of analysts across different regulatory proposals. In this respect, a two-level process – to use Thacher and Rein's (2004) terminology – might 'cycle' through different values, emphasising democratic responsiveness in one regulatory proposal and effectiveness in another. It could also be what Thacher and Rein call 'hybridisation' if the two values can be reconciled and emphasised simultaneously. Due to the benefits of using both types of comments processing, the two-level approach has the advantage of addressing risks that come with an either/or approach.

DISCUSSION AND CONCLUDING REMARKS

Based on the question, 'how do algorithmic tools that engage with public input affect public values in decision-making processes?', we make three observations in the case of regulations. gov:

1. Public participation without the digital dimension has value trade-offs that are present, but not actively acknowledged in the digital version. This includes aspects of participation dynamics (who initiates, who participates, and who decides) as well as how issues are portrayed and understood.
2. The invitation for digital public feedback creates an administrative challenge to the government due to the sheer volume of comments, but also the responsibility of processing them in a meaningful way. Due to procedure alone, trade-offs are being made to handle comments either manually or automatically.
3. Using AI to process comments layers trade-offs that have been made prior to introducing the technology. This implies that value trade-offs need to be highlighted when introducing AI, but also their relationship with those made in the process itself – the choice to crowd-source feedback and the area in which public participation is wanted.

These observations can be understood as both conscious and unconscious forms of public value 'consumption'. They are evolving strategies for making value trade-offs at the organisational and at the individual levels. These strategies are needed to deal with competing values and avoid having too many salient values leading to paralysis (Thacher and Rein, 2004). Thacher and Rein (2004) identified three strategies: cycling, firewalls, and casuistry. Stewart (2006) later added three other strategies: bias, hybridisation, and incrementalism. In our case analysis we focused on casuistry, cycling and hybridisation but we see some elements of all the strategies. The case suggests several strategies played a role; the case itself can be regarded as an example of casuistry. This refers to a situational solution for dealing with value conflicts and is evidenced here by resolving value trade-offs at the level of the case rather than opting for resolving them at a more generalised level. Next, the firewall strategy reveals how different teams of analysts may be set up to safeguard one or some of the values, particularly to fulfill legal responsibilities or to manage the administrative burdens of processing large amounts of information. This compartmentalisation of values can be an effective strategy, but this is also where the legacy of the pre-algorithm situation plays a role. Whereas it is effective for the trade-offs with respect to, for example, representation and usefulness of comments generally, the introduction of algorithms shifts the value trade-offs to the data analyst. Lastly, the incrementalism strategy, referring to increasing emphasis on some values, appears in both the general movement towards digital public comments and in the subsequent need to employ tools to handle the resulting information overload. The first leads to extra emphasis on the value of participation, the second on the value of effectiveness in dealing with the results, which may negatively impact participation-related values over time. These signs of incrementalism point to perhaps the biggest challenge for using algorithms in this domain: by keeping the balance between values stable as based on the pre-algorithms stage, the way that values affected (promoted or challenged) by algorithms are considered only as part of the use of algorithms, rather than seen as portraying a need to re-assess which value trade-offs are made for the entire practice of participation through algorithm-supported processing of public comments.

Taken together, there is more (digital) input by the public than capacity on the government side to meaningfully process this 'crowd knowledge'. Given this processing gap, algorithmic tools are seen as a valuable addition to bridge the gap and give insights into public comments and sentiment. However, the algorithmic tools come with practices suggesting a specific set of values, uncertainties and assumptions. This has to do with the nature of the technical workings of applications, but also due to the fact that the technology is offered by third-party stakeholders. The questions raised in this scenario are directly related to public values in terms of whether transparency and accountability values can be upheld if there is ML processing by third parties with a focus on efficiency and speed. Another question is whether reading and potentially skipping comments due to capacity issues gives too little space to participation values in policymaking, which can potentially be facilitated by ML tools. Basically, whether the uncertainties and public values each process brings – the public participation and ML processes – add up to a more balanced, value-oriented way of policymaking or whether they cancel out relevant values in each other's processes. This is something to pay close attention to as algorithmic tools in this space evolve and public officials become more equipped to understand and use these tools in participatory processes.

REFERENCES

Arnaboldi, M., Busco, C., and Cuganesan, S. (2017). Accounting, accountability, social media and big data: Revolution or hype? *Accounting, Auditing & Accountability Journal*, 30(4), 762–776.

Arnstein, S. R. (1969). A ladder of citizen participation. *Journal of the American Institute of Planners*, 35(4), 216–224.

Balla, S. J. (2015). Political control, bureaucratic discretion, and public commenting on agency regulations. *Public Administration*, 93(2), 524–538.

Bannister, F., and Connolly, R. (2014). ICT, public values and transformative government: A framework and programme for research. *Government Information Quarterly*, 31(1), 119–128. https://doi.org/10.1016/j.giq.2013.06.002

Barredo Arrieta, A., Díaz-Rodríguez, N., Ser, J. Del, Bennetot, A., Tabik, S., Barbado, A., ... Herrera, F. (2020). Explainable Artificial Intelligence (XAI): Concepts, taxonomies, opportunities and challenges toward responsible AI. *Information Fusion*, 58, 82–115.

Bartneck C., Lütge C., Wagner A., and Welsh S. (2021). Trust and fairness in AI systems. In: *An Introduction to Ethics in Robotics and AI*. Springer Briefs in Ethics. Springer, Cham.

Benouaret, K., Raman V.-R., and Charoy, F. (2013). CrowdSC: Building smart cities with large-scale citizen participation. *IEEE Internet Computing*, 17(6), 57–63.

Bertot, J. C., Jaeger, P. T., and Grimes, J. M. (2010). Using ICTs to create a culture of transparency: E-government and social media as openness and anti-corruption tools for societies. *Government Information Quarterly*, 27(3), 264–271.

Bingham, L. B., Nabatchi, T., and O'Leary, R. (2005). The new governance: Practices and processes for stakeholder and citizen participation in the work of government. *Public Administration Review*, 65(5), 547–558.

Bozeman, B. (2002). Public-value failure: When efficient markets may not do. *Public Administration Review*, 62(2), 145–161.

Brabham, D. C. (2013). *Crowdsourcing*. Cambridge: MIT Press.

Bryer, T. A. (2013). Public participation in regulatory decision-making: Cases from regulations.gov. *Public Performance & Management Review*, 37(2), 263–279.

Bryson, J. M., Crosby, B. C., and Bloomberg, L. (2014). Public value governance: Moving beyond traditional public administration and the new public management. *Public Administration Review*, 74(4), 445–456.

Bryson, J. M., Quick, K. S., Slotterback, C. S., and Crosby, B. C. (2013). Designing public participation processes. *Public Administration Review*, 73(1), 23–34.

Busuioc, M. (2021). Accountable artificial intelligence: Holding algorithms to account. *Public Administration Review*, 81(5), 825–836.

Chen, Y.-C., and Hsieh, T.-C. (2014). Big data for digital government. *International Journal of Public Administration in the Digital Age*, 1(1), 1–14.

Clark, S. D., Morris, M. A., and Lomax, N. (2018). Estimating the outcome of UK's referendum on EU membership using e-petition data and machine learning algorithms. *Journal of Information Technology & Politics*, 15(4), 344–357.

Cleaver, F. (2005). The inequality of social capital and the reproduction of chronic poverty. *World Development*, 33(6), 893–906.

Coglianese, C., Kilmartin, H., and Mendelson, E. (2008). Transparency and public participation in the federal rulemaking process: Recommendations for the new administration. *Geo. Wash. L. Rev.*, 77, 924.

Cunningham, J. V. (1972). Citizen participation in public affairs. *Public Administration Review*, 32, 589–602.

Dahl, R. A. (1994). A democratic dilemma: System effectiveness versus citizen participation. *Political Science Quarterly*, 109(1), 23–34.

De Bruijn, H. (2002). Performance measurement in the public sector: Strategies to cope with the risks of performance measurement. *International Journal of Public Sector Management*, 15(7), 578–594.

De Graaf, G., and Van der Wal, Z. (2010). Managing conflicting values in public policy. *The American Review of Public Administration*, 40(6), 623–630.

Desmarais, B. A., Harden, J. J., and Boehmke, F. J. (2015). Persistent policy pathways: Inferring diffusion networks in the American states. *American Political Science Review*, 109(2), 392–406.

Dumas, C. L., LaManna, D., Harrison, T. M., Ravi, S. S., Kotfila, C., Gervais, N., ... and Chen, F. (2015). Examining political mobilization of online communities through e-petitioning behavior in We the People. *Big Data & Society*, 2(2), 2053951715598170.

Dutil, P. (2015). Crowdsourcing as a new instrument in the government's arsenal: Explorations and considerations. *Canadian Public Administration*, 58(3), 363–383.

Epstein, D., Farina, C., and Heidt, J. (2014). The value of words: Narrative as evidence in policy making. *Evidence & Policy: A Journal of Research, Debate and Practice*, 10(2), 243–258.

Farina, C. R., Newhart, M., and Heidt, J. (2012). Rulemaking vs. democracy: Judging and nudging public participation that counts. *Mich. J. Envtl. & Admin. L.*, 2, 123.

Farina, C. R., Newhart, M. J., Cardie, C., and Cosley, D. (2010). Rulemaking 2.0. *U. Miami L. Rev.*, 65, 395.

Fiorina, M. (1999). Extreme voices: A dark side of civic engagement. In Theda Skocpol and Morris P. Fiorina (eds), *Civic Engagement in American Democracy*, pp. 395–426. Washington, DC: Brookings Institution Press.

Giest, S., and Klievink, B. (2022). More than a digital system: How AI is changing the role of bureaucrats in different organizational contexts. *Public Management Review*, https://doi.org/10.1080/14719037.2022.2095001.

Greene, K. T., Park, B., and Colaresi, M. (2019). Machine learning human rights and wrongs: How the successes and failures of supervised learning algorithms can inform the debate about information effects. *Political Analysis*, 27(2), 223–230.

Hagen, L., Harrison, T. M., and Dumas, C. L. (2018). Data analytics for policy informatics: The case of e-petitioning. In *Policy Analytics, Modelling, and Informatics* (pp. 205–224). Springer, Cham.

Ingrams, A. (2019). Big Data and Dahl's challenge of democratic governance. *Review of Policy Research*, 36(3), 357–377.

Ingrams, A. (2022). Do public comments make a difference in open rulemaking? Insights from information management using machine learning and QCA analysis. *Government Information Quarterly*, 101778.

Ingrams, A., Kaufmann, W., and Jacobs, D. (2020). Testing the open government recipe: Are vision and voice good governance ingredients? *Journal of Behavioral Public Administration*, 3(1), https://doi.org/10.30636/jbpa.31.114

Ingrams, A., and Klievink, B. (2022). Transparency's role in AI governance. In Justin B. Bullock and others (eds), *The Oxford Handbook of AI Governance* (online edn, Oxford Academic, 14 Feb. 2022), https://doi.org/10.1093/oxfordhb/9780197579329.013.32.

Janssen, M., van der Voort, H., and Wahyudi, A. (2017). Factors influencing big data decision-making quality. *Journal of Business Research*, 70, 338–345.

Kitchin, R. (2014). *The Data Revolution: Big Data, Open Data, Data Infrastructures and Their Consequences*. London: Sage.

Krippendorff, K. (2013). *Content Analysis. An Introduction to its Methodology*. Thousand Oaks, CA: Sage.

Liebwald, D. (2015). On transparent law, good legislation and accessibility to legal information: Towards an integrated legal information system. *Artificial Intelligence and Law*, 23(3), 301–314.

Linders, D. (2012). From e-government to we-government: Defining a typology for citizen coproduction in the age of social media. *Government Information Quarterly*, 29(4), 446–454.

Liu, H. K. (2016). Exploring online engagement in public policy consultation: The crowd or the few? *Australian Journal of Public Administration*, 76(1), 33–47.

Liu, H. K. (2017). Crowdsourcing government: Lessons from multiple disciplines. *Public Administration Review*, 77(5), 656–667.

Lodge, M., and Wegrich, K. (2015). Crowdsourcing and regulatory reviews: A new way of challenging red tape in British government? *Regulation & Governance*, 9(1), 30–46.

Long, E., and Franklin, A. L. (2004). The paradox of implementing the government performance and results act: Top-down direction for bottom-up implementation. *Public Administration Review*, 64(3), 309–319.

Long, W.J., and Quek, M.P. (2002). Personal data privacy protection in an age of globalization: The US-EU safe harbor compromise, *Journal of European Public Policy*, 9(3), 325–344.

O'Flynn, J. (2007). From new public management to public value: Paradigmatic change and managerial implications. *Australian Journal of Public Administration*, 66(3), 353–366.

O'Neil, C. (2016). *Weapons of Math Destruction: How Big Data Increases Inequality and Threatens Democracy*. London: Penguin.

Office of the Federal Registrar (2011). A Guide to the Rulemaking Process. Washington, DC: Office of the Federal Registrar. https://www.federalregister.gov/uploads/2011/01/the_rulemaking_process.pdf

Okwir, S., Nudurupati, S., Ginieis, M., and Angelis, J. (2018). Performance measurement and management systems: A perspective from complexity theory. *International Journal of Management Reviews*, 20(3), 731–754.

Panagiotopoulos, P., Bowen, F., and Brooker, P. (2017). The value of social media data: Integrating crowd capabilities in evidence-based policy. *Government Information Quarterly*, JAI 34: 601–12.

Panagiotopoulos, P., Klievink, B., and Cordella, A. (2019). Public value creation in digital government. *Government Information Quarterly*, 36(4), 101421. https://doi.org/10.1016/J.GIQ.2019.101421

Prpić, J., Taeihagh, A., and Melton, J. (2015). The fundamentals of policy crowdsourcing. *Policy & Internet*, 7, 340–61.

Ranerup, A., and Henriksen, H. Z. (2019). Value positions viewed through the lens of automated decision-making: The case of social services. *Government Information Quarterly*, 36(4). https://doi.org/10.1016/j.giq.2019.05.004

Redden, J. (2018). Democratic governance in an age of datafication: Lessons from mapping government discourses and practices. *Big Data & Society*. https://doi.org/10.1177/2053951718809145

Schlosberg, D., Zavestoski, S., and Shulman, S. W. (2008). Democracy and e-rulemaking: Web-based technologies, participation, and the potential for deliberation. *Journal of Information Technology & Politics*, 4(1), 37–55.

Shulman, S. W. (2007). Whither deliberation? Mass e-mail campaigns and US regulatory rulemaking. *Journal of E-Government*, 3(3), 41–64.

Steenhuisen, B., and van Eeten, M. (2008). Invisible trade-offs of public values: Inside Dutch railways. *Public Money & Management*, 28(3), 147–152.

Stewart, J. (2006). Value conflict and policy change. *Review of Policy Research*, 23(1), 183–195. doi:10.1111/j.1541-1338.2006.00192.x

Thacher, D., and Rein, M. (2004). Managing value conflict in public policy. *Governance*, 17(4), 457–486.

van den Berg, A. C., Giest, S. N., Groeneveld, S. M., and Kraaij, W. (2020). Inclusivity in online platforms: Recruitment strategies for improving participation of diverse sociodemographic groups. *Public Administration Review*, 80(6), 989–1000.

Van den Berg, A.C., Giest, S., and Kraaij, W. (2022). Assessing inclusivity in online platforms through usability evaluation with Google Analytics. *Policy & Internet*, 15(1), 55–77.

Vydra, S., Poama, A., Giest, S., Ingrams, A., and Klievink, B. (2021). Big Data ethics: A life cycle perspective. *Erasmus Law Review*. DOI: 10.5553/ELR.00

Welch, E. W. (2012). The relationship between transparent and participative government: A study of local governments in the United States. *International Review of Administrative Sciences*, 78(1), 93–115.

Young, M. M., Bullock, J. B., and Lecy, J. D. (2019). Artificial discretion as a tool of governance: A framework for understanding the impact of artificial intelligence on public administration. *Perspectives on Public Management and Governance*, 2(4), 301–313.

9. Artificial intelligence and its regulation in representative institutions

Fotios Fitsilis and Patricia Gomes Rêgo de Almeida

INTRODUCTION

Artificial Intelligence (AI) does not constitute a single technology but a whole area of methods, patterns and approaches that are fine-tuned to mimic and approximate human-like behaviour in solving complex problems (Winston, 1992; Nilsson, 2009). As these are developing at a high pace, the associated tools and services are becoming production-ready, gradually finding their way into the public sector (De Sousa et al. 2019; Van Noordt and Misuraca, 2022). Such technologies have the potential to revolutionise governance institutions, both on the production and delivery side of public services. Nonetheless, one particular sector that is usually left out of the broader equation is representative institutions.

The term 'representative institution' is not placed here by chance, as it may characterise national or supra-national parliaments (EU, UN), as well as institutions of regional or local self-government. Inevitably, due to the number of existing Information and Communications Technology (ICT) applications, technology screening starts at the level of national institutions, yet the extrapolation of AI solutions to fit into the specific context of different levels of representative institutions is considered realistic as they can become beacons of change and form knowledge hubs. Though parliaments seem to acknowledge the necessity for introducing AI into their realm (IPU, 2020, 2021), the pertinent literature contains only limited examples of actual AI implementation (Fitsilis (2021) studied the interaction of the Committee for the Future at the Finnish Parliament with an AI chatbot). On the other hand, there seems to be not much interest from the industry to invest in the development of AI-based parliamentary technology, a sub-sector of *ParlTech*. One reason for this is that the Return on Investment (RoI), achieved by a relatively small number of cases worldwide, is not appealing enough and might defer larger companies from investing in related solutions.

In the following sections, unless stated otherwise, the terms 'parliament' and 'representative institution' will be used interchangeably. However, representative institutions at all levels possess significant similarities, for instance in the structure of debates, the issuing of regulatory documents and the use of controlling functions such as posing questions and requesting administrative documents. From this perspective, the RoI for AI-empowered digital solutions that can accommodate and handle common, basic representation features across institutions might constitute a game changer and spark a race for the digital transformation of representative institutions. Several incremental steps have already been taken to facilitate the above, such as the mapping of parliamentary functions and their matching with respective AI-based solutions, as well as first surveys to prioritise AI technology for parliaments (Koryzis et al., 2021).

This chapter aims first at providing a concise and state-of-the-art picture of AI technology in parliaments with links to possible interfaces with government systems and platforms. The goal is to frame realistic expectations around what is possible with current AI tools and what is not.

In doing so, based on a series of case studies, a series of underlying technologies, tools, and services will be discussed. Inevitably, any AI-based solutions in this domain cannot be generic but will rely on generated big open legal (parliamentary) data turning them into tangible information with added value for Members of Parliament (MPs), parliamentary professionals and society at large. Such solutions can be replicated in representative institutions of all sorts. For this, significant factors required to successfully implement AI systems in complex organisational environments are listed and discussed. Moreover, this contribution showcases inherent limitations but also considerable opportunities that span out of the use of AI in the parliamentary workspace. These are discussed and analysed.

It is also imperative to stress the role of representative institutions, vis-à-vis the Executive, in the regulation of AI technologies (see in this regard, Fitsilis, 2019). Hence, several regulatory aspects that place representative institutions at the centre of the relevant discussion around AI regulation are assessed and highlighted. Ultimately, it is argued that it is possible to develop an AI-driven, unified yet customisable and low-cost platform to pave the way towards the 'parliament of the future'. However, a broader assessment on how the basics of parliamentary representative democracy are enhanced or diminished by AI cannot be supported by the current data set nor is this assessment in the chapter's scope.

REPRESENTATIVE INSTITUTIONS AS USERS OF AI

Driven by the fact that parliaments are multifaceted public organisations aiming, among other priorities, to establish legal rules through debates among citizens' representatives (legislative function), or scrutinise governmental actions or omissions (Norton, 1990), the goals for their digital services may differ from those of e-Government services. This chapter exclusively deals with the evolution and analysis of AI-based solutions in the parliamentary environment, circumventing the necessity for a lengthy presentation of 'classic' ICT in the parliamentary workspace. For a comprehensive discussion of the latter, one may consult Missingham (2011), as well as Williamson and Fallon (2011).

There is limited knowledge and experience regarding the implementation of AI-based solutions in the parliamentary workspace. Ziouvelou, Giannakopoulos, and Giannakopoulos (2022) provide an overview of parliamentary functions that AI can support along with a broader framework to classify such uses. In fact, a 2022 study found more than 200 potential uses for AI in the parliamentary workspace (von Lucke, Fitsilis, and Etscheid, 2022). These range from services to supporting MPs in their parliamentary work or representative function, to sophisticated tools for citizens' engagement in political debates and the law-making process. In recent years, one has seen many digital solutions aimed at raising accountability and transparency and to create digital channels for citizen interaction with the parliament. Moreover, there were several independent approaches for the digital transformation of the legislative process, which has become increasingly complex over the years. Many of the above include the development of digital platforms that display similar design characteristics and have in common the fact that they are powered by AI algorithms.

In addition, due to the increase of digital inclusion and the strengthening of public sector accountability mechanisms, the overall level of access to information has increased significantly. As a consequence, the mission of representing citizens has become more complex. Among others, analyses of vast data sets in a shorter time are necessary to keep pace with the society. AI-related tools and services have the potential to provide satisfactory responses to these challenges.

To understand the state-of-play of AI in representative institutions and attempt any extrapolations, one needs field evidence and a broad sample. For this, a series of various AI-based tools and services in parliaments across the globe have been screened. In the Appendix, one may find these use cases presented in alphabetical order of the countries of origin. A mixed-method approach was used for qualitative and quantitative data collection that includes access to public domain data sources, literature research, expert interviews and information retrieval through the Open Data Hub, a thematic hub of Inter-Parliamentary Union's (IPU) Centre for Innovation in Parliaments. Despite the authors' attempts, this list is far from exhaustive. Actually, this is the short list of an earlier longer version of AI solutions already employed in parliaments. Inevitably, several of the original cases had to be removed due to low maturity of the technology (either in the early design phase or relating to developing specifications), the lack of detailed information, or missing clearance. The main parameters that were collected are: identification, description, technology, and maturity.

The identification of the parliamentary institution includes its name, level, and geographical location. The description contains details about the name and functionality of the AI-based app, tool, or service. The technology parameter indicates the main technology used. Finally, the level of maturity is indicated. Due to the difficulty in assessing different grades of maturity, two levels have been possible: 'in use' (productive operation) or 'project' (pilot or demonstrator phase).

Ten legislative chambers, also including a supra-national parliament, from eight countries responded to the general call for information via the Open Data Hub (30 legislative chambers as members; AI assimilation rate: 33 per cent). However, due to the advanced technological affinity of the hub's members, such an overall extraordinarily high assimilation rate of AI cannot be considered representative across the IPU's entire member population (178 as of 2022). Hence, the responding chambers can be rather considered as early adopters and the collection of data resembles an expert survey approach. With Estonia, Finland, Italy, and the Netherlands, Europe is over-represented in this study. North America has a single representative (Canada), while South America has two, Argentina and Brazil. Africa is represented through Angola. Brazil is the only country represented by two legislative chambers, the Chamber of Deputies and the Senate. The European Parliament is the only supra-national parliament that took part in this study. The Asian countries in the hub, that is Indonesia and Israel, have not declared any AI-based systems.

Overall, 39 AI-based systems were recorded (N=39), which results in a mean average of four systems per parliament. However, this is a rather misleading figure as four chambers (40 per cent of the examined ones) implement 23 AI-based solutions (or 59 per cent of all captured ones). The top-three leaders in AI-adoption are Brazil (both parliaments, nine systems), Canada (House of Commons, seven systems), and Italy (Senate, six systems). Interestingly, apart from the Netherlands, all the rest implement at least one AI project. This indicates a rather high plateau of technological maturity and an increased innovation potential. In other words, parliaments would act with more caution when dealing with emerging *ParlTech* if both of the above are not the case. This is also supported by the maturity parameter: 24 systems out of 39 (62 per cent) have already reached production status, which is considered to be an extraordinarily high figure.

When studying the specific technologies, the majority of the solutions, i.e. 30, or 77 per cent, implement Natural Language Processing (NLP) algorithms. In this context, the Generative Pre-trained Transformer 3 (GPT-3) utilised by the Finnish Eduskunta is also thought to belong to NLP-based systems (Fitsilis, 2021). This is attributed to the maturity of the underlying algorithms, as well as to the large number of existing applications in the governance or business sector. A significant number of systems use cognitive AI, i.e. 7, or 18 per cent.

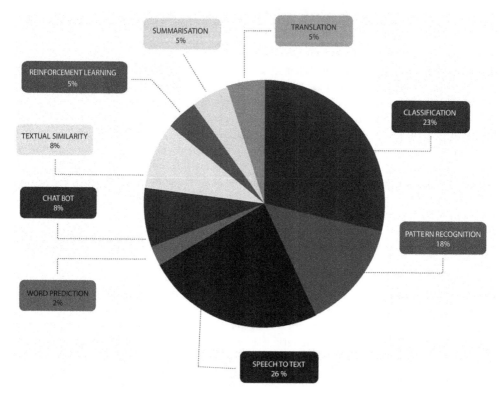

Figure 9.1   *Main functionality of parliamentary AI-based systems*

Yet the most significant outcome from the point of view of representative institutions is undoubtedly the functionality of systems envisaged by early adopters. For the sake of simplicity, each system was assigned a primary functionality. Figure 9.1 shows the distribution of the systems' functionality across the 39 systems. The top-three functionalities are speech to text transformation (ten systems, or 26 per cent), text classification (nine systems, or 23 per cent), and pattern recognition (seven systems, or 18 per cent). Those three functionalities together are implemented in 67 per cent of all the systems studied. Here, it needs to be noted that topic modelling is also under 'text classification', while 'pattern recognition' includes, voice, images, objects, and facial recognition.

Other applications represented are chatbots that have all been implemented in the European context, in Italy, Finland and in the European Parliament. Automatic summarisation and textual similarity constitute significant features for text analytics and were originally considered by the research team to be top candidates for implementation in *ParlTech*. Reality however is different. Both were clearly captured among the AI-tools but were just above the visualisation threshold, with two and three appearances respectively.

Interested representative institutions can draw important lessons from this analysis for the future utilisation of AI technologies. From the bird's eye view perspective, despite different institutional cultures and sizes of chambers, there are common elements in the use of AI by the parliaments of the sample. First, processes and tasks associated with legislative procedures were prioritised, especially for law-making and deliberation, plenary sittings and committee meetings. The second major focus was on digital services to citizens, for instance in improving citizens' access to information and vice-versa on analysing the information received from the citizens by representative institutions. Both approaches fit the parliament's greater missions to represent citizens and to regulate. Interestingly, the analysed sample did not include AI systems dedicated to the oversight of government. Given the significance of the oversight function, this is a remarkable output that needs to be investigated further, since it is not clear if it constitutes a bigger trend. The sectoral distribution of AI-based systems will be further investigated in the section that refers to their regulation in the parliamentary workspace and beyond.

FACTORS NEEDED TO SUCCESSFULLY IMPLEMENT AN AI SYSTEM

AI services are highly dependent on reliable data, which again results in the need for effective data-governance and data-management processes. In the data-governance dimension, the main challenges in engaging parliament stakeholders include data-ownership, data-treatment and of course, the appropriate level of data-protection and transparency. The data-management process also requires special attention to the recruiting of skilled people to deal with data quality and data-protection (Janssen et al. 2020). Such challenges also demand processes to assess risks and ethical principles associated with data-governance (Kuziemski and Misuraca, 2020; Alshahrani, Dennehy, and Mäntymäki, 2021; Medaglia, Gil-Garcia, and Pardo, 2021; Vetrò, Torchian, and Mecati, 2021). When dealing with AI in legislative processes, defining complete data models, including metadata, is a task that becomes more complex in bicameral parliaments, since negotiation between both houses must be established.

When there are AI services that make use of personal data, measures must be taken to (pseudo-) anonymise those data before applying any advanced algorithm to them. In parliaments, such situations may arise when reporting/commenting on confidential documents or placing comments on e-participation platforms. Such situations require a data quality process that is synchronised with a personal data-protection process (ISO, 2021).

Another action that requires a substantial amount of resources is the application of a set of procedures to avoid, or at least reduce, biases. From a practical perspective, such actions combine statistics with process management that consider the context of the problem for which the AI system will be implemented (González, Ortiz, and Ávalos, 2020). Often, many rehearsals are required to evolve the relevant ICT and business units, which also continue when the system is already launched. Hence, a continuous oversight process becomes mandatory along the entire lifecycle of the AI system.

All actions and processes mentioned need a continuously updated data catalogue that includes business and technical metadata. A reliable data catalogue depends on an integrated view of the business processes that will support the new AI service and the data models designed by the technical team. Therefore, parliaments can support such tasks by building joint working groups of experts in information and data science.

In every substantial organisational system, a responsible, all-around risk management process ought to be applied. As the majority of AI system classification methods consider the level of risk (Wirtz, Weyerer, and Geyer, 2019; European Commission, 2022), a risk management process becomes imperative, covering not only the entire system development life cycle but also the AI service life cycle (after the system is available to the users) (Zuiderwijk, Chen, and Salem, 2021). Once risk management is established, a change management must also take place, considering variables like algorithmic performance, security, and the context in which the service is immersed. The higher the risk level of an AI service, the higher the importance of a change management process.

Parliaments have adopted different strategies on developing AI systems: internal development; partnerships; or commercial software. Any internal development of AI-based systems allows for full control of data governance and management, overall increasing organisational transparency and reducing risk associated with off-the-shelf alternatives. However, it may be problematic to recruit or train experts to develop and maintain these systems. Commercial AI systems, on the other hand, can be a practical option to overcome these obstacles. However, the high number of different tasks and competencies, and the evolving nature of representative institutions can make the search for exclusively proprietary solutions a nearly impossible task. The building of partnerships (for instance with universities, research institutions, and other civil society organisations) can form a viable alternative for the development of AI tools and services. Unless there is an in-house development process, every AI adoption strategy should allow for substantial data and knowledge transfer between the partner institutions. This might affect the data and system protection risk level but in the long-term, in-house solutions could prove to be more secure and efficient. Considering, however, that these strategies are not exclusive, a hybrid approach can be considered.

REGULATORY ASPECTS

Representative Institutions as Regulators of AI

With AI tools and services coming into mainstream application and consumption, state actors and entities could not exercise apathy nor delay their involvement, be it for the purpose of regulation (Clarke, 2019; Fitsilis, 2019) or harvesting the technologies' unexplored potential, for which the term 'AI governance' has been coined. For instance, AI has long entered the area of political communication and already showcased its huge potential in influencing political campaigns (Neudert and Marchal, 2019). At the same time, it may seriously affect other key inter-state activities such as diplomacy, thus forming powerful external policy tools (Franke, 2021).

Aiming to increase the likelihood of reliable AI (i.e. AI that is safe and follows ethical principles) (AI HLEG, 2019), regulation efforts have been implemented in two types of initiatives: legislation (hard law) and soft law. Representative institutions may have decisive roles in both.

Regarding legislative action, different approaches are observed on AI regulation. Currently, relevant bills are being discussed in several legislative houses (OECD, 2022a). In some cases, national legislatures have passed laws for specific AI applications such as autonomous systems, drones and face recognition (Husch and Teiden, 2017; German Federal Government, 2021).

In others, a wider approach was opted for using a cross sectional model as a basis for future specific laws. In April 2021, following comprehensive public consultation, the European Commission brought forth a proposal for the Artificial Intelligence Act (AI Act) that is yet to be considered by the European Parliament. In this regard, it needs to be considered that the European Parliament might very well be the most thoroughly informed representative institution on issues around AI, with multiple related resolutions and a sufficiently staffed and capable parliamentary administration, i.e. the European Parliament Research Service (European Parliament, 2022).

Yet, in the case of AI, soft law seems to be predominant, indicating a more cautious approach by legislatures of all levels. Sensing the pressure from society, parliaments responded by studying the opportunities and challenges in the use of AI. In 2020, the Parliamentary Assembly of the Council of Europe embraced a set of practical proposals, in the form of resolutions and recommendations, to counterbalance the risks posed by the application of AI in democratic rights and environments (PACE, 2020). These proposals have also increased reuse potential by representative and other public institutions.

While larger assemblies may be better positioned in terms of resources to respond to those challenges, smaller yet decisive legislatures have begun studying them in an effort to increase their understanding of the matter and plan their digital evolution accordingly (see for example, Parliament of Victoria, 2018). For the same reason, the Organisation for Economic Co-operation and Development (OECD) Global Parliamentary Network, a legislative learning hub, founded a thematic parliamentary group on AI (OECD, 2022b) in 2019.

When it comes to AI, there are several possible layers of parliamentary involvement, for instance regulation; parliamentary oversight of governmental AI; ethical position and constraints. A recent study of the parliamentary research service of the Parliament of New South Wales (NSW), Australia, found that the application of automated decision-making by the government has no explicit legal basis in NSW (Montoya and Rummery, 2020). This legal 'grey zone' might very well reflect the legal situation in most legal orders around the globe.

There are diverse opinions about parliamentary legislative involvement in scrutinising the use of AI by the government. For instance, according to the Law Society of England and Wales:

> there is no obvious reason why the growth of AI and the use of data would require further legislation or regulation (Artificial Intelligence Committee, 2017).

The same UK parliamentary AI Committee recommended that Government's AI-specific policies should be reported to Parliament annually. Notably, Le Sueur (2016) stated that:

> [a]pps should, like other forms of legislation, be brought under democratic control.

Regardless of the approaches adopted, representative institutions cannot keep pace with technology production. A realistic regulation scenario would consider incremental development that combines soft and hard law. As soft laws are flexible norms, often seen as strategies, guidelines, conduct codes and standards, they are suitable to be applied to disruptive technologies, as a complement to AI-related legislation, as well as a temporary solution while bills (hard law) are being debated to avoid blocking technology development (Marchant, 2019). However, the regular legislative process cannot be discarded, considering that soft law offers rather low legal certainty to deal with any conflicts of a penal or civil nature (Hagendorff, 2020; De Almeida, dos Santos, and Farias, 2021).

Additionally, it would involve several stakeholders including legislatures; governmental bodies; independent state bodies that act as regulatory agencies; and organisations in charge of tests, certifications and auditing such as for technical, safety and ethical issues. Furthermore, societal stakeholders and academia can also play an important role, contributing to the bills as well as to eventual recommendations, assessment and auditing processes by regulatory agencies (De Almeida, dos Santos, and Farias, 2021). In particular, contributions by civil society organisations to bills at parliamentary committees may offer rich opportunities to spark and improve the ethical debate, as sometimes, even when referring to the same situation, ethical approaches can be conflicting (Bench-Capon and Modgil, 2017).

Stakeholders and Dimensions of the Regulatory Process

Parliaments, as representative institutions, may act in two major dimensions: as lawmakers (regulatory dimension) and as public organisations incorporating and/or providing AI services (functional dimension) (see Figure 9.2). For each dimension, there are possible regulatory setups and outcomes.

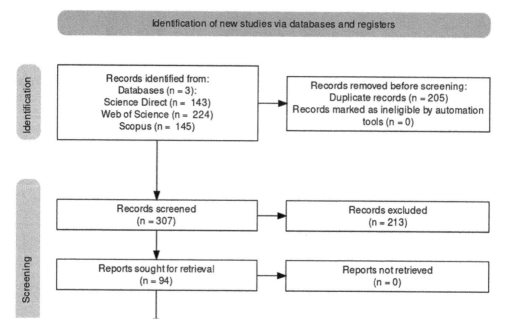

Figure 9.2   *Functional and regulatory dimensions for AI in representative institutions*

In the regulatory dimension, parliaments, in a partnership with other regulatory bodies (or similar governmental organisations), work by exchanging information in a continuous process in order to validate the effectiveness of bills and improve current legislation with new technical patterns and requirements. They can encompass laws and regulations for AI governance as well as other laws associated with the AI law, i.e. personal data protection, security, digital market, data governance etc. (Bogucki et al. 2022). In the context of AI law, one can find general AI laws, or laws for specific AI applications or specific fields of knowledge (health, national security, for instance). Insofar as the AI legislation becomes mature, it is expected that other related new laws are defined and old ones are adjusted (Bogucki et al., 2022). One of the most relevant instances of such relations is the EU Data Act and the EU Cybersecurity Act. Georgieva, Timan, and Hoeckstra (2022) highlight many changes necessary in such Acts in order to harmonise them and to avoid inconsistencies among them. In the European Parliament report of amendments on the AI Act, their level of dependence becomes tangible. Technological, social, and ethical aspects may also be considered as part of the sub-set of legislation. Hence, parliamentary openness, and maybe anticipation, to receive and process society's and academia's contributions become crucial parameters of the law-making process.

As public organisations that implement AI-based systems, legislatures can use AI to support and improve their institutional functions (functional dimension). There are several possibilities for placing AI-based systems in the parliamentary workspace (von Lucke, Fitsilis, and Etscheid, 2022; Ziouvelou, Giannakopoulos, and Giannakopoulos, 2022). After combining new with previous data, the authors came up with seven major sectors for the implementation of AI-based systems in the parliamentary workspace. These are clustered in three pillars covering institutional functions, with an additional horizontal sector for administrative and general purpose tasks. The first pillar contains the systems for the legislative, the oversight and the diplomacy functions of parliaments. The second pillar is all about citizen engagement, civic education and culture. The third pillar is dedicated to parliamentarians and includes the functions that are necessary for them to perform their representative and parliamentary duties. Parliamentary research units can be placed in this column as they are often entrusted with the provision of research and information support services to parliamentarians. Regarding administrative processes, AI systems for increasing transparency and budget management could be determined, yet there are a broad number of alternatives to be explored, for instance cyber security and internal auditing. It is worth noting that the prioritisation of transparency can be explained, since it is a basic requirement with regard to accountability.

One can observe the absence of AI systems for government oversight in the collected data, a phenomenon that requires some attention in order to establish possible causes. A first question one might ask regards the existence of available data in the government institutions that the parliament is allowed to access (and process) with its AI systems. A second issue to be considered is the quality of government department/agencies data, since missing or incorrect data can make AI systems unreliable or even impossible to be implemented. Obstacles can also be found when government institutions are not integrated within a structure of national data governance. In such situations, inter-institutional data exchange becomes extremely difficult and problematic. Similarly, parliamentary systems that tackle mis- and dis-information are missing from the sample, yet they could constitute irreplaceable working tools in the near future. At the institutional level, such systems could be utilised, for example in parliamentary research services that prepare informative notes and reports, and in parliamentary press offices that analyse and communicate parliamentary activity. Particularly for political parties and individual MPs, there is ample evidence that mis- and dis-information activities can seriously affect electoral processes (Fitsilis, 2019).

As any organisation that has decided to focus on trustworthy AI, parliaments need to be aware of technological, social and ethical aspects of their implementation. For that, they need to follow ethical principles, processes and practices (in other words, they need to apply 'soft law'), as well as legislation (hard law). More precisely, it is recommended that parliamentary AI systems should both be in compliance with AI laws as well as follow any relevant regulatory agency recommendations. Still, as public organisations, parliaments must provide their own AI governance considering internal strategies, policy, guidelines and norms, i.e. their own soft laws that apply to their organisation's units.

Acting in both dimensions implies being well skilled, in terms of human resources and properly equipped, in terms of software and hardware. While hardware can be conveniently procured once the necessary funding becomes available, the recruitment of AI specialists and the development of dedicated AI-based applications and services need a more elaborate approach. Specifically with regard to the up-skilling of their human resources, representative institutions will unlikely enter a bidding race to secure top AI experts. Therefore, it is highly recommended that parliaments co-ordinate efforts through peer-to-peer partnerships or knowledge hubs such as the ones formed under IPU's Centre for Innovation in Parliament.

Ethics is embedded in everything humans do, including their conduct with AI, which requires a multidisciplinary approach (Dignum, 2022). Ethical requirements can be part of the legislation, the guidelines, the strategy, the policy, and the systems (Hagendorff, 2020). The specific approach or the level of analysis for each type of ethical manifestation can be different and regulatory agencies need to assess those in a reliable and socially responsible manner. This also includes the assessment of algorithm 'trustworthiness' (see, for instance, the case of Z-inspection, Zicari et al. 2021), stakeholders' impact analysis, ethical dilemmas' formal analysis (De Almeida, dos Santos, and Farias, 2021), or the very notion of AI 'explainability' (Goebel et al., 2018).

In the case of representative institutions, actors rarely claim the responsibility of ethical leadership and it remains questionable whether they are up to it when it comes to the implementation of AI tools and services. While there have been calls to establish, also on behalf of the authors, the implementation of ethical committees in parliament (Fitsilis, 2019), this inter-sectoral, controversial and deeply human matter evades the scope of this chapter. Moreover, the issuing of ethical positions is not to be confused with institutional preparedness to belong to the early adopters of AI-related *ParlTech*. The ability to do the latter does not imply the (moral) obligation to express the former.

LIMITATIONS, RISKS, OPPORTUNITIES, AND TECHNICAL REQUIREMENTS

More than just representative institutions at large, parliaments are public organisations that heavily rely on tradition (Fitsilis et al., 2017). Bearing this in mind, a cautious approach to the adaptation of technology-induced changes in established processes and practices is understandable and indeed desirable. This was the original understanding as this study was initiated. However, as several institutions initiated experimentation with such technologies in the parliamentary workspace, it becomes apparent that, to a certain degree, parliaments opt to act first than to adopt a more passive stance.

In this regard, it is maybe interesting to note that parliaments entail notions of democracy even in governance regimes that cannot be immediately identified as 'democratic' in the classic sense. Hence, any wrongful implementation of AI-based solutions can be associated with democratic shortcomings and cause damage to the institutional reputation. After all, also in relation to AI, parliaments may act as beacons of society. If they get it wrong, this will send out conflicting messages and potentially negatively characterise entire scientific sectors.

In any case, there are certain prerequisites for parliaments to enter the AI era. One does not simply change from a paper-dominated organisation to an AI-supported workspace. Apart from the – rather self-evident – technological maturity and technical standards, there are additional factors that may play an important role in moving forward with the use of AI in parliaments. It all starts with the strive for organisational and procedural innovation and the necessary political will for moving forwards. If at least one of those is missing, then one should not bother to attempt to employ AI technologies.

To these requirements also belong the level of existing digitalisation and the ICT expertise within the organisation. A well-established ICT backbone needs to be present, with sufficiently skilled ICT professionals in place, not only to facilitate the transition and/or AI integration process but also to handle the related challenges and perils such as advanced data-management, personal data-protection issues, aspects of cyber security and others. Next, AI necessarily works with data; big data. Thus, the existing ICT infrastructure, tools and services must produce big open legal data (BOLD), i.e. the digital representation of parliamentary products. Without digital, structured, and validated parliamentary data in the proper formats such as OASIS or W3C standards, the application of AI *ParlTech* is not even possible. Furthermore, an embedded, progressive and versatile parliamentary digital strategy must be in place, placing AI at the end of the road, as the goal, rather than at the beginning. This strategy can be in-line with national or supra-national strategies.

It is misleading to assume that parliaments (or representative institutions in the broader sense) should strive to achieve taking-up the institutional lead in this technologically-dominated field. This, however, should not prevent them from massively stacking up their relevant administrative capacities, for instance in internal technical knowledge and expertise. In the short to medium term, this is easier said than done. Instead, a more feasible AI strategy could be paved by advancing collaboration with different societal stakeholders that may include academia, research institutions, private and the public sector, civil society organisations and citizen networks, for instance through crowdsourcing. The *Hellenic OCR Team*, https:// hellenicOCRteam.gr, is a characteristic example of the latter.

Nonetheless, a possible strategic goal for parliaments worth planning for, could be to reach role model status in governance. This would enable the export of know-what and know-how to other public entities, both domestic and international, while strengthening their institutional status. For this, software design and the AI solution implementation have to be structured to allow for a potential exportation. In other words, they need to be, among others, scalable (up and down), modular (include changeable components with standardised interfaces) and configurable (adaptable to different users and institutional environments). Other requirements to AI-based tools and services may include user friendliness, data-first and mobile-first approaches. In any case, these would have to match institutional demands, a broad aspect that evades the scope of this chapter.

In the opinion of the authors, the question as to whether or not parliamentarians possess the necessary technical skills and knowledge to regulate AI is a false one. A great part of today's legislative production is highly technical and this has never been a serious obstacle for parliaments to legislate on, due to the expertise available at their disposal. Yet, the complexity, non-linearity and 'black-box'-type of AI systems do call for a fundamentally different approach of regulation by parliaments.

The institutional capacity needs to be advanced by all available means. On the one hand, this may include co-operation schemes with national and international academic and research institutes (see, for instance, the case of the National Graduate Institute for Policy Studies (GRIPS) in Japan and its co-operation with the National Diet). On the other hand, the development of a relevant internal knowledge-base seems inevitable and of course desirable. A dedicated unit is not necessarily important for this. The primary role could be handed over to the parliamentary research services that need to be substantially strengthened, in terms of mandate and scientific personnel. These again would have to cooperate with the rest of the administration for acquiring, developing and operating AI-based tools and services.

Furthermore, it is imperative to attempt to advance or build from scratch relevant parliamentary working bodies (or Committees) that will deliberate on AI-related issues in a structured and transparent manner. In this regard and closely depending on the individual goals, parliaments may want to orient themselves to the example of the AI APPG (All-Party Parliamentary Group) of the UK Parliament (APPG, 2022) or the Committee of the Future in the Finnish Parliament, which has been hailed as a model for advanced 'foresight practices' by the European Parliamentary Research Service (Eduskunta, 2022). In the first case, a particular topic (AI in this case) is handled by informal cross-party groups, while the latter forms a standing committee deliberating on a variety of emerging and cross-cutting societal and technological topics using sometimes unusual methodologies (Koskimaa and Raunio, 2020).

Having analysed the aforementioned AI use cases, one could possibly conclude that the similarity of the approaches and the rather limited scope of intervention would make them easily adaptable, and thus reusable, at the same or different level of representative institutions. However, while integration of AI solutions into different specific contexts and environments might be realistic, this is still challenging from a system and software development standpoint, something that may have a deterrent effect on the organisations' decision-making. Hence, it can be deduced that the next big thing in the evolution of the workings of parliaments might be an open digital platform that supports different AI-based modules that offer customised solutions for specific user needs. The development of such a platform, the conception of the institutional processes that are necessary to accommodate it within any given parliamentary workspace, as well as the ethical framework required for its operation could be the focus of a global cross-cutting parliamentary research agenda that has yet to be defined.

The potentially open source nature of the platform, or its components and features, could make it accessible to all representative institutions, while at the same time providing lots of incentives for the private sector in terms of advanced customisation and innovative proprietary solutions offered as dedicated modules. The latter could be accessible from dedicated or supporting application marketplaces, or other interoperable consumer applications and platforms (Leventis, Fitsilis, and Anastasiou, 2021). An open digital platform, also available as a Software as a Service (SaaS) alternative, could constitute a low-cost, user-friendly alternative to existing customised ICT solutions, thus promoting the democratisation of AI use in the parliamentary workspace.

REFERENCES

Agnoloni, T., Bartolini, R., Frontini, F., Montemagni, S., Marchetti, C., Quochi, V., Ruisi, M., and Venturi, G. (2022a). Making Italian parliamentary records machine-actionable: The construction of the ParlaMint-IT corpus. *Proceedings of the Workshop ParlaCLARIN III within the 13th Language Resources and Evaluation Conference, Marseille, France*, 117–124. European Language Resources Association. Retrieved from https://aclanthology.org/2022.parlaclarin-1.17

Agnoloni, T., Marchetti, C., Battistoni, R., and Briotti, G. (2022b). Clustering similar amendments at the Italian Senate. *Proceedings of the Workshop ParlaCLARIN III within the 13th Language Resources and Evaluation Conference, Marseille, France*, 39–46. European Language Resources Association. Retrieved from https://aclanthology.org/2022.parlaclarin-1.7

[AI HLEG] High-Level Expert Group on Artificial Intelligence (2019). *Ethics Guidelines for Trustworthy AI*. Retrieved from https://ec.europa.eu/newsroom/dae/document.cfm?doc_id=60419

All-Party Parliamentary Group [APPG] (2022). *Artificial Intelligence APPG*. Retrieved from https://www.parallelparliament.co.uk/APPG/artificial-intelligence

Alshahrani, A., Dennehy, D., and Mäntymäki, M. (2021). An attention-based view of AI assimilation in public sector organizations: The case of Saudi Arabia. *Government Information Quarterly*, 39(4), 101617. Retrieved from https://doi.org/10.1016/j.giq.2021.101617

Artificial Intelligence Committee (2017, April 16). *AI in the UK: Ready, Willing and Able?* Report of Session 2017, 19, HL Paper 100, UK Parliament. Retrieved from https://publications.parliament.uk/pa/ld201719/ldselect/ldai/100/10002.htm

Bench-Capon, T. and Modgil, S. (2017). Norms and value based reasoning: Justifying compliance and violation. *Artificial Intelligence & Law Review*, 25, 29–64. Retrieved from https://doi.org/10.1007/s10506-017-9194-9

Bogucki, A., Engler A., Perarnaud, C., and Renda, A. (2022) *The AI Act and Emerging EU Digital Acquis: Overlaps, Gaps and Inconsistencies* (September 2022). Center for European Policy Studies. Retrieved from https://www.ceps.eu/ceps-publications/the-ai-act-and-emerging-eu-digital-acquis/

Clarke, R. (2019). Regulatory alternatives for AI. *Computer Law & Security Review*, 35(4), 398–409. Retrieved from https://doi.org/10.1016/j.clsr.2019.04.008

De Almeida P. G. R. (2021). El caminho hacia um parlamento inteligente – Cámara de Diputados de Brasil. *Red Información* (pp. 4–12). Retrieved from https://www.redinnovacion.org/revista/red-informaci%C3%B3n-edici%C3%B3n-n%C2%B0-24-marzo-2021

De Almeida, P. G. R., dos Santos, C. D., and Farias, J. S. (2021). Artificial Intelligence regulation: A framework for governance. *Ethics and Information Technology*, 23, 505–525. Retrieved from https://doi.org/10.1007/s10676-021-09593-z

De Almeida P. G. R., Vaz, R., and Kimaid, L. (2020). What a completely virtual parliament looks like. *Apolitical*. Retrieved from https://apolitical.co/solution-articles/en/what-a-completely-virtual-parliament-looks-like

De Sousa, W. G., de Melo, E. R. P., Bermejo, P. H. D. S., Farias, R. A. S., and Gomes, A. O. (2019). How and where is artificial intelligence in the public sector going? A literature review and research agenda. *Government Information Quarterly*, 36(4), 101392. Retrieved from https://doi.org/10.1016/j.giq.2019.07.004

Dignum, V. (2022). Relational Artificial Intelligence. Retrieved from https://doi.org/10.48550/arXiv.2202.07446

Eduskunta (2022, July 2). *The European Parliamentary Research Service Raises the Committee for the Future as a Model for the Development of Strategic Foresight in EP*. Retrieved from https://www.eduskunta.fi/EN/tiedotteet/Pages/EPRS-raises-the-Committee-for-the-Future-as-a-model-for-the-development-of-strategic-foresight-in-EP.aspx

European Commission (2022, November 9). *A European Approach to Artificial Intelligence*. Retrieved from https://digital-strategy.ec.europa.eu/en/policies/european-approach-artificial-intelligence

European Parliament (2022). *Proposal for a Regulation on a European Approach for Artificial Intelligence*. Retrieved from https://www.europarl.europa.eu/legislative-train/theme-a-europe-fit-for-the-digital-age/file-regulation-on-artificial-intelligence

Fitsilis, F. (2019). *Imposing Regulation on Advanced Algorithms*. Cham: Springer.

Fitsilis, F. (2021). Artificial Intelligence (AI) in parliaments – Preliminary analysis of the Eduskunta Experiment. *The Journal of Legislative Studies*, 27(4), 621–633. Retrieved from https://doi.org/10.1080/13572334.2021.1976947

Fitsilis, F., Koryzis, D., Svolopoulos, V., and Spiliotopoulos, D. (2017). Implementing digital parliament innovative concepts for citizens and policy makers. In Nah, F. H. and Tan, C. H. (eds), *HCI in Business, Government and Organizations. Interacting with Information Systems* (pp. 154–170). Cham: Springer. Retrieved from https://doi.org/10.1007/978-3-319-58481-2_13

Franke, U. (2021). *Artificial Intelligence Diplomacy: Artificial Intelligence Governance as a New European Union External Policy Tool.* (Report No. PE 662.926). Policy Department for Economic, Scientific and Quality of Life Policies, Directorate-General for Internal Policies. Retrieved from https://www.europarl.europa.eu/RegData/etudes/STUD/2021/662926/IPOL_STU(2021)662926_EN.pdf

Georgieva, T., Timan, T., and Hoekstra, M. (2022). *Regulatory Divergences in the Draft AI Act: Differences in Public and Private Sector Obligations.* (Report No. PE 729.507). European Parliamentary Research Service. Retrieved from https://www.europarl.europa.eu/thinktank/en/document/EPRS_STU(2022)729507

German Federal Government (2021). *Road Traffic Act.* Retrieved from http://www.gesetze-im-internet.de/englisch_stvg/print_englisch_stvg.html

Goebel, R., Chander, A., Holzinger, K., Lecue, F., Akata, Z., Stumpf, S., Kieseberg, P., and Holzinger, A. (2018). Explainable AI: The new 42? In *International Cross-domain Conference for Machine Learning and Knowledge Extraction* (pp. 295–303). Cham: Springer. Retrieved from https://doi.org/10.1007/978-3-319-99740-7_21

González, F., Ortiz, T., and Ávalos, R. S. (2020). *Responsible Use of AI for Public Policy: Data Science Toolkit.* OECD and IDB. Retrieved from http://dx.doi.org/10.18235/0002876

Hagendorff, T. (2020). The ethics of AI ethics: An evaluation of guidelines. *Minds and Machines*, 30, 99–120. Retrieved from https://doi.org/10.1007/s11023-020-09517-8

Husch, B., and Teiden, A. (2017). Regulating autonomous vehicles. *LegisBrief*, 25(13). Retrieved from https://www.ncsl.org/research/transportation/regulating-autonomous-vehicles.aspx

Inter-Parliamentary Union [IPU] (2020). Artificial Intelligence: Innovation in parliaments. *Innovation Tracker*, 4. Retrieved from https://www.ipu.org/innovation-tracker/story/artificial-intelligence-innovation-in-parliaments

Inter-Parliamentary Union [IPU] (2021). *World E-parliament Report 2020.* Geneva: IPU. Retrieved from https://www.ipu.org/resources/publications/reports/2021-07/world-e-parliament-report-2020

International Organization for Standardization [ISO] (2021). *Information Technology – Artificial Intelligence – Process Management Framework for Big Data Analytics* (ISO/IEC 24668:2022(en)). Retrieved from https://www.iso.org/standard/78368.html

Janssen, M., Brous, P., Estevez, E., Barbosa, L. S., and Janowski, T. (2020). Data governance: Organizing data for trustworthy Artificial Intelligence. *Government Information Quarterly*, 37(3), 101493. Retrieved from https://doi.org/10.1016/j.giq.2020.101493

Koryzis, D., Dalas, A., Spiliotopoulos, D., and Fitsilis, F. (2021). ParlTech: Transformation framework for the digital parliament. *Big Data and Cognitive Computing*, 5(1), 15. Retrieved from https://doi.org/10.3390/bdcc5010015

Koskimaa, V. and Raunio, T. (2020). Encouraging a longer time horizon: The Committee for the future in the Finnish Eduskunta. *The Journal of Legislative Studies*, 26(2), 159–179. Retrieved from https://doi.org/10.1080/13572334.2020.1738670

Kuziemski, M. and Misuraca, G. (2020). AI governance in the public sector: Three tales from the frontiers of automated decision-making in democratic settings. *Telecommunications Policy*, 44(6), 101976. Retrieved from https://doi.org/10.1016/j.telpol.2020.101976

Le Sueur, A. (2016). Robot government: Automated decision-making and its implications for parliament. In Horne, A. and Le Sueur, A. (eds), *Parliament: Legislation and Accountability* (pp. 183–202). Oxford and Portland: Hart Publishing.

Leventis, S., Fitsilis, F., and Anastasiou, V. (2021). Diversification of Legislation Editing Open Software (LEOS) using software agents – transforming parliamentary control of the hellenic parliament into big open legal data. *Big Data and Cognitive Computing*, 5(3), 45. Retrieved from https://doi.org/10.3390/bdcc5030045

Marchant, G. (2019). 'Soft Law' governance of artificial intelligence. *UCLA: The Program on Understanding Law, Science, and Evidence (PULSE)*. Retrieved from https://escholarship.org/uc/item/0jq252ks

Medaglia, R., Gil-Garcia, J. R., and Pardo, T. A. (2021). Artificial intelligence in government: Taking stock and moving forward. *Social Science Computer Review*, 1–18. Retrieved from https://doi.org/10.1177/08944393211034087

Missingham, R. (2011). E-parliament: Opening the door. *Government Information Quarterly*, 28(3), 426–434. Retrieved from https://doi.org/10.1016/j.giq.2010.08.006

Montoya, D., and Rummery, A. (2020). *The Use of Artificial Intelligence by Government: Parliamentary and Legal Issues* (e-brief 02/2020). NSW Parliamentary Research Service. Retrieved from https://www.parliament.nsw.gov.au/researchpapers/Pages/The-use-of-AI-by-government-parliamentary-and-legal-issues.aspx

Neudert, L. M. and Marchal, N. (2019). *Polarisation and the Use of Technology in Political Campaigns and Communication*. (Report No. PE 634.414). European Parliamentary Research Service. Retrieved from https://www.europarl.europa.eu/RegData/etudes/STUD/2019/634414/EPRS_STU(2019)634414_EN.pdf

Nilsson, N. J. (2009). *The Quest for Artificial Intelligence*. Cambridge University Press.

Norton, P. (1990). Parliaments: A framework for analysis. *West European Politics*, 13(3), 1–9. Retrieved from https://doi.org/10.1080/01402389008424803

Organisation for Economic Co-operation and Development [OECD] (2022a). *Policies, Data and Analysis for Trustworthy Artificial Intelligence*. Retrieved from https://oecd.ai/en/

Organisation for Economic Co-operation and Development [OECD] (2022b). *The OECD Global Parliamentary Group on AI*. Retrieved from https://oecd.ai/en/parliamentary-group-on-ai

Parliament of Victoria (2018). *Artificial Intelligence Primer*. Retrieved from https://www.parliament.vic.gov.au/publications/research-papers/download/36-research-papers/13863-artificial-intelligence-primer

Parliamentary Assembly of the Council of Europe [PACE] (2020). *Artificial Intelligence: Ensuring Respect for Democracy, Human Rights and the Rule of Law*. Retrieved from https://pace.coe.int/en/pages/artificial-intelligence

Silva, N. F. F., Silva, M. C. R., Pereira, F. S. F., Tarrega, J. P. M., Beinotti, J. V. P., Fonseca, M., de Andrade, F. E., and de Carvalho, A. C. P. de L. F. (2021). Evaluating topic models in Portuguese political comments about bills from Brazil's chamber of deputies. In Britto, A. and Valdivia Delgado, K. (eds), *Intelligent Systems* (pp. 104–120). Cham: Springer. Retrieved from https://doi.org/10.1007/978-3-030-91699-2_8

Souza, E., Moriyama, G., Vitório, D., de Carvalho, A. C., Félix, N., Albuquerque, H. O., and Oliveira, A. L. (2021a). Assessing the impact of stemming algorithms applied to Brazilian legislative documents retrieval. In *Anais do XIII Simpósio Brasileiro de Tecnologia da Informação e da Linguagem Humana* (pp. 227–236). Porto Alegre: Sociedade Brasileira de Computação. Retrieved from https://doi.org/10.5753/stil.2021.17802

Souza, E., Vitório, D., Moriyama, G., Santos, L., Martins, L., Souza, M., Fonseca, M., Felix, N., Carvalho, A. C. P. L. F., Albuquerque, H. O., and Oliveira, A. L. (2021b). An information retrieval pipeline for legislative documents from the Brazilian chamber of deputies. In *Legal Knowledge and Information Systems* (pp. 119–126). Amsterdam: IOS Press. Retrieved from https://doi.org/10.3233/FAIA210326

Van Noordt, C. and Misuraca, G. (2022). Exploratory insights on Artificial Intelligence for government in Europe. *Social Science Computer Review*, 40(2), 426–444. Retrieved from https://doi.org/10.1177/0894439320980449

Vetrò, A., Torchiano, M., and Mecati, M. (2021). A data quality approach to identifying discrimination risk in automated decision-making systems. *Government Information Quarterly*, 38(4), 101619. Retrieved from https://doi.org/10.1016/j.giq.2021.101619

von Lucke, J., Fitsilis, F., and Etscheid, J. (2022). Using artificial intelligence for legislation-thinking about and selecting realistic topics. *EGOV-CeDEM-ePart 2022*, 32–42. Retrieved from https://dgsociety.org/wp-content/uploads/2022/09/CEUR-proceedings-2022.pdf#page=46

Williamson, A., and Fallon, F. (2011). Transforming the future parliament through the effective use of digital media. *Parliamentary Affairs*, 64(4), 781–792. Retrieved from https://doi.org/10.1093/pa/gsr028

Winston, P. H. (1992). *Artificial Intelligence* (3rd ed.). Addison-Wesley Publishing Co.

Wirtz, B. W., Weyerer, J. C., and Geyer, C. (2019). Artificial intelligence and the public sector – applications and challenges. *International Journal of Public Administration*, 42(7), 596–615. Retrieved from https://doi.org/10.1080/01900692.2018.1498103

Zicari, R. V., Brodersen, J., Brusseau, J., Düdder, B., Eichhorn, T., Ivanov, T., ... and Westerlund, M. (2021). Z-Inspection®: A process to assess trustworthy AI. *IEEE Transactions on Technology and Society*, 2(2), 83–97. Retrieved from https://doi.org/10.1109/TTS.2021.3066209

Ziouvelou, X., Giannakopoulos, G., and Giannakopoulos, V. (2022) Artificial intelligence in the parliamentary context. In Fitsilis, F. and Mikros, G. (eds), *Smart Parliaments*, 43–53. Brussels: European Liberal Forum. Retrieved from https://liberalforum.eu/wp-content/uploads/2022/11/Smart-Parliaments_ELF-Study_Techno-Politics_vol.4.pdf#page=58

Zuiderwijk, A., Chen, Y., and Salem, F. (2021). Implications of the use of artificial intelligence in public governance: A systematic literature review and a research agenda. *Government Information Quarterly*, 38(3), 101577. Retrieved from https://doi.org/10.1016/j.giq.2021.101577

APPENDIX

Collected and analysed AI use cases in parliament

Parliament	AI system functionality	Technology	Maturity
Angola – National Assembly	Facial recognition to confirm attendance of the Assembly's staff	Computer vision – facial recognition	In use
	Speech recognition in plenary sittings and committee meetings	NLP – Speech to text	In use
Argentina – Chamber of Deputies[1]	Indexation of legislative process information	NLP – Text classification	Project
	Smart Parliament app – Organisation of legislative information in topics	Latent Dirichlet Allocation, NLP Topic classification	Project
Brazil – Chamber of Deputies[2]	Ulysses 1 – Classification of thematic web pages according to citizens' interest	NLP – Text classification	In use
	Ulysses 2 – Automatic distribution of parliamentarians' requests for new bill to lawmaker expert groups best skilled to draft it (according to bill subject)	NLP – Text classification	In use
	Ulysses 3 – Look for similar technical studies or bills at the law-making process[3]	NLP – Named entities recognition; NLP – Semantic textual similarity	Project
	Ulysses 5 – Speech recognition in plenary sittings and committee meetings	NLP – Speech to text	Project
	Ulysses 6 – Automatic analysis of citizens' contribution/opinion to a bill[4]	NLP – Topic modelling	Project
	Ulysses 7 – Facial recognition through liveness detection allows parliamentarians to authenticate when using Infoleg App – attendance registration, voting and election at plenary sitting and committee meetings[5]	Computer vision – Facial recognition	In use
Brazil – Senate[6]	Automatic distribution of parliamentarians' requests for new bill to lawmaker expert groups best skilled to draft it	NLP – Text classification	In use
	Parliamentarians' facial recognition for attendance registration at plenary sittings and committee meetings	Computer vision – Facial recognition	Project
	Speech transcription to text at plenary sittings and committee meetings.	NLP – Speech to text	Project
	Prediction of next words	NLP – Word prediction	Project

Parliament	AI system functionality	Technology	Maturity
Canada – House of Commons	Parlvu – Voice recognition to produce closed captioning	NLP – Speech to text – Custom built with NRC and CRIM Canada	In use
	PRISM – Automatic translation using the parliamentary knowledge base	NLP – Semantic textual similarity; NLP – Text translation	In use
	Physical security pattern recognition	Cognitive AI – Image and pattern recognition	In use
	CyberSecurity – Behavioural analysis and indicators of compromise discovery	Cognitive AI	In use
	PRISM – Speech recognition in plenary sittings and committee meetings	NLP – Speech to text	Project
	Automatic analysis on the free text indexation and summarisation	NLP – Clustering machine learning; summarisation	Project
	E-Vote – Facial recognition through liveness detection allows parliamentarians to authenticate when using the E-Voting app	FaceTec – facial recognition	In use
Estonia – Riigikogu	Speech recognition in plenary sittings and committee meetings	NLP – Speech to text	In use
	Subtitles' generation during remote plenary sittings and committee meetings	NLP – Speech to text	In use
European Parliament	Text summariser for the European Parliament archive documents, reducing the original size and facilitating EU citizens' research[7]	NLP – Summarisation	In use
	Archibot – EU Parliament chatbot for questions about the Archives content	NLP – Conversational agent	In use
	Topic identification and document classification on parliamentary questions stored in historical archives	NLP – Text classification	Project
	Placing jobs for translators	Reinforcement learning	Project
Finland – Eduskunta	Automation of accounting, payments and invoicing	NLP – Reinforcement learning	In use
	Speech recognition	NLP	In use
	Automatic translation	Neural Machine Translation	In use
	Committee of the Future conversational experience with AI 'personalities'	GPT-3 – Conversational agent	Project

Parliament	AI system functionality	Technology	Maturity
Italy – Senate	Automatic bill classification	NLP – Text classification	In use
	Linkoln – Identification of references to European and Italian laws, and other types of acts, in a given text fragment; automatic mark-up of each reference as a hyperlink[8]	NLP – Text similarity	In use
	Organisation of amendments in a sequence according to the Rules of Procedure[9]	NLP	In use
	Similis – Look for similar texts among amendments in parliamentary committees[10]	NLP – Text similarity	In use
	Chatbot 'discussing' contents of the institutional website	NLP – Chatbot	Project
	Photo recognition of archive's pictures	Computer vision – Object recognition	Project
	Transcription of audio of committees, and for converting stenotyping machine outputs in textual drafts of verbatims	NLP – Speech to text	In use
The Netherlands – House of Representatives	peach2Write – Automatic Speech Recognition to transcribe audio to text, automated editing of these transcripts	NLP – Speech to text	In use

Notes:
1   For more details on the AI solutions of the Parliament of Argentina, see: https://diplab.hcdn.gob.ar/proyectos #inteligencia-artificial
2   A concise description of the Ulysses system(s) is provided by De Almeida (2021).
3   The algorithmic processing of legislative documents in Brazil is described by Souza et al. (2021a, 2021b).
4   Silva et al. (2021) offer an evaluation of topic models for analysing political comments.
5   See De Almeida et al. (2020).
6   For details on the AI initiatives of the Brazilian Senate, see: https://www12.senado.leg.br/transparencia/gestgov/ planejamento-estrategico
7   The dashboard for the European Parliament archives can be found here: https://142m8225d1.execute-api.eu -central-1.amazonaws.com/v1/ep-archives-anonymous-dashboard
8   See https://ittig.github.io/Linkoln/ and https://www.normattiva.it/
9   See Agnoloni et al. (2022a).
10 See Agnoloni et al. (2022b).

10. Personalised public services powered by AI: the citizen digital twin approach

Aleksi Kopponen, Antti Hahto, Tero Villman, Petri Kettunen, Tommi Mikkonen and Matti Rossi

INTRODUCING CITIZEN DIGITAL TWIN: A NEW CONCEPT FOR PERSONALISED PUBLIC SERVICES

Providing cost-effective public services that fit citizens' real needs has been a persistent challenge in developed countries. With the development of technology and the better availability of digital information, the utilisation of artificial intelligence for these services has become a realistic possibility. One widely accepted idea has been to use the information about the persons themselves to target services (Margetts and Dorobantu, 2019; Zuiderwijk et al., 2021). However, current service provision often relies on data from individual customer events, rather than a comprehensive understanding of the person's situation, leading to a lack of targeted services. The Citizen Digital Twin (CDT) concept is presented as a solution to this problem, offering proactive service orchestration based on a holistic view of a citizen's real situation.

Citizen Digital Twin is a concept helping people to create an informed and digitised picture of their own lives, represented as a CDT (Kopponen et al., 2022a). The CDT, based on the digital twin paradigm (Glaessgen and Stargel, 2012) originating from the industry, or organisational digital twin (Parmar et al., 2020), allows a citizen to create a digital replication (El Saddik, 2018) of themselves with all the data that pertains to the citizen, including information beyond the public sector. The CDT helps a person perceive their own situation by going beyond analysing narrow perceptions, such as health information, to see their own situation holistically and to become empowered to act for their own good (Janowski, 2015; World Economic Forum, 2019). For service providers, seeing citizens through clusters of the CDTs sharing similar characteristics provides an informed basis for strategic guidance of service development and boosts Transformational Government or T-Gov (Omar et al., 2020) to reform public service delivery for the better of citizens. The CDT also enables automatic provision of public and private services to the citizen in various situations and events in life. The CDT supports the citizen to reflect on existential questions in which a person should be aware of their own situation, but in such a way that does not affect their own well-being negatively. By citizen-controlled sharing of the CDT information with service providers, citizens can receive suitable services from service ecosystems at the right times, leading to a situation where citizens have the capacity to act in the society for their own good and they are given assistance by service providers in a beneficial and non-intrusive manner. Support can be targeted especially to those whose own capacity to perceive necessary and useful services is limited (see the nursing child case example later in this chapter). In some cases, citizens do not even know what services they are entitled to receive. The CDT can act as everyday support for such situations.

The CDT also supports people's ability to make informed choices to improve their own situation by leveraging services that take the individual toward their own goals. Thus, when forming a service offering, the target CDT state of the individual must also affect the services provided. For example, if an individual wants to become a doctor, it makes more sense to recommend a high school than a vocational school.

In tailoring service ecosystems in a people-related yet proactive way by utilising the CDT concept, data of various origins needs to be combined so that service providers in different sectors can consider the overall situational context when providing their services fitting people's real needs, while considering the legal limitations as well as regulative responsibilities of data utilisation as well as the incentives to share data across organisational boundaries.

The more people's relative quality of life increases, the less heavy and expensive public services are needed. However, public services are also needed for a normal and prosperous life. Then it is as important that any public service is provided on time and as needed. By improving the accuracy of service delivery and reducing the number of people running in the wrong services at the wrong time (Seddon, 2003) with the help of artificial intelligence and machine learning, we can significantly improve the efficiency of our service delivery and increase the value delivery potential for people in the years to come.

In this chapter we look at the possibilities of supporting citizens in their life through their CDTs originally proposed in Kopponen et al. (2022a), at the level of an abstract blueprint. We chart the possibilities of helping citizens in their life events through AI augmented service orchestration that adjusts service provision to their individual circumstances to support people moving towards their personal goals. As new contributions, the chapter refines the concept and technical blueprint of CDT that allows a citizen to create a digital twin with all the data that pertains to the citizen themselves, similar to MyData initiatives (Hsien-Lee, 2021). Moreover, a validating example is presented.

The chapter is structured as follows. First, we give background and motivation to understand the transformative nature of the CDTs and AI augmented service offering. Then, we present the concept of augmenting proactive service delivery with CDT. The Finnish National Artificial Intelligence Programme AuroraAI (Ministry of Finance, Finland, 2022a), in which the AuroraAI Network has been built to enable a proactive and cross-sectoral service orchestration in people's life events, demonstrates the concept. Then, we provide implications for implementing the proposed concept and finally we wrap up with a few conclusions.

BACKGROUND AND MOTIVATION

Digital government transformation (DGT) may bring even paradigm shifts towards augmented governments to provide citizens with more tailored public services (Eom and Lee, 2022). The relationships between citizens and governmental service providers could change fundamentally by enabling predictive capabilities for public administration for better or for worse from a people perspective (Kopponen et al., 2022b). Overall, DGT may lead to fundamental redesigns of the information systems architectures and their constituting technological components where data is collected efficiently and utilised seamlessly across processes ('government as a platform') (Eom and Lee, 2022). However, there the AI-based digital transformations entail more than just advanced technologies. For instance, the government employees should be willing to use AI-based systems and data in their service work. DGTs thus also entail risks and potential downsides (for example adverse 'algorithmic bureaucracy', imbalanced data stewardships) (Eom and Lee, 2022).

Digital transformation can therefore lead to different results depending on what driving forces control service ecosystems around people (Butollo and Schneidemesser, 2022). The first driving force is business-centricity, in which private platform companies' key interest is to control service ecosystems and multiply their share values through their platform-based solutions (Vesnic Alujevic et al., 2019). The second driving force of the digital transformation is governance-centricity, in which, for example, authoritarian states utilise service ecosystems to tighten control over people. The third driving force of the digital transformation, which is argued for in this chapter, is human centricity, which incentivises service ecosystems to strengthen people's well-being. Human-centricity encourages service providers to design their operating models and solutions from the perspective of people's real needs.

There are also economic grounds for supporting and maintaining people's well-being proactively. Referring to the OECD (Organisation for Economic Cooperation and Development) report (OECD, 2021), the average per capita spending on health care grew by 2.7 per cent across OECD countries. At the same time, for example in Finland, the general government budgetary position begins to weaken over the medium term, and the debt-to-GDP ratio will start to grow. The aging population is the main factor that raises healthcare and nursing expenditure, which we cannot handle with the current total tax ratio in the coming decades (Ministry of Finance, Finland, 2022b). One factor contributing to the increase in costs is people's ability and desire to take care of their own well-being, which surprisingly has not improved in decades (Coe et al., 2022), even though average life expectancy and healthy years have increased by 19 years since the 1960s. This also indicates that current means of improving people's quality of life at the population level are not working as desired. A notable part of the cost of social and health care seems to be that people in one way or another neglect to take care of their own well-being. For example, an unhealthy diet and immobility provide fertile ground for type 2 diabetes to develop (Simpson et al., 2003). Even though we live in a time when people are better able to access knowledge that strengthens well-being than ever before, the amount of relative well-being is still not increasing.

Personalised Public Services

So how does looking at the service ecosystem from different perspectives change the need for the service offering? If you look at the service offering from an individual's perspective, the need for services is typically related to different situations and events in life. Since life can be viewed as a series of different life situations and events, the provision of services should also be designed from the point of view of these events (Kopponen et al., 2022). Today, service providers are providing siloed services based on the tasks assigned to the organisation and its mandates. The current way of organising public service production is customer-oriented, where customer relationships are usually defined from the perspective of the tasks or mandates of the organisations. For example, a hospital may be interested in the care path for a depressed person with the services they offer, while they are not responsible for depression as a life event that may involve other challenges in a personal relationship, work life, or other life areas. Thus, the hospital takes care of the customer-oriented service process precisely in terms of the tasks for which they are responsible, and the person is seen as a patient and an object of the service process rather than as a person or a subject.

Efforts towards seamless customer experiences often occur within organisations, but cross-organisational services often lack coordination, leading to a poor customer experience. People require smooth service chains for their life events, which involve services from various sectors. Thus, individual services should be integrated as parts of a holistic service ecosystem to provide meaningful human-centric service processes for different situations and events in life.

In a vision of a human-centric and proactive society (presented in Ministry of Finance, Finland, 2018), people also should have a better ability to take care of themselves and their own well-being, and service providers should be better able to respond to people's real needs with their own services (Rousku et al., 2019). One should be served holistically in different situations and events in life, which in practice means that the services and their orchestration must have a view of the person, not as an object of a customer process. Creating a public service offering around people's life events is a challenging task because legislation behind each authority draws the attention of public authorities to matters within their mandates. In principle, this is a good thing because it limits the authority's power over its citizens and businesses. Unfortunately, the limitation of power and data usage ties the hands of the authority to work more innovatively towards addressing the real needs of the people.

A life-event based approach to building a range of services is used around the world. For example, New Zealand launched SmartStart in 2016 (Andrews, 2017), which supported New Zealanders to go through the life event of having a child. The service provided life event-related information as well as three integrated services. In Singapore, government services have been similarly grouped into different life situations and events with a service called LifeSG, which is also available as an application (Government of Singapore, 2023). The service informs the user about current administration issues. In both cases, the service offering focuses on governance services. From a people's perspective, however, services are required from all different sectors in different life events. While cross-sectoral cooperation can be extraordinarily complex and difficult, it is needed today more than ever before (Bryson et al., 2015).

In addition to meeting people's real needs, the service offering must be provided in a timely and proactive manner. Taiwan, for example, began to pay attention to the reactive nature of services (pull) to provide services proactively (push) instead (Linders et al., 2018).

Everyday service paths are rarely limited to public or private services, but life consists of combinations of these services, and these combinations also vary depending on the characteristics and needs of the person using the services, because people and their lives are unique. Similarly, the current way of thinking about customer orientation at worst only accelerates the flow of people from door to door, no matter how customer-oriented these hatches are. The so-called 'one-stop service experience' is not a credible concept for life event service entities, as services change and evolve, and in a one-stop shop philosophy this would mean a single entity.

It is plausible to think that we could create a service orchestration that mimics the ways in which existing platform services, such as Amazon, optimise their service ecosystems. According to previous studies (Adner, 2017; Jacobides et al., 2018), the formation of an ecosystem is driven by the special and value-strengthening bonds formed between those involved in the ecosystem. In a human-centric service ecosystem, the service offering is optimised for different situations and events in life from the perspective of strengthening people's well-being. In practice, people themselves need to have a better ability to perceive their own situation, and service providers need to have a better ability to understand the characteristics and needs of the population in different life situations and events.

To understand people holistically, we must first have an idea of what data would help us look at people holistically. The idea of human integrity requires the utilisation of analytics, as the amount of data collected from people in organisations is constantly increasing and at the same time the possibilities for refining the understanding of large masses of data to support decision-making in ethically sustainable ways are increasing. Large data sets will not be useful unless they are suitable for statistical analysis and the use of machine learning models. The usefulness of the models depends, among other things, on the quality, quantity, and usability of the input data. In addition, the data currently held by service providers supports their own customer processes and is intended only for a specific use, which may not allow the data to be used as such to form an overall picture of people, in this case as a CDT.

There seldomly exists an optimal single service, or service provider, to provide optimal support for a life situation. Furthermore, a service that has been originally designed with a one-size-fits-all design ideology (for example, national unemployment services for unemployed), is harder to tailor for individual users' personal needs in an effective manner. A person is seen as a customer of a single entity, be it a public or commercial service, ignoring complex interplay of all the other stakeholders affecting the user's daily life at any given time.

With a life-event approach, we present a modelling method for automatically defining the user's current situation and their desired goals for selecting optimal supportive service combinations in a computationally solvable manner. Applying the method to orchestrating services increases the likelihood that people will select and utilise services that, based on feedback from previous service users, have added value in that life event. The section Conceptual Design Idea and Development, presents a practical example of Finland's National Artificial Intelligence Program AuroraAI, which creates the technical infrastructure to enable the intelligent interaction of services directly in different life situations and events (Digital and Population Data Services Agency, Finland, 2023a; Rousku et al., 2019).

Digital Twins

To solve the problem of data relevance, the data must be viewed from the perspective of people. Here, the CDT – based on a digital twin concept – helps to form an understanding of a person from her own starting points. Nowadays, digital twin technology is increasingly studied and applied in public sector domains to enhance and improve service design and provision, for example in Japan (Obi and Iwasaki, 2021). Smarter cities could be achieved with AI-DT collaborations, and the labour productivity of the government could be improved with AI. However, they argue that the effects of digital twins should be evaluated considering their convenience for users. They see a need for standards and convergence of platforms for digital twins in smart cities.

Furini et al. suggest digital twins of students could help in delivering more effective, personalised educational services (Furini et al., 2022). The general idea is that the service system could suggest and recommend for each individual student suitable learning models based on AI-analysis of the student's digital twin information (for example, past behaviour on campus premises). Also, Human Digital Twin (Shengli, 2021) is a novel concept to construct a virtual counterpart of a person.

Anshari and Hamdan examined the potential of digital twins in e-government to improve public services and well-being (Anshari and Hamdan, 2022). In their vision, digital twins are built and operated through e-government and infrastructure systems managing the relationship between service providers and citizens. The general idea is that digital twins enable capturing the citizens' historical and current behaviour in digital activity processes that help analyse them across all available e-services. When critical issues or problems are discovered, the digital twin can alert and present alternative solutions and recommendations to the (physical) user (citizen) based on the gathered data. The citizens can then determine their chosen best course of action for their next steps. In that way, individual citizens can understand themselves better and improve their own performances based on comprehensive, or even real-time data, and develop accordingly.

CONCEPTUAL DESIGN IDEA AND DEVELOPMENT

The AuroraAI network, developed under Finnish National Artificial Intelligence Program AuroraAI, aims to help its users in a broad range of different life events, by creating and orchestrating tailored service combinations meeting users' personal needs (Ministry of Finance, Finland, 2022a). This connectivity functionality is designed to be added to thousands of already existing public services, combined with relevant private and third sector services to form viable service ecosystems around people's life events (Figure 10.1).

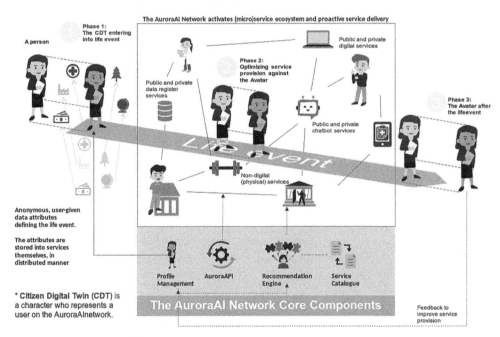

Source: The National Artificial Intelligence Programme AuroraAI (Ministry of Finance, Finland, 2022a).

Figure 10.1   The AuroraAI Network brings a person to the right services when the life situation changes

Let us assume that citizens have CDTs at their disposal. The public service providers can use them in the provision of services to citizens, enabled by The AuroraAI Network. When the CDT is being defined as a collection of user attributes and service provisioning (Figure 10.1), utilising services offered further modifies and alters the CDT (causing an impact to the user). In the future, the user attributes could also contain dynamic data such as people's self-defined goals and feelings. Thus, CDT can be seen as a dynamic digital profile of its user's historical and current behaviour that supports the optimisation of business performance (Anshari and Hamdan, 2022). When the user utilises the services offered, data is collected about the use of the services and their impact on the person, which can be returned to the CDT to be evolved after the use of the services. In Phase 1 (see Figure 10.1), a person defines their situation with the CDT. Through a dialogue between a person and their CDT, Profile Management updates the CDT to enable Phase 2, where the service ecosystem is optimised by Recommendation Engine from available service space found in Service Catalogue to provide proactive services. Depending on the maturity level of services in the service ecosystem, the AuroraAI Network enables services to interact with each other by utilising AuroraAPI. Then, public, and private chatbot services connected to the AuroraAI Network can recommend those services to the user. In Phase 3, utilised services and their contribution to the person's life is a basis for the CDT after the life event.

The operating principles of the AuroraAI Network (Figure 10.1) are as follows:

1. A service connected to the AuroraAI network proposes a service recommendation to the user.
2. The user may provide additional information about him/herself in numerous services connected.
3. Recommendation Engine further utilises the user's information, orchestrating an optimal service combination from the Service Catalogue based on this distributed user profile.
4. The user chooses to use the recommended service or services.
5. The user's information is transferred to the recommended service.

Any person is, at any given time, in a certain life situation (state) defined by the user attributes and attribute changes. It is worth mentioning that the states are not discrete but continuous: life events do not have a rigid start and end but rather, the user resides simultaneously in many events and situations gradually morphing into others. Intuitively, it is difficult to model a combination of all these life events and there resides temptation to oversimplify. A faulty assumption of a single isolated life situation unfolding at a time, benefitting from services – or any single service – targeted to that specific situation only, would not result in truly holistic well-being. Similarly, having no 'memory' of the past events would not lead to meaningful life improvements. This continuous migration from one state to another, facilitated by continuous and personalised service provisioning, is here approximated as a state-machine. With this approach, we reduce the problem to be solvable by automated means. Optimising service space can be seen as adjusting probabilities of a state-transition table for a given similar peer-group. The peer group, or user segment, is obtained from the CDT.

AI Augmented Service Orchestration with CDTs

The AI augmented personalised public services are composed by orchestrating optimal service combinations in the AuroraAI Network. This overall solution belongs to a well-known AI sub-category: automated planning and scheduling, as utilised for example in robotics (Chien et al., 1998; Hahto et al., 2011a, 2011b). The service offering is thus viewed from a human perspective as a relevant life event projected onto the AuroraAI network. As stated earlier, a life event is not a fixed set of services, but any service combination can be triggered onto the AuroraAI network, leveraging data from others who have experienced similar life situations.

Different techniques can be used to optimise the service offering. The operations of the AuroraAI network are based on a state machine. Traditionally, state machines are used in computer science and any technical systems utilising sequential logic, but their application to societal level problems has been, to the best of the authors' knowledge, non-existent. User journey mapping is a common tool in service design, modelling the sequence of services in similar fashion, but having manually pre-defined, static structures with no flow control or probabilistic transitions. Furthermore, experts in their own domain, not considering thousands of different services from various service providers, define service journey maps. Customer journey maps are tailored to fit individual user needs in a limited fashion, but are not proactive (service recommendation vs. listing of services) nor even reactive (reacting to users' changing needs).

Let us consider a life situation as a state of a state machine, consisting of many minor and major life situations and transitions between those. The state transitions are hereby defined as life events and in this context, 'state' is defined as aggregate of all the information AuroraAI services have stored from the user in a distributed manner (in Figure 10.1 'user attributes', or state variables). This aggregate data is represented as the user's digital twin (CDT). The AI-based service orchestration utilises CDT as input: users having similar twins will have similar service combinations offered. On the other hand, CDT can be seen as an interface between the actual user and the service ecosystem.

Service orchestration and recommendation overlap as concepts but have some crucial differences. Even though service recommender provides a visible end-result (for example, recommended service combination) to the end-user, recommendation itself acts as an aggregate being constructed from many smaller services. This tailoring is done on a user-level; personalised service is attained by 'constructing' in-situ an aggregate service against CDTs to be then recommended. When the overall services are constructed, joining those from a pool of available ones, this usually also requires services to interact with each other for acting as a single seamless unit (for example, exchange information with each other using AuroraAPI, dependency solving and execution order solving).

A conception of service is defined here in a broad manner: a self-contained entity to provide utility to the end user or other services, be it a technical service (such as data source, computation or UX) or non-technical (such as customer service, a local ice hockey club or a swimming hall). Services are considered as a main interface and embodiment of a society to its members.

When services are considered connected, hereby defined as service chains, they constitute a graph with services as nodes and transitions between services as edges. The transitions are probabilistic, zero probability value indicating disconnection. State transitions can be considered to fulfil Markov property: the next potential nodes of the chain only depend on the current location (life situation) and probability of the transitions. This relaxes the problem to be solved with any current recommendation algorithms: a service chain can be constructed as a recursive sequence, considering the user's current service, user attributes and historical data. The overall process is stochastic, such as life and its events.

State of Service Orchestration Practice in the AuroraAI Network

The first implementations of the AuroraAI Network core components have been developed, with open-source code published in 2022. Similarly, first reference implementations utilising the network's capabilities, in addition to some 10 pilot projects for converting legacy services to the new paradigm, are underway.

The AuroraAI Network consists of loosely coupled services, including four core components (see Figure 10.1) to provide basic functionality for orchestrating the service chains in life events and situations:

1. **Profile Management** handles distributed identity and establishes a mechanism to match services from Service Catalogue against the CDT. User data consists of both validated (register data, for example) and user-given attributes. The data is not collected to a central repository or any single organisation but rather, in the control of the user themselves.
2. **AuroraAPI** establishes a standard way to operate all the services in society, be it digital or physical, and enables service discovery. Data and functionality are separated from their providers (institutions). This dismantles traditional organisational silos and establishes truly holistic well-being as a product of cross-sectoral cooperation supported by technical means.
3. **Recommendation Engine** suggests service combinations from a pool of available ones. The AuroraAI Network connected services, or the user utilising said service thereof, may obtain 'best service combination' to meet their demand, with 'best possible' relating to search criteria and user attributes given. As the effects on winning combinations are often delayed and no clear cause-effect relationship can be established, best combinations are obtained with reinforcement learning.
4. **Service Catalogue** includes descriptions and necessary information on AuroraAI services, making those searchable and machine-readable. One instance of such a component is Suomi.fi Finnish Service Catalogue (FSC) (Digital and Population Data Services Agency, 2023b).

The user can obtain service recommendations by using any user interface (such as chatbots) of a service integrated in the AuroraAI Network. Recommendations are based on their current CDT data (in Figure 10.1, Optimising Service Provision against the CDT), to help the user progress towards self-given desired states (in Figure 10.1, The CDT after the life event) and to avoid undesired ones. As the Recommendation Engine gets feedback from people using services, it begins to learn with the help of machine learning from various user segments utilising certain service combinations and benefitting from those. The more feedback the Recommendation Engine gets, the better chance to establish a role model library with CDT archetypes (an AI Lenses concept presented in Kopponen et al., 2022b). In the future, we can utilise the library for better end-user experience: the user may select a desired archetype in a very intuitive way, for obtaining service recommendations and advancing towards the selected target. CDT could develop a better ability to understand its user than the user can have themselves, at least in limited cases, such as today's wearable technology that knows better than its users when the optimal time is to go to sleep.

Evaluating 'good' service combinations is difficult, as this is very subjective. This also poses many ethical considerations. As the services are being aggregated with heterogeneous types and have non-deterministic execution times, it is exceedingly difficult to pinpoint any sole source causing the exact impact. An orchestrated aggregate might include both physical and digital services, some lasting several months such as 'career counselling' or 'psychotherapy' but also services such as 'obtaining tax ID' or 'reading data value from a register' being instantaneous. Fortunately, we can reduce the problem with reinforcement learning: as we evaluate combinations (aggregates) for leading towards positive end results, it does not matter what single service was the source (if there was any). Here, a fitness function requires multiple components: user opinion gives some value (for example, thumbs up), but on its own is far from sufficient. Other sources might include historical A/B data, for example. Before usage data starts accumulating, 'good' combinations are taught in a distributed manner, using an expert teaching tool (for example, a single expert can only teach combinations their service is having a part in).

As the AuroraAI Network enters the scaling phase, it is populated by new services around strategically chosen life events by the next Finnish Government. As the services vary from each other (compare, say, a swimming hall to automatically applying for a new company registration number) connecting services is a case-by-case process with unique characteristics.

Scaling is done both bottom-up and top-down: any new service added will benefit from previously added life situations and events, as it will automatically be included in the suitable service chains for providing new value and new combinations. On the other hand, we aim to integrate service combinations in tandem to specifically target new life events or situations: therefore, the user gains immediate help with good pre-set combinations to specific problems out of the box but on the other hand, when the services are integrated once, those can be re-used with any new combination targeting other life-events. Finally, manually defining or labelling new life events is not necessary at all: the AuroraAI Network aims to find best service combinations from a pool of existing services in any situation, whether a human-defined discrete label or not.

It is envisioned that the AuroraAI Network and the AuroraAI Operating model, with all the tools developed in the project, will be utilised as a backbone in future government programs, such as National Digital Compass (Finnish Government, 2022), driven by the European Commission Digital Compass Initiative, with 40 additional life events to be integrated. Furthermore, AuroraAI as a programme focused primarily on the public sector services is due to practical limitations: during the scaling phase, it is expected services from any sector will join, achieving a truly cross-sectoral cooperation for the person's well-being, facilitated by the infrastructure and organisational tools developed.

A Case Example of the CDT Building: Nursing Child

As a practical pilot example with a pre-chosen service offering, the CDT was demonstrated in the so-called 'nursing child' segment which was revealed through wide data analysis (City of Tampere, 2022), where a young person was identified as a person who must take an unusually significant role in his family, for example in caring for his parents or siblings. A member of the target group does not necessarily know that she is a caring young person, in which case the young person may not be able to apply for services or support suitable for their situation. Correspondingly, the service system is unable to identify the persons in the situation. As a solution, the group of young people was offered the opportunity to examine their own situation with the help of a comprehensive well-being questionnaire application (shown in Figure 10.2), in which the young person answers the questions presented to them. Based on the questions, a CDT is formed about the respondent, which is compared to the relevant target segment. If the CDT belongs to the target segment, the application activates the service offering reserved for the target group for the person to use. The demonstration also subsidised the services offered to a selected target group who lived in a certain area in Finland. As a result of the demonstration, the young person developed a better ability to understand their own situation, and the service production system gained an understanding of how to contact the people in the target segment, so that the intersection of services could also be resolved, and services known in advance from different sectors could be offered for the young person to use.

In this pilot, a pre-selected service offer was used. Thus, AI-based service orchestration (in this article, Recommendation Engine in Figure 10.1) was not yet needed. The main goal of this pilot was to investigate if a young person in a tricky situation could be supported better than at present through the CDT approach and to suggest suitable services in a chosen situation. In the next phase, the Recommendation Engine (see Figure 10.1) in the AuroraAI Network can be applied to enable optimal service offering from the Service Catalogue and based on the CDT of the user.

Figure 10.2   *User interface images from the demonstration of building the CDT (corresponding Phase 1 in Figure 10.1) out of real use case (a nursing child). The user answers questions based on which a CDT is formed about the user, against which a service offer is formed (corresponding Phase 2 in Figure 10.1)*

DISCUSSION

The introduction of Citizen Digital Twins (CDT) will have several implications for public administration, public and private sector services, service providers, and most importantly, citizens using and/or needing the services.

CDT As a Key in Orchestrating Personalised Public and Private Services

People go through different life situations and events that together form a chain of life, including slower, faster, minor, and major life changes. Proactive public services need to understand where a person is coming from, where they are and where they are going or want to go to be able to provide truly personalised services. If a person's dreams and goals are clear, the services must be able to travel along the way as a reliable and desirable partner to help them progress. If one's dreams and goals are unclear for one reason or another, personalised public services should help the person identify favourable directions for themselves to further develop their understanding and abilities.

Improving one's own sense of their real situation and planning their own future can also involve tensions. Although improving one's own knowledge management can be thought to improve well-being in general, dealing with the real situation can be stressful, even painful, and there is not necessarily the will nor the capacity to take the necessary measures to improve the situation. For some, it may make sense to live their own lives dreaming of a better one and at the same time doing well enough in their own lives. Some want an honest situation analysis of their own lives (for example, a Cooper test result), some want indicative information on how to act (for example, a suggestion to go to sleep earlier). In some situations, things need to be looked at over a brief period, for example in the event of sudden changes requiring a fast response, although building awareness, identifying the desired direction, and developing needed capabilities over a longer period would be the real goal. In a way, people move from one life situation or event to another, while their CDT travels with them in the background. The CDT should help a person identify paths that are favourable to them to choose from, and help them make no-regret decisions, which are beneficial to them no matter what happens in life.

Personalising public service delivery through CDTs and by better understanding the real needs of people with the help of AI and, even further, attracting cross-sectoral service ecosystems directly in people's life events, would fundamentally challenge current public administration policies in service provision. It could significantly improve people's ability to make their own lives as meaningful as possible by offering them relevant and timely services and to move towards their personal goals, as depicted in the AI Lenses concept in Kopponen et al. (2022b). Similarly, improving a person's own awareness of their situation enables an even larger part of the population to make informed decisions to support their own well-being, which will reduce the need for heavy and expensive public services in cases where people do not pay attention to their own well-being proactively. The drivers that guide individual life and service provision would be the real needs of the people instead of aiming to meet the responsibilities or goals of public administration or a private company.

The desire of service providers to offer services is based, for example, on the law or the need to succeed in the market. In both cases, the service provider tries to ensure that its own services can be found and used by its own target group. However, point-of-care services compete for the individual's attention and use of time, so from the individual's point of view, the utilisation of the services is not optimal. With the help of CDT, a new opportunity opens for service providers to identify people's real needs through various data analyses, and thus to formulate services and entities that are as accurately as possible suitable for different target groups, which can be targeted directly at users of CDTs. In such a market, those services that have the greatest welfare impact on the real individuals behind the CDTs will succeed. CDT gives the public administration better opportunities to target statutory services timelier and more proactively than at present, so that heavy and expensive public services are not needed as much as when people's well-being deteriorates.

Emphasis on the Role of the User of CDT and Ethical Questions

In the demonstration of the 'nursing child' (see case example in section 'A Case Example of the CDT Building: Nursing Child') target segment, it was possible to resolve the issue of services in favour of a young person in a tricky situation. The traditional running from one service to another turned into proactive recognition of the situation and the provision of services suitable for the situation. For the user of CDT, it practically means a growing interest in their own situation and the utilisation of services suitable for it, which gives the potential to greatly increase people's ability and desire to take care of themselves thus avoiding situations in which their well-being would deteriorate and the subsequent need for heavy public services would increase.

Benefitting from the CDT concept requires an active role from the citizen themselves. Personalised public services cannot be obtained if a person is not interested in their own situation and so thereby form a CDT from it. Also, the public self-image may also be quite different from the real self and the CDT might be formed very differently depending on what kind of data Profile Management (Figure 10.1) gets from a person. If they form their CDT based on the actual situation, it differs from the public image in which, at worst, the person may have covered the actual situation, resulting in a quite different service offering. As with any new service, citizens should be provided with support and training in setting up their own CDT using services proactively.

Although artificial intelligence can be considered to play a significant role and CDT as a concept can be viewed from a technological point of view, it is a broader social change where technological solutions are only one part of the whole. The change should also be examined critically from the point of view of ethics, among other things. As an example, the independent ethics group of the AuroraAI program supported the implementation of the program by examining ethical issues and making recommendations to support the implementation. The utilisation of CDT has the potential for far-reaching and deep change, first in the operation of the public administration, but also in the everyday life and operating environment of private service providers and citizens, while ensuring privacy issues and citizens control data flows.

Potential Benefits and Benefitters

CDTs can be used as a concept either with a precisely defined focus, such as 'a nursing child' (see case example in section 'A Case Example of the CDT Building: Nursing Child') or in broader, even surprising contexts. So far, the discussions in Finland have been divided strongly between the two interpretations. In more precisely defined use cases, the concrete implementation of CDT has been a very pragmatic mapping and reflection of the person's situation, for example in pilots carried out at confirmation camps in Finland in 2022. As a broader concept, CDT has not yet been concretely implemented, so the debate has taken place on a conceptual level. In Finland, one can see at least two-way views on which line is desirable and which is not. For example, information management of one's own life with the help of a concept like CDT has been seen as harmful to the person in some cases. Not all people have the ability or even the desire to understand their own situation, and when they understand the weakness of the situation in relation to their reference group, their well-being may collapse without solid support from society. Others think that people's ability to make better informed decisions to strengthen their own well-being in turn strengthens the well-being of civil society and the direction towards a more sustainable public economy.

At this early stage of the concept, it can be said that we need much more evidence of what can and cannot be expected from CDTs. It must also be understood that the utilisation of data-based CDTs is strongly tied to the social context. For example, a CDT carried out in Finland can be successful in a quite unique way compared to a country where citizens' trust in the authorities is not at the same level. Thus, the concept can also provoke backlash, especially in societies where trust between government and citizens is not in a decent shape. Gathering comprehensive information about the individual in a country whose government might use the CDT concept for their own purposes or even against their citizens, does not necessarily lead to the strengthening of well-being, but even to the curtailment of human rights.

Societal Implications of CDTs

The more accurate the Recommendation Engine's (see Figure 10.1) understanding of the human situation (with the CDT), the more optimal the service offering can be tailored from the known services in the service network. However, it is paramount to consider privacy issues when forming a CDT. One must be able to control one's own information flows, and to manage and utilise the CDT formed from them. Minimum Viable Data (MVD) thinking could work well here, referring to the minimum data needed to train the machine learning model (van Allen, 2018). In an analogue world, the police officer who writes you a speeding ticket needs your identification, but the fisher selling you some fish only needs money from you. Preventing the formation of a Big Brother society is key to building a human-centric and proactive society. It must be possible to create segment-level profiles from CDTs whose data cannot be linked to a specific person. Segment-level data can also be used to create synthetic profiles based on a data model, against which service development can be made without worries. At its best, the service offering is optimised for millions of CDTs, and the identity of the people behind them does not need to be revealed when the service offering is formed. The Recommendation Engine (see Figure 10.1), machine learning models, and service provision outcomes should be regularly and transparently audited.

There seems to be a consensus in Finland that better targeting of public services will improve the effectiveness of services to people who need services in a particular situation in their own lives. The optimisation of society's service offering to support people's well-being and the achievement of their own goals creates a new kind of well-being market, where service providers in different sectors compete for the best possible service offerings for people in different life situations and events. At the same time, the use of public services at the wrong time and need is reduced. Also, better segment analysis of the population improves the ability of public service providers to develop services to meet people's real needs and provide proactively different life situations to people who need them the most, thus, realising citizen centricity in public services.

CONCLUSIONS

In this chapter, we have outlined how AI and Citizen Digital Twin (CDT) augmented human-centric, proactive public services can be provided in combination with other relevant services. It offers many potential benefits both for citizens and the service providers, such as meeting public service provision for the real needs of people and at the right time. In Finland, such capabilities for public service provision and orchestration have started to form under the national AI program AuroraAI. However, the practical implementation of a human-centric and proactive society requires several further measures. The technical and semantic interoperability of services, the orchestration of services, and the change in service production and the transformation of the service providers' operations are examples of the drivers of change in human-centric service ecosystems. The ability of service providers to understand the situation of people holistically needs to be increased by building situational analysis of the target population to which the organisation targets services. Similarly, companies need to be given a better understanding of other service providers which provide services to similar target groups for an organisation to have a better ability to perceive the service ecosystem that will form around its chosen target population.

The orchestration of services based on the real situation of people results in the genuine ability of service providers to provide services directly to the situations and events in people's lives where their services are typically most needed, and where services provide the most value to people. AI plays a key role in improving the match accuracy of the service orchestration, utilising data about the users of the services and user feedback on the effectiveness of the service offerings on the actual need. Similarly, as service providers' understanding of people's life situations and needs is increased, services are also expected to evolve and be better targeted to meet service needs. Together, these reduce the so-called failure demand for services, where a person exploits the wrong services at the wrong time, making the disorder a waste of time and resources that, from the service provider's point of view, the service is not designed for. A better understanding of people's needs and a better understanding of the provision of services can also form a basis for optimal service combinations directly for different life situations and events, which at the same time improves the matching of services.

In the future, the optimisation of the service offering with the CDTs could learn to consider personal goals in life, in which case the service offering also supports the achievement of the person's goals in the longer term, and not only considers the current situation. Improving people's ability to take care of their own well-being and those of their loved ones and enabling them to live their lives towards their own dreams can truly establish a better society that supports a better quality of life through relevant public and private services throughout a lifetime.

REFERENCES

Adner, R. (2017). Ecosystem as structure: An actionable construct for strategy. *Journal of Management*, *43*(1), 39–58. https://doi.org/10.1177/0149206316678451

Andrews, P. (2017). SmartStart: A federated service life event story. *New Zealand Government*. https://www.digital.govt.nz/blog/smartstart-a-federated-service-life-event-story/

Bryson, J., Crosby, B., and Stone, M. (2015). Designing and implementing cross-sector collaborations: Needed and challenging. *Public Administration Review*, *75*(5), 647–663. http://dx.doi.org/10.1111/puar.12432

Butollo, F., and Schneidemesser, L. (2022). Who runs the show in digitalized manufacturing? Data, digital platforms and the restructuring of global value chains. *Global Networks*, *22*(4), 595–614. http://dx.doi.org/10.1111/glob.12366

Chien, S., Smith, B., Rabideau, G., Muscettola, N., and Rajan, K. (1998). Automated planning and scheduling for goal-based autonomous spacecraft. *IEEE Intelligent Systems and their Applications*, *13*(5), 50–55. https://doi.org/10.1109/5254.722362

City of Tampere (2022). Management with information and regional inequality. Tampere Junior development program. https://www.tampere.fi/organisaatio/tampere-junior-kehitysohjelma/tiedolla-johtaminen-ja-alueellinen-eriarvoistuminen

Coe, E., Dewhurst, M., Hartenstein, L., Hextall, A., and Latkovic, T. (2022). Adding years to life and life to years. McKinsey Health Institute, Report. https://www.mckinsey.com/mhi/our-insights/adding-years-to-life-and-life-to-years

Digital and Population Data Services Agency, Finland (2023a). *AuroraAI-verkkoon liittymisen aloitus-paketti*. https://www.suomidigi.fi/ohjeet-ja-tuki/auroraai-verkkoon-liittymisen-aloituspaketti

Digital and Population Data Services Agency (2023b). Suomi.fi Finnish Service Catalogue (FSC). https://www.suomi.fi/services/suomi-fi-finnish-service-catalogue-fsc-digital-and-population-data-services-agency/d93be162-07a2-45f2-84b3-f794da852b58

El Saddik, A. (2018). Digital twins: The convergence of multimedia technologies. *IEEE MultiMedia*, *25*(2), 87–92. https://doi.org/10.1109/MMUL.2018.023121167

Eom, S. and Lee, J. (2022). Editorial, Digital government transformation in turbulent times: Responses, challenges, and future direction. *Government Information Quarterly*, *39*(2), Article 101690. https://doi.org/10.1016/j.giq.2022.101690

Finnish Government (2022). Valtioneuvoston selonteko Suomen digitaalisesta kompassista. 2022:65. http://urn.fi/URN:ISBN:978-952-383-906-9

Furini, M., Gaggi, O., Mirri, S., Montangero, M., Pelle, E., Poggi, F., and Prandi, C. (2022). Digital twins and artificial intelligence as pillars of personalized learning models. *Communications of the ACM*, *65*(4), 98–104. https://doi.org/10.1145/3478281

Glaessgen, E. and Stargel, D. (2012). The digital twin paradigm for future NASA and U.S. Air Force vehicles. *53rd AIAA/ASME/ASCE/AHS/ASC Structures, Structural Dynamics and Materials Conference 20th AIAA/ASME/AHS Adaptive Structures Conference 14th AIAA*, 1818. http://dx.doi.org/10.2514/6.2012-1818

Government of Singapore (2023). *Government Services that Fit Your Life*. https://www.life.gov.sg/

Hahto, A., Rasi, T., Mattila, J., and Koskimies, K. (2011a). Service-oriented architecture for embed-ded machine control. 2011 *IEEE International Conference on Service-Oriented Computing and Applications (SOCA)*, 1–4, https://doi.org/10.1109/SOCA.2011.6166246

Hahto, A., Aha, L., Nurminen, T., Aaltonen, A., Heikkilä, L., Mattila, J., Siuko, M., Saarinen, H., and Semeraro, L. (2011b). Supervisory system for DTP2 remote handling operations. *Fusion Engineering and Design*, *86*(9–11), 2047–2050. https://doi.org/10.1016/j.fusengdes.2011.02.051

Hsien-Lee, T. (2021). A personal data innovative government digital service in Taiwan: Study of MyData services. *The 22nd Annual International Conference on Digital Government Research*, 273–280. https://doi.org/10.1145/3463677.3463727

Jacobides, M., Cennamo, C., and Gawer, A. (2018). Towards a theory of ecosystems. *Strategic Management Journal*, *39*(8), 2255–2276. http://dx.doi.org/10.1002/smj.2904

Janowski, T. (2015). Digital government evolution: From transformation to contextualization. *Government Information Quarterly*, *32*(3), 221–236. https://doi.org/10.1016/j.giq.2015.07.001

Kopponen, A., Hahto, A., Kettunen, P., Mikkonen, T., Mäkitalo, N., Nurmi, J., and Rossi, M. (2022a). Empowering citizens with digital twins: A blueprint. *IEEE Internet Computing*, *26*(5), 7–16. https://doi.org/10.1109/MIC.2022.3159683

Kopponen, A., Villman, T., Kettunen, P., Mikkonen, T., and Rossi, M. (2022b). Artificial intelligence lenses: Citizens' guide to the futures with citizen digital twins. *AI and Society: Tensions and Opportunities*. Chapter 6. http://dx.doi.org/10.1201/9781003261247-8

Linders, D., Liao, C., and Wang, C. (2015). Proactive e-Governance: Flipping the service delivery model from pull to push in Taiwan. *Government Information Quarterly*, *35*(4), Supplement. S68–S76. https://doi.org/10.1016/j.giq.2015.08.004

Margetts, H. and Dorobantu, C. (2019). Rethink government with AI. *Nature, 568*(7751), 163–165 568. http://dx.doi.org/10.1038/d41586-019-01099-5

Ministry of Finance, Finland (2018). *A Human-Centric and Proactive Society.* https://vm.fi/ ihmiskeskeinen-yhteiskunta

Ministry of Finance, Finland. (2022a). *National Artificial Intelligence Programme AuroraAI.* https://vm .fi/en/national-artificial-intelligence-programme-auroraai

Ministry of Finance, Finland (2022b). *Economic Survey, Spring 2022.* http://urn.fi/URN:ISBN:978-952 -367-227-7

Muhammad, A. and Mahani, H. (2022). Enhancing e-government with a digital twin for innovation management. *Journal of Science and Technology Policy Management.* https://doi.org/10.1108/JSTPM-11 -2021-0176

Obi, T. and Iwasaki, N. (2021). Smart Government using Digital Twin in Japan. 2021 International Conference on ICT for Smart Society (ICISS). 1–4. https://doi.org/10.1109/ICISS53185.2021 .9533190

OECD (2021). *Health at a Glance 2021: OECD Indicators*, OECD Publishing, Paris. https://doi.org/10 .1787/ae3016b9-en

Omar, A., Weerakkody, V., and Daowd, A. (2020). Studying transformational government: A review of the existing methodological approaches and future outlook. *Government Information Quarterly, 37*(2), Article 101458. https://doi.org/10.1016/j.giq.2020.101458

Parmar, P., Leiponen, A., and Thomas, L. D. (2020). Building an organizational digital twin. *Business Horizons, 63*(6), 725–736. http://dx.doi.org/10.1016/j.bushor.2020.08.001

Rousku, K., Andersson, C., Stenfors, S., Lähteenmäki, I., Limnéll, J., Mäkinen, K., Kopponen, A., Kuivalainen, M., and Rissanen, O.-P. (2019). Glimpses of the future: Data policy, artificial intelligence and robotisation as enablers of wellbeing and economic success in Finland. *Publications of the Ministry of Finance*, 2019, 39. http://urn.fi/URN:ISBN:978-952-367-021-1

Seddon, J. (2003). *Freedom from Command and Control.* Vanguard Press: Buckingham.

Shengli, W. (2021). Is Human Digital Twin possible? *Computer Methods and Programs in Biomedicine Update, 1*, Article 100014. https://doi.org/10.1016/j.cmpbup.2021.100014

Simpson, R. W., Shaw, J. E., and Zimmet, P. Z. (2003). The prevention of type 2 diabetes – lifestyle change or pharmacotherapy? A challenge for the 21st century. *Diabetes Research and Clinical Practice, 59*(3), 165–180. https://doi.org/10.1016/s0168-8227(02)00275-9

van Allen, P. (2018). Prototyping ways of prototyping AI. *Interactions, 25*(6), 46–51. https://doi.org/10 .1145/3274566

Vesnic Alujevic, L., Stoermer, E., Rudkin, J., Scapolo, F., and Kimbell, L. (2019). The future of government 2030+: A citizen-centric perspective on new government models. *Publications Office of the European Union, Luxembourg*, p. 23. http://dx.doi.org/10.2760/145751

World Economic Forum (2019). *Leading through the Fourth Industrial Revolution: Putting People at the Centre.* https://www.weforum.org/whitepapers/leading-through-the-fourth-industrial-revolution -putting-people-at-the-centre/

Zuiderwijk, A., Chen, Y. C., and Salem, F. (2021). Implications of the use of artificial intelligence in public governance: A systematic literature review and a research agenda. *Government Information Quarterly, 38*(3), Article 101577. https://doi.org/10.1016/j.giq.2021.101577

11. Enterprise data governance for artificial intelligence: implications from algorithmic jobseeker profiling applications in government

Luis Felipe Luna-Reyes and Teresa M. Harrison

INTRODUCTION

Governments around the world have adopted Artificial Intelligence (AI) applications given their potential to improve government operations, policy and decision making, as well as citizen services (Dwivedi et al., 2021; West and Allen, 2020). Examples of such applications can be seen in many domains of government activity, and range from the very visible smart chatbots that help citizens to navigate government portals and find relevant information and services, to the much less visible applications of AI that help governments to make decisions on a variety of issues such as assessing eligibility for services (for example, social security benefits, employment services, or parole), resource allocation (for example, policing, inspections, auditing) or managing repetitive tasks (for example, classifying email) (West and Allen, 2020).

Data is a fundamental asset to build AI applications in any domain (Crawford, 2021; Harrison et al., 2019; Stoyanovich et al., 2020). Unfortunately, data is also one of the major sources of uncertainty for AI applications because of several technical, managerial and contextual issues (Dwivedi et al., 2021), including problems related to data gathering, curation and distribution (Lane, 2020), issues associated with data fragmentation and storage (Domeyer et al., 2021), and policies and practices for data management (Domeyer et al., 2021; Dwivedi et al., 2021; Harrison et al., 2019). As a result of these concerns, data governance constitutes a key success factor for AI applications, which requires an enterprise view of data management and data architecture (Harrison et al., 2019; Janssen et al., 2020).

However, national, state and local governments are complex organisations composed of multiple, relatively independent agencies that typically have disparate missions, goals and values. In addition, government policies and management practices need to respond to a set of stakeholders that also represent a complex set of contextualised perspectives, values and interests that are frequently in conflict (Sun and Medaglia, 2019). Historically, each agency has focused on the development of their own data management practices and information technology capabilities (Lane, 2020), creating an environment where promoting enterprise-wide data governance is a challenging task. Given these complexities, defining the government enterprise is not an easy task, and many researchers have called for a systems view of data management and governance (Dwivedi et al., 2021; Janssen et al., 2020).

This chapter takes a conceptual approach to this call and, adopting a systems perspective, provides a set of principles, concepts and tools that have the potential to deal with the complexity of building an enterprise data architecture for AI in government. The chapter begins by considering what is meant by 'enterprise data governance' and by acknowledging the characteristics of administrative organisations and the nature of AI that make it challenging to achieve. The following section includes a description of systems views and concepts as they relate to the governance of complex systems (Calida et al., 2016; Checkland and Holwell, 1998; Guevara et al., 2020; Keating and Katina, 2019; Moldogaziev and Resh, 2016). The chapter continues with a closer look at the characteristics of, and experiences with, one internationally applied government AI use case, profiling in public employment services. The case is then used to illustrate how a pluralistic systems approach may prove valuable to public administrators in dealing with the complexity proper of AI applications to government and data governance. Although there is potential value from all systems approaches, a pluralistic systems view that involves tools, methods and approaches to facilitate conversations and sensemaking is more suitable to address the problems of AI ethics and data governance. The chapter concludes with a brief summary and suggests the next steps for research that aims to further this line of thought.

THE CONCEPT OF ENTERPRISE DATA GOVERNANCE AND ITS CHALLENGES FOR AI

Corporations have long appreciated the benefits of an 'enterprise' approach to data management, which is focused on creating unified views of data and data infrastructure across an organisation (Davenport, 1998). But a focus on data, rather than technology, is still a relatively new perspective within the broad scope of information technology management in government organisations (Harrison et al., 2019; Janssen et al., 2020). Such a perspective, upon which successful AI applications of any kind depend, foregrounds quantity and quality of data as well as all related operations including data stewardship, data governance, data standards, data quality management, data architecture, and security. Achieving the goals of an enterprise approach encompasses the necessity of substantial organisational change.

What is Enterprise Data Governance?

'Enterprise data governance' can be defined as a model of information systems management in organisations that seeks to manage data from heterogeneous sources, validate data quality, create a common data model, and manage metadata (Sivaprakasam, 2010). In such information management systems, the objective is to create a data environment integrated across the enterprise that ensures consistent information with a single version of truth (Sivaprakasam, 2010). In the corporation, the enterprise system has been viewed as a way of replacing previously disparate and often idiosyncratic information systems in an effort to share information across multitudes of business functions, such as sales, manufacturing, suppliers, and accounting and across hierarchical levels (Olson and Kesharwani, 2009). As Davenport (1998) suggested, an enterprise system offers a chance to reconsider the company's strategy and organisation. In making decisions about type, definition, form, structure, quantity, quality, and flow of information as well as where and how to standardise, changes inevitably need to be made in how organisational units conduct work, from job design, work sequencing, and training to the possibility of organisational restructuring (Markus and Tanis, 2000).

With respect to data governance, Janssen and his colleagues (2020) identified three different developmental approaches: (1) planning and control, (2) organisational, and (3) risk-based.

The planning and control approach is based on the annual cycle of project planning, with a focus on the processes of goal definition, budget allocation, project selection, implementation, monitoring and evaluation; organisational priorities and projects can be adapted in each cycle, and departments within the organisation compete for resources every cycle as well. The organisational approach emphasises roles and responsibilities, as well as accountability and reporting; key elements of the approach involve decision makers in the organisational structure such as a Chief Data Officer or a Chief AI Officer, among others. Finally, the risk-based approach is based on the analysis and management of risk along the data life cycle. This last approach is becoming popular for AI projects given its usefulness in analysing risks at any stage of data preparation and algorithmic testing (Janssen et al., 2020). These approaches to data governance are rarely used individually; it is most common for organisations to combine them in a complementary way.

Given the nature of the government enterprise as described above, any 'enterprise' approach may need to consider a collaborative approach involving more than one government agency, and potentially private partners. Collaborative approaches to public administration have emerged as a response to the 'wicked'[1] nature of problems faced by contemporary government organisations on the assumption that coordinated action is needed. The literature in public management and digital government refers to these approaches as 'Collaborative Governance' (for example, Emerson et al., 2012), 'Public Value Governance' (for example, Bryson et al., 2014), 'Joined-up government' (for example, Bogdanor, 2005) or 'Whole-of-Government' (for example, Christensen and Lægreid, 2007). Although all these frameworks differ on specific aspects of collaboration, they also have similarities and focus on common topics such as the initial conditions and drivers, collaboration processes and capacities, leadership, technology, and governance (for example, Bryson et al., 2006; Gasco-Hernandez et al., 2022). In this way, developing an enterprise view of data governance may involve a collaborative and iterative process of designing and making decisions around aspects of data life cycle and project associated risks, organisational structures for decision making and accountability, and processes of resource allocation and project implementation, monitoring, and evaluation (Janssen et al., 2020; Lawton, 2016; Ojo et al., 2011).

Developing an enterprise view for data governance in government is, if not a wicked problem, at least a daunting task that requires a long-term investment and effort (Lawton, 2016). Developing the collaborative structures and processes necessary to build enterprise governance are challenging themselves and highly consistent with calls for systems perspectives as well (for example, Bryson et al., 2006; Richardson et al., 2015). Some of the key challenges of building such an enterprise view are introduced in the next section.

Enterprise Data Governance Challenges for AI

Successful AI application development depends on characteristics of the data in several ways. First, AI depends upon the availability, usability, fitness for task, and integrity of the data itself. AI applications cannot proceed beyond preprocessing without datasets that exist in sufficient quantity and quality to enable developers to apply AI's computational strategies. Further, the greatest value obtained in using AI often comes from integrating volumes of data

---

[1]   The term was introduced by Rittel and Webber (1973), and was used to refer to intractable, hard if not impossible to solve, problems.

from multiple sources, a task that brings its own set of challenges. Government must marshal and deploy the required data in order to pursue AI benefits.

In one respect, government would seem to be up to the task since agencies create very large data resources while carrying out their missions. However, at the same time, critics have charged that government agencies do not typically possess data resources that are appropriately curated (Mehr, 2017). Government data is scattered in registers among agencies that are siloed, making it difficult to determine what registers exist and identify which data are contained in which register. As one critic put it, 'This means there is little transparency on whether a specific data point is available somewhere in the government, whether it is available in multiple registers, or where the most current data can be found' (Domeyer et al., 2021).

Further, there are few unified technical formats and shared semantic meanings for data registers so similar data sets may be incapable of being used by other agencies, much less shared (West and Allen, 2020), defying technical interoperability. Compounding these issues, lack of legal interoperability suggests that it is often unclear what data can be legally shared, accessed, exchanged or combined between agencies (Domeyer et al., 2021; Dwivedi et al., 2021). Historically, agencies have tended to focus on data practices that support their own missions, which makes sharing data resources a challenging task. It is worth noting that lack of data sharing, collaboration among government agencies, interoperability, and shared data governance are familiar and recurrent problems identified in the literature of e-government (for example, Pardo et al., 2006).

Although recent trends show that governments are working on more centralised structures for managing their information resources (for example, Office of the Spokesperson, 2021), integrating data management across boundaries is very much a challenge (West and Allen, 2020). However, even assuming that technically adequate datasets can be obtained, successful government AI applications using that data must conform to democratic values, and often legal requirements, for outcomes consistent with fairness, privacy, and transparency. Unfortunately, more serious and fundamental data issues arise as a function of interdependencies between datasets for training and learned models and AI's current computational strategies. The challenges of achieving outcomes consistent with democratic values have fuelled substantial interest in ensuring that AI can be trustworthy and ethically sound (for example, Harrison and Luna-Reyes, 2022; Kearns and Roth, 2019).

Further, the inherent cultural and political situatedness of datasets means that data and its attributes reflect the societies from which they are collected. Numerous scholars have noted that when data are taken from their original sites of production and used to enable AI products in other domains, the outcomes can distort, stigmatise, and discriminate (for example, Crawford, 2013; Dawes and Helbig, 2015; Erickson et al., 2018; Lageson, 2016). This suggests that significant care must be taken in repurposing data collected for governments' mission-related purposes to achieve AI-fuelled objectives.

However, this situatedness also means that bias is an inherent characteristic of datasets. Pointing to training datasets at the core of most machine learning systems, Crawford (2021) argues that the 'origins of the underlying data in a system can be incredibly significant and there are no standardised practices to note where all this data came from or how it was acquired – let alone what biases or classificatory politics these datasets contain that will influence all the systems that come to rely on them' (p. 103). Even attempts to remove classificatory information of gender, race, or religion can fail since other characteristics covarying with them can introduce potential sources of bias. So far, efforts aimed at ensuring that algorithms produce legally equitable results, such as 'fair machine learning,' have not produced guarantees, although some strategies may be better than others under given circumstances (Corbett-Davies and Goel, 2018). Given this situation, algorithms used in government profiling and service targeting are susceptible to the possibility of reducing citizen equality in order to achieve efficiencies (for example, Henman, 2019).

Safeguarding privacy poses another significant challenge. Beyond the dangers of data breaches and the sometimes faulty assurances of anonymisation, another recurrent issue is the danger of inferred identity that can occur as a consequence of AI computational strategies. Identity inference can take place when learned models are reverse engineered, when models are overfitted, and, as requirements for transparency increase thus producing more publicly available models (Kearns and Roth, 2019; Yeom et al., 2018).

The challenges above are now widely acknowledged and generate considerable discourse over technical solutions that might ameliorate their worst manifestations. But technical solutions may not be sufficient by themselves, and they will not by themselves address historically entrenched patterns of behaviour and rigid bureaucratic structures that must change in ways commensurate for obtaining appropriate data for incorporation in AI and finding ways to work ethically with the difficulties presented by AI. As Crawford (2021, pp. 147–148) has observed, decisions need to be made by individuals that can assess the impact of AI systems interacting with social processes: 'Making these choices about which information feeds AI systems to produce new classifications is a powerful moment of decision making: but who gets to choose and on what basis? The problem for computer science is that justice in AI systems will never be something that can be coded or computed. It requires a shift from assessing systems beyond optimisation metrics and statistical parity and an understanding of where the frameworks of mathematics and engineering are causing the problems. This also means understanding how AI systems interact with data, workers, the environment, and the individuals whose lives will be affected by its use and deciding where AI should not be used.'

The authors of this chapter argue that an enterprise data governance approach in organising systems for AI development is required to enable public administrators to be sensitised to the interdependencies between the AI strategies contemplated, the nature of the data currently available or newly created, and policy implications of the use cases under consideration. Dawes (2009) argued over ten years ago that future digital government infrastructure requires an enterprise view that encompasses all parts of a government to form an interconnected whole functioning within a complex social and economic environment. This vision of the future is one that also includes the theme of public/private/civic sector relationships and collaboration that are focused on 'sharing responsibilities and exchanging information among networks of diverse organizations in ways that generate public value and satisfy public requirements for fairness, accountability, and competence' (Dawes, 2009, p. 258).

SYSTEMS APPROACHES TO MANAGEMENT

Past and current research calls for a systems approach to respond to the challenges described in the previous section. However, many different systems approaches exist. This section describes a pluralistic view of systems approaches. It starts by describing the diversity of systems approaches in management and continues by focusing on one potentially useful way of applying these approaches to the complex problem of enterprise data governance.

Table 11.1   A system of systems methodologies

		Participants		
		Unitary	Pluralistic	Coercive
Systems	Simple	Operational Research Systems Engineering	Soft Systems Thinking	Emancipatory Systems Thinking
	Complex	System Dynamics Organisational Cybernetics Complexity Theory		Postmodern Systems Thinking

Source: Adapted from Jackson, 2003.

Hard vs. Soft vs. Emancipatory Systems Approaches

Systems approaches emerged in the first half of the 20th century as a reaction against the traditional scientific method, which was criticised for using a reductionist approach to develop and evaluate theories of the world through generating and testing hypotheses. According to critics, although highly effective in advancing our understanding of causality in the world, the approach was less effective in helping us to understand complex behaviours of biological and social systems (Jackson, 2003). Ludwig Von Bertalanffy and Norbert Wiener were important pioneers of the systems approach in the areas of biology and engineering respectively. The major contribution of Von Bertalanffy was the premise that most complex systems share characteristics and organising principles that can be modelled mathematically (Von Bertalanffy, 1969); Wiener introduced the concepts of purposeful systems, communication, and control in social and organisational systems (Wiener, 2013).

These seminal works have inspired the development of what Jackson calls Applied Systems Thinking (Jackson, 2000, 2003). Applied Systems Thinking is a set of systems approaches that, according to Jackson's premise, constitute a toolset of methods that can be used in tackling different types of management problems or used in different contexts. Table 11.1 introduces what Jackson calls a System of Systems Methodologies (Jackson, 2000), which constitutes a map of the toolset. In this map, Jackson maps systems approaches to types of problems (or contexts), using a 2x3 grid of types of problems based on the levels of complexity of the problem and conflict among participants.

Complexity of problems is defined on the basis of the number of elements or components within the problem. Repairing an oven or a bicycle, or managing a small NGO or business may be examples of simple problems. Developing advanced information systems such as AI applications in government organisations is most likely a complex problem involving, as described above, the integration of diverse sources of data as well as the involvement of a diverse group of stakeholders and policy makers. Conflict, on the other hand, is measured as the level of agreement on the system's purposes among problem owners and problem participants. When all actors in the problem situation agree on the goals unanimously, Jackson classifies the problem as Unitary; when there is diversity of perspectives about the goal that can be harmonised, Pluralistic; and when power imbalances make consensus impossible, Coercive. It can be assumed that actors and stakeholders in the development of AI applications in government are at least a pluralistic group of actors, although some of the AI research suggests that there are multiple situations where stakeholders and actors face a coercive situation of perpetuation of power (Eubanks, 2018; Fountain, 2021).

The framework in Table 11.1 is not only useful as a map of systems approaches, but it can also be used as a way of describing the main categories of systems approaches: (1) systems approaches to improve goal seeking and viability, (2) systems approaches for exploring and clarifying goals among stakeholders, and (3) systems approaches to ensure fairness and promote diversity (Jackson, 2003).

The first type of systems approaches – those interested in improving goal seeking – is located in the first column in Table 11.1. Common applications of operational research and systems engineering used a variety of mathematical modelling tools to optimise organisational outputs and improve efficiencies in the use of resources. Similarly, system dynamics and complexity theory apply mathematical models to the understanding of complex systems behaviours. Finally, approaches such as organisational cybernetics define key functions necessary for an effective organisation (Keating and Katina, 2019). In general, this family of systems approaches shares the assumption that system behaviour is the result of the interaction of an identifiable set of components within the system. In this way, all these approaches provide practical methods to identify those components and model their interactions.

The second type of systems approaches emerged as a reaction to the main criticisms of the first type. Systems thinkers like Peter Checkland (2000) pointed out a major problem in what he referred to as Hard Systems Thinking: it is uncommon that social and organisational actors are in full agreement about the main goals and ways of measuring them. In addition, he also recognised the difficulties of identifying crisp components within the system and modelling their relationships as objective reality. As a result, he developed the Soft Systems Methodology, founded on the principle of dialogue and learning among actors in order to learn about the problem and potential solutions. Many other 'soft' systems thinking approaches have been developed, and many of the traditionally 'hard' approaches have developed participatory modelling techniques, involving stakeholders in the exploration of the problem and the solutions (Jackson, 2003; Vennix et al., 1994).

Soft systems approaches' main criticism lies in the fact that all of them assume that it is always possible to reach agreement about goals among problem stakeholders (Jackson, 2000), giving birth to the last type of systems approaches. In this last type of approach, conflict and power imbalances are openly recognised, promoting the need for an active search for fairness and diversity from a pluralistic perspective. The next section of the paper briefly describes some basic characteristics of this emancipatory and pluralistic approach.

A Pluralistic View of Systems Intervention

The pluralistic systems intervention that is proposed in this section of the paper is based on the postmodern systems approaches (Taket and White, 2000), which promotes pluralism and diversity in the nature of the client, the use of methods, the modes of representation employed and the facilitation process (Jackson, 2003). Being plural in terms of the nature of the client means not only to ensure the widest possible range of viewpoints in the discussion of the problem, but also acknowledging that consensus may be impossible, and thus accepting that satisficing[2] solutions can be adopted with the consent of participants. Pluralism in methods consists of using all possible systems approaches not only for different aspects of the inter-

---

[2]   The use of the term 'satisficing' here follows the concept introduced by Herbert Simon (1956), assuming the possibility of a solution that complies with a threshold of acceptability for all stakeholders.

vention, but using different methods to approach the same task using different lenses. In addition, the selection of methods should be based on the nature of the problem, but also from the preferences of facilitators and stakeholders. Pluralism in terms of the representations used involves the use of a mix of verbal (stories and narratives), visual (diagrams and pictures), and kinesthetic (sociodrama) representations. Finally, being pluralistic in terms of the facilitation process involves flexibility to adapt to the situation, challenging the process and results when appropriate, keeping sense of purpose and reflecting on fairness and equitable participation.

A systems view of this nature will take advantage of many of the soft systems approaches to facilitate dialogue and extended participation. Moreover, such participative approaches may be used together with any of the hard approaches that have been traditionally less inclusive. One hard view that may be potentially useful to organise plural discussions about data governance for artificial intelligence is Complex System Governance (CSG) (Calida et al., 2016; Keating and Katina, 2019). CSG incorporates principles and concepts from organisational cybernetics to think about the main components and functions of governance. According to Calida and colleagues (2016), a governance concept for complex systems should examine the governed system (structure and activities), the governing system (controller, provides regulatory capacity), a meta-governance system (main functions and principles of governance), and the contextual environment. From a pluralistic view, all these components and functions need to be negotiated and developed from diverse perspectives as described in the previous paragraph.

Several collections of tools and systems approaches applied to public management exist. Bryson and colleagues' (2015) have edited a collection of such approaches from the perspective of Public Value Management, which constitutes their own perspective on a whole-of-government perspective. The Cabinet Office in the United Kingdom maintains an initiative to increase the use of systems thinking and systems approaches to public policy (see https://systemsthinking.blog.gov.uk/). More specifically in the domain of information technologies implementation, the Center for Technology in Government has been collecting and applying systems tools in partnership with many government partners (Dawes et al., 2004).

USE CASE: ALGORITHMIC JOBSEEKER PROFILING

The aim of this section is to create a better understanding of how a systems approach to designing enterprise data governance for AI applications could produce organisational systems that minimise uncertainty, better balance benefits with risks, and do so within frameworks of democratic values. This goal is accomplished through the analysis of a use case that illustrates the multiple organisational interdependencies involved in AI application development; certain decision choices in application model, design, and administration; the role of humans working with algorithm-driven applications; and data analytic issues, along with their legal implications, that have the potential to undermine model validity and democratic values. Employing a use case to discuss enterprise data governance takes the risk-based approach (see Janssen et al., 2020) as the starting point, by focusing on risks of a single application and its life cycle, and building on the lessons learned from the specific case to develop more general governance principles in an iterative way (for example, Lawton, 2016).

Unfortunately, a thorough understanding of the various contexts in which AI has been deployed or the extensiveness with which AI has been applied in government does not yet exist. But it is known that AI driven profiling for the purpose of decision making has been applied across numerous agencies. Profiling systems are often used in government services where assessing eligibility is a common task (for example, Eubanks, 2018). In the US, some of the most recognised applications include the determination of state and local welfare payments and fraud detection (Gilman, 2020), potential fraud detection in financial transactions by the Securities Exchange Commission, facial recognition systems and traveller risk profiling by the US Customs and Border Control, and selecting candidates for adjudication hearings by the Social Security Administration (Engstrom et al., 2020). But so far research in the US has not told us much about the way that AI is used for profiling across these endeavours.

However, European governments have used algorithmic profiling of jobseekers registered in public employment agencies as a basis for making employment service-related decisions. Here, a growing body of quantitative and qualitative research has examined profiling systems used in Australia, Austria, Belgium, Poland, Portugal, and the Netherlands, among others. Consistent with the examples of Kuziemski and Misuraca (2020) and Dahlin (2021), the authors draw on research that has described some of these cases, focusing primarily on Austria and Poland, to illustrate below the goals of profiling; the kinds of data that are used, how algorithms using this data are deployed, the stakeholders affected, and some significant risks and challenges of these applications.

According to Büchi et al. (2021), profiling is defined as the 'systematic and purposeful recording and classification of data related to individuals.' AI-based profiling and large quantities of diverse data are used in countries such as Austria to predict the likelihood that jobseekers will find new employment, which then guides subsequent service-related decision making. Administrative profiling, such as that used in Poland, creates groups based on administrative eligibility criteria such as demographic information as well as personal attributes (Delobelle et al., 2021). Governments adopt profiling to predict how jobseekers will fare in the job market (Desiere and Struyven, 2021) and then often use that information to determine the level and/or types of services provided based upon the assigned category.

Profiling and Its Goals

Typically, employment services offered by governments are under-resourced and over-subscribed. Profiling in this domain is frequently motivated by a desire to reduce the costs of providing unemployment services or to better allocate scarce resources. Fiscal austerity has been the primary driver for the Public Employment Service Austria, which rolled out a test phase of its profiling system in 2018, but was then blocked in 2021 by the Austrian Data Protection Authority; as of May 2022, the profiling system was not yet in use (Scott et al., 2022). At one time it was anticipated that more might be served with the AI system, but more recently it has been envisioned to justify budget cuts (Allhutter et al., 2020).

In Austria, AI profiling was to be used to classify unemployed individuals into three predictive categories: Group 1, those with high probability (greater than 66 per cent) of finding employment of at least three months within the next seven months; Group 2, those with mediocre chances of finding employment; and Group 3, those who are not likely to find employment (less than 25 per cent chance) of at least three years duration in the next two years (Allhutter et al., 2020). Services are provided largely to those in the middle category on the grounds that members of the first category have less need and members of the third category are unlikely to make the best use of services. According to researchers, 'High investments in these two groups are not deemed cost-effective' (Allhutter et al., 2020).

In contrast, the Polish Ministry of Labour and Social Policy intended their profiling system to enable labour offices to better diagnose problems of the unemployed and adjust the services offered to the situation of each specific person, so that individuals thought to be more easily employed would receive fewer services in favour of those who would have a harder time securing employment (Niklas et al., 2015).

In Poland's system, which was declared unconstitutional and dismantled in 2019, jobseekers were classified into one of three profiles. Profile 1 (approximately 2 per cent of jobseekers) included individuals with both qualifications and interpersonal skills who also lacked life problems that would make it difficult to find a job. Profile 2 (approximately 33 per cent of registrants) were those with professional skills but who had worked a long time for one company or were redundant on the labour market but otherwise promising. Profile 3 (65 per cent of registrants) were those with serious life problems or who were unwilling to cooperate with labour offices. Those in Profile 1 were assumed not to need intensive support from labour offices, while those categorised in Profile 3, were granted access to employment support programs that, in practice, labour offices were often unwilling to launch. They were often not offered any attractive type of support (Niklas, 2019).

Often those most in need of services are from vulnerable or marginalised populations (Zejnilović et al., 2020). Decision makers tend to perceive AI systems as neutral or objective, thus seeming to offer the possibility of ensuring that those predicted to become long-term unemployed are treated similarly by the agency, in contrast to caseworkers whose personal proclivities may lead, for example, to prioritising young versus old jobseekers (Desiere and Struyven, 2021). In practice, researchers found that caseworkers in Poland chose to focus more heavily on individuals in Profile 2 since they were more likely to be employable, which helped caseworkers to demonstrate their job success (Niklas, 2019).

Data and Algorithms

Data for profiling is obtained from the jobseeker upon initial registration in the public employment system or upon meeting with a caseworker. The data typically consisted of standard demographics, such as age, gender, education level, and nationality/origin, as well as professional background information, employment history, and periods of unemployment.

In Austria, no information uniquely related to the profiling algorithm or its improvement is collected; information used for the algorithm is personal data from registration and from an employment history re-purposed from other uses and provided by other government offices such as social security services (Allhutter et al., 2020; Zejnilović et al., 2020). Profiling through the algorithm is accomplished using data from the experiences of past jobseekers. Thus, a jobseeker's personal data and previous employment history is compared with data accumulated by Austria's Public Employment Service over time, and category assignments reflect how the labour market has reacted to jobseekers in the past.

Poland's system was similar to those of other countries in the kinds of demographic data collected during registration. However, further data was collected during a structured interview administered by a labour office counsellor who asked seemingly open-ended questions, but recorded answers on computer forms requiring selection from a limited drop-down list, thus making it difficult to fully reflect the unique characteristics of a jobseeker (Niklas et al.,

2015; Niklas, 2019). Once this data was collected, the system automatically determined the profile. Clients were not informed that the data was collected for the purpose of determining their placement within the three-tiered profiling system that would then determine the extent of their access to labour services (Dahlin, 2021), and they were not informed of their score.

Diverse types of analytical approaches are applied to data to develop the models (or train in the use of the models) that produce the scores by which jobseekers are classified, although more specific information about the models is often not available. In Austria, for example, logistic regressions were used to determine which factors best predicted chances of finding employment and associated coefficients (Lopez, 2019). However, Austria has released only two of 96 statistical models that are claimed to be used in assessing jobseekers (Kayser-Bril, 2020). In Poland, the algorithm used to make decisions as well as the rules guiding its use were unavailable to labour office staff and clients (Kuziemski and Misuraca, 2020).

What is not yet known about either Austria or Poland is whether new data was ever entered into a jobseeker's profile (if, for example, a jobseeker acquired a new degree), whether individuals' profiles were re-computed over time (to reflect amount of time in the system), or whether models were ever retrained for changing economic conditions.

Stakeholders

The stakeholders mentioned in discussions of algorithmic profiling systems include the following user groups: unemployed jobseekers, employees that work with jobseekers (caseworkers, counsellors, etc.), technical staff who have designed and/or operated profiling systems, and policymakers at a variety of levels. Jobseekers' rights are discussed in the next section. Suffice it to say that none of the research that has been examined for this chapter discussed designing profiling systems in a way that took into consideration the needs or interests of jobseekers themselves (Scott et al., 2022). Neither are technical staff or policy makers discussed. Only caseworkers that work with jobseekers are explicitly discussed in the literature.

Although there are some exceptions, the EU prohibits entirely automated decision-making for individuals. In countries such as Austria and Poland, caseworkers can, in principle, overrule the judgement of the algorithm (Kayser-Bril, 2020; Zejnilović et al., 2020), thus inserting 'humans-in-the-loop' and maintaining the legality of the AI approach.

In Austria, the system is framed as a 'support system' to the judgement of the caseworker which assists them in fulfilling their responsibility. Caseworkers also take note of a jobseeker's soft skills, because the automated system cannot accommodate this information, and thus serve as 'correctives' to the shortcomings of the system. However, such interventions run counter to the system's avowed goals for increased efficiency and effectiveness (Allhutter et al., 2020); caseworkers had to request permission from a supervisor to overrule the profiling decision (Haeri et al., 2022).

In Poland, counsellors could change jobseekers' profile assignments, but changes had to be justified in writing according to a specialised rubric; this option was used in just under 1 in 100 cases (Niklas et al., 2015; Niklas, 2019). Counsellors seldom made changes, in part, due to lack of time in their interviews with clients to find a basis for an alternative score (Sztandar-Sztanderska and Zielenska, 2022). Further, management in Poland sent strong signals about how such alterations would be scrutinised, which had a chilling effect that discouraged changes in profile placement (Sztandar-Sztanderska and Zielenska, 2022). Even though they did not always trust the products of the algorithms, caseworkers also did not understand how the scores were produced due to the opacity with which the system is managed. And even if they did wish to exercise discretion, they did not necessarily understand the reasons given in the system that could justify overriding the system score. Thus, in the majority of cases, it was far easier for the caseworkers to accept the algorithmic score and detach themselves from decision making (Zejnilović et al., 2020).

Risks and Challenges

In the US, administrative government law is committed to values of fairness, transparency, and accountability. Similarly, the European Union has promulgated a set of values required for trustworthy AI which includes fairness, transparency, and accountability, as well as privacy and data governance, and the preservation of human agency and oversight. Thus, government applications of AI will be judged by a substantive set of ethical values and are likely to be challenged in court, as they were in Poland and Austria.

Procedural rights. In the case of Poland's dismantled system, jobseekers had no right to information about how the system established their profiling scores and no right to contest the decision received (Niklas, 2019). Further, unemployed individuals were not allowed to express opinions about the determinations made by the system or request a re-verification of the assigned profile (Niklas et al., 2015). Opting out of the system meant forgoing unemployment benefits.

Indeed, the inability of Poland's system to create a non-discriminatory system and the failure to fully appreciate the importance of legal guidelines regarding data appears to have been responsible for the decision by Poland's Constitutional Court that the profiling system was a breach of the Polish constitution; the system was subsequently scrapped (Niklas, 2019).

In Austria, documents describing the system made no provision for formalised processes for explaining outcomes or justifying them to jobseekers. However, researchers note that this could not be expected to happen given the numerous factors in the algorithm that produced results and the technical language and documentation that a jobseeker would have to be able to understand (Allhutter et al., 2020).

Accuracy-equity trade-off. In the US and Europe, it is illegal to include variables such as gender, age, and ethnicity into AI models because of their discriminatory potential (Desiere and Struyven, 2021). However, variables such as gender and ethnicity are often correlated with other predictors in the model, such as proxies for local labour market conditions, which can then be used to identify minorities (Desiere and Struyven, 2021). While work-arounds have been suggested, the result of using them is a sacrifice in accuracy. Thus AI-based statistical profiling and selection rules 'inevitably entail statistical discrimination' while other options tend to reduce the accuracy of the model producing greater numbers of misclassifications (Desiere and Struyven, 2021) which may unfairly limit the resources available to jobseekers. How this trade-off is adjudicated is a decision that should be made by policy makers rather than model developers.

Discrimination. Critics charge that the use of algorithms to construct profiles introduces choices reflecting social values into the system, producing conditions in which individuals may be misclassified potentially reinforcing patterns of discrimination in society. In the Austrian system, attributes such as disability and women with care responsibilities are inscribed into the system through the data they are based on and the way the data is processed, making it more likely that such individuals are classified into the riskiest group (Allhutter et al., 2020). An unemployed woman is more likely to be assigned to a lower group when her experience and qualifications are equivalent to that of a man (Kayser-Bril, 2020). Further, women in technical occupations and women with migration backgrounds along with other marginalised groups received lower scores on certain indexes of value (Delobelle et al., 2021).

As Lopez (2019) points out, jobseekers whose employment history is 'fragmented,' as it may be for young people who have no employment history or immigrants with no employment history in Austria, or jobseekers returning to work after a long period of time, are removed from the population of continuously employed people, and analysed in a different model variant, and thus may be assumed to have a greater risk of being assigned to Group 3, although the information needed to assess this is not available.

Far from being free of human discretion, the process of algorithm construction involves normative decisions such as choosing what data to include, defining outcome variables, constructing decision rules, and setting category cut-off points. Thus, some recommend that a continuous dialogue within a design context needs to take place between data analysts, policy makers, and caseworkers (Desiere and Struyven, 2021). With respect to the consequences of algorithmic profiling, which were not assessed in Poland or Austria, Dahlin (2021) argues that AI design cannot be separated from its social impacts and designers must recognise that AI models will influence the social practices that shape society. This means AI projects should incorporate social analyses of the technical design from the outset.

TOWARDS A SYSTEMS APPROACH TO ALGORITHMIC JOBSEEKER PROFILING AND ITS IMPLICATIONS FOR ENTERPRISE DATA GOVERNANCE

This section of the chapter discusses structures, process, and design choices that may be introduced by a pluralistic systems approach to enterprise governance during the development of an AI statistical profiling system.

Setting the Stage: Basic Structures and Processes

Several basic requirements are necessary to benefit from a systems perspective. First, the complexities and interdependencies associated with the data needed to develop the application, as well as the risks and challenges described in the previous section, call for a team effort. In other words, any effort to develop an AI application in government requires the involvement of a team of managers from both the business and information technology areas within the agencies involved in the problem (Lawton, 2016). Although external technology partners may be included in these efforts, experiences at the Center for Technology in Government suggest that their involvement needs to be carefully managed and developing an initial understanding of the problem and requirements is an important prerequisite for their involvement. Team approaches are also a requirement from a pluralistic systems perspective (for example, Richardson et al., 2015; Richardson and Andersen, 1995).

A second important requirement for the development of an enterprise view of data governance is leadership. The collaborative governance literature suggests that shared leadership is an important factor in the development of information technology initiatives in government (Gasco-Hernandez et al., 2022). Shared leadership involves both vertical and horizontal coordination across and within government agencies. Vertical coordination calls for a high-level sponsor for any AI and data governance initiative. This sponsor provides a vision, as well as the necessary political capital to ensure that resources and other enablers for the project are available. Horizontal shared leadership involves interactions within the team. Although best practices in information technology governance suggest that the leadership of these teams should come from the business side of the team (Weill and Ross, 2009), the IT side plays a key leadership role providing understanding and know-how in the selection of specific technology tools. Finally, whole-of-government activities, such as enterprise data governance, require an operational leader that facilitates and promotes collaboration within the agency and potentially across agencies to improve data management practices. The creation of these units is a common element of whole-of-government approaches (Christensen and Lægreid, 2007). A Chief Data Officer may be an appropriate leader to facilitate this process (Harrison et al., 2019).

A third basic requirement consists of developing the necessary capacities for collaboration and project development. Two main capacities are relevant to the development of enterprise data governance: data literacy and systems tools to facilitate collaboration. An emphasis on understanding data as a key asset across the organisation is critical to improving data quality as well as for the development of the necessary stewardship and frameworks to ensure privacy, accountability, and the ethical use of data (Harrison and Luna-Reyes, 2022). In addition, training in systems tools is also necessary. Many approaches are available to accomplish this task. Maybe a notable example is the previously mentioned effort on systems thinking for public policy approach adopted by the United Kingdom.

A final core requirement, maybe the most important, to develop a systems view of enterprise data governance is a vision and a map for that vision. Research in digital government has proposed frameworks and approaches to develop information technology governance in general (for example, Juiz et al., 2022; Ojo et al., 2011), and data governance in particular (for example, Janssen et al., 2020; Lawton, 2016). These frameworks may be considered long-term visions that require a core set of principles and values that provide a basic map to build the vision over time. The core set of values and principles are typically embedded in data strategy documents (see for example the data strategy in the United States https://strategy.data.gov/, Canada https://www.canada.ca/en/privy-council/corporate/clerk/publications/data-strategy.html, and the United Kingdom https://www.gov.uk/guidance/national-data-strategy).

Understanding Risks: The Role of Stakeholders

Given the inherent cultural and political situatedness of datasets, uncovering the meanings of data itself as well as interpreting the patterns that AI algorithms may uncover require the involvement of many different stakeholders that participate in the production, collection, and analysis of data. In this way, a pluralistic systems approach to statistical profiling systems would require extensive and careful thinking to identify the stakeholders, and how they should be involved in the process. Stakeholders in the system would include not only the caseworkers serving the clients looking for jobs, but also the providers of the services that support the job seeking and placement process. Clients looking for employment and potential employers would be two other important stakeholder groups. Involvement of all those different stakeholders is important because they are producing the important data through their actions in the system, and their knowledge is key to making proper interpretation of the patterns in the data, as well as identifying when those patterns are only artifacts of data quality problems (Hagen et al., 2019). Those patterns represent the activities and idiosyncrasies of system participants. Systems approaches include plenty of tools for stakeholder analysis; a very widely known one in public management is John Bryson's approach to identify stakeholders that matter (Bryson, 2004). Identifying important stakeholders and engaging in conversations with them to understand the risks, impacts, and unintended consequences of the use of data and AI applications is a primary responsibility of the core project team developing the application.

Contesting System Goals

Stakeholders in this system have many different goals, and developing more efficient processes for helping citizens to find a job is only one of them. Other potentially important goals in the system are the following: (1) employers within the community most likely want to get the best possible employees, (2) employees most likely are looking for a job that suits their needs and provides them with a sense of fulfillment, (3) service providers in this system may have the goal of providing the most relevant skills to their clients, and helping them to be successful in job placement, as well as (4) representatives of other government entities that contribute data to the modelling, and thus need to be consulted regarding the characteristics and scope of that data, and (5) policymakers carrying out political mandates and seeking solutions to political problems.

Even from the perspective of cost savings and producing efficiencies in the system, system goals can be contested. For example, previous research suggests that job placement efficiency constitutes only one component of the problem, and that savings in this component of the system may backfire by increasing client recidivism (Zagonel et al., 2004). This same research suggests then that investments in supporting clients after job placement is a more effective way of reducing costs in the system when compared with investments in increasing the efficiency in job placement.

Incorporating all these perspectives in defining goals of the system requires the use of both a diverse set of system representations and a diverse and flexible set of facilitation techniques. Soft systems approaches provide many tools to be used in the process, many of them successfully used already in developing public policy (Andersen and Richardson, 1997; Richardson et al., 2015; Richardson and Andersen, 1995; Rouwette et al., 2016; Vennix et al., 1994). Prototypes and other models have also proven to be effective tools to understand and define goals in technology projects (for example, Gil-Garcia et al., 2007; Luna-Reyes et al., 2021; Lyons et al., 2005).

Governing Data and Algorithms

Complex System Governance (CSG), as described in previous sections, is a systems approach that has been used successfully in developing governance of complex systems (Calida et al., 2016; Keating and Katina, 2019) such as those that are necessary for the development of profiling systems in government. The approach may be useful not only as a tool to identify the main components of the governed system (data, algorithms, goals, people, etc.), but also in identifying the meta-functions that produce control, communication, coordination, and integration of the system.

From the pluralistic perspective, these components need to be continuously audited and redesigned to ensure system viability and sustainability over time. Design principles that may be perceived as important at first may prove to have no effect in reaching the goals of the system. For example, current regulations forbid the use of demographics as data inputs for AI profiling algorithms. Nonetheless, and given that race and gender are correlated with many other data elements associated with an individual, current research suggests that incorporating those data elements in a transparent way may be a way of reducing bias and promoting fairness (Kearns and Roth, 2019).

Once more, soft systems approaches may be useful in the definition of components and processes for data governance. Some of these approaches are already in the early stages of experimentation, showing promising results (Martin Jr. and Moore, 2020).

CONCLUSION

In this chapter, some of the main challenges of data governance for the development of fair and transparent AI applications in government have been described. To tackle those challenges, the authors sketched the potential benefits and core requirements of an approach based on a pluralistic view of systems approaches to management. The use of AI poses entirely new risks and challenges which, in order to avoid or minimise, will require substantial reorganisation of the historical practices and structures of numerous government entities as well as public-private partnerships. Trustworthy AI will certainly not be achieved overnight and may instead require experimenting with incremental enterprise changes and frequent assessment of their impacts. Future research and government practice should incorporate general ideas of pluralistic systems approaches to enterprise data governance in more specific designs to be tested in the development of AI systems.

REFERENCES

Allhutter, D., Cech, F., Fischer, F., Grill, G., and Mager, A. (2020). Algorithmic profiling of job seekers in Austria: How austerity politics are made effective. *Frontiers in Big Data*, *3*. https://www.frontiersin.org/article/10.3389/fdata.2020.00005
Andersen, D. F., and Richardson, G. P. (1997). Scripts for group model building. *System Dynamics Review (Wiley)*, *13*(2), 107–129.
Bogdanor, V. (ed.) (2005). *Joined-up Government*. Oxford University Press.
Bryson, J. M. (2004). What to do when stakeholders matter: Stakeholder identification and analysis techniques. *Public Management Review*, *6*(1), 21–53. https://doi.org/10.1080/14719030410001675722
Bryson, J. M., Crosby, B. C., and Bloomberg, L. (2014). Public value governance: Moving beyond traditional public administration and the new public management. *Public Administration Review*, *74*(4), 445–456. https://doi.org/10.1111/puar.12238
Bryson, J. M., Crosby, B. C., and Bloomberg, L. (eds) (2015). *Public Value and Public Administration* (illustrated edition). Georgetown University Press.
Bryson, J. M., Crosby, B. C., and Stone, M. M. (2006). The design and implementation of cross-sector collaborations: Propositions from the literature. *Public Administration Review*, *66S*, 44–55. https://doi.org/10.1111/j.1540-6210.2006.00665.x
Büchi, M., Fosch-Villaronga, E., Lutz, C., Tamò-Larrieux, A., and Velidi, S. (2021). Making sense of algorithmic profiling: User perceptions on Facebook. *Information, Communication & Society*, *0*(0), 1–17. https://doi.org/10.1080/1369118X.2021.1989011

Calida, B. Y., Jaradat, R. M., Abutabenjeh, S., and Keating, C. B. (2016). Governance in systems of systems: A systems-based model. *International Journal of System of Systems Engineering, 7*(4), 235. https://doi.org/10.1504/IJSSE.2016.080313

Checkland, P. (2000). Soft systems methodology: A thirty year retrospective. *Systems Research and Behavioral Science, 17*(S1), S11–S58.

Checkland, P., and Holwell, S. (1998). *Information, Systems and Information Systems – Making Sense of the Field*. John Wiley & Sons.

Christensen, T., and Lægreid, P. (2007). The whole-of-government approach to public sector reform. *Public Administration Review, 67*(6), 1059–1066. https://doi.org/10.1111/j.1540-6210.2007.00797.x

Corbett-Davies, S., and Goel, S. (2018). The measure and mismeasure of fairness: A critical review of fair machine learning. *ArXiv:1808.00023 [Cs]*. http://arxiv.org/abs/1808.00023

Crawford, K. (2013, April 1). The hidden biases in big data. *Harvard Business Review*. https://hbr.org/2013/04/the-hidden-biases-in-big-data

Crawford, K. (2021). *Atlas of AI: Power, Politics, and the Planetary Costs of Artificial Intelligence*. Yale University Press.

Dahlin, E. (2021). Mind the gap! On the future of AI research. *Humanities and Social Sciences Communications, 8*(1), Article 1. https://doi.org/10.1057/s41599-021-00750-9

Davenport, T. H. (1998, July 1). Putting the enterprise into the enterprise system. *Harvard Business Review, July–August*. https://hbr.org/1998/07/putting-the-enterprise-into-the-enterprise-system

Dawes, S. S. (2009). Governance in the digital age: A research and action framework for an uncertain future. *Government Information Quarterly, 26*(2), 257–264. https://doi.org/10.1016/j.giq.2008.12.003

Dawes, S. S., and Helbig, N. (2015). The value and limits of government information resources for policy informatics. In E. W. Johnston (ed.), *Governance in the Information Era* (pp. 25–44). Routledge. https://doi.org/10.4324/9781315736211-11

Dawes, S. S., Pardo, T. A., Simon, S., Cresswell, A. M., LaVigne, M. F., Andersen, D. F., and Bloniarz, P. A. (2004). *Making Smart IT Choices: Understanding Value and Risk in Government IT Investments*. http://www.ctg.albany.edu/publications/guides/smartit2

Delobelle, P., Scott, K. M., Wang, S. M., Miceli, M., Hartmann, D., Yang, T., Murasso, E., and Berendt, B. (2021). *Time to Question If We Should: Data-driven and Algorithmic Tools in Public Employment Services*, 8. https://feast-ecmlpkdd.github.io/archive/2021/papers/FEAST2021_paper_5.pdf

Desiere, S., and Struyven, L. (2021). Using artificial intelligence to classify jobseekers: The accuracy-equity trade-off. *Journal of Social Policy, 50*(2), 367–385. https://doi.org/10.1017/S0047279420000203

Domeyer, A., Hieronimus, S., Klier, J., and Weber, T. (2021, September 20). Government data management for the digital age. *McKinsey Insights*. https://www.mckinsey.com/industries/public-and-social-sector/our-insights/government-data-management-for-the-digital-age?cid=other-eml-alt-mip-mck&hdpid=faf57223-411c-4522-a595-23ac64af0812&hctky=1195042&hlkid=b51d7cf5d52d41c684e834f73a649835

Dwivedi, Y. K., Hughes, L., Ismagilova, E., Aarts, G., Coombs, C., Crick, T., Duan, Y., Dwivedi, R., Edwards, J., Eirug, A., Galanos, V., Ilavarasan, P. V., Janssen, M., Jones, P., Kar, A. K., Kizgin, H., Kronemann, B., Lal, B., Lucini, B., … Williams, M. D. (2021). Artificial Intelligence (AI): Multidisciplinary perspectives on emerging challenges, opportunities, and agenda for research, practice and policy. *International Journal of Information Management, 57*, 101994. https://doi.org/10.1016/j.ijinfomgt.2019.08.002

Emerson, K., Nabatchi, T., and Balogh, S. (2012). An integrative framework for collaborative governance. *Journal of Public Administration Research & Theory, 22*(1), 1–29.

Engstrom, D. F., Ho, D. E., Sharkey, C. M., and Cuéllar, M.-F. (2020). Government by algorithm: Artificial intelligence in federal administrative agencies. *SSRN Electronic Journal*. https://doi.org/10.2139/ssrn.3551505

Erickson, L. C., Evans Harris, N., and Lee, M. M. (2018, March 23). It's time for data ethics conversations at your dinner table [Blog]. *Tech at Bloomberg*. https://www.techatbloomberg.com/blog/time-data-ethics-conversations-dinner-table/

Eubanks, V. (2018). *Automating Inequality: How High-tech Tools Profile, Police, and Punish the Poor*. St. Martin's Press.

Fountain, J. E. (2021). The moon, the ghetto and artificial intelligence: Reducing systemic racism in computational algorithms. *Government Information Quarterly, 39*(2), 101645. https://doi.org/10.1016/j.giq.2021.101645

Gasco-Hernandez, M., Gil-Garcia, J. R., and Luna-Reyes, L. F. (2022). Unpacking the role of technology, leadership, governance and collaborative capacities in inter-agency collaborations. *Government Information Quarterly*, *39*(3), 101710. https://doi.org/10.1016/j.giq.2022.101710

Gil-Garcia, J. R., Pardo, T. A., and Baker, A. (2007). *Understanding Context Through a Comprehensive Prototyping Experience: A Testbed Research Strategy for Emerging Technologies*. IEEE, 104b (1–10).

Gilman, M. (2020, February 14). *AI Algorithms Intended to Detect Welfare Fraud Often Punish the Poor* [The Conversation]. US News & World Report. https://www.usnews.com/news/best-states/articles/2020-02-14/ai-algorithms-intended-to-detect-welfare-fraud-often-punish-the-poor-instead

Guevara, J., Garvin, M. J., and Ghaffarzadegan, N. (2020). The forest and the trees: A systems map of governance interdependencies in the shaping phase of road public–private partnerships. *Journal of Management in Engineering*, *36*(1), 1–16. https://doi.org/10.1061/(ASCE)ME.1943-5479.0000726

Haeri, M. A., Hartmann, K., Sirsch, J., Wenzelburger, G., and Zweig, K. A. (2022). Promises and pitfalls of algorithm use by state authorities. *Philosophy & Technology*, *35*(2), 33. https://doi.org/10.1007/s13347-022-00528-0

Hagen, L., Seon Yi, H., Pietri, S., and E. Keller, T. (2019). Processes, potential benefits, and limitations of big data analytics: A case analysis of 311 data from City of Miami. *Proceedings of the 20th Annual International Conference on Digital Government Research*, 1–10. https://doi.org/10.1145/3325112.3325212

Harrison, T. M., and Luna-Reyes, L. F. (2022). Cultivating trustworthy artificial intelligence in digital government. *Social Science Computer Review*, *40*(2), 494–511. https://doi.org/10.1177/0894439320980122

Harrison, T. M., Luna-Reyes, L. F., Pardo, T., De Paula, N., Najafabadi, M., and Palmer, J. (2019). The data firehose and AI in government: Why data management is a key to value and ethics. *Proceedings of the 20th Annual International Conference on Digital Government Research*, 171–176. https://doi.org/10.1145/3325112.3325245

Henman, P. (2019). Of algorithms, apps and advice: Digital social policy and service delivery. *Journal of Asian Public Policy*, *12*(1), 71–89. https://doi.org/10.1080/17516234.2018.1495885

Jackson, M. C. (2000). *Systems Approaches to Management* (2000 edition). Springer.

Jackson, M. C. (2003). *Systems Thinking: Creative Holism for Managers* (1st edition). John Wiley & Sons.

Janssen, M., Brous, P., Estevez, E., Barbosa, L. S., and Janowski, T. (2020). Data governance: Organizing data for trustworthy Artificial Intelligence. *Government Information Quarterly*, *37*(3), 101493. https://doi.org/10.1016/j.giq.2020.101493

Juiz, C., Duhamel, F., Gutiérrez-Martínez, I., and Luna-Reyes, L. F. (2022). IT managers' framing of it governance roles and responsibilities in Ibero-American higher education institutions. *Informatics*, *9*(3), Article 3. https://doi.org/10.3390/informatics9030068

Kayser-Bril, N. (2020). The year algorithms escaped quarantine: 2020 in review. *Algorithm Watch*. https://algorithmwatch.org/en/review-2020/

Kearns, M., and Roth, A. (2019). *The Ethical Algorithm: The Science of Socially Aware Algorithm Design*. Oxford University Press.

Keating, C. B., and Katina, P. F. (2019). Complex system governance: Concept, utility, and challenges. *Systems Research & Behavioral Science*, *36*(5), 687–705. https://doi.org/10.1002/sres.2621

Kuziemski, M., and Misuraca, G. (2020). AI governance in the public sector: Three tales from the frontiers of automated decision-making in democratic settings. *Telecommunications Policy*, *44*(6), 101976. https://doi.org/10.1016/j.telpol.2020.101976

Lageson, S. E. (2016). Found out and opting out: The consequences of online criminal records for families. *The ANNALS of the American Academy of Political and Social Science*, *665*(1), 127–141. https://doi.org/10.1177/0002716215625053

Lane, J. (2020). *Democratizing Our Data: A Manifesto*. The MIT Press.

Lawton, J. (2016). Four critical success factors to effectively managing data as an asset. *Journal of Government Financial Management*, *65*(3), 34–39.

Lopez, P. (2019). Reinforcing intersectional inequality via the AMS algorithm in Austria. In *Critical Issues in Science, Technology, and Society Studies, Proceedings of the STS Conference*, 289–309.

Luna-Reyes, L. F., Andersen, D. F., Black, L. J., and Pardo, T. A. (2021). Sensemaking and social processes in digital government projects. *Government Information Quarterly*, *38*(2), 101570. https://doi.org/10.1016/j.giq.2021.101570

Lyons, A. C., Coronado Mondragon, A. E., Bremang, A., Kehoe, D. F., and Coleman, J. (2005). Prototyping an information system's requirements architecture for customer-driven, supply-chain operations. *International Journal of Production Research*, *43*(20), 4289–4319. https://doi.org/10.1080/00207540500142365

Markus, M. L., and Tanis, C. (2000). The enterprise system experience – From adoption to success. In R. W. Zmud and M. F. Price (eds), *Framing the Domains of IT Research: Glimpsing the Future Through the Past* (pp. 173–207). Pinnaflex Educational Resources.

Martin Jr., D., and Moore, A. (2020, October 28). AI engineers need to think beyond engineering. *Harvard Business Review*, 2–5.

Mehr, H. (2017). *Artificial Intelligence for Citizen Services and Government*. Ash Center for Democratic Government and Innovation: Harvard. https://ash.harvard.edu/files/ash/files/artificial_intelligence_for_citizen_services.pdf

Moldogaziev, T. T., and Resh, W. G. (2016). A systems theory approach to innovation implementation: Why organizational location matters. *Journal of Public Administration Research & Theory*, *26*(4), 677–692. https://doi.org/10.1093/jopart/muv047

Niklas, J. (2019, April 16). Poland: Government to scrap controversial unemployment scoring system. *Algorithm Watch*. https://algorithmwatch.org/en/poland-government-to-scrap-controversial-unemployment-scoring-system/

Niklas, J., Sztandar-Sztanderska, K., and Szymielewicz, K. (2015). *Profiling the Unemployed in Poland: Social and Political Implications of Algorithmic Decision Making*. Fundacja Panoptykon.

Office of the Spokesperson. (2021, September 27). The department unveils its first-ever enterprise data strategy. *United States Department of State*. https://www.state.gov/the-department-unveils-its-first-ever-enterprise-data-strategy/

Ojo, A., Janowski, T., and Estevez, E. (2011). Whole-of-government approach to information technology strategy management: Building a sustainable collaborative technology environment in government. *Information Polity*, *16*(3), 243–260. https://doi.org/10.3233/IP-2011-0237

Olson, D. L., and Kesharwani, S. (2009). *Enterprise Information Systems: Contemporary Trends and Issues* (illustrated edition). World Scientific Publishing Company.

Pardo, T. A., Cresswell, A. M., Thompson, F., and Zhang, J. (2006). Knowledge sharing in cross-boundary information system development in the public sector. *Information Technology and Management*, *7*(4), 293–313. https://doi.org/10.1007/s10799-006-0278-6

Richardson, G. P., and Andersen, D. F. (1995). Teamwork in group model building. *System Dynamics Review (Wiley)*, *11*(2), 113–137.

Richardson, G. P., Andersen, D. F., and Luna-Reyes, L. F. (2015). Joining minds: Group system dynamics modeling to create public value. In J. M. Bryson, B. C. Crosby, and L. Bloomberg (eds), *Valuing Public Value*. Georgetown University Press.

Rittel, H. W., and Webber, M. M. (1973). Dilemmas in a general theory of planning. *Policy Sciences*, *4*(2), 155–169.

Rouwette, E., Bleijenbergh, I., and Vennix, J. (2016). Group model-building to support public policy: Addressing a conflicted situation in a problem neighbourhood. *Systems Research & Behavioral Science*, *33*(1), 64–78. https://doi.org/10.1002/sres.2301

Scott, K. M., Wang, S. M., Miceli, M., Delobelle, P., Sztandar-Sztanderska, K., and Berendt, B. (2022). Algorithmic tools in public employment services: Towards a jobseeker-centric perspective. *2022 ACM Conference on Fairness, Accountability, and Transparency*, 2138–2148. https://doi.org/10.1145/3531146.3534631

Simon, H. A. (1956). Rational choice and the structure of the environment. *Psychological Review*, *63*(2), 129–138. https://doi.org/10.1037/h0042769

Sivaprakasam, S. R. (2010). *Enterprise Data Management: A Comprehensive Data Approach for CSPs*. Infosys Viewpoint.

Stoyanovich, J., Howe, B., and Jagadish, H. V. (2020). Responsible data management. *Proceedings of the VLDB Endowment*, *13*(12), 3474–3488. https://doi.org/10.14778/3415478.3415570

Sun, T. Q., and Medaglia, R. (2019). Mapping the challenges of Artificial Intelligence in the public sector: Evidence from public healthcare. *Government Information Quarterly*, *36*(2), 368–383. https://doi.org/10.1016/j.giq.2018.09.008

Sztandar-Sztanderska, K., and Zielenska, M. (2022). When a human says 'no' to a computer: Frontline oversight of the profiling algorithm in public employment services in Poland. *Sozialer Fortschritt, 71*, 465–487. https://doi.org/10.3790/sfo.71.6-7.465

Taket, A., and White, L. (2000). *Partnership and Participation: Decision-making in the Multiagency Setting* (1st edition). Wiley.

Vennix, J. A. M., Andersen, D. F., Richardson, G. P., and Rohrbaugh, J. (1994). Model building for group decision support: Issues and alternatives in knowledge elicitation. In J. Morecroft and J. D. Sterman (eds), *Modeling for Learning Organizations*. Productivity Press.

Von Bertalanffy, L. (1969). *General System Theory: Foundations, Development, Applications* (revised edition). George Braziller Inc.

Weill, P., and Ross, J. W. (2009). *IT Savvy: What Top Executives Must Know to Go from Pain to Gain* (unknown edition). Harvard Business Press.

West, D. M., and Allen, J. R. (2020). *Turning Point: Policymaking in the Era of Artificial Intelligence*. Brookings Institution Press.

Wiener, N. (2013). *Cybernetics: Second Edition: Or the Control and Communication in the Animal and the Machine* (2nd edition). Martino Fine Books.

Yeom, S., Giacomelli, I., Fredrikson, M., and Jha, S. (2018). Privacy risk in machine learning: Analyzing the connection to overfitting. *2018 IEEE 31st Computer Security Foundations Symposium (CSF)*, 268–282. https://doi.org/10.1109/CSF.2018.00027

Zagonel, A. A., Rohrbaugh, J., Richardson, G. P., and Andersen, D. F. (2004). Using simulation models to address 'what if' questions about welfare reform. *Journal of Policy Analysis and Management*, *23*(4), 890–901.

Zejnilović, L., Lavado, S., Martínez de Rituerto de Troya, Í., Sim, S., and Bell, A. (2020). Algorithmic long-term unemployment risk assessment in use: Counselors' perceptions and use practices. *Global Perspectives*, *1*(1). https://doi.org/10.1525/gp.2020.12908

PART III

FORWARD-LOOKING RESEARCH ON AI IN PUBLIC MANAGEMENT

12. Taking stock and looking ahead – developing a science for policy research agenda on the use and uptake of AI in public sector organisations in the EU

Luca Tangi,[1] Peter Ulrich, Sven Schade and Marina Manzoni

INTRODUCTION

Artificial Intelligence (AI) is considered one of the key technologies of our time. AI already fundamentally changes many aspects of daily life, and this trend is expected to continue. As part of this AI-led transformation of our society, public sector organisations are also increasingly making use of AI-based solutions for addressing both internal operational needs and the provision of public services. Many scholars and practitioners expect AI to radically change public sector management and the way public sector organisations develop, and deliver their services.

The European Commission's Joint Research Centre (JRC) has been monitoring the uptake and use of AI in the public sector closely,[2] in order to collect scientific evidence of AI opportunities and challenges applied to the public sector and provide policy advice on the topic. Providing scientific evidence throughout the whole policy cycle is crucial to ensuring policies are informed by factual and independent knowledge. This holds particularly true in the field of AI fostered by public sector organisations, where such emerging and rapidly developing technology promises great benefits to society on the one hand, but poses equally great risks on the other – also given that it is used by organisations that provide essential services to the public that cannot easily be substituted. To put it in different words: the stakes are high for using AI in the public sector, as it has a unique mandate enshrined in the 'rule of law' that can directly intervene in, and have a strong impact on many sensitive and critical aspects of citizen and business life.

The defining feature of AI that makes it unique is that it does not follow the simple 'if-then (-else)' logic of other digital technologies. Hence, systems are no longer simple artefacts, but a new kind of organisational agent (Desouza et al., 2020; Maragno et al., 2022; Raisch and Krakowski, 2021).

The complexity of the subject requires a strong collaboration between research and policy, based on complementary strategies and instruments. If on the one hand policymakers should rely on the existing research for developing informed policies, on the other hand researchers

---

[1]   The copyright for this chapter belongs to the European Union.
[2]   More details on the Innovation in Public Governance website at https://joint-research-centre.ec .europa.eu/scientific-activities-z/innovations-public-governance_en

should investigate topics reflecting priorities and related policy needs. Such complementarity and mutual support is needed in order to ensure the development of relevant policy regulations and their successful implementation. This aspect is where the contribution of this book chapter focuses, alongside what determines its scope.

To support the uptake of trustworthy AI in European public sector organisations with scientific evidence, this chapter develops a science for policy research agenda. A science for policy research agenda is a research agenda designed from the policy angle. In other words, the topics and research questions that the research agenda addresses, not only consider gaps in the existing literature but also, and above all, reflect on the challenges to be tackled and knowledge needed by policymakers when approaching specific topics and related implications. The agenda we propose in this chapter is based on the experiences of two major science-for-policy projects (AI Watch, and Innovative Public Services[3]) that investigated the use and uptake of AI and other emerging technologies in the public sector. Both feature the input of a wide community of stakeholders, from policymakers and public managers, to practitioners, user representatives and researchers regarding AI application in public sector organisations.

Working along a research for policy agenda is an invitation to all researchers in the field to help policymakers take evidence-based decisions. It should inform the research community of the needs of policymakers for factual and objective evidence and, in this specific case, stimulate a collective effort by the research community to support public sector organisations in their transition towards the use of trustworthy AI. To do that, the research agenda needs to 'moderate' research with the specific needs and questions faced by policy makers in response to societal challenges, and anticipate and forecast emerging trends that will require an informed policy response for the future.

Leading up to the discussion of the science for policy research agenda in this chapter, we will first provide the current state of use and uptake of AI in public sector organisations in Europe (Section 2). This offers a necessary reality check of where we currently stand. After this overview, we will introduce the most important policy developments at the level of the European Union, in order to introduce the relevant policy context (Section 3) to the need for a science for policy agenda. Following the policy context, we will discuss the most important challenges for the use and uptake of AI by public sector organisations (Section 4). Building upon the outcomes from this discussion, we shaped the science for policy agenda which is at the core of the chapter and presented in Section 5. Section 6 outlines some conclusions from the discussion and underpinning context.

STATE OF PLAY OF AI IN THE PUBLIC SECTOR

The JRC has been monitoring the uptake and use of AI in the public sector in Europe since 2019 (Misuraca and van Noordt, 2020). During this time, use cases across Europe were extensively mapped to create a landscape of 686 cases (at the time of writing).[4] This data is

---

[3]   AI WATCH: https:// ai -watch .ec .europa .eu/ index _en; Innovative Public Services: https:// joinup.ec.europa.eu/collection/innovative-public-services
[4]   The latest updates to the database are available on the Public Sector Tech Watch Observatory at https://joinup.ec.europa.eu/collection/public-sector-tech-watch

available openly in the JRC data catalogue[5] and an analysis thereof is available in a dedicated report (Tangi et al., 2022). While we cannot claim the representativeness or completeness of this data, it is nevertheless the most complete and extensive overview today. We are hereby reporting some insights that would serve as a starting point to set the scene and draw our research for policy agenda. For more details about the data collection, analysis, methodology and resulting implications please refer to the dedicated report (Tangi et al., 2022).

The AI in the public sector landscape maps 686 cases of adoption from 30 different countries across several common variables – for example the country where the case is located, the level of government the case is managed at, and the AI enabled technology the case is using. As mentioned above, this landscape does not claim completeness or representativeness, hence, this exercise cannot be used for benchmarking or drawing comparisons across countries. It can however give indications and show overall trends of how AI is currently being applied in the public sector.

The main takeaways from this analysis are (Figure 12.1):

- Since 2015, we can observe an exponential growth in the number of cases, with 167 new cases being added in 2021 alone (the last year for which data was available).
- A third (38 per cent) of the cases identified have already been implemented and are used in daily operations. However, a considerable amount is still in their pilot phase (30 per cent) or under development (25 per cent).
- More than half of the overall cases are initiatives launched at the national level. This might point to the resource's capacity needed for developing or managing AI enabled solutions. Nevertheless, a considerable number of initiatives are developed at subnational level. Hence, regions, cities and municipalities, can just as well make use of AI enabled solutions to improve internal processes or deliver public services.
- Machine Learning (ML) and Natural Language Processing (NLP) are the two most widely used AI technologies.
- Regarding what the cases are trying to achieve by deploying AI solutions, a large share aims to support innovative public services and engagement. The following categories, in decreasing order, are law enforcement, data analysis, monitoring and regulatory research, and internal management.
- In terms of the main recipients of an AI based solution, almost half the AI cases have internal government actors as the main recipient, while of the remaining cases more than half target either citizens or businesses.
- Most cases analysed aim at improving administrative efficiency, or the quality of public services. Cases aiming at improved government capacity for more openness, such as increasing transparency, participation or public control, are still a minority.

Overall, the analysis indicates that the uptake and use of AI in the public sector is rapidly evolving with an increasing number of cases becoming part of daily operations, suggesting that AI in the public sector is evolving from an experimental outlier to becoming an established and widely used technology at all operational levels of government. Nevertheless, most examples are internally oriented and aimed at improving efficiency in public organisations themselves.

---

[5]   https://data.jrc.ec.europa.eu/dataset/7342ea15-fd4f-4184-9603-98bd87d8239a

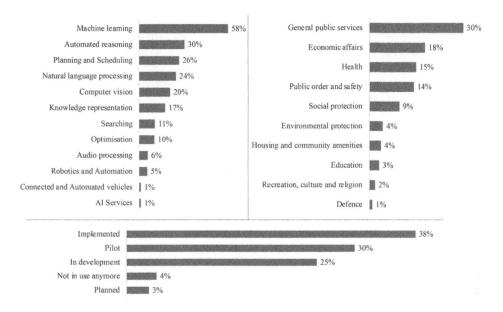

Source: Tangi et al., 2022.

Figure 12.1   Statistics on the use cases collected

POLICY BACKGROUND

After having established the state of play of AI use and uptake in public sector organisations in the EU, we now turn to the policy developments relevant to this context. Our analysis focuses on current and upcoming policy developments, regulations, and other non-binding strategies, as well as on specific programs at EU level. For the purpose of this chapter, national policies, although relevant and impactful within their national borders, are not within the scope of this analysis, and neither are other international strategies that are not led by the EU Programs. For a more in-depth analysis of the international policy background and National Strategies, you can refer to the dedicated reports (Jorge Ricart et al., 2022; Manzoni et al., 2022; Tangi et al., 2022).

Table 12.1 and Table 12.2 summarise the main policies described in this section, with all information updated at the time of writing, i.e. March 2023.

Table 12.1   Main European policies and initiatives on AI

Policy	Year	Main goal
Declaration of Cooperation on AI	2018	Boosting Europe's technological and industrial capacity in AI and its uptake.
Communication by the European Commission 'Artificial Intelligence for Europe'	2018	Proposing an overall strategy on AI for Europe and in particular to create the ideal conditions for the development and implementation of AI in Europe.

Policy	Year	Main goal
Coordinated Plan on the Development and Use of Artificial Intelligence	2018 [revision 2021]	Providing a shared policy collaboration framework and encouraging all Member States to develop national AI strategies.
Recommendations of the High-Level Expert Group (HLEG) on AI	2019 [1st deliverable]	Putting forward a human-centric approach to AI listing requirements and recommendations.
White Paper on Artificial Intelligence	2020	Identifying policy options for ensuring the development of AI is trustworthy, secure, and in line with the values and rights of EU citizens.
Adopt AI program	2021	Supporting the public sector in the procurement of AI.
Artificial Intelligence Act (AI Act)	Proposed 2021 – to be approved	Promoting transparency and compliance with ethical requirements for AI systems that interact with humans by following a risk-based approach.

Table 12.2   *Main European policies affecting the adoption of AI in the PS*

Policy	Year	Main goal
European Strategy for Data	2020	Creating a single market for data that will ensure Europe's global competitiveness and data sovereignty.
Berlin Declaration	2020	Taking the user-centricity principles formulated in the Tallinn Declaration a step further by strengthening the pioneering role of public administrations in driving a value-based digital transformation of our European societies.
Strasbourg Declaration	2022	Underling overarching support of open source and interoperability within the public sector.
Digital Europe Programme	2021	Bringing digital technology to businesses, citizens, and public administrations.
Data Act	2022	Establishing a harmonised framework for industrial, non-personal data sharing in the European Union.
Digital Services Act	2022	Create a safer digital space where the fundamental rights of users are protected and to establish a level playing field for businesses.
Digital Market Act	2022	Ensure that large online platforms behave in a fair way online.
Interoperable Europe Act	Proposed 2022 – to be approved	Ensuring a consistent EU approach to interoperability and establishing an EU-wide interoperability governance structure.

The year 2018 was a true milestone for policies on AI in Europe. The first policy building block for harnessing the potential of this emerging technology in Europe was the *Declaration of Cooperation on AI*. This document aims at boosting Europe's technological and industrial capacity in AI developments and uptake. It was adopted on 10 April, 2018 by all EU Member States, Norway, Switzerland, and the United Kingdom. It was immediately followed on 25 April, 2018 by the *Communication by the European Commission 'Artificial Intelligence for Europe'* (COM/2018/237). The Communication proposes an overall strategy on AI for Europe and, in particular, it intends to create the ideal conditions for the development and implementation of AI in Europe.

The same year the Declaration of Cooperation and the Communication on Artificial Intelligence were adopted, the Commission released the Coordinated Plan on the Development and Use of Artificial Intelligence (COM/2018/795). This plan provides a shared policy collaboration framework, and, at the same time, it encourages all Member States to develop national strategies dedicated to AI. The coordinated plan was updated in 2021 ('Coordinated Plan on Artificial Intelligence 2021 Review'). The review included joint actions for how to create EU global leadership on trustworthy AI. Among those actions, one – action 14 – aims at making the public sector a 'trailblazer for using AI'.

In 2020 the Commission added the White Paper on Artificial Intelligence – a European approach to excellence and trust (COM/2020/65) – to the previous plans and communications. This document presents policy options ensuring the development of AI is trustworthy, secure, and in line with the values and rights of EU citizens. The white paper also includes a specific section dedicated to the adoption of AI by the public sector. The public consultation on the white paper highlighted the importance of the public sector in ensuring trustworthy AI in Europe. The white paper was complemented in the same year by the Communication on a European Strategy for Data (COM/2020/66). The communication emphasises the need to capitalise on the use of data and the importance of embracing cloud technologies to deploy AI for improving decision-making and public services, and updating regulations.

Those policy documents are flanked by the recommendations and considerations of the **High-Level Expert Group (HLEG) on AI**, reported in four deliverables published from 2019 onwards. Those recommendations aim to develop, use, and scale trustworthy AI, leading to AI-based public services that are human-centric and would safeguard the fundamental rights of the beneficiaries of AI-based public services. Furthermore, the Berlin Declaration on Digital Society and Value-based Digital Government also acknowledges the importance of creating value-oriented, human-centric AI systems for use by the public sector. The declaration stresses the importance of ensuring responsible, accountable, transparent, and explainable use of AI, and that unlawful discrimination by AI used in the public sector should be minimised. In general, the Berlin Declaration sees the public sector as a catalyst for sustainable growth and innovation, and a strategic use of public procurement to fund innovation is part of this view. A first report monitoring the progress of the MSs in the Berlin Declaration was published in 2022.[6] Most recently, the **Strasbourg Declaration** on the Common Values and Challenges of European Public Administrations, calls for 'Mobilising emerging technologies, such as artificial intelligence, to improve the effectiveness and efficiency of public service, and ensuring they are used in an ethical, accountable, and inclusive manner to build better digital services for all citizens and businesses'.

These broad strategic lines can be operationalised through a number of programs at the EU level. The Digital Europe Programme (DEP), for example, enables the experimentation of AI within cities through the Large-Scale Pilots initiative. In addition, the new EU GovTech Incubator of the DEP can support the development of new interoperable solutions and AI for the public sector, through cooperation with start-ups and SMEs. Those solutions will become part of the portfolio offered by the Common Services Platform defined under the Digital Europe Programme. Some Member States have used the funds available through the EU Recovery and Resilience Facility (RRF) to support AI policies in their countries. Spain, for example, is supporting the implementation of its national AI Strategy through this instrument. Through the forthcoming Adopt AI program, public sector organisations are supported in procuring AI systems. Furthermore, the European Digital Innovation Hubs (EDIHs) intend to support the uptake of AI by the public sector, for example by helping cities and communities implement AI-enabled urban digital services and urban digital twins, on top of interoperable urban digital platforms.

---

[6]   https://joinup.ec.europa.eu/collection/nifo-national-interoperability-framework-observatory/berlin-declaration-monitoring-mechanism

Moreover, it is here worth mentioning the Digital Service Act and the Digital Market Act, two legislations that combined aim at creating a safer digital space where the fundamental rights of users are protected and establishing a level playing field for businesses. Even if not directly affecting the public sector, they set regulatory implications relevant for suppliers and partners of public organisations. Companies replying to tenders, especially if they provide AI solutions, are likely to fall under the scope of these acts. In this sense, public service development and provision and other public tasks might be indirectly affected.

Any use of AI either in the public or in the private sector, takes place in a regulatory context. At the time of writing, two regulations are in the making that will have an impact on the development, uptake and use of AI in the public, as well as the private sector. In February 2022, the European Commission proposed the new Data Act. Data are a fundamental resource for AI development and implementation. According to this Act, public sector organisations will get access to the data held by the private sector in case of exceptional circumstances and emergencies, such as floods and wildfires, or to implement a legal mandate if data are not otherwise available.

AI development goes hand-in-hand with interoperability. Interoperability policies have been evolving in recent years at the European level. It was recognised that a stronger legal framework is needed to support interoperability, and thus the European Commission proposes the Interoperable Europe Act. The aim is to ensure a consistent EU approach to interoperability, establish an EU-wide interoperability governance structure, and also to set up an ecosystem of reusable and interoperable solutions for public administrations that will apply also to AI based solutions.

The biggest impact on AI from EU regulations, however, is represented by the Artificial Intelligence Act (AI Act), proposed by the Commission in April 2021. The new AI Proposal for a European Regulation laying down harmonised rules on Artificial Intelligence aims to promote transparency and compliance with ethical requirements for AI systems that interact with humans, by following a risk-based approach. The AI Act introduces a practical 'product safety regime' modelled around four risk categories: unacceptable risk, high risk, limited risk, and minimal risk. While the deployment of AI based systems bearing unacceptable risks is forbidden, the Act imposes requirements for market entrance and certification for High-Risk AI Systems. Consequently, the AI Act affects any organisation with EU market exposure that develops or wants to adopt AI. Such requirements are even more important when applied to public sector organisations.

In addition, the AI Act also considers an AI system being at high-risk if it is used as a safety component of a product, or if it is covered by one of 19 specified sectors of EU single market harmonisation legislation (for example, aviation, cars, and medical devices).

CHALLENGES FOR THE UPTAKE AND USE OF AI BY THE PUBLIC SECTOR

In the previous two sections, we presented the current landscape of deployment of AI in the public sector and introduced the relevant policy context. These showed that there is a policy commitment to using trustworthy AI in the EU, and that the public sector should play a key role in buying, developing, and using this technology to the highest possible compliance to, and in respect of, human rights and digital principles.

What we see are significant expectations about how public sector organisations should contribute to the development of AI (being a trailblazer), and how they should use the underpinning technology (in a trustworthy and value driven way). Yet, when it comes to the actual implementation of AI in public sector organisations there is still a lot of uncertainty about how this should look in practice.

In the case of AI in public sector organisations, we should include the uncertainty about how this technology should be used in support of decision making, the difficulties in managing the integration and use of AI in organisational structures, processes and procedures (Dwivedi et al., 2019; Maragno et al., 2022; Sun and Medaglia, 2019), and the difficulties in involving citizens (Medaglia and Tangi, 2022). We therefore need now to have a look at the challenges encountered for the uptake and use of AI by the public sector, as it is precisely these challenges that a science for policy research agenda has to address, especially in this area (see also the unique features, specific risks and barriers, and recommendations described in Manzoni et al., 2022).

Wirtz et al. (2019) identify four main classes of challenges:

1. **Societal**, for example, related to social acceptance of AI, such as trust in technology or fear of losing one's job due to a wrong algorithm.
2. **Ethical**, including the risk of encountering issues like discrimination or value judgements induced by machines.
3. **Regulatory**, related to legal or responsibility questions, for example, privacy or accountability.
4. **Technological**, related to the difficulties of the implementation of technological solutions, such as data integration or technical skills of public employees.

Mikalef et al. (2021) add to the above challenges the need for funding and incentives, the degree of innovative culture, and possible pressure given by political priorities. Ahn and Chen (2021) highlight the importance of training and education on AI, and de Bruijn, Warnier, and Janssen (2021) identify a set of challenges for better explaining AI to non-experts and users. On the same lines, Grimmelikhuijsen (2022) highlighted that algorithmic explainability must be addressed to ensure trustworthiness. In other words, the assumption is that AI will be more acceptable to users if it is transparent, and its purpose and use should be explained to all the actors involved – public servants, public managers, citizens, etc.

While all the elements above have their specific AI dimension, not all of them are unique to AI but some are shared by many emerging developments in the process of digital government transformation (see, for example, Eom and Lee, 2022; Tangi et al., 2021).

Taking into account what we learnt from the landscape of AI in the public sector, from the policy context, and from literature, we understand that the challenges regarding the use and uptake of AI in public sector organisations are mostly related to the following instrumental processes:

- **Bringing AI into public sector organisations through innovation and experimentation practices**. As we could see from the landscape (Tangi et al., 2022), about a third (31 per cent) of cases identified were already implemented and in daily use. Therefore, this specific phase of adoption and use still requires special attention as it also needs to take into account specific guidelines and regulations.

- **Managing the implementation and integration of AI in a public organisation**. As we just saw, the literature places a lot of attention on elements such as skills, capacities, training, and funding, as well as other management-related issues, such as data integration. Considering the state of uptake of AI as shown by the AI landscape, integrating AI into the day-to-day operations of a public sector organisation seems a crucial challenge.
- **The role of policy in steering the deployment of AI in public sector organisations**. As we showed in previous sections, there is a rich policy context where the public sector can find support to foster AI deployment within its organisations for both internal and external purposes. This includes existing policies for which impact can already be measured, and upcoming policies, such as the AI Act, for which the potential impact is still to unfold.
- **Trustworthiness and human centricity as cross-cutting principles to respect a lawful and safe use of AI by the public sector**. As we explained above, trustworthiness of AI is an issue high on the policy agenda and features prominently among the challenges identified by literature. We understand trustworthiness as a challenge that is not specific to any particular AI enabled technology or solution in the public sector, as all of them should be human centered, but it is rather its intended use that is relevant across the board.

RESEARCH FOR POLICY AGENDA

In the previous section, we identified the challenges that a science for policy research agenda for the fostering of AI by public sector organisations needs to address. In this section, we will develop the research agenda itself, following the challenges identified above and drawing from the input from policymakers that we engaged with over the past three years. The research agenda is not limited to being implemented by any specific research institution, it is rather an invitation addressed to researchers in the field, to help policymakers take more evidence-based decisions and develop evidence-driven policy agendas.

Figure 12.2 summarises the research agenda graphically. First, it highlights that all aspects of research in support of the deployment of AI by the public sector should take place under the umbrella of the trustworthiness principle. Second, it defines the three main pillars that contain key research for policy questions: enabling innovation, management and governance, and policy and regulation. Third, it highlights the methods that are needed to implement this research. For the remainder of the section, we will describe in detail each of the elements shown in Figure 12.2. We do not claim that those research questions cover every aspect of research imaginable. We do believe, however, that they address the most pressing issues at this point in time.

Overarching Principle: Trustworthiness and Human Centricity

AI requires a change of paradigm in understanding the relation between humans and machines. In a nutshell, AI is not infallible and should rather be considered as a new kind of agent in the organisation that, like human agents, can make mistakes and lead to wrong decisions, i.e. the so-called algorithm biases. Even with good intentions, AI misuse can cause unintentional harm. A direct consequence of this is the need to ensure trust in the AI based system, by putting human values at the centre, and human supervision at the core of any AI solution.

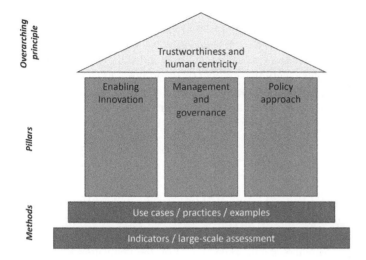

Figure 12.2   Research for policy agenda on AI in public sector organisations

The High-Level Expert Group on AI (HLEG) wrote the 'ethics guidelines for trustworthy AI' (2018). Already in its introduction, the guidelines clearly state:

> Trustworthiness is a prerequisite for people and societies to develop, deploy and use AI systems. Without AI systems – and the human beings behind them – being demonstrably worthy of trust, unwanted consequences may ensue, and their uptake might be hindered, preventing the realisation of the potentially vast social and economic benefits that they can bring. To help Europe realise those benefits, our vision is to ensure and scale Trustworthy AI.

Trustworthiness, as defined by the HLEG, is an overarching principle that embraces three components: (i) lawfulness, i.e. compliance with laws and regulations, (ii) ethics, i.e. adherence to ethical principles and values, and (iii) robustness, i.e. performing in a secure and reliable manner. Going deeper into the ethical values and principles, the HLEG identifies respect for human autonomy, prevention of harm, fairness and explicability.

The public sector, even more so than other sectors, cannot afford any type of discrimination or unfair use of AI. Despite the short history of AI use in the public sector, there have already been a number of examples of systems being discontinued due to algorithmic discrimination. For example, in the Netherlands the District Court of the Hague stopped an AI system named SyRI for having violated privacy and transparency rights.[7] Similarly, in France the Régie Autonome des Transports Parisiens (RATP) put on hold a system monitoring the wearing of a mask as it was considered too intrusive.[8]

Hence, the proposed research agenda highlights trustworthiness – as defined by the HLEG – as the overarching principle, which should serve as an umbrella and guiding light for any research on the topic of AI deployed by public sector organisations. Only by developing,

---

[7]   https://www.nysingh.nl/blog/steem-risico-indicatie-syri-is-strijd-evrm/

[8]   https:// www .bfmtv .com/ tech/ trop -intrusives -les -cameras -de -detection -de -masques -desactivees-a-paris-et-a-cannes_AN-202006220163.html

adopting, and using trustworthy AI solutions can the public sector be considered as a true pioneer for the respect of digital rights and principles (such as safety and security, solidarity, inclusion, etc.) without risking the opposite effect, i.e. to undermine and threaten them.

Researchers are required to pursue the same professional effort and cultural change that is required from policymakers and implementers and consider trustworthiness as the keystone of any research on AI. Trustworthiness has become the higher, peculiar, and distinctive principle for AI implementation, especially in the public sector; hence it must also be the higher, peculiar, and distinctive principle for any research addressing AI development, and especially its use by the public sector.

Pillar: Enabling Innovation

AI in the public sector is an innovative topic. Our inventory of cases shows that the vast majority are either in a piloting phase or still under development. AI technology is evolving fast and so is its application in the public sector, with changing and new possibilities being discovered continuously. This means that researchers should keep an eye on the innovation angle, the new possibilities arising from AI, and how public organisations can discover and deploy them. Table 12.3 summarises the different challenges and the main research questions still open that feed our research for policy agenda.

Table 12.3   Enabling innovation: challenges and research questions

Challenges	Suggested research questions
Identifying and anticipating trends and sustainability in the use of AI in the public sector in Europe.	• Which are the trends and developments in the deployment of AI in the public sector?
Developing, testing, and acquiring AI sustainable solutions by the public sector.	• How can public sector organisations procure trustworthy and sustainable AI? • How can public sector organisations use sandboxing to experiment and measure impact and sustainability of AI solutions?
Partnerships and alliances for innovating with AI in the public sector.	• How to involve users, including internal to public organisations, in the development of trustworthy AI solutions? • How to collaborate with academia, research institutions, and the private sector for developing trustworthy AI solutions for the public sector?

First, AI is not represented by a single technology, but rather by a fast evolving mix of technologies, systems and solutions. Therefore, scholars should not focus exclusively on the dynamics and the changes that AI individual technology innovations could bring to public sector organisations. Research should take a more holistic and, at the same time, nuanced look, understanding which AI technologies are to be used where, how, and for solving which problems. We expect the landscape of AI deployment in the public sector to be quite dynamic and change over time along with the maturity of AI underpinning technologies. We suggest a continuous mapping of those trends in order to highlight new possibilities for deployment of AI in the public sector as they emerge.

When investigating AI applied to the public sector through the lens of innovation, we need to understand also how AI solutions could be best introduced in the public sector in order to solve a particular problem. This refers to a large extent to procurement, and especially to Public Procurement of Innovation. Policymakers need to better understand how to procure trustworthy AI, the underlying framework conditions and possible related clauses. To our best knowledge, except for experimentation instances in a few European cities, little research is currently addressing this topic, even though public organisations are struggling with the identification of the proper approach toward the procurement of AI solutions. We invite researchers to fill this gap between research and actual practice on this process. To complement the need for a better understanding of procurement processes, other elements for developing and testing AI need to be explored. This can, for example, include sandboxing, or other approaches for testing and experimenting with new solutions, in a controlled environment yet with real working conditions in addressing concrete issues.

Only very few public sector organisations demonstrate the capacity and resources to develop AI systems themselves. Therefore, they strongly rely on cooperation with external partners, in the private sector or academia. This might include elements of GovTech with the involvement of start-ups, or a science-policy interface (Kuziemski et al., 2022; Mergel et al., 2022). In addition, in order to develop relevant, successful and trustworthy AI systems, we also need to consider the involvement of end-users, such as citizens and business, including public sector officers. Applying participatory approaches required for the co-creation (from design to delivery) of AI enabled public services need more efforts (Medaglia and Tangi, 2022). In actual fact, even though there are policy recommendations for the development of participatory approaches, its actual realisation does not seem to be so easy and so widespread (Medaglia and Tangi, 2022). More research is needed to find ways to address this shortcoming, and one way could be by devoting more research to identify and develop collaborative schemes based on complementarity of efforts, common interest and challenges and, above all, shared values.

Pillar: Management and Governance

A report by the JRC emphasises the need to carefully manage the transition from piloting to implementing AI in the public sector (Molinari et al., 2021). Since only a third of all cases have been fully implemented in public sector organisations, there is still little experience and knowledge regarding how to manage AI in public sector organisations. From the evidence available thus far, we observe that implementing AI in public sector organisations requires significant changes in structures, processes, and procedures. At the same time, using AI in the public sector will also trigger unexpected changes that will transform the way the public sector works. Table 12.4 goes more into depth about these different challenges and suggests related research questions.

Table 12.4   *Management and governance: challenges and research questions*

Challenges	Suggested research questions
Developing skills and competences of public sector employees for the correct development and use of AI solutions.	• Which skills and competences are needed for the development and the use of AI-based solutions?
	• How far do AI skills already exist in the public sector in Europe?
	• How are public administrations developing AI skills among their workforces?
Managing organisational change for the effective use of AI solutions.	• How is AI changing tasks, roles, and structures, in public organisations?
	• What would be public officials' tasks and roles for ensuring trustworthiness?

Challenges	Suggested research questions
Understanding public sector transformation triggered by the adoption of AI.	• How will AI change the way the public sector is working and responding to users' needs?
	• How will AI adoption affect public administrations' multi-level governance?
	• How will AI adoption affect the relations between the private and the public sector?
Effectively governing data and processes for trustworthy AI.	• How is data governed? From data collection to its use in an ethical and trustworthy manner.

The lack of relevant skills in the public sector is often cited as one of the main barriers to a successful digital transformation thereof. This holds true especially for AI due to the novelty and complexity of the technology, and its potential role and responsibility as an organisational agent within the administration. This might include reorganising processes that include AI-based decisions and questions about human oversight that stem from it. Therefore, the skills and competencies needed for using AI in public sector organisations do not just include technical or IT skills, although those are certainly crucial. Equally important are skills in change management, stakeholder communication, project and process management, and more. In addition to skills, effective AI use might require the creation of entirely new job profiles in the administration, such as algorithm trainers (Maragno et al., 2022).

In order to effectively make use of AI solutions, public sector organisations need to adapt tasks, roles, structures, and processes. Developing and using AI in the public sector also raises questions about the creation of new AI-teams and their integration into existing organisational structures (Maragno et al., 2022).

While a wise and effective use of AI in public sector organisations might require active and conscious change, AI might also lead to unexpected transformations of the public sector over time. This might include changing relations between the public and the private sectors, or different approaches to strategic planning. Regarding the role of the private sector in this development there are several crucial questions, for example about the ownership of data, who trains and runs an algorithm, and more. There is also the possibility that the extended use of AI in the public sector might change multi-level governance and the sharing of responsibilities between different levels of administration.

Data is the fuel of digital transformation, in the public sector and elsewhere. This is especially the case when applying AI solutions. Data is crucial for training algorithms to perform a particular task. In addition, for AI techniques such as predictive analytics or machine learning, quality data is the input needed for AI to perform tasks correctly. Concrete examples might be fraud detection or environmental planning. AI-based solutions raise questions for the public sector related to the availability of data and its strategic management, including integration of datasets, sharing of data within and between public sector bodies, as well as with the private sector, data protection and privacy, and data ownership in the public vs the private sector.

Pillar: Policy and Regulation

The adoption of AI in the public sector takes place in the context of specific policies and regulations. A research for policy agenda on this subject needs to engage with policy and regulation in a circular manner. We need to understand the impact of policy and regulation on the adoption of AI in the public sector and identify the evidence needed to adapt policies or create new ones accordingly. Table 12.5 goes more into depth about these different challenges and suggests related research questions.

Table 12.5   *Policy and regulation: challenges and research questions*

Topic	Research question(s)
Understanding the role of the regulatory context	• To what extent will AI and other relevant acts and regulations affect AI adoption by the public sector? • What effects will the upcoming AI Act have on the uptake of AI in the public sector? How can public sector organisations assess the risk level of AI-based solutions? • Which measures do public administrations need to develop to be compliant with the AI Act?
Analysing the role of National Recovery and Resilience Plans	• How are RRPs supporting the uptake of AI by the public sector? What evidence in this direction is reported in the national plans? • What are the effects of the budget devoted to the uptake of AI through RRPs?
Monitoring strategies and policy impacts	• How do policies support the uptake of AI in the public sector? • Are there any measurable impacts of political directives and pressure on AI uptake?
Algorithm registries and other facilitating measures	• Which facilitating measures can be promoted at a political level to support a trustworthy uptake of AI? • How might the setup of algorithm registries become a policy to foster transparency, and how should they be implemented?

Often, new technologies outpace the regulatory context in which they are embedded. This holds true especially for AI due to the speed of development of more complex and advanced solutions. There is, for example, uncertainty around the impact GDPR has on the implementation of novel and more advanced AI solutions. Moreover, scholars need to acknowledge that the consequence of the AI Act makes a clear distinction amongst the risks brought about by the different AI solutions; there are solutions that are riskier than others, hence different approaches and dynamics will need to be put in place by public administrations, hence these differences should be mirrored in the research on the topic. In this context, AI systems that fall under the high-risk category need to follow strict obligations. Some use cases of AI in the public sector will most likely fall under the high-risk category. Other systems instead fall under the transparency-risk category; hence, they must fulfil transparency obligations. For example, the AI Act clearly indicates that all the chatbots (more than 70 chatbots in public administrations in Europe were identified) have to respect transparency obligations. Beyond the AI Act, there will be strict transparency obligations to respect, especially in the public sector where transparency is one of the driver values to follow.

In this respect, discussion about the AI Act is still ongoing and modifications will be applied to the regulation. However, what is already clear is that the AI Act will significantly affect the AI uptake by the public sector. In conclusion, scholars need to carefully consider the effect of the regulatory environment in researching the challenges and opportunities for the adoption and the consequent impacts of AI use by the public sector (Manzoni et al., 2022).

Besides the legislation in place, the Recovery and Resilience facility is currently one of the EU's main instruments for facing the socio-economic crisis the world is undergoing. Part of the reforms and investments in the national recovery plans are earmarked to address the modernisation of the public sector with digital technologies. In fact, 21.2 billion euros have been allocated to governments' digital modernisations. Questions on the impact of the RRF on wider AI deployment by the public sector are still open. First, to our knowledge no studies are available, from a policy perspective, on how governments intend to use this amount of money for fostering the uptake of AI, and what would be the differences among countries; second, no measurement or anecdotal evidence is available to demonstrate which effect this injection of money is to bring on AI integration in the public sector.

The AI Watch has been monitoring the political intentions through the analysis of the national AI strategies (Jorge Ricart et al., 2022; Tangi et al., 2022). However, the national strategies represent only a small portion of the policies designed and the evidence collected can be considered only a starting point in understanding the role of policies and policy documents and their impact (Manzoni et al., 2022). Not only official policies but also political attitudes, facilitating measures, and promotion activities can foster or hinder the uptake of AI in government (Sun and Medaglia, 2019).

Conversely, the role and the impact of AI on politics are still unclear and deserve further research. In this direction, algorithm registries have emerged as promising approaches to increase transparency and trust in AI-based solutions in the public sector and beyond (Manzoni et al., 2022). One such registry will likely be implemented at EU level to capture high risk cases across the Union. Further research should focus on the potential of algorithm repositories, their strengths and weaknesses, to develop recommendations for their application across the EU.

Development Methods

Above we introduced the challenges, topics, and questions related to the development of a science for policy research agenda under the umbrella of trustworthiness as the overarching principle. Here we will describe the cross-cutting methodological approach needed to develop it. The two main building blocks being, (1) use cases, practices, and examples, and (2) indicators, large-scale assessment, and framework conditions.

Use cases, practices, and examples

As more and more cases of AI in the public sector emerge, we need to move towards a more efficient and structured way of identifying them. To enrich the landscape meaningfulness one path could be developing a structured analysis of public procurement data for identifying instances where AI related products or services were purchased.

Further we need to look under the surface and undertake deep dives into selected cases. We need to understand the internal workings of public sector organisations in relation to AI through interviews, document in-depth analysis, and other qualitative methods of investigation. The in-depth scrutiny of case studies provides evidence for understanding the innovation processes in public sector organisations needed for the adoption of AI, as well as the organisational transformations implemented also in relation to new roles and functions.

Moreover, another important step would be the identification of best practice cases and examples and their presentation. Based on a clear set of criteria for selecting them, best practice cases have an important communicative effect. They can highlight particular elements of the innovation processes and how public sector organisations are adopting and using AI, allowing policy makers to identify the objectives and the path to follow when developing innovation agendas and related policies.

Indicators and large-scale assessment

AI is often described as a disruptive technology. Even if we ignore for a moment the question of whether we really want the public sector to be 'disrupted', we still get a sense of the high expectations associated with AI applied to the public sector. At the moment, even with an extensive and in-depth mapping of AI cases, we cannot make a meaningful enough assessment of the impact of AI. Developing dedicated indicators needs to be part of future science for policy research effort. In fact, by having access to more AI specific indicators and combining them with existing indicator sets specific to digital government and public sector performance measurement, we would be able to assess the impact of AI in the public sector and thus, incentives of data-driven policy making.

To carry out assessment exercises, we can partially rely on existing indicator systems and benchmarks measuring public sector performance and digital government transformation, such as the Digital Economy and Society Index (DESI), the eGovernment benchmark, and by monitoring through the European Interoperability Framework (EIF) and Berlin Declaration. These instruments would need to be complemented with indicators specific to the use of AI by the public sector, for example, as an evolution to the AI Watch Index[9] that so far does not explicitly address the public sector. This could for example include also a specific indicator about the funds going into public procurement of AI systems and services. Such an indicator could be based on a systematic analysis of procurement data. Another indicator could be the share of AI systems used in the public sector that are considered high-risk according to the definition of the forthcoming AI Act. Such an indicator would be informed by introducing reporting obligations on high-risk systems. These are just examples of the kinds of indicators that would be needed in order to fully understand the impact of AI on the public sector and the citizens and business it serves.

CONCLUSIONS

In this chapter, we developed the concept of a science for policy agenda for the uptake and use of AI by the public sector, intended as a research agenda driven by the needs of policy to develop regulations supported by relevant and objective evidence for an effective governance of public good. This chapter represents the first attempt to introduce this concept. We understand our research for policy agenda as an invitation to the research community to engage with and support policymakers with independent scientific evidence.

At the basis of this agenda, we argue that trustworthiness needs to be the principle underpinning any research effort on AI in general and even more when applied in the public sector. Within the context of trustworthiness, we cluster the proposed science for policy efforts into three pillars: Enabling Innovation, Management and Governance, and Policy and Research. The research agenda proposes building the research on two methodological approaches: the collection and analysis of use cases, and the development and use of indicators and dedicated assessment frameworks.

It is important to note here that many of the issues encountered in the deployment of AI by the public sector have in one way or another already been addressed by previous research efforts. The aim of this chapter is therefore not to reinvent the wheel, but to identify what is truly unique about this particular technology (for example, the risk created by algorithmic biases) and from this perspective reinterpret knowledge created in the tradition of eGovernment. We

---

[9]   https://ai-watch.ec.europa.eu/publications/ai-watch-index-2021_en

invite researchers to follow the same approach and also to not treat AI as one uniform block, but to acknowledge the different types of AI (natural language processing, machine learning, etc.) and understand the specificities of each of these different AI technologies.

While we do not claim that the proposed research for policy agenda includes every imaginable research angle and view, we argue that it covers many fundamental ones. Further research is needed to strengthen the agenda by enriching and prioritising the various challenges and research questions that emerged. The research agenda proposed here is just a snapshot at the moment of writing, and new pillars, challenges, and gaps might emerge in the future. Continuous work is needed to keep the agenda up to date to continue positive cross-fertilisation between research and policy.

Despite those limitations, we hope readers will find this research for policy agenda stimulating and hope for a constructive dialogue on this concept in the following years.

REFERENCES

Ahn, M. J., and Chen, Y.-C. (2021). Digital transformation toward AI-augmented public administration: The perception of government employees and the willingness to use AI in government. *Government Information Quarterly*, 101664. https://doi.org/10.1016/j.giq.2021.101664

de Bruijn, H., Warnier, M., and Janssen, M. (2021). The perils and pitfalls of explainable AI: Strategies for explaining algorithmic decision-making. *Government Information Quarterly*, 101666. https://doi.org/10.1016/j.giq.2021.101666

Desouza, K. C., Dawson, G. S., and Chenok, D. (2020). Designing, developing, and deploying artificial intelligence systems: Lessons from and for the public sector. *Business Horizons*, *63*(2), 205–213. https://doi.org/10.1016/j.bushor.2019.11.004

Dwivedi, Y. K., Hughes, L., Ismagilova, E., Aarts, G., Coombs, C., Crick, T., Duan, Y., Dwivedi, R., Edwards, J., Eirug, A., et al. (2019). Artificial Intelligence (AI): Multidisciplinary perspectives on emerging challenges, opportunities, and agenda for research, practice and policy. *International Journal of Information Management*, *August*, 101994. https://doi.org/10.1016/j.ijinfomgt.2019.08.002

Eom, S.-J., and Lee, J. (2022). Digital government transformation in turbulent times: Responses, challenges, and future direction. *Government Information Quarterly*, 101690. https://doi.org/10.1016/j.giq.2022.101690

Grimmelikhuijsen, S. (2022). Explaining why the computer says no: Algorithmic transparency affects the perceived trustworthiness of automated decision-making. *Public Administration Review*, puar.13483. https://doi.org/10.1111/puar.13483

Jorge Ricart, R., Van Roy, V., Rossetti, F., and Tangi, L. (2022). *AI Watch – National Strategies on Artificial Intelligence: A European Perspective, 2022 Edition*. EUR 31083 EN, Publications Office of the European Union, Luxembourg, ISBN 978-92-76-52910-1, Doi: 10.2760/385851, JRC129123.

Kuziemski, M., Mergel, I., Ulrich, P., and Martinez, A. (2022). *GovTech Practices in the EU*. EUR 30985 EN, Publications Office of the European Union, Luxembourg, ISBN 978-92-76-47234-6, doi:10.2760/74735, JRC128247.

Manzoni, M., Medaglia, R., Tangi, L., van Noordt, C., Vaccari, L., and Gattwinkel, D. (2022). *AI Watch. Road to the Adoption of Artificial Intelligence by the Public Sector*. EUR 31054 EN, Publications Office of the European Union, Luxembourg, ISBN 978-92-76-52132-7, doi: 10.2760/288757, JRC129100.

Maragno, G., Tangi, L., Gastaldi, L., and Benedetti, M. (2022). AI as an organizational agent to nurture: Effectively introducing chatbots in public entities. *Public Management Review*, 1–31. https://doi.org/10.1080/14719037.2022.2063935

Medaglia, R., and Tangi, L. (2022). The adoption of artificial intelligence in the public sector in Europe: Drivers, features, and impacts. *15th International Conference on Theory and Practice of Electronic Governance*, 10–18. https://doi.org/10.1145/3560107.3560110

Mergel, I., Ulrich, P., Kuziemski, M., and Martinez, A. (2022). *Scoping GovTech Dynamics in the EU*. EUR 30979 EN, Publications Office of the European Union, Luxembourg, ISBN 978-92-76-47059-5 (Online), Doi:10.2760/700544 (Online), JRC128093.

Mikalef, P., Lemmer, K., Schaefer, C., Ylinen, M., Fjørtoft, S. O., Torvatn, H. Y., Gupta, M., and Niehaves, B. (2021). Enabling AI capabilities in government agencies: A study of determinants for European municipalities. *Government Information Quarterly*, 101596. https://doi.org/10.1016/j.giq .2021.101596

Misuraca, G., and van Noordt, C. (2020). *AI Watch – Artificial Intelligence in Public Services* (JRC EUR 30255). Publications Office of the European Union. https://ec.europa.eu/jrc/en/publication/eur -scientific-and-technical-research-reports/ai-watch-artificial-intelligence-public-services

Molinari, F., van Noordt, C., Vaccari, L., Pignatelli, F., and Tangi, L. (2021). *AI Watch. Beyond Pilots: Sustainable Implementation of AI in Public Services*. EUR 30868 EN, Publications Office of the European Union, Luxembourg. https://doi.org/ISBN 978-92-76-42587-8, doi:10.2760/440212, JRC126665.

Raisch, S., and Krakowski, S. (2021). Artificial intelligence and management: The automation – augmentation paradox. *Academy of Management Review*, *46*(1), 192–210. https://doi.org/10.5465/amr .2018.0072

Sun, T. Q., and Medaglia, R. (2019). Mapping the challenges of Artificial Intelligence in the public sector: Evidence from public healthcare. *Government Information Quarterly*, *36*(2), 368–383. https:// doi.org/10.1016/j.giq.2018.09.008

Tangi, L., Janssen, M., Benedetti, M., and Noci, G. (2021). Digital government transformation: A structural equation modelling analysis of driving and impeding factors. *International Journal of Information Management*, *60*, 102356. https://doi.org/10.1016/j.ijinfomgt.2021.102356

Tangi, L., van Noordt, C., Combetto, M., Gattwinkel, D., and Pignatelli, F. (2022). *AI Watch. European Landscape on the Use of Artificial Intelligence by the Public Sector*. EUR 31088 EN, Publications Office of the European Union, Luxembourg, 2022, ISBN 978-92-76-53058-9, Doi:10.2760/39336, JRC129301.

Wirtz, B. W., Weyerer, J. C., and Geyer, C. (2019). Artificial intelligence and the public sector – applications and challenges. *International Journal of Public Administration*, *42*(7), 596–615. https://doi.org/ 10.1080/01900692.2018.1498103

13. Analysis of driving public values of AI initiatives in government in Europe[1]

Colin van Noordt, Gianluca Misuraca and Ines Mergel

INTRODUCTION

Artificial intelligence (AI) promises disruptive changes to the way the public sector designs and operates its internal processes and delivers public services to businesses and citizens. The changes range from proactive delivery of services (Androutsopoulou et al., 2019) to automation of tasks (Engin and Treleaven, 2019) and disruption of work (Sun and Medaglia, 2019), among others. While some applications of data analytics based on machine learning already exist in some countries, and several pilots are emerging, in general, public administrations have only recently started to explore the implementation of AI technologies and have therefore not realised its potential in use. Empirical evidence is in fact missing to understand what these AI-supported public service delivery projects look like and how – or whether – they deliver public value. While some scholars argue that AI might disrupt not only how services are delivered, but also how value is created for the public (Ojo, Mellouli and Ahmadi Zeleti, 2019), we also witness potential threats to the quality-of-service delivery and emerging risks or unintended negative consequences that can be generated by the adoption of AI in the public sector, as some recent cases have demonstrated (Misuraca and van Noordt, 2020).

Whereas research on AI in the private sector is generally more widespread and advanced (Collins et al., 2021; Loureiro, Guerreiro and Tussyadiah, 2021), it is questionable whether copying approaches and practices from the private sector is sufficient in understanding public sector use of AI (Zuiderwijk, Chen and Salem, 2021). The public sector operates in a unique setting, where public services and policy (supported by AI and other ICT) should not only be based on economic values such as profit, but also on democratic and social values, such as the rule of law. Innovation in the public sector has also been argued to occur differently than the private sector due to the specific culture, goals and constraints the public sector operates in (Bugge and Bloch, 2016; De Vries, Bekkers and Tummers, 2016), which is why research insights from the private sector cannot be directly transferred to the public sector context (Medaglia, Gil-Garcia and Pardo, 2021). In fact, while a lot of attention to the potential societal impacts of AI is given in the literature (Zuiderwijk, Chen and Salem, 2021), empirical research testing these assumptions is only slowly emerging (Aoki, 2020). What this early research has found is a too limited view, focusing exclusively on the economic benefits of the use of AI systems that may limit awareness and perspectives of other important public values, such as ignoring legality, within the scope of the development and implementation

[1] Work on this chapter has benefitted in part from the activities conducted by two of the authors within the framework of the AI for the public sector research task of the AI Watch, a joint initiative of DG CONNECT and the European Commission's Joint Research Centre.

of such a solution, leading to destructive results as seen in the case of Robodebt in Australia (Rinta-Kahila et al., 2021).

As such, research on AI in government is growing, but a clear understanding on both how to assess the impact of AI in government and which effects materialise after adoption and deployment is still lacking (Zuiderwijk, Chen and Salem, 2021). It is often still unclear how positive and negative impacts can be identified, given the potential positive, negative, and unintended consequences AI brings in a public sector setting. While there is plenty of work on the theoretical effects of AI deployed in government, linking it clearly with the actual deployment of AI in government is limited. As such, research is quite aware of what public value AI could create, but there is limited evidence of which value is being (or attempting to be) created.

This chapter, therefore, aims to tackle this research gap by assessing which public value existing AI use cases, found in public administrations around Europe, aim to create. Through a landscaping exercise of AI use in public services across the EU, we have extracted cases and conducted an analysis of a set of 549 identified use cases. Using a public value framework derived from the existing literature (Rose et al., 2015), we identify how AI public service delivery plans contribute to the professionalism of public values, efficiency-related public values, the service-related public values and/or engagement-related public values. This is especially relevant in order to minimise 'administrative evil' and to maximise good governance, as public values may be threatened by the implementation of AI technologies (Schiff, Schiff and Pierson, 2021). Furthermore, it provides an overview of which values may be under and overrepresented, especially since in the strategic documents surrounding AI, a too strong economic perspective is often present whilst other important goals, such as strengthening the rule of law, sustainability, citizen participation and democracy, are severely overlooked in the narratives (Toll et al., 2020; Guenduez and Mettler, 2022; Wilson, 2022).

Next, we provide an overview of the state of play by reviewing the literature on public sector AI, and outline how various forms of public value could be created by utilising AI within public administrations. We then present the research design and our methodological approach followed by the discussion of the main findings of the analysis. Then we derive implications of the study for both policy makers and public managers who are implementing AI initiatives and propose new avenues for future research.

LITERATURE REVIEW

AI in the Public Sector

The use of AI technologies and applications in government has been argued both by academics and practitioners to be capable of improving government tasks and processes in significant ways. Despite AI being often used as an umbrella term to describe a variety of different technologies, AI is often understood as ICT systems which are capable of perceiving their environment and taking actions to complete tasks, which are regarded to require some form of human intelligence or rationality (Sun and Medaglia, 2019). In this respect, a diverse set of AI applications has been emerging in public sector settings for purposes such as assisting in policy making processes (Wirtz, Weyerer and Geyer, 2019; Valle-Cruz et al., 2020), direct public service delivery (Aoki, 2020; Kuziemski and Misuraca, 2020), internal process management of public administrations (Lima and Delen, 2020; Pencheva, Esteve and Mikhaylov, 2020), and public procurement (van der Peijl et al., 2020).

Compared to other ICT used by public administrations, AI can be much more impactful for citizens due to its direct support in decisions affecting citizens, the likely deployment in core functions of governmental organisations which originally required human expertise (Veale and Brass, 2019; Engstrom et al., 2020). Despite the positive potential impact and discourse, an increasing amount of research warns of the negative consequences of the use of AI within the public sector context (Hartmann and Wenzelburger, 2021). If used irresponsibly, there are risks of amplifying (existing) discrimination within society by using biased data in automated decision making (Liu, Lin and Chen, 2019), making decisions more opaque, and reducing citizens' privacy through large-scale data collection, which can increase the feeling of surveillance and paradoxically reduce transparency in government (Barocas and Selbst, 2016; Dwivedi et al., 2019). Moreover, the possible loss of control through AI-mandated decisions and the low capacity to manage complex AI-enabled operations may undermine the trust relationship between the public sector and the citizens (Janssen et al., 2020) or even exclude citizens entirely (Larsson, 2021).

In this still emergent field, we have little empirical insight into the implications that the adoption of this new set of technologies can have in terms of public value creation in society. In general terms, it could indeed be assumed that the implementation of AI in public administrations will follow the general strategic goals and discourse laid out by policy documents. Studies reviewing AI strategy documents found in fact that AI is often described as an enabler of efficiency and effectiveness in the public sector (Fatima, Desouza and Dawson, 2020), but not regarded as an enabler for increasing citizen engagement in general (Toll et al., 2019; Wilson, 2021). As there is a significant interplay between the values involved in the design and roll-out of ICT technologies, understanding which values are driving the deployment of AI in the public sector will give a noteworthy preview of the impact that can be expected from AI in general (Viscusi, Rusu and Florin, 2020), and in specific domains, such as in the case of social services and care (Misuraca and Viscusi, 2020), a domain that will likely hold great potential for AI implementation and the possibility to enhance social values and citizens' well-being.

Public values in the use of AI

AI, similar to other types of public sector innovations, is generally deemed to be 'of value' because it is innovative, dynamic, changes the previous status of service delivery, or is generally agreed upon as the next wave of technology use in government (see, for example, De Vries, Bekkers and Tummers, 2016). However, it is often unclear what kind of outcome new technologies have on the organisation, their stakeholders or society at large.

Such a debate is like earlier discussions on the purpose and goal of e-Government initiatives, as a similar debate was held on what were the main values, purposes and visions found in such e-Government initiatives (Bannister and Connolly, 2014; Rose et al., 2015). Such values are commonly associated with certain assumptions on how technology will improve the functions of government, strongly linked to the technological frames of technology, and e-Government more closely (Criado and O.de Zarate-Alcarazo, 2022). Such technological frames can provide powerful cognitive structures on the expected applications as well as consequences of their deployment, as seeing technology primarily as a tool for automation will change the perceptions, scopes, and objectives of the e-Government initiatives.

How AI initiatives in government are thus perceived as well, and which objectives and values they attempt to achieve, further brings insights into how AI may be seen as a tool to improve the quality of government and increase public value. We therefore set out to better understand what public value might be created – or potentially destroyed – by the use of technology that replaces human interaction in public service provision processes, as it allows for better understanding of the underlying purposes and motivations beyond individual project goals (Rose et al., 2015). In fact, first explorations on the expected benefits of AI of CIOs show that efficiency benefits is the highest perceived one, whereas citizen participation and trust were the least (Criado and O.de Zarate-Alcarazo, 2022) – which may possibly reflect the way AI is planned to be deployed in their administrations and which public value they aim to achieve.

Public value is generally defined as the additional value that public managers provide through their actions to society – and is seen as equivalent to shareholder value held on a company's assets (see Moore, 1995). While the research on e-Government, as well as practitioners, has aimed to follow the experiences and practices of ICT in the private sector, to the public sector, directly copying the practices may not be as desirable as expected as public organisations ought to create public value – which goes beyond merely the market-related objectives that the private sector ultimately values (Pang, Lee and DeLone, 2014; MacLean and Titah, 2021).

Based on Moore's initial definition, scholars have created theoretical frameworks of public value(s), that include long lists of potentially distinguishable 'value-dimensions' in large public value inventories (see, for example, Bozeman, 2007; Jørgensen and Bozeman, 2007). Most of these values have not been empirically tested yet – given the rather implicit nature of most of them (see, for example, Panagiotopoulos, Klievink and Cordella, 2019). However, for public value creation to occur, public administration will have to implement these AI technologies, changing their operations and strategy of public services to consequently improve citizen satisfaction (van Noordt and Misuraca, 2020; Chatterjee, Khorana and Kizgin, 2021).

The public administration literature distinguishes between public value and public values (Bryson, Crosby and Bloomberg, 2014; Nabatchi, 2018). Public value itself is defined as the beneficial outcomes through the strategic activities of public administrations. These can be numerous and more specific, which are particularly useful for analysing the success and objectives of specific AI initiatives and goals (Jørgensen and Bozeman, 2007; Rose et al., 2015; Twizeyimana and Andersson, 2019). The deployment of AI, or any ICT for that matter, will have implications for public values, including transparency, equality, integrity, and human connectivity, amongst many others. Such (theoretical) effects have been discussed in previous literature on the implications of information systems and e-Government (Bannister and Connolly, 2014), similar to the discussions held now on how AI technologies positively or negatively impact certain public values (Zuiderwijk, Chen and Salem, 2021). For instance, there is the expectation that AI will have a positive impact on efficiency but a negative impact on the equity of government operations (Gaozhao, Wright and Gainey, 2023).

Public values, on the other hand, are used as a label for the normative principles that underlie these activities and help 'to guide and justify the behavior of individuals, governments and societies' (Nabatchi, 2018, p. 61). These values are seen as more broad in nature, transcending specific actions and their outputs. In a way, they act as value drivers which underpin e-Government initiatives in general (Misuraca and Viscusi, 2015), linking to broader ideal public values driving such as the core values of public management of *sigma*, *theta* and *lambda*-type values (Hood, 1991), as the main 'input' for the activity (Chantillon, Crompvoets and Peristeras, 2020).

In order to understand what the values are that AI use in public administrations might follow, we follow the four value positions as identified by Rose et al. (2015), which integrated the main value traditions in public administration literature with assumptions of the benefits of technology in government.

Professionalism value ideal

The professionalism value originates from the traditional bureaucratic values as coined by Weber. These imply that decisions are based on law and policy and that decision-makers base their decision on good information. The key values of this ideal type are that governments act durably by ensuring a robust, resilient, and competent public service supported by an accurate public record, a focus on equity by ensuring honest, fair and impartial civil servants, legality and accountability so that decisions follow the chain of command and are properly documented (Rose et al., 2015). These values are important to ensure that government remains 'fair and honest' and 'robust and resilient' (Hood, 1991). Technology could support such values by allowing for a better identification of citizens, improving data security, ensuring more accountability and governance by better recording governmental actions and supporting standardised administrative procedures. AI technologies could, despite the remarks that bureaucracy could disappear due to technological change, reinforce these bureaucratic values rather than replace them by making more rules and procedures formalised (Newman, Mintrom and O'Neill, 2022). Limiting, or even replacing, potentially biased civil servants using their discretionary decision making by technology could be a main driver to introducing AI technology in the administration, consequently improving equity and procedural fairness.

At the same time, the inscrutability of AI systems and their unclear role in workflows may lead to less formalisation within bureaucracies as civil servants find their work content altered in unforeseen ways (Giest and Klievink, 2022). Furthermore, there is the often pointed out risk that despite the attempts to improve fairness, equity and objective decision-making, the use of AI may increase inequalities due to biases in historical datasets or the disproportioned targeting of certain demographics with AI (Schiff, Schiff and Pierson, 2021).

Efficiency ideal

Through New Public Management, traditional bureaucratic values were challenged by focusing more on introducing private sector values and market mechanisms within the public sector. Economic value focuses on the indicators that show how efficient and effectively public administrations deliver public services (Alford and O'Flynn, 2009) and whether they have achieved these goals. Typical goals as part of the efficiency ideal are to have adequate value for money, achieving cost reductions, and enhancing productivity and performance. Efficiency values have been at the forefront of the e-Government narrative and initiatives as the main purpose of IT is often to improve the effectiveness and efficiency of the state (Cordella and Bonina, 2012). The same narrative is often highlighted in the case of AI applications, such as in strategic documents where the economic value of AI is often strongly highlighted (Wilson, 2022). This is unsurprising since the main benefits of AI are being able to automate or speed up tasks, a technological frame often connected with efficiency ideals (Medaglia, Gil-Garcia and Pardo, 2021). Indeed, within the debate, the main benefit of AI often focuses on the reduction of personnel through automation of tasks or decision making with the use of technology (Schiff, Schiff and Pierson, 2021).

Service ideal

As such, the too strong focus on the economic values, sometimes undermining the rule of law and decreasing accountability of government, risks limiting crucial bureaucratic values at the cost of economic interests – sometimes without empirical evidence that such privatised ways of working are in fact better (Rose et al., 2015). Therefore, government officials should aim to search and implement public value; an ill-defined yet crucial objective ensuring that civil servants do not merely follow the decisions of policy or pursue the most efficient options. Instead, they should aim for commitment to the public interest, respect individual citizens and ensure that their expectations are met or consensus made (Bannister and Connolly, 2014; Rose et al., 2015). Value for citizens is thus generated when citizens have access to a service, they have the right to, and access is not denied due to high expectations of administrative literacy or unreasonable administrative burden (Bryson, Crosby and Bloomberg, 2014). The role of technology in government has been further included to improve the availability, accessibility, and usability of their services to citizens compared to traditional, offline, public service delivery. Artificial Intelligence may further tap into the increased possibility to improve the quality of services, and in particular the information provision, as it could provide more accurate and relevant information for citizens (Kuziemski and Misuraca, 2020) through, for instance, Chatbots (van Noordt and Misuraca, 2019a; Aoki, 2020).

Through automatic translation or rewriting bureaucratic sentences, interpreting sign language, etc., AI could be used to make the service and information more accessible for those facing difficulties with traditional or previous digital public service delivery. At the same time, however, is that the use of AI limits possibilities for achieving citizen value, as not the individuals but their data points will determine how services are delivered (Peeters and Widlak, 2018), limiting human responsiveness and reactivity. Furthermore, despite the possibility to have AI make public services more citizen-centric, it is often the case that citizens are excluded from the design and development choices or only play a marginal role in the testing of the system.

Engagement ideal

Building on top of the earlier emphasis on ensuring collaboration with citizens, the engagement ideal takes it further and highlights that serving the public is through co-production and citizen empowerment. In this perspective, government should run like a democracy rather than a business (Rose et al., 2015), and thus actions that support transparency, inclusive participation, democratic engagement, deliberation, and citizen rights support the engagement ideal (Bozeman, 2007, 2019). Many e-participation and e-democracy initiatives that strengthen citizen involvement in policy could be regarded as having the engagement ideal as their driver.

However, despite the potential public value creation through AI, it is important to highlight the difference between the expected, potential effects of technology (and thus the intended public value) and the actual effects and realisation of public value. In fact, all too often, only the potential benefits of technology are considered and it is assumed they will (always) materialise, but it has been well established that technology used in government does not necessarily lead to any value, but the transformation enabled by the technology does (Nograšek and Vintar, 2014; Tangi et al., 2020), with expected and unexpected effects only materialising over time, affecting different groups in varying ways, which depends on an interaction of various factors (MacLean and Titah, 2021). As many of the AI projects are still in an emerging stage, it is, without closer examination, too challenging to assess the realised public value, but it is possible to assess the expected and potential public value as this is more readily available.

When public values are not realised, or certain public values are over or underrepresented in AI, it may lead to a failure in public value creation later on when efficiency-related values at the cost of the other main values, such as bureaucratic values, ensure fairness of government practices (Schiff, Schiff and Pierson, 2021). Conflicts may indeed emerge when multiple public values are desirable but cannot be fulfilled at the same time (Chantillon, Crompvoets and Peristeras, 2020) which is likely to occur within design considerations and objectives of AI initiatives within the public sector. Potential trade-offs within the design of AI in government could be aiming to maximise (algorithmic) efficiency and effectiveness by utilising more deep learning models at the cost of opacity and accountability (de Bruijn, Warnier and Janssen, 2021) or designing and introducing AI to augment existing workers rather than replace or overrule them (Kuziemski and Misuraca, 2020; Giest and Klievink, 2022). As such, understanding which public values are the main drivers of current AI initiatives within public administrations in Europe could provide a telling insight into the main motivations of public administrations aiming to introduce AI and also where possible tensions may arise. For instance, if many AI initiatives within government are introduced with efficiency-related goals in mind, it may come at the cost of other values or may simply be wasteful endeavours (Meijer and Thaens, 2020).

RESEARCH DESIGN

In the following, we describe the overall research design including the steps of the data collection, the analytical steps and also highlight potential limitations of the chosen approach and how the research team aimed to mitigate them.

Data Collection

This chapter follows a mixed-method research design, consisting of a secondary data analysis of AI use cases gathered as part of the AI Watch research activities in the public sector collected by the Joint-Research Centre between 2019 and 2022. This inventory of AI use cases (N = 686) is the result of a research activity to gather and analyse adoption and implementations of AI currently in use by various public administrations across the European Union, first started in Misuraca and van Noordt (2020) and later continued in Tangi et al. (2022). This inventory is the result of a variety of data collection efforts to fill the gap of missing structured information of AI use in the public sector.

Firstly, desktop research was used through an internet search of news articles on AI use in the public sector, as well as policy documents and practitioner-generated reports describing use cases, such as those on the European AI Alliance platform of the European Commission. Several governmental innovation websites or dedicated AI registers were also included in this desktop search to identify as many use cases as possible. Secondly, additional cases were gathered based on submissions from EU country representatives who added their national cases to the resulting AI Watch database, either via email and/or shared during the four workshops organised by the AI Watch research group (van Noordt and Pignatelli, 2020; van Noordt et al.,

2020, 2021; Manzoni, Medaglia and Tangi, 2021). Thirdly, a survey was held as part of the AI Watch research to gain more information on barriers for AI adoption which also allowed for the gathering of some additional use cases which were consequently added to the inventory as well (Medaglia and Tangi, 2022).

Each of the cases went through a procedure to ensure the validation of the use cases so that all the information was double-checked and information of earlier gathered use cases confirmed later within the process to ensure the information was up to date. Consequently, this inventory is a great starting point to assess currently known use of AI in the public sector and the public value aim. However, the inventory suffers from several limitations, due to the targeted and therefore potentially biased nature of the data collection in the form of self-reports from the EU member states, making it very likely that many initiatives are not included in the inventory, especially those implemented at local/municipal level which are more difficult to be identified by the research team. Other limitations might include language barriers of the research team, so that the assessment of each country's policy documents might be limited in its depth and breadth. The research team however made their best effort using deepl.com to translate as many relevant sections of websites and cases as possible.

It is also noteworthy that different initiatives are included or not included due to the wide-varying understandings of the term AI: not every administration refers to AI in the same way, but might have described other types of technologies, with those not fitting the categories of the inventory not included (van Noordt, 2022). Challenges also emerged in gathering reliable information with regards to the maturity and local actors involved in the implementation of AI. It is possible that not a public administration, but in fact a private vendor was tasked with developing or using the AI solution within a public service, without clear understanding if public administrations in fact, do. Lastly, it may very well be that initiatives in the inventory have already been discontinued due to various reasons. For the scope of this chapter, the research team decided to include the case if it had a clear public service delivery connection and thus excluded initiatives with no public service component or use, for instance when the case was used in hospital services or in schools which are not considered public administrations. This resulted in the removal of 137 cases, leaving 549 for the analysis.

Overall, the inventory includes all 27 EU countries, as well as the United Kingdom, Norway, Switzerland and Ukraine, as all countries have either submitted their current AI use case descriptions to the database or the use cases were identified through desk research. However, the inventory is not evenly distributed across the different countries, as there are more use cases of AI from the Netherlands (114), Estonia (47), Italy (43), Portugal (40), Germany (35), Belgium (34), France (32) and Finland (31), whereas in many other countries less than 10, or even only 1, use cases could be identified. As such, the inventory should not reflect the actual status of use of AI yet merely reflect which use cases could be identified through the data collection methods. On average, for each country 18.3 use cases of AI are included in the inventory. An overview of the cases per country can be seen in Figure 13.1 below.

Data Analysis

Each individual case in the inventory was reviewed and assessed based on its title and submitted description to evaluate whether there is an (implicit or explicit) expectation that the AI case will add or is driven by either the professionalism, efficiency, service or engagement value, following the four types of main public values highlighted in the literature review (see Rose et

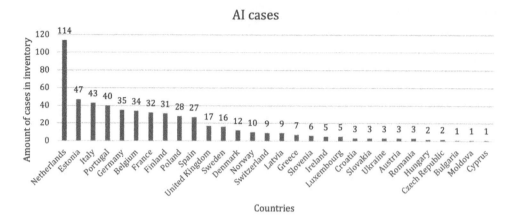

Figure 13.1   AI cases in inventory per country

al., 2015). In this coding step, it became obvious that individual AI use cases are driven by one or more public values. Consequently, the analysis is not restricted to the most prevalent public value type. Each of the cases have been discussed among the authors and any differences in coding deliberated to ensure accuracy and reliability in the labelling (see Burla et al., 2008). An example of such a coding would be:

Table 13.1   Example of coding process with one use case

Name	Description	Value driver(s)
EE Parliament – A system for preparing of verbatim reports	The speech recognition system helps transcribe the speeches given at the rostrum of the Estonian Parliament (Riigikogu). The Chancellery of the Riigikogu is currently required to publish a verbatim report within one hour from the end of the sitting. It takes a lot of human effort to do that, and the burden falls on stenographers. By deploying speech recognition, it will increase the efficiency and accuracy in transcripts of the sessions. Also, the plan is to start providing verbatim recordings as machine-readable open data, so other systems can use that data freely as well.	Professionalism value Efficiency value Engagement value

In addition to the thematic coding described in the first step, in a second step the research team identified several illustrative cases to exemplify the resulting value categories. These cases were selected from the inventory to highlight the possible public value created by AI technologies, but also identify how these values may be challenged in practice.

FINDINGS

In this section, we provide an overview of the main findings. These include an overview of the coded initiatives, starting with those driven by professionalism public values, then the efficiency-related public values, the service-related public values and lastly those driven by engagement public values. In each of these sections AI use cases derived from the AI Watch inventory are described to complement the coding. Following, a discussion is held on how some of the intended purposes of the AI systems may in fact contribute to public value destruction.

A fair portion (70 out of 549) of the cases analysed in the inventory support the professionalism values. Many of the use cases, for instance, aim to strengthen the data quality of the public administration so as to have more accurate records of citizens, businesses or other such groups as identifying and removing errors in business statements in the Danish Business Authority. Similarly, the Swiss Federal Office for Statistics uses machine learning algorithms to improve their data quality by returning wrong or likely incorrect data to the data providers. AI may also be deployed to make public service delivery fairer than traditional services, as in Belgium a system has been deployed to decide the registration of children in a school system. This system is based on several factors which is seen as fairer than registering children in-person which has led to parents sleeping in tents outside of schools to secure a spot. Similarly, several AI initiatives are being introduced to ensure existing rules are being reinforced, such as the use of satellite imagery to check farmers' compliance to subsidy requirements as in Walloon and Estonia, or the use of computer recognition to standardise the vaccination registration process in the Flemish Child and Family Agency. Other use cases aim to facilitate the professionalisation of the civil service staff, such as the deployment of a chatbot called RenoiRH within the French Interministerial Centre for IT Services to provide information regarding the mobility and career development of their staff members. Lastly, there are several use cases aiming at strengthening the resilience of public administrations, in particular cybersecurity, such as the sensor technology to detect cyber attacks in the Norwegian National Security Authority.

The driving public values identified among the cases focus predominantly on achieving efficiency values, supporting the effectiveness or cost-effectiveness of the administration, the services or the policy. In fact, of the overall 549 cases, in 431 AI applications some form of efficiency-driven values could be identified. This shows the prevalence of the expected efficiency gains provided by AI in many of the identified and described AI use cases in the inventory and is in line with the previous dominant perspective of ensuring efficiency gains in public administration through digital technologies. This shows that public administrations are attempting to use AI to create economic value to reduce costs, for example by replacing human workers by automating tasks with various AI technologies. An example of having AI take over mundane and redundant tasks of civil servants is the deployment of the Chatbot UNA in Latvia, which is now used to answer many frequently asked questions with regards to the process of registering a business. Now, public servants have freed up time to answer more specific requests which are considered more value-adding and thus reorganise how the work gets organised internally (van Noordt and Misuraca, 2019b). Others, for instance, suggest the automatic processing of citizen applications, such as the case in the municipality of Trelleborg in Sweden (Ranerup and Henriksen, 2019). Several cases further highlight making the existing policy options more effective as more data could be utilised, or the risk of fraud strongly limited, limiting the misallocation of public resources.

In 132 of the use cases, references to service public values were identified. In many of these use cases, service value is expected when administrative processes will be simplified for citizens, reducing their waiting time or difficulties in filling in forms. This aim to ensure the utility of government for citizens through qualitative and accessible public service aligns well with the role of technology as a service enabler for governmental organisations, continuing the legacy of e-Government to create public value through the provision of services to citizens (Bannister and Connolly, 2014; Rose et al., 2015). In this respect, chatbots or other forms of virtual assistants are seen as the main form of AI technology to improve accessibility of public information or understandability of various administrative processes. Examples include the Voicebot used in the Irish Revenue Commission to provide a more efficient and effective service to citizens using their telephone services, or Taxana used in the Slovakian Financial Administration to facilitate communication with citizens.

Despite the emphasis to improve the service quality to citizens, it is to be noted that very often the AI is also introduced to not only make the service more accessible or easier for citizens, but also to reduce the administrative burden for the administration itself as it lessens the workload of the staff members. Whereas in some cases the Chatbots seem to be introduced as a pure quality improvement, in several cases the main goal of the AI systems is to either automate or lessen the workload of civil servants, highlighting the strong prevalence of the efficiency values even in AI systems aiming to improve the service quality to citizens. Other use cases aiming to achieve service-related public values are diverse in scope and include many forms of making existing public services more accessible, in particular to citizens with disabilities, by enabling automatic subtitles on public and internal videos of the Finnish Tax Administration, allowing an AI-based interpreting service for deaf communicating with the Flemish Agency for Persons with Disabilities, automatic translation services such as on the Official Gazette of Estonia to English to support foreign businesses, or providing advice to businesses such as an AI system that provides advice on the chances of success for a craftsman based on a given location used in France.

The use of AI in public administrations to better connect with citizens through enhanced deliberation, participation, and other goals more linked with citizen participation is very rarely mentioned at all. Only in a minor number of cases was AI connected with the engagement public values, namely only 19 out of the 549 cases. One such example is the AI system *The Dublin Beat* that analyses citizen opinions in the Dublin region to provide an overview of their most pressing concerns. The tool is based on a combination of both natural language processing and machine learning to categorise the unstructured tweets of citizens, providing an overview of key issues such as how people feel about environmental issues, cultural events or city region developments expressed in online media (Kirchner, 2020).

Another example of an AI use case which aims to support democracy is the speech recognition system in place in the Estonian Parliament, capable of transcribing the parliamentary sessions taking place in the parliament called HANS (Plantera, 2019). This AI system has been put in use as an effort to make the work of the stenographers more effective as it significantly speeds up the transcription work previously done by the four stenographers (Plantera, 2019). Next to the expected economic gains, the project has been linked strongly with enhancing the transparency of the democratic system of Estonia. The transcriptions made by HANS are planned to be released in machine-readable open data format, so that they are suitable for additional data analysis or for use in other information systems (Plantera, 2019). Next to the parliament, there are expectations that the same solution might be used in other public sector organisations as well, increasing the efficiency of transcription processes and allowing higher degrees of transparency (Pau, 2020).

In summary, the following graphic provides an overview of finding 2 – the driving public values in the AI use cases.

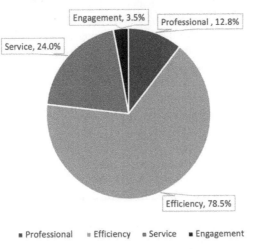

Figure 13.2   Driving public values in AI use cases

Risks of Public Value Destruction through AI

Despite the positive public value drivers underpinning the various AI use cases in the public sector, there are several key considerations to be held that emerge from either tension between the different objectives the AI initiatives aim to achieve or due to the potential risks that deploying AI-based public sector innovation holds (Mikalef et al., 2022). Whereas this overview does not hold all the potential tensions and trade-offs which may occur during the development and deployment of AI (Madan and Ashok, 2022), several considerations did stand out.

The first risk comes from the prevalence of many of the AI initiatives to support efficiency-related goals. As previous work on e-Government showed, efficiency values dominate not only the expected gains of digitalisation of the public sector, but when in conflict or tension with other important public values, public managers tend to value the efficiency-related values more strongly than others. With the use of AI however, a too strong emphasis on reducing costs or being more efficient could lead to illegal practices of data gathering, the lack of responsiveness towards citizens and not ensuring the AI systems work as they are supposed to (Rinta-Kahila et al., 2021). Other risks of focusing too strongly and seeing AI technologies as a quick win for limiting costs through automation means that a wider picture of digital transformation through multiple stakeholders may get lost or additional costs needed to make the AI system run completely overlooked (Maragno et al., 2022). It may also be the case that many AI-innovations will not see themselves adopted within the public administration if they do not have a strong efficiency-related focus. Some use cases in the inventory are aware of these risks, such as the AI system in use in the city of Amsterdam, the Netherlands, tasked with tracking down people illegally renting out their homes via platforms, such as Airbnb (Volkskrant, 2020). However, there are risks to public value destruction, of which the city is already aware (Amsterdam, 2020). Therefore, personal data such as birth, nationality and others are not included in the algorithm, aiming to limit prejudice of the algorithm to a certain demographic or increasing privacy concerns (Meijer, 2020).

In fact, these challenges may occur especially in the cases that aim to support both the professionalism and efficiency public values, namely 38 (out of the 70). These cases often revolve around fraud prevention due to the automatic verification, checks and analysis of data and documentation, aiming to both make the record-keeping of the administration more correct while at the same time making the fraud prevention processes more efficient and effective as well as minimising the risk of misallocation of public funds. However, it remains controversial to assume that striving to achieve both these values may be done so successfully as some discontinued use cases already highlight (Giest and Klievink, 2022; Simonofski et al., 2022).

Secondly, there may be an overexcitement for the deployment of AI tools to support the quality and accessibility of public services. Whereas Chatbots and other AI-tools may indeed support the information provision to citizens, it may be an open question to what extent citizens may want to talk to a Chatbot rather than a person and in which scenarios (Aoki, 2020). This is particularly true when the introduction of new AI-enabled technologies also aim to relieve or automate tasks of staff members. Performance of Chatbots may also vary greatly (Wang, Zhang and Zhao, 2020) depending on the in-house resources of the organisation. Furthermore, there are questions to be raised regarding to what extent new technological innovations may immediately resolve difficulties in citizen unwillingness to use e-services, such as the lack of trust in government (de Walle et al., 2018).

Thirdly, despite the potential and interest to use smart technologies in such ways as to facilitate inclusion and participation of citizens in public-sector decision making processes (Criado and Gil-Garcia, 2019), the analysis of the AI use cases suggest that the role of AI deployed by public administrations does not necessarily aim to improve engagement and citizen participation. While the intent of the AI system may be to make public administrations more responsive and accepting of citizen needs, it is, in the end, not the citizens who are meaningfully participating in policy processes, but merely their online data is passively used without additional explanations and often without their knowledge and consent (Cardullo and Kitchin, 2019).

Lastly, in some cases, public values are not explicitly mentioned and the underlying goal of the initiative risks self-referential, with the data analysis or the development of the system being the aim, with the expectation that 'something' will come out of it and provide patterns and indications for further research or policy action, doing innovation for the sake of innovation (Meijer and Thaens, 2020). In that respect, several of the AI use cases aimed to create some form of dashboards where AI-based analysis could be conducted or where the results of such analysis could be found. It is, however, often unclear how the creation of these dashboards link with the actual organisational workflows, how it is supposed to change the work of the organisation, or of which aims the dashboard is supposed to be supportive. This highlights a disconnect between the effective adoption and implementation, and the real public service transformation that could be generated from the insights emerging from the use of AI systems.

This risk is reinforced when the development of the AI systems is completely outsourced by private organisations, and it is not always clear what the contribution of public organisations is, or whether they play an active role in the public value creation when the system is put in active use. There is a risk that public administrations only act as a funding or sparring partner, rather than being actively involved in using these developed systems themself. While there is public value to be created during co-creation and co-design (Crosby, 't Hart and Torfing, 2017; Rösler et al., 2021), leaving non-governmental organisations the main actors for the development and the implementation of the AI systems may lead to further accountability issues or the privatisation of public services later. For instance, several cases in the inventory focus on energy services, waste management and the water supply. Whilst considered public services or supervised by ministries of their countries, these are often in fact already private services due to historical outsourcing.

CONCLUDING REMARKS

The analysis of the findings shows a high heterogeneity of AI use across Member States in the EU and a still unclear understanding of the public value that is effectively created. In particular, despite the strong potential of AI to transform public services and make them more citizen-oriented (Dwivedi et al., 2019; Veale and Brass, 2019), public administrations are predominantly applying AI technology to produce economic value. However, while AI systems may contribute to the improvement of higher-level public values, such as inclusiveness in terms of enhancing outreach and improving user satisfaction, they rarely involve citizens directly in their design or implementation.

Nevertheless, it seems that there is a gap between the transformative potential to generate public value that AI technologies promise and the observable adoption and use of AI. This has implications for the value-orientation of the initiatives under investigation, which are to a great extent focusing their attention on increasing performance (efficiency and effectiveness) by generating economic and administrative value, as seen in our analysis. The evidence shows instead a less prevalent – direct – focus on the citizen and societal values, that when present are driven by a greater emphasis on other dimensions and value drivers, such as openness and transparency, trust and legitimacy and also inclusiveness and diversity. This calls for further research through in-depth case studies to explore more in detail these dimensions of analysis as well as a further empirical application of the framework suggested. Specific attention should also be given to AI initiatives implemented at the local and municipal levels, also considering the diverse values that are associated with different sectoral policy domains.

Future research should therefore further elaborate on the framework and may infer theoretical implications from the findings gathered. For this purpose, in this chapter we developed a baseline for the use of AI in public services which might serve as a future research framework or even as the basis for future benchmarking. However, a robust methodology to assess social and economic impacts of AI in public services is still strongly required, and in our opinion, it should build on a public value perspective that can benefit the analysis provided in this chapter to categorise potential benefits, while also considering risks and possible negative side-effects that could lead to value destruction if not well assessed and/or anticipated.

The results of our analysis provide an important contribution to advance knowledge in the field of AI-enabled innovation in the public sector, that we consider as a form of ICT-enabled innovation to be addressed from a multidisciplinary perspective. In particular, the categories of analysis proposed and the underlying framework for public value assessment suggested, are suitable to provide the basis for additional comparative analysis. The current findings provide insights for future evaluations of the functional use of AI in public services stemming from the insights that resulted from the exploratory approach we have taken. In this respect, our findings confirm the growing interest in the use of AI in the public sector to redesign internal processes, enhance policy-making mechanisms and improve public services delivery – even though this is clearly still an emerging practice among public sector organisations. In line with the search for 'best practices', which is started at both academic and policy levels, it becomes clear from our analysis that there is a strong need to learn from in-depth case studies and to identify the key dimensions and barriers to be overcome, transfer and potentially replicate success stories across the public sector. This includes not only the potential for 'scale-up', but also the 'scale deep' and the 'scale-out' of initiatives, beyond the 'ever-piloting' paradox that is instead often limiting the adoption of AI, and ICT-enabled innovation in general.

REFERENCES

Alford, J. and O'Flynn, J. (2009) Making sense of public value: Concepts, critiques and emergent meanings, *International Journal of Public Administration*, 32(3–4), 171–191. doi: 10.1080/01900690902732731.

Alshahrani, A., Dennehy, D. and Mäntymäki, M. (2021) An attention-based view of AI assimilation in public sector organizations: The case of Saudi Arabia, *Government Information Quarterly*, (July). doi: 10.1016/j.giq.2021.101617.

Amsterdam, C. of (2020) *Holiday Rental Housing Fraud Risk – Amsterdam Algoritmeregister.* Available at: https://algoritmeregister.amsterdam.nl/en/holiday-rental-housing-fraud-risk/ (accessed: 12 October 2020).

Androutsopoulou, A. et al. (2019) Transforming the communication between citizens and government through AI-guided chatbots, *Government Information Quarterly*, 36(2), 358–367. doi: 10.1016/j.giq.2018.10.001.

Aoki, N. (2020) An experimental study of public trust in AI chatbots in the public sector, *Government Information Quarterly*, 37(4), 101490. doi: 10.1016/j.giq.2020.101490.

Bailey, D. E. and Barley, S. R. (2019) Beyond design and use: How scholars should study intelligent technologies, *Information and Organization*, 30(2), 100286. doi: 10.1016/j.infoandorg.2019.100286.

Bannister, F. and Connolly, R. (2014) ICT, public values and transformative government: A framework and programme for research, *Government Information Quarterly*, 31(1), 119–128. doi: 10.1016/j.giq.2013.06.002.

Barocas, S. and Selbst, A. D. (2016) Big data's disparate impact, *Calif. Law Rev.*, 104(3), 671. doi: 10.15779/Z38BG31.

Bozeman, B. (2007) Public values and public interest: Counterbalancing economic individualism, in *Public Values and Public Interest: Counterbalancing Economic Individualism.* doi: 10.1057/ap.2009.14.

Bozeman, B. (2019) Public values: Citizens' perspective, *Public Management Review*, 21(6), 817–838. doi: 10.1080/14719037.2018.1529878.

Bryson, J. M., Crosby, B. C. and Bloomberg, L. (2014) Public value governance: Moving beyond traditional public administration and the new public management, *Public Administration Review*, 74(4), 445–456. doi: 10.1111/puar.12238.

Bugge, M. M. and Bloch, C. W. (2016) Between bricolage and breakthroughs – framing the many faces of public sector innovation, *Public Money and Management*, 36(4), 281–288. doi: 10.1080/09540962.2016.1162599.

Burla, L. et al. (2008) From text to codings: Intercoder reliability assessment in qualitative content analysis, *Nursing Research.* doi: 10.1097/01.NNR.0000313482.33917.7d.

Cardullo, P. and Kitchin, R. (2019) Being a 'citizen' in the smart city: Up and down the scaffold of smart citizen participation in Dublin, Ireland, *GeoJournal*, 84(1), 1–13. doi: 10.1007/s10708-018-9845-8.

Chantillon, M., Crompvoets, J. and Peristeras, V. (2020) Prioritizing public values in e-government policies: A document analysis, *Information Polity*, 25(3), 275–300. doi: 10.3233/IP-190126.

Chatterjee, S., Khorana, S. and Kizgin, H. (2021) Harnessing the potential of artificial intelligence to foster citizens' satisfaction: An empirical study on India, *Government Information Quarterly*, 101621. doi: 10.1016/j.giq.2021.101621.

Collins, C. et al. (2021) Artificial intelligence in information systems research: A systematic literature review and research agenda, *International Journal of Information Management*, 60(July), 102383. doi: 10.1016/j.ijinfomgt.2021.102383.

Cordella, A. and Bonina, C. M. (2012) A public value perspective for ICT enabled public sector reforms: A theoretical reflection, *Government Information Quarterly*, 29(4), 512–520. doi: 10.1016/j.giq.2012.03.004.

Criado, J. I. and Gil-Garcia, J. R. (2019) Creating public value through smart technologies and strategies: From digital services to artificial intelligence and beyond, *International Journal of Public Sector Management*, 32(5), 438–450. doi: 10.1108/IJPSM-07-2019-0178.

Criado, J. I. and O.de Zarate-Alcarazo, L. (2022) Technological frames, CIOs, and Artificial Intelligence in public administration: A socio-cognitive exploratory study in Spanish local governments, *Government Information Quarterly*, 39(3), 101688. doi: 10.1016/j.giq.2022.101688.

Crosby, B. C., 't Hart, P. and Torfing, J. (2017) Public value creation through collaborative innovation, *Public Management Review*, 19(5), 655–669. doi: 10.1080/14719037.2016.1192165.

de Bruijn, H., Warnier, M. and Janssen, M. (2021) The perils and pitfalls of explainable AI: Strategies for explaining algorithmic decision-making, *Government Information Quarterly*, (March), 101666. doi: 10.1016/j.giq.2021.101666.

de Sousa, W. G. et al. (2021) Artificial intelligence and speedy trial in the judiciary: Myth, reality or need? A case study in the Brazilian Supreme Court (STF), *Government Information Quarterly*, 101660. doi: 10.1016/j.giq.2021.101660.

De Vries, H., Bekkers, V. and Tummers, L. (2016) Innovation in the public sector: A systematic review and future research agenda, *Public Administration*, 94(1), 146–166. doi: 10.1111/padm.12209.

de Walle, S. et al. (2018) Explaining non-adoption of electronic government services by citizens: A study among non-users of public e-services in Latvia, *Information Polity*, 23(4), 399–409. doi: 10.3233/IP-170069.

Dwivedi, Y. K. et al. (2019) Artificial Intelligence (AI): Multidisciplinary perspectives on emerging challenges, opportunities, and agenda for research, practice and policy, *International Journal of Information Management*, (August), 101994. doi: 10.1016/j.ijinfomgt.2019.08.002.

Engin, Z. and Treleaven, P. (2019) Algorithmic government: Automating public services and supporting civil servants in using data science technologies, *Computer Journal*, 62(3), 448–460. doi: 10.1093/comjnl/bxy082.

Engstrom, D. F. et al. (2020) Government by algorithm: Artificial intelligence in federal administrative agencies, *SSRN Electronic Journal*. doi: 10.2139/ssrn.3551505.

Fatima, S., Desouza, K. C. and Dawson, G. S. (2020) National strategic artificial intelligence plans: A multi-dimensional analysis, *Economic Analysis and Policy*, 67, 178–194. doi: 10.1016/j.eap.2020.07.008.

Gaozhao, D., Wright, J. E. and Gainey, M. K. (2023) Bureaucrat or artificial intelligence: People's preferences and perceptions of government service, *Public Management Review*, 00(00), 1–28. doi: 10.1080/14719037.2022.2160488.

Giest, Sarah N. and Klievink, B. (2022) More than a digital system: How AI is changing the role of bureaucrats in different organizational contexts, *Public Management Review*, 00(00), 1–20. doi: 10.1080/14719037.2022.2095001.

Guenduez, A. A. and Mettler, T. (2022) Strategically constructed narratives on artificial intelligence: What stories are told in governmental artificial intelligence policies? *Government Information Quarterly*, (May), 101719. doi: 10.1016/j.giq.2022.101719.

Hartmann, K. and Wenzelburger, G. (2021) Uncertainty, risk and the use of algorithms in policy decisions: A case study on criminal justice in the USA, *Policy Sciences*, 0123456789. doi: 10.1007/s11077-020-09414-y.

Höchtl, J., Parycek, P. and Schöllhammer, R. (2016) Big data in the policy cycle: Policy decision making in the digital era, *Journal of Organizational Computing and Electronic Commerce*, 26(1–2), 147–169. doi: 10.1080/10919392.2015.1125187.

Hood, C. (1991) A public management for all seasons?, *Public Administration*, 69(2), 3–19.

Janssen, M. et al. (2020) Data governance: Organizing data for trustworthy Artificial Intelligence, *Government Information Quarterly*, 37(3), 101493. doi: 10.1016/j.giq.2020.101493.

Jørgensen, T. B. and Bozeman, B. (2007) Public values, *Administration & Society*, 39(3), 354–381. doi: 10.1177/0095399707300703.

Kirchner, L. (2020) *Smart Dublin Explores How AI and Social Media Can Help Improve the City Region*, *Dublin Economic Monitor*. Available at: http://www.dublineconomy.ie/2020/02/06/smart-dublin -explores-how-ai-and-social-media-can-help-improve-the-city-region/ (accessed: 12 October 2020).

Kuziemski, M. and Misuraca, G. (2020) AI governance in the public sector: Three tales from the frontiers of automated decision-making in democratic settings, *Telecommunications Policy*, 44(6), 101976. doi: 10.1016/j.telpol.2020.101976.

Larsson, K. K. (2021) Digitization or equality: When government automation covers some, but not all citizens, *Government Information Quarterly*, 38(1), 101547. doi: 10.1016/j.giq.2020.101547.

Lima, M. S. M. and Delen, D. (2020) Predicting and explaining corruption across countries: A machine learning approach, *Government Information Quarterly*, 37(1), 101407 [1–15]. doi: 10.1016/j. giq.2019.101407.

Liu, H. W., Lin, C. F. and Chen, Y. J. (2019) Beyond State v Loomis: Artificial intelligence, government algorithmization and accountability, *International Journal of Law and Information Technology*, 27(2), 122–141. doi: 10.1093/ijlit/eaz001.

Loureiro, S. M. C., Guerreiro, J. and Tussyadiah, I. (2021) Artificial intelligence in business: State of the art and future research agenda, *Journal of Business Research*, 129, 911–926. doi: https://doi.org/10 .1016/j.jbusres.2020.11.001.

MacLean, D. and Titah, R. (2021) A systematic literature review of empirical research on the impacts of e-government: A public value perspective, *Public Administration Review*, (Icis 2007). doi: 10.1111/ puar.13413.

Madan, R. and Ashok, M. (2022) AI adoption and diffusion in public administration: A systematic literature review and future research agenda, *Government Information Quarterly*, (November 2021), 101774. doi: 10.1016/j.giq.2022.101774.

Manzoni, M., Medaglia, R. and Tangi, L. (2021) *AI Watch Artificial Intelligence for the Public Sector Report of the '4th Peer Learning Workshop on the Use and Impact of AI in Public Services', 28 October 2021*. doi: 10.2760/142724.

Maragno, G. et al. (2022) AI as an organizational agent to nurture: Effectively introducing chatbots in public entities, *Public Management Review*, 00(00), 1–31. doi: 10.1080/14719037.2022.2063935.

Medaglia, R., Gil-Garcia, J. R. and Pardo, T. A. (2021) Artificial intelligence in government: Taking stock and moving forward, *Social Science Computer Review*, 089443932110340. doi: 10.1177/08944393211034087.

Medaglia, R. and Tangi, L. (2022) *The Adoption of Artificial Intelligence in the Public Sector in Europe: Drivers, Features, and Impacts*, *Icegov 2022*. Association for Computing Machinery. doi: 10.1145/3560107.3560110.

Meijer, A. and Thaens, M. (2020) The dark side of public innovation, *Public Performance & Management Review*, 0(0), 1–19. doi: 10.1080/15309576.2020.1782954.

Meijer, E. (2020) *Amsterdam zet algoritme in voor opsporing illegale vakantieverhuur – AG Connect*, *AGConnect*. Available at: https://www.agconnect.nl/artikel/amsterdam-zet-algoritme-voor-opsporing -illegale-vakantieverhuur (accessed: 12 October 2020).

Mikalef, P. et al. (2022) Thinking responsibly about responsible AI and 'the dark side' of AI, *European Journal of Information Systems*, 31(3), 257–268. doi: 10.1080/0960085X.2022.2026621.

Misuraca, G. and van Noordt, C. (2020) *AI Watch – Artificial Intelligence in Public Services*, *EU Science Hub*. Luxembourg. doi: 10.2760/039619.

Misuraca, G. and Viscusi, G. (2015) Shaping public sector innovation theory: An interpretative framework for ICT-enabled governance innovation, *Electronic Commerce Research*, 15(3), 303–322. doi: 10.1007/s10660-015-9184-5.

Misuraca, G. and Viscusi, G. (2020) AI-enabled innovation in the public sector: A framework for digital governance and resilience, in Pereira, G. V. et al. (eds) *Electronic Government: Proceedings of the 19th IFIP WG 8.5 International Conference, EGOV 2020*. Cham, Switzerland: Springer International Publishing, pp. 110–120. doi: 10.1007/978-3-030-57599-1_9.

Nabatchi, T. (2018) Public values frames in administration and governance, *Perspectives on Public Management and Governance*, 1(1), 59–72. doi: 10.1093/ppmgov/gvx009.

Newman, J., Mintrom, M. and O'Neill, D. (2022) Digital technologies, artificial intelligence, and bureaucratic transformation, *Futures*, 136(April 2021), 102886. doi: 10.1016/j.futures.2021.102886.

Nograšek, J. and Vintar, M. (2014) E-government and organisational transformation of government: Black box revisited? *Government Information Quarterly*, 31(1), 108–118. doi: 10.1016/j.giq.2013.07.006.

Ojo, A., Mellouli, S. and Ahmadi Zeleti, F. (2019) A realist perspective on AI-era public management*, in Chen, Y.-C., Salem, F., and Zuiderwijk, A. (eds) *20th Annual International Conference on Digital Government Research on - dg.o 2019*. New York, New York, USA: ACM Press (dg.o 2019), pp. 159–170. doi: 10.1145/3325112.3325261.

Panagiotopoulos, P., Klievink, B. and Cordella, A. (2019) Public value creation in digital government, *Government Information Quarterly*, 36(4), 101421 [1–8]. doi: 10.1016/j.giq.2019.101421.

Pang, M.-S., Lee, G. and DeLone, W. H. (2014) IT resources, organizational capabilities, and value creation in public-sector organizations: A public-value management perspective, *Journal of Information Technology*, 29(3), 187–205. doi: 10.1057/jit.2014.2.

Pau, A. (2020) *Riigikogu võtab kasutusele neli robotstenografisti – kolme inimkolleegi pole enam vaja (24) [The Riigikogu will introduce four robotic stenographers – three human colleagues are no longer needed]*, *Forte*. Available at: https://forte.delfi.ee/news/tehnika/riigikogu-votab-kasutusele-neli-robotstenografisti-kolme-inimkolleegi-pole-enam-vaja?id=91038989 (accessed: 12 October 2020).

Peeters, R. and Widlak, A. (2018) The digital cage: Administrative exclusion through information architecture – The case of the Dutch civil registry's master data management system, *Government Information Quarterly*, 35(2), 175–183. doi: 10.1016/j.giq.2018.02.003.

Pencheva, I., Esteve, M. and Mikhaylov, S. J. (2020) Big Data and AI – A transformational shift for government: So, what next for research? *Public Policy and Administration*, 35(1), 24–44. doi: 10.1177/0952076718780537.

Plantera, F. (2019) *Introducing HANS, the New AI Support Tool for Estonian Lawmakers – e-Estonia*. Available at: https://e-estonia.com/hans-ai-support-tool-for-estonian-parliament/ (accessed: 12 October 2020).

Ranerup, A. and Henriksen, H. Z. (2019) Value positions viewed through the lens of automated decision-making: The case of social services, *Government Information Quarterly*, 36(4), 101377 [1–13]. doi: 10.1016/j.giq.2019.05.004.

Rinta-Kahila, T. et al. (2021) Algorithmic decision-making and system destructiveness: A case of automatic debt recovery, *European Journal of Information Systems*, 31(3), 313–338. doi: 10.1080/0960085X.2021.1960905.

Rose, J. et al. (2015) Managing e-Government: Value positions and relationships, *Information Systems Journal*, 25(5), 531–571. doi: 10.1111/isj.12052.

Rose, J., Persson, J. S. and Heeager, L. T. (2015) How e-Government managers prioritise rival value positions: The efficiency imperative, *Information Polity*, 20(1), 35–59. doi: 10.3233/IP-150349.

Rösler, J. et al. (2021) Value co-creation between public service organizations and the private sector: An organizational capabilities perspective, *Administrative Sciences*, 11(2). doi: 10.3390/admsci11020055.

Schiff, D. S., Schiff, K. J. and Pierson, P. (2021) Assessing public value failure in government adoption of artificial intelligence, *Public Administration*, (April), 1–21. doi: 10.1111/padm.12742.

Sharma, G. D., Yadav, A. and Chopra, R. (2020) Artificial intelligence and effective governance: A review, critique and research agenda, *Sustainable Futures*, 2(November), 100004. doi: 10.1016/j.sftr.2019.100004.

Simonofski, A. et al. (2022) Balancing fraud analytics with legal requirements: Governance practices and trade-offs in public administrations, *Data & Policy*, 4. doi: 10.1017/dap.2022.6.

Sun, T. Q. and Medaglia, R. (2019) Mapping the challenges of Artificial Intelligence in the public sector: Evidence from public healthcare, *Government Information Quarterly*, 36(2), 368–383. doi: 10.1016/j.giq.2018.09.008.

Tangi, L. et al. (2020) Barriers and drivers of digital transformation in public organizations: Results from a survey in the Netherlands, in Viale Pereira, G. et al. (eds) *Electronic Government: Proceedings of the 19th IFIP WG 8.5 International Conference, EGOV 2020*. Cham: Springer International Publishing (Lecture Notes in Computer Science), pp. 42–56. doi: 10.1007/978-3-030-57599-1.

Tangi, L. et al. (2022) *AI Watch European Landscape on the Use of Artificial Intelligence by the Public Sector*. Luxembourg. doi: 10.2760/39336.

Toll, D. et al. (2019) Artificial intelligence in Swedish policies: Values, benefits, considerations and risks, in Lindgren, I. et al. (eds) *Electronic Government: Proceedings of the 18th IFIP WG 8.5*

International Conference, EGOV 2019. Cham, CH: Springer, Cham (Lecture Notes in Computer Science), pp. 301–310. doi: 10.1007/978-3-030-27325-5_23.

Toll, D. et al. (2020) Values, benefits, considerations and risks of AI in government: A study of AI policy documents in Sweden, *eJournal of eDemocracy and Open Government*, 12(1), 40–60. doi: 10.29379/jedem.v12i1.593.

Twizeyimana, J. D. and Andersson, A. (2019) The public value of E-Government – A literature review, *Government Information Quarterly*, 36(2), 167–178. doi: 10.1016/j.giq.2019.01.001.

Valle-Cruz, D. et al. (2020) Assessing the public policy-cycle framework in the age of artificial intelligence: From agenda-setting to policy evaluation, *Government Information Quarterly*, 37(4), 101509. doi: 10.1016/j.giq.2020.101509.

van der Peijl, S. et al. (2020) *Study On Up-take of Emerging Technologies in Public Procurement*. European Commission.

van Noordt, C. (2022) Conceptual challenges of researching Artificial Intelligence in public administrations, in *DG.O 2022: The 23rd Annual International Conference on Digital Government Research (dg.o 2022)*. New York. doi: doi.org/10.1145/3543434.3543441.

van Noordt, C. et al. (2020) *Report of the '1st Peer Learning Workshop on the Use and Impact of AI in Public Services'*. Seville.

van Noordt, C. et al. (2021) *AI Watch Artificial Intelligence for the Public Sector Report of the '3rd Peer Learning Workshop on the Use and Impact of AI in Public Services', 24 June 2021*. doi: 10.2760/162795.

van Noordt, C. and Misuraca, G. (2019a) New wine in old bottles: Chatbots in government: Exploring the transformative impact of chatbots in public service delivery, in *Lecture Notes in Computer Science (including subseries Lecture Notes in Artificial Intelligence and Lecture Notes in Bioinformatics)*. Springer, pp. 49–59. doi: 10.1007/978-3-030-27397-2_5.

van Noordt, C. and Misuraca, G. (2019b) New wine in old bottles: Chatbots in government, in Panagiotopoulos, P. (ed.) *Electronic Participation. ePart 2019. Lecture Notes in Computer Science*. Springer, Cham, pp. 49–59. doi: 10.1007/978-3-030-27397-2_5.

van Noordt, C. and Misuraca, G. (2020) Evaluating the impact of Artificial Intelligence technologies in public services: Towards an assessment framework, in Charalabidis, Y., Cunha, M. A. and Sarantis, D. (eds) *13th International Conference on Theory and Practice of Electronic Governance (ICEGOV 2020)*. New York, NY, USA: Association for Computing Machinery (ICEGOV 2020), pp. 8–16. doi: 10.1145/3428502.3428504.

van Noordt, C. and Pignatelli, F. (2020) *Report of the 2nd Peer Learning Workshop on the Use and Impact of AI in Public Services, 29 September 2020*. Available at: https://publications.jrc.ec.europa.eu/repository/handle/JRC120315.

Veale, M. and Brass, I. (2019) Administration by algorithm? Public management meets public sector machine learning, *Algorithmic Regulation*, 1–30. doi: 10.31235/OSF.IO/MWHNB.

Viscusi, G., Rusu, A. and Florin, M.-V. (2020) Public strategies for artificial intelligence: Which value drivers? *Computer*, 53(10), 38–46. doi: 10.1109/MC.2020.2995517.

Volkskrant (2020) *Amsterdam komt met algoritme tegen illegale vakantieadressen | De Volkskrant*. Available at: https://www.volkskrant.nl/nieuws-achtergrond/amsterdam-komt-met-algoritme-tegen-illegale-vakantieadressen~bca70b1f/ (accessed: 12 October 2020).

Wang, Y., Zhang, N. and Zhao, X. (2020) Understanding the determinants in the different government AI adoption stages: Evidence of local government chatbots in China, *Social Science Computer Review*, 089443932098013. doi: 10.1177/0894439320980132.

Wilson, C. (2021) Public engagement and AI: A values analysis of national strategies, *Government Information Quarterly*, (June 2020), 101652. doi: 10.1016/j.giq.2021.101652.

Wilson, C. (2022) Public engagement and AI: A values analysis of national strategies, *Government Information Quarterly*, 39(1), 101652. doi: 10.1016/j.giq.2021.101652.

Wirtz, B. W., Weyerer, J. C. and Geyer, C. (2019) Artificial intelligence and the public sector – applications and challenges, *International Journal of Public Administration*, 42(7), 596–615. doi: 10.1080/01900692.2018.1498103.

Zuiderwijk, A., Chen, Y. and Salem, F. (2021) Implications of the use of artificial intelligence in public governance: A systematic literature review and a research agenda, *Government Information Quarterly*, (March), 101577. doi: 10.1016/j.giq.2021.101577.

14. Challenges and design principles for the evaluation of productive AI systems in the public sector

Per Rådberg Nagbøl, Oliver Krancher and Oliver Müller

INTRODUCTION

Governmental organisations and businesses are increasingly using Artificial Intelligence (AI) systems to automate and support various tasks across different domains (Berente et al., 2021; Sun and Medaglia, 2019). While empirical research to date has focused on the development, adoption, and implementation of AI systems (Asatiani et al., 2021; Sun and Medaglia, 2019; van den Broek et al., 2021), less attention has been paid to the maintenance phase, i.e., the part of an AI system's lifecycle that starts after the system has been implemented in an organisation and ends with its decommissioning. Given the high costs associated with building AI systems, the maintenance phase is critical because the longer an AI system can be productively used, the more likely it is that the initial cost will be recovered. Moreover, a focus on the maintenance phase is essential given that productive AI systems (i.e., AI systems in the maintenance phase) may cause harm, such as by making decisions that discriminate against particular social groups (Hill, 2020; Mayer et al., 2020). Preventing such harm is important throughout the entire lifecycle of an AI system.

A key activity during the maintenance phase is the evaluation of AI systems. Evaluation has been defined as the cybernetic process of assessing the performance of a system in relation to performance expectations (Doshi-Velez and Kim, 2017; Eisenhardt, 1985; Kirsch, 2004). In the context of AI systems, evaluation involves, thus, an assessment of the performance characteristics of an AI system, such as its accuracy, fairness, and transparency (Lipton, 2018; Russell and Norvig, 2002) in relation to stakeholders' performance expectations. Evaluation during the maintenance of an AI system is not only an opportunity to discover performance issues not found during development, it is also critical to prevent a decrease in performance (for example, a decrease in accuracy or fairness) over time. Performance may decrease due to environmental changes that lead production data to drift away from the AI system's training data. For example, the performance of an AI system trained to recognise signatures may decrease if the technologies through which citizens sign applications change. If such environmental changes are not detected, the organisation may be unaware of running a productive AI system that makes poor decisions. Performance may also decrease because of changes in behaviours, standards, and laws, which might cause the AI systems to enforce an old and incorrect version of the law.

Despite the recent surge of interest in AI systems, relatively little research has focused on evaluating the performance of AI systems during maintenance. Socio-technical AI research has focused on issues such as top management involvement (Li et al., 2021), collective learning (Fügener et al., 2021; van den Broek et al., 2021), delegation and augmentation (Baird and Maruping, 2021; Jussupow et al., 2021; Teodorescu et al., 2021), pre-production risk assessment and mitigation (Asatiani et al., 2020, 2021; Nagbøl et al., 2021), and unexpected outcomes (Mayer et al., 2020; Strich et al., 2021) without explicit attention to evaluation during maintenance. Technical research has explored strategies for evaluating AI systems (Doshi-Velez and Kim, 2017; Hernández-Orallo, 2017), though without focusing on the issues that arise when organisations attempt to implement these strategies in organisational realities throughout the lifecycle of a system.

Although existing work does not explicitly focus on the evaluation of AI systems during maintenance, it offers a critical insight relevant to the design of evaluation systems, namely that effective use of AI requires integrating domain and AI knowledge. For example, a study on the design of pre-production risk assessment emphasises the importance of a multi-perspective expert assessment involving both AI and domain specialists. Such multi-perspective expert assessments go beyond accuracy metrics and rely on the stakeholders' diverse experience and expertise for assessing AI systems (Nagbøl et al., 2021). An ethnographic study describes the interplay of machine learning (ML) expertise and domain expertise in AI-supported hiring. It finds that developers and domain experts are in an interdependent relationship where domain experts contribute to defining, evaluating, and complementing machine input and output, while developers contribute novel ML-based insights from the data (van den Broek et al., 2021). Based on archival data on drug development, Lou and Wu (2021) similarly claim that the development and use of AI systems require integrating the knowledge of AI and medical experts. Lebovitz et al. (2021) warn against treating ground truth as objective when the ground truth is based on uncertain knowledge. They point to a tension between how domain experts evaluate their work according to know-how and how AI systems are evaluated according to the quality of know-what and ground truth measures. They recommend that humans make the final judgement in areas of high uncertainty. At the same time, AI systems in fields with more established knowledge claims should be trained and validated according to quality measures representing the know-how and standard of the expert's practical performance (Lebovitz et al., 2021). Doshi-Velez and Kim propose a three-level taxonomy of interpretability evaluation (applications-grounded evaluation, human-grounded metrics, functionally-grounded evaluation), highlighting that evaluation strategies may differ in the way they involve human domain expertise (Doshi-Velez and Kim, 2017).

While these studies provide important background knowledge, we know little about how organisations can ensure the effective ongoing evaluation of their AI systems in production. This study aims to address this knowledge gap by exploring the following two research questions: (1) What are the challenges in planning and enforcing the evaluation of productive AI systems? (2) What are the design principles for AI evaluation infrastructure that address these challenges?

We addressed these questions through an Action Design Research (ADR) study in the Danish Business Authority (DBA). ADR provides a good fit for the research project because it allows for studying the planning and execution of evaluation under authentic circumstances. The DBA is an ideal setting, being a front-running organisation[1] in a world-leading country in e-government (Nations, 2018; United Nations & Department of Economic and Social Affairs,

---

[1]   The DBA was nominated for the Danish digitisation prize sammenhængsprisen for the public sector (2022) for their AI supported work with COVID-19 compensation https:// www .d igitaliser ingsprisen.dk/

2020), providing rare opportunities for exploring issues of evaluating AI systems in production. In the remainder of this chapter, we present our ADR methods, report our findings about challenges and solution strategies in AI evaluation, and discuss these findings.

METHODS

Research Design

The project's methodological approach is Action Design Research (ADR) which creates generalisable knowledge by solving practical problems through the combination of action and design research (Sein et al., 2011). Key outcomes of ADR are one or more artifacts and design principles. In our case, the artifact is a method for evaluating productive AI systems, which we call Evaluation Plan (see the section on the design artifact below for more details). ADR proceeds along the four stages of (1) problem formulation, (2) building, intervention and evaluation (BIE), (3) reflection and learning, and (4) formalisation of learning.

The first stage, problem formulation, is initiated through engagement with a practical problem and scoping the project (Sein et al., 2011). The stage is based on two principles. Principle 1: Practice-inspired research turns a non-unique practical problem into a knowledge-creation opportunity by treating the problem as an instance of a class of problems. Through our existing collaboration with the DBA on issues of AI management, we identified the evaluation of AI systems as a key challenge in public-sector organisations relying on the AI system, suggesting that artifacts and design principles developed through the research project could be of value to organisations other than the DBA (Sein et al., 2011). Principle 2: Theory-ingrained artifact emphasises that the artifact should not be purely based on the designer's creativity or practical requirements but also grounded in literature and theory (Sein et al., 2011). In line with the principle of theory-ingrained artifact, we integrated our emerging findings on challenges and solution strategies with theories that can explain and inform the challenge or the solution strategies and thus inform the artifact.

The second stage, building, intervention, and evaluation (BIE), describes an iterative process of building the artifact, intervening in the organisation, and continuously evaluating both the problem and artifact, ultimately leading to the realised design of the artifact. It relies on Principle 3: Reciprocal Shaping, Principle 4: Mutually Influential Roles, and Principle 5: Authentic and Concurrent Evaluation. Reciprocal shaping focuses on the mutual influence that the two domains, in the form of the IT artifact and organisational context, have on each other. The principle of mutually influential roles emphasises the necessity of mutual learning among the participants in the design project where different actors provide different perspectives on the project. In line with this principle, data scientists, domain experts, and managers from the DBA contributed insights into their requirements, methods, and challenges, while the researchers contributed knowledge about the literature and theories on AI systems and on theories that shed light on the emerging findings. Authentic and Concurrent Evaluation represents the idea that the evaluation of the artifact (i.e., the evaluation of the Evaluation Plan) is not a stage in a process but an ongoing endeavour (Sein et al., 2011). Consistent with this principle, the decisions about designing, shaping, and reshaping the Evaluation Plan and implementing it into organisational work practices were accompanied by an ongoing evaluation.

The third stage, reflection and learning, runs in parallel to stages 1 and 2 but focuses on the insights that result from the development of the artifact through reflections about the problem scope, the ingrained theories, and the emerging ensemble artifact and its evaluation. It relies on Principle 6: Guided Emergence, which recognises that the learnings are the product not only of the researcher but also of its organisational use, the participants' perspectives, authentic outcomes, and concurrent evaluation (Sein et al., 2011). In line with these principles, reflection and learning occurred through an ongoing dialogue between the researcher and participants at the DBA, the work on and use of the Evaluation Plan, and its evaluation.

The fourth stage, formalisation of learning, involves a conceptual move from one instance of a problem to a general solution applicable to a class of problems to satisfy Principle 7: Generalised Outcomes (Sein et al., 2011). Following this principle, we moved from our instance of the problem – the use of the Evaluation Plan at the DBA – to design principles that can help inform the evaluation of AI systems in organisations more generally.

Empirical Work

The first author of this article has been working with the DBA since September 2017, initially as an external consultant and from August 2018 as a collaborative Ph.D. fellow, spending about half of his time in the Machine Learning Lab at the DBA where he took part in everyday work-life activities. He kept a field diary with notes from observations in the organisation and meetings and conversations with colleagues and consultants. These were supplemented with insights from reading and writing emails and documentation on platforms such as Git, Teams, Outlook, Jira, and Confluence.

Design Artifact

The design artifact, the Evaluation Plan, is part of a broader framework for responsible AI use named X-RAI (Nagbøl and Müller, 2020). One element of X-RAI is the Artificial Intelligence Risk Assessment (AIRA) tool (Nagbøl et al., 2021), which supports AI risk assessment before production, and thus creates the foundation for post-production evaluation and the retraining of AI systems. The Evaluation Plan inherits, due to its supplementary nature, the theory ingrained into AIRA, including principles such as multi-expert assessment and structured intuition (i.e., providing some structure while leaving experts room for judgement) (Nagbøl et al., 2021). In line with the principle of structured intuition, the Evaluation Plan is a questionnaire that provides some structure while leaving room for expert judgement. Table 14.1 shows the Evaluation Plan implemented at the DBA during iteration 3 (see below for a description of iterations).

BIE Iterations

The initial work of designing the artifact (the Evaluation Plan) started in February 2019 in close collaboration with stakeholders from the company registration (business unit), a product owner, and the Machine Learning Lab. The Evaluation Plan was designed to accompany the Evaluation Framework and the Retraining Framework in a three-framework process. The process was expanded with a fourth framework for Artificial Intelligence Risk Assessment (AIRA) (Nagbøl et al., 2021) inspired by the Canadian Algorithmic Impact Assessment tool

Table 14.1   Evaluation plan artifact

Question No.	Question
Q1	Who should participate in the evaluation (e.g., application manager, relevant business unit, ML lab)?
Q2	Who owns the model/the solution (usually the business)?
Q3	When should the first evaluation meeting take place?
Q4	What is the expected meeting frequency (how often should you meet and evaluate)?
Q5	What is the current threshold setting for the AI system?
Q6	What is the basis for the evaluation (e.g., logging data, annotated evaluation data, i.e., data where human categorisation is compared with the model)?
Q7	Is data unbalanced to a degree where this must be taken into account when fabricating data for evaluation and retraining? If so, how?
Q8	What resources are needed (e.g., who can make evaluation data, is evaluation data provided internally or externally, how much needs to be evaluated, what is the cost in time/money)?
Q9	What resources are expected to be needed for the evaluation?
Q10	Is the model visible or invisible to external users?
Q11	Does the model receive input from other models? If so, which ones?
Q12	What are success and error criteria (e.g., when does a model perform well/poorly, what percentage, business value, labour waste)?
Q13	Is there any future legislation that will impact the model's performance (e.g., new requirements, abolition of requirements)?
Q14	Are there other future factors that affect the model's performance (e.g., bias, circumstances, data, standards)?
Q15	When should the model be retrained?
Q16	When should the model be muted or deactivated?

(Secretariat, Treasury Board of Canada, 2020) and further developed into the X-RAI (Nagbøl and Müller, 2020) method. The intervention occurred using the Evaluation Plan on 16 AI systems in the DBA. In three iterations, the artifact was evaluated with three different foci: usability and content (iteration 1), behavioural impact (iteration 2), and challenges (iteration 3).

Iteration 1: Usability and content
We evaluated the Evaluation Plan following the ADR principles of authentic and concurrent evaluation. The Evaluation Plan was introduced to organisational work practices in a word format. In this phase, the evaluation focused on the understandability of the questions and on their suitability for estimating the resource needed. The evaluations led to minor changes to the artifact. Afterwards, the artifact was transformed into YAML format, which facilitates integration into an IT infrastructure.

Iteration 2: Behavioural impact
The second evaluation iteration focused on evaluating the extent to which the Evaluation Plan fulfilled its expected behavioural impact, i.e., the impact of securing and structuring the evaluation of AI systems in the DBA. To this end, we gathered the compiled Evaluation Plans and other relevant documentation, such as Evaluation Schemas. We then analysed the compiled Evaluation Plan frameworks. The analysis revealed that 16 AI systems had compiled an Evaluation Plan stating the time for the first evaluation and the expected following evaluation frequency. There were, to our awareness, only three AI systems with filled-out evaluation frameworks, one of which filled out the evaluation framework only partially. The two full evaluations of the AI systems had taken place before COVID-19. The lockdown of society, the

working-from-home situation caused by COVID-19, and the intense attention on developing the COVID-19 compensation system increased the difficulties in maintaining an overview of the status of the different AI systems. Therefore, we decided to conduct formal interviews to validate our findings from previous evaluations, discover overlooked practices, and gain a deeper understanding of causes and reasons.

Iteration 3: Challenges

The third evaluation iteration focused on discovering overlooked evaluation practices and gaining a deeper insight into the circumstances impacting evaluation. Therefore, we conducted seven semi-structured interviews in January and February 2022 with stakeholders named in the Evaluation Plans. The stakeholders held diverse positions related to IT development, the ML Lab, and different departments using AI systems. Interview durations varied from 44 to 80 minutes. The interviews were structured around the following themes: introduction questions and background, purpose and use of AI systems, quality assurance, evaluation, accountability, risk, challenges, and trust. The interviews were transcribed and coded in Nvivo. In coding, we followed an inductive process where we aggregated lower-level challenges and design principles into a few higher-order categories, similar to data analysis approaches in case study research and grounded theory research (Charmaz, 2006; Yin, 2009). The design principles are planned to be implemented in a subsequent, digitised version of the Evaluation Plan.

FINDINGS: CHALLENGES AND SOLUTIONS

Figure 14.1 provides an overview of our findings. Our data analysis led us to identify the five challenges shown on the left-hand side of Figure 14.1. These challenges can be addressed by an Evaluation Plan infrastructure based on five design principles shown on the right-hand side of Figure 14.1. The arrows show which design principles help address which challenges.

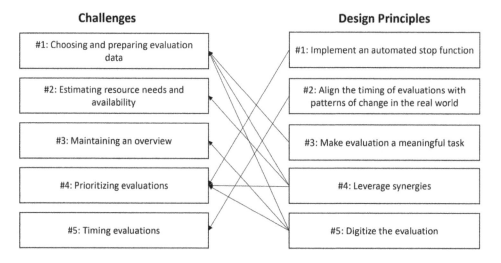

Figure 14.1   Challenges of and design principles for AI systems evaluation

Challenges

#1: Choosing and preparing evaluation data

Several informants mentioned challenges in choosing and preparing the data needed to evaluate a productive AI system. These challenges revolved around tedious annotation work and bias in the available data.

Our participants perceived annotating data for supervised ML as a rather tedious, resource-intensive task. Much like during the initial training of an AI system, post-production evaluation involved selecting data and providing ground truth about the data. One domain specialist highlighted that annotation activity during the evaluation was very time-consuming, requiring domain specialists to 'read … these 10,000–15,000 lines' and 'put a number here and a cross there' (Daniel). This work was sometimes considered tedious and frustrating, especially when looking for small minority classes: 'They wanted me to … look through 100 lines once a month. But almost none of the lines was related to [a specific type of record]. It might be valuable for the model, … [but] there was no [record] that exactly fit what we needed. Then you're lost.' (Daniel)

Other participants mentioned difficulties in choosing and preparing data related to bias in the available data. For instance, one participant mentioned a potential source of bias in data obtained from another public-sector organisation. They said employees of the other organisation would likely focus their checks on those companies that were most likely to submit incorrect reports. As a result, using these data as a basis for annotation during evaluation could result in 'a massive bias' (Rikke), given that the data from companies that were likely to submit accurate reports were underrepresented in the data.

#2: Estimating resource needs and availability

Our informants reported that it was often difficult to anticipate the resources available and needed for evaluation because the use of AI fundamentally changed business processes and priorities. For instance, Torben mentioned that the work in his team increased rather than decreased after AI was introduced. AI provided the opportunity of more effectively detecting fraudulent applications early in the process, helping employees 'to take out the right ones' early in the process rather than to 'waste a lot of businesses' time' or to perform manual checks later. Because of this more effective, AI-enabled checking process, the DBA found it economically advantageous to increase the team size from 4 to 18 employees, who were now responsible for following up on the alarms triggered by the system. These and other fundamental changes in the business process and the role of human labour in the business process would have made it very difficult, if not impossible, for the DBA to anticipate what amount of resources would be available for evaluation and not bound by the new work activities that are enabled by the AI system.

#3: Maintaining an overview

The analysis of the filled-out Evaluation Plan revealed that it was increasingly difficult to maintain an overview of the status of AI system evaluations. As the number of productive AI systems increased and as these systems evolved, the Evaluation Plans increasingly became historical documents displaying an intention to evaluate rather than a tool for monitoring the evaluation. In this situation, maintaining an overview was difficult for several reasons. First, as the use of AI increased, so did the number of AI systems, data scientists, and business processes supported by AI. Second, the COVID-19 crisis required the DBA to direct managerial attention to urgent issues, such as systems supporting the allocation of compensation packages for companies suffering from the pandemic. This drew attention away from the evaluation of AI systems. Thirdly, AI systems were not only added but also paused or retired, making it more difficult to maintain an overview. Some AI systems were periodically switched on and off: 'They are not retired, just temporarily switched off ... the intention is that it is periodically switched on but not permanently ... it is one of the things we will have periodically switched on, for example, from April to June' (Torben). Fourth, staff changed as described by an informant while looking at the Evaluation Plan 'Liselotte on Y has left, and Harald has left ML Lab, ... and Maria is to my knowledge still here, but I have not seen her for a long time, but I believe she is still employed ...' (Kim).

#4: Prioritising evaluations

The Evaluation Plans were initially followed until the start of the COVID-19 pandemic. The pandemic caused an exceptional situation at the DBA where enormous resources were needed to rapidly develop systems, such as systems for administering the compensation packages the Danish government granted to businesses suffering from lockdowns. This exceptional situation made it difficult for the DBA to allocate resources to evaluate existing AI systems.

It was not only the COVID-19 pandemic that bound resources; so did the development of a new digital platform (the Intelligent Control Platform) that was introduced to make AI systems and their evaluations and retraining more effective and efficient in the future: 'There has not been time ... it has been flagged, but it has not been prioritised. There has been put more will towards things that had to be built ... we have been living with compensation (COVID-19) for almost two years. And there has been a new platform (Intelligent Control Platform) that had to be built... We were about to find a routine if you go two years back for how everything should be evaluated ...' (Theo). Developing this required refactoring all the existing AI systems.

While the pandemic and the development of the new digital platform were one-off events that bound resources, our informants also described the challenges of mobilising sufficient resources for evaluation in organisational realities. For instance, one informant said: '... the challenge is that if ... we start to be pressured on the resources on task and on time and when one can see that an evaluation of a model is going to take around 20 hours and these are hard to find, then we might end up not doing it ...' (Torben).

#5: Timing evaluations

There was substantial uncertainty about when to evaluate. Initially, a rule of thumb was that the first evaluation should occur 14 days after go-live and that subsequent evaluations should be performed every third month. Our informants agreed that deciding on the time and scope for the first evaluation was difficult. For example, are child diseases and early implementation issues something to include, or should the first evaluation only touch on matters aligned with the subsequent evaluations? Some informants argued that 14 days was too early for some AI systems: 'I think it is a little optimistic ... there might still be some issues and minor mistakes that must be corrected right when the model is put in production ... I also think that the business unit would need some time to look at the cases' (Rikke). Another informant pointed to the scarcity of available data when systems are evaluated too early: 'We often first know our models' effect when the caseworkers have worked the cases flagged by the model' (Theo).

Not only were decisions about the timing of the first evaluation challenging, but so were decisions about the timing of subsequent evaluations because 'the models will automatically perform worse over time' (Oscar), making it required to time ongoing evaluations before performance decreases substantially. As one informant said, 'You do not know when the fraud patterns are changing ... it can change the day after the evaluation' (Ida).

Design Principles

Informed by the challenges described in the previous section, our engagement in the DBA and our analysis of interview data suggest that the challenges can be addressed by an Evaluation Plan and underlying infrastructure based on the design principles shown in Table 14.2. We describe these design principles according to the schematic guidelines suggested by Gregor et al. (2020).

#1: Implement an automated stop function
A key challenge, especially during the COVID-19 pandemic, was ensuring evaluations receive sufficient priority. To address this challenge, the DBA chose to implement an automated emergency stop function in its Intelligent Control Platform, i.e., the infrastructure developed to digitise the Evaluation Plan. The automated stop function is a feature that ensures a productive AI system stops running if it is not evaluated as per the evaluation plan. Such a function is similar to an automatic train stop system, which stops a train automatically if the train conductor fails to push a button regularly. As one informant told us: '[The head of the department] is going towards setting something up in the Intelligent Control Platform so that we switch off a model if it is not confirmed that the model has been evaluated' (Ida).

#2: Align the timing of evaluations with patterns of change in the real world
Another key challenge was to decide on the timing of evaluations. The evaluation timing is essential for ensuring that AI systems maintain their standards and perform when needed. Through our engagement in evaluating 16 AI systems, we learned that there are multiple logics for timing the evaluation of productive AI systems and that different AI systems need different logics. For example, AI systems that build on trends, such as fraud detection systems where fraudsters change behaviour over time, have other needs for evaluation and retraining than the industrial classification code system where it will not be necessary to retrain and evaluate the system before the standards change. The idea that different AI systems require different temporal evaluation logics is consistent with representation theory (Recker et al., 2019), which holds that information systems, including AI systems, are representations of certain real-world phenomena. Whether the representation of reality (i.e., the AI system) needs to be reassessed depends on the pattern of change in the real-world phenomenon.

While the timing of the first evaluation often depended on the question of when enough data is available, the timing of subsequent evaluations followed one of the following logics: frequency-based, event-based, seasonal, and autonomous-driven. Frequency-driven evaluation implies that evaluations are conducted as a reoccurring event after a fixed timespan, for example, every third month. Our informants pointed to several considerations to be made when deciding on the frequency. One question is how long it is tolerable to run on a false premise, given that the pattern in behaviour could, in principle, change the day after the evaluation. A question to ask when planning the evaluation is 'for how long can we tolerate that

Table 14.2   *Design principles*

Principle	Aim	Mechanism	Rationale
#1: Implement an automated stop function	To enforce compliance with the Evaluation Plan …	… ensure that the AI system cannot run in production without being evaluated by humans as per the Evaluation Plan.	As (semi-)autonomous systems, AI systems can cause undesired consequences. Emergency stop measures known from other dangerous machines like power saws or lawn mowers can help prevent some of these consequences.
#2: Align the timing of evaluations with the patterns of change in the real world	To make sure that the AI system is up to date when needed …	… consider event-based and frequency-based timing strategies in line with expected real-world changes.	According to representation theory (Recker et al., 2019), the fundamental purpose of any information system, including AI-based systems, is to represent certain real-world phenomena faithfully. Hence, AI systems need to be re-evaluated and, if needed, retrained whenever the real-world phenomenon they represent changes.
#3: Make evaluation a meaningful task	To ensure motivated evaluators …	… design the annotation task so that it is an opportunity for autonomy, competence, and relatedness.	According to self-determination theory (Ryan and Deci, 2000), satisfying the basic psychological needs for autonomy, competence, and relatedness can increase people's intrinsic motivation for a given task.
#4: Leverage synergies between AI system evaluation, human training, human work, and AI system training	To reduce costs and make evaluation work less tedious …	… recycle data between work, evaluation, and training activities.	According to representation theory (Recker et al., 2019), information systems represent real-world work systems. Hence, the task of training and assessing an AI-based decision-making system (a type of information system) has important parallels to the task of training and assessing a human decision-making system, suggesting that synergies between these two can be leveraged, e.g., by reusing the products of human training efforts for AI training or assessment.
#5: Digitise the evaluation	To ensure compliance with Evaluation Plans and maintain an overview …	… implement a digital platform that automatically collects data about evaluation activities and outcomes.	According to control theory (Eisenhardt, 1985), accurate information about a controlee's behaviour makes it more likely that the controlee will engage in the desired behaviours. Digitising the evaluation infrastructure helps make information about evaluation activities transparent and thus encourages evaluators (i.e., controlees) to comply with Evaluation Plans.

it answers incorrectly [and for how long are we willing] … to live with not discovering that there suddenly is something that we do not catch although we think we catch right ...' (Ida). Our informants mentioned the impact of the AI system, the thoroughness of prior evaluations, and the amount of dynamism as further factors that affect the needed frequency: 'How big an impact it has but also how the earlier assessments have looked like. If we had the first evaluation rather quickly and then held another one after three months, and everything looks fine, and this is not an area where something is going to happen, and it is probably business as usual, then there is no reason we should meet again in three months, and then we can set it up to be biannual' (Torben).

Event-driven evaluation is based on events that impact the AI system's performance or change the context of the AI systems so that the predictions are no longer suitable. Examples of such events include changes in technical standards and industrial classification codes: 'We also have XBRL with taxonomies that are changing all the time' (Daniel), '... revision of industrial classification code, yes, we know that would happen in 2024, I think, maybe 2025 ...' (Oscar).

Other AI systems have a seasonal flow, with activity fluctuating depending on the time of the year or other recurrences. It is essential to consider when planning the evaluation: 'I will say that there should be more meetings the closer we get to the big filling period occurring from around the end of April until the end of June ...' (Daniel).

Lastly, the DBA considered using autonomous monitoring of AI systems for detecting changing behaviour of the AI system. Abnormalities or changes in the distribution of, for example, positive and negative classifications can be an indicator of a need for evaluation. 'There is an alarm that looks at the probability returned by the model if they suddenly change a lot ... If something is flagged ... If ... the model has this amount of true positives in this quarter, but in another quarter it had only so many true positives, why is that? So again, create some rules for when it must be flagged' (Theo).

While the properties of the real-world phenomenon represented in the AI system may affect the evaluation logic, our interviews also suggested other considerations. One important consideration was resource availability. As one informant shared: 'If there is an office that has five different [AI systems], then one would probably prefer having spread the evaluation work across the months' (Ida). Another important consideration is the interrelatedness of AI systems. For example, if the output of one AI system is the input of another AI system, these dependencies would need to be considered when scheduling the evaluation of the two systems.

#3: Make evaluation a meaningful task

As discussed above, one challenge was that choosing and preparing evaluation data was often seen as a time-consuming and tedious task that, though tedious, required highly skilled labour, such as an employee with a legal or audit background. When reflecting on this challenge, our interviewees suggested several strategies for making evaluation work a meaningful task. These strategies can be well explained by self-determination theory, which suggests that people will find work enjoyable if the work provides opportunities for autonomy, competence, and relatedness (Ryan and Deci, 2000). For instance, evaluation can be framed as an opportunity for competence development by emphasising that the evaluator will obtain a first-hand feeling of how the AI system performs on negative and positive classifications. Evaluation can also be framed as an opportunity for autonomy by communicating that the evaluator plays the role of an educator of the AI system by ingraining their expert knowledge or by including the management of running AI systems into individuals' job descriptions. Moreover, evaluation can be seen as an opportunity for relatedness by involving multiple evaluators, which may provide opportunities for knowledge sharing and learning from each other. While these strategies may help make evaluation work more enjoyable, other strategies focus on communicating the benefits and rewards of evaluation. For example, it may be helpful to communicate why the evaluation is essential, how it benefits the quality of everyday work, and what consequences can occur without evaluation.

#4: Leverage synergies between regular work, AI system evaluation, human training, and AI system training

While it was difficult to ensure sufficient, motivated resources were available (as captured through challenges #1, #2, and #4), our informants shared that several strategies help leverage synergies between evaluation and other activities, which may help relax resource issues and reduce tedious elements of evaluation work. Specifically, our informants recommended leveraging synergies between regular work, AI system evaluation, human training, and AI system training. Human oversight was often a mandatory quality insurance and validation mechanism for at least one of the classification categories (typically for negative classifications, for example, for rejected applications) and, in some AI systems, both for negative and positive classifications. The informants considered quality insurance critical. Indeed, there were different kinds of ongoing quality insurance and evaluation mechanisms of the AI systems despite the lack of use of X-RAI's evaluation framework. 'In the audit unit, we have weekly meetings about the model and our experiences with the model both on the caseworker level and with our boss ... We conduct these meetings, among other things, to collect and deliver feedback back to ML (ML lab)' (Kim). Hence, meetings that aimed at reflecting on and improving AI-enabled work practices provided important potential input for evaluations.

Our informants also pointed us to potential synergies between evaluation and human training. Indeed, the formalised and standardised evaluation flow allowed acquiring, storing, and sharing of knowledge and experience from the evaluation of the AI system, contributing to continuous individual and organisational learning and the development of best practices, including utilising the experiences already ingrained in the evaluation schema. For example, evaluation activities can be included in individual competence development processes: 'We have just hired a new employee in the team who needs training. We always focus them on [the AI system] because there are some good cases to get out about training' (Torben). The data annotation is an opportunity to work dedicated to one specific interpretation of, for example, a law repeatedly, thus stipulating learning. It is then relevant when working through the cases to annotate the data.

Another synergy is to store and declare annotated evaluation data so that it can be recycled as training data when retraining the AI system. Hence, a retraining procedure starts with deciding which evaluation data to recycle. Integration of evaluation into the regular workflow is an option '... the best in the world would be that our case management is constructed in a way if I, for example, had processed a case in the signature [AI system], then I could, while closing my handling of the case, do some evaluations of the positives' (Torben).

#5: Digitise the evaluation

Among the most important challenges related to evaluation were the difficulties of maintaining an overview of and prioritising evaluation activities. The DBA reacted to these difficulties by introducing the Intelligent Control Platform, a digitised infrastructure for managing AI systems evaluation. As control theory suggests (Eisenhardt, 1985), controlees (for example, evaluators) are more likely to show the expected behaviours (for example, evaluating AI systems when needed) if the information about the controlees' behaviours is transparent. Hence, a digitised evaluation infrastructure can be an important element for not only maintaining an overview of evaluation activities but also for enforcing that evaluations are conducted as required. Interestingly, the platform also helped make evaluation and retraining more straightforward (see the link between challenges #1 and #5: Digitise the evaluation in Figure 14.1) because it allowed the evaluator to annotate relevant data in a system that automatically stored it and made it accessible for retraining purposes, which further helped cope with resource bottlenecks. As Daniel put it: 'We want that four eyes have a look at a case .... We should have created ... a GUI [Graphical User Interface] ... , where we could annotate: I think this [company] here is fictitious [based on the AI system prediction].Then your colleague could go into the tool and say: This is correct ... and starts a case' (Daniel). The DBA started building an infrastructure for evaluating and retraining AI systems. That infrastructure should allow for easier evaluation and faster adaptation of AI systems to changes in their environment. The expectation was that the new platform will allow for better monitoring, evaluation, and retraining: 'It makes it easier for us to evaluate the possibility because we are sitting with it closely now. It becomes easier to update the model when we discover that the model starts to perform worse, making it easier to put a new model in production. It is easier to retrain the models because everything is in one place in our repository' (Oscar).

DISCUSSION

This chapter was motivated by the observation that little work has examined the evaluation of productive AI systems in organisational realities, even though evaluating productive AI systems is critical for avoiding harm and ensuring benefits from AI systems. Against this background, we explored the challenges organisations face in planning and enforcing the evaluation of productive AI systems and design principles for an AI evaluation infrastructure that helps address these challenges. We relied on Action Design Research to answer these research questions. We built, implemented, and evaluated our design artifact, the Evaluation Plan in the Danish Business Authority (DBA), which included conducting seven semi-structured interviews. The DBA, with its high amount of productive AI systems, was a unique environment for studying changes in the ongoing evaluation of productive AI systems and design principles that help address these challenges.

Implications

Challenge #1: Choosing and preparing evaluation data relates to prior research emphasising the importance and difficulties of preparing labelled data for training or evaluation (Lebovitz et al., 2021). While existing work highlights the potentially problematic nature of ground truth and the difficulties that uncertain ground truth creates for labelling (Lebovitz et al., 2021), our findings point to another challenging facet of labelling work: its tedious, effortful nature. We not only reveal this as a factor that challenges the evaluation of AI systems; we also propose design principles for evaluation infrastructure that can help address this challenge. Specifically, our data suggest that the tedious nature of evaluation work can be mitigated by a digitised evaluation infrastructure that enables evaluation planners to make evaluation more meaningful and leverage synergies between evaluation and human and AI training. These insights align with, but also go beyond, prior research that emphasises the tightly connected nature of human and AI learning in AI implementations (Lebovitz et al., 2021; Lou and Wu, 2021; Nagbøl et al., 2021; van den Broek et al., 2021).

Challenge #2: Estimating resource needs and availability highlights the difficulties of planning and ensuring the availability of resources for evaluation. This finding echoes socio-technical research showing that system implementations often yield many planned and unplanned changes (Lehrig and Krancher, 2018; Orlikowski, 1996; Robey et al., 2002). It may, hence, be of little surprise that work systems after implementing an AI system may look different from what the designers of the systems had anticipated, which also implies that it is difficult to plan the resources required for evaluation. Challenge #2 also resonates with project management research that generally emphasises the difficulties of ensuring domain expert availability during IS projects (for example, Wallace et al., 2004). Going beyond these findings, however, our study highlights that, for AI systems, the availability of domain experts is a key challenge not only during development but also during the maintenance of AI systems, given the continuous need for domain experts to ascertain that the systems work as intended.

Challenge #3: Maintaining an overview and Challenge #4: Prioritising evaluations, point to two further difficulties in organisational realities after the go-live of AI systems. Given the relatively scant focus on maintenance (Luccioni et al., 2022) and on the social context (Selbst et al., 2019) in most existing AI research, we are not aware of prior work that has pointed to these two challenges, which arise as the number of live AI systems in organisations is increasing. Nonetheless, our chapter suggests that existing organisational theories may be well suited for explaining the organisational structures required to ensure coordination of and focus on evaluations. Control theory (Eisenhardt, 1985; Kirsch, 1996; Krancher et al., 2022) can help explain the information systems required to ensure enough focus on evaluation. Organisational research on the role of slack in improvement activities (for example, Repenning and Sterman, 2002) can help explain why slack resources (i.e., domain experts having capacity beyond their daily tasks) can be an essential foundation for evaluations.

Last but not least, Challenge #5: Timing evaluations and the design principles of aligning the timing of evaluations with patterns in the real world raises the timing of evaluation as an important issue that has yet to be addressed by AI research. We propose that representation theory (Recker et al., 2019) can be a fruitful theoretical basis for future research on the issue.

PRACTICAL CONTRIBUTION

Our chapter and the collaborative development of X-RAI with the DBA offer several practical implications for organisations setting up or needing to improve structures to evaluate productive AI systems. First, they should consider implementing an automated stop function that switches off critical AI systems if they are not evaluated. Second, they should consider the pattern of change in the application domain of a system and align the timing of evaluations with that pattern. Third, they design work arrangements that make evaluations a meaningful task despite its potentially tedious nature. Fourth, they should leverage synergies between regular work, AI system evaluation, human training, and AI system training. Fifth, they should consider building digital infrastructures for AI system evaluations, which help provide an overview of evaluations and make use of the data generated during evaluation and during human-in-the-loop activities.

The use of the X-RAI artifact (Nagbøl and Müller, 2020; Nagbøl et al., 2021) with its four elements – Artificial Intelligence Risk Assessment, Evaluation Plan, Evaluation, and Retraining Frameworks – has contributed to the recognition of the DBA as an industry leader in AI Ethics. The Joint Research Center under the European Commission has found the DBA's Ethical Data Governance to be the most advanced among public sector organisations within the European Union (Tangi et al., 2022). In addition, the consultancy firm Gartner has suggested that AI Leaders adopt the DBA approach to ensure an ethically defensible development and use of AI Systems (Gartner, 2021). The importance of this topic for the industry is evident for Gartner, including it in their Top 10 Strategic Technology Trends for 2023 as AI Trust, Risk and Security Management (AI TRiSM). Furthermore, Gartner highlights the DBA's methodological framework as an example of how to tie ethical principles to concrete actions (Gartner, 2022).

Limitations and Boundary Conditions

In this ADR study, we focused on challenges and design principles that help address them, as our work with the artifact and interview data indicated. Implementing an artifact that fully embodies these design principles remains future work. As such, it is possible that implementing an artifact based on the design principles proposed here may produce unanticipated effects and call for further changes to the artifact. Similarly, it is worth highlighting that our artifact, the Evaluation Plan, was subject to authentic, concurrent evaluation by examining its use in action at the DBA and deriving design principles from these observations. A rigorous summative evaluation of the effect of the Evaluation Plan on outcomes such as decision accuracy or harm is beyond the possibilities of this study. It is also important to point out that this study solely focused on evaluation based on the X-RAI framework as an artifact according to the design principles of ADR. The quality insurance mechanism and evaluation of governmental conduct and work in the DBA were beyond the scope of this study. Pointing toward a lack of formal evaluation of a given AI system must not be interpreted as a lack of quality insurance.

CONCLUSION AND FUTURE RESEARCH

While most existing research on AI focuses on technical issues or on socio-technical aspects of the development and adoption of AI, our study reveals challenges that arise post-implementation when organisations rely on a multitude of AI systems and make efforts to ensure the proper functioning of these systems through evaluation. The challenges and design principles for addressing the challenges open up many avenues for future research. For example, researchers interested in the future of work and humanistic aspects of work could explore how individuals cope with the tedious nature of evaluation work and how organisations can further address these challenges beyond the strategies unveiled in this chapter. Researchers interested in organisational structures and control could explore portfolios of control mechanisms that help ensure sufficient evaluation. Researchers interested in dynamics and formal systems could expand on the evaluation timing strategies uncovered in our study and examine the effectiveness and efficiency of these strategies. Design researchers could focus on infrastructure that integrates an organisation's AI systems and organises the data required for evaluation in an efficient, user-friendly way. Further research could focus on conducting and optimising the post-production performance evaluations to secure continued fulfillment of the business objectives, how to performance measure AI systems where the business value differentiates within the positive or negative categories and how to continuously monitor business objectives going beyond the accuracy of the AI system such as systematically checking and mitigating for bias and other harmful outcomes.

REFERENCES

Asatiani, A., Malo, P., Nagbøl, P. R., Penttinen, E., Rinta-Kahila, T., and Salovaara, A. (2020). Challenges of explaining the behavior of black-box AI systems. *MIS Quarterly Executive, 19*(4), 259–278.

Asatiani, A., Malo, P., Nagbøl, P. R., Penttinen, E., Rinta-Kahila, T., and Salovaara, A. (2021). Socio-technical envelopment of artificial intelligence: An approach to organizational deployment of inscrutable artificial intelligence systems. *Journal of the Association for Information Systems, 22*(2), 325–352. https://doi.org/10.17705/1jais.00664

Baird, A., and Maruping, L. M. (2021). The next generation of research on IS use: A theoretical framework of delegation to and from agentic IS artifacts. *MIS Quarterly, 45*(1).

Berente, N., Gu, B., Recker, J., and Santhanam, R. (2021). Managing artificial intelligence. *MIS Q, 45*(3), 1433–1450.

Charmaz, K. (2006). *Constructing Grounded Theory: A Practical Guide Through Qualitative Analysis.* Sage.

Doshi-Velez, F., and Kim, B. (2017). Towards a rigorous science of interpretable machine learning. *ArXiv:1702.08608 [Cs, Stat].* http://arxiv.org/abs/1702.08608

Eisenhardt, K. M. (1985). Control: Organizational and economic approaches. *Management Science, 31*(2), 134–149.

Fügener, A., Grahl, J., Gupta, A., and Ketter, W. (2021). Will humans-in-the-loop become borgs? Merits and pitfalls of working with AI. *Management Information Systems Quarterly (MISQ)-Vol, 45.*

Gartner. (2021). *Case Study: How to Apply Ethical Principles to AI Models (Danish Business Authority)* (Case Study No. G00749866). Gartner. https://www.gartner.com/en/documents/4004387

Gartner. (2022). *Top Strategic Technology Trends 2023.* https://www.gartner.com/en/information-technology/insights/top-technology-trends

Gregor, S., Kruse, L. C., and Seidel, S. (2020). Research perspectives: The anatomy of a design principle. *Journal of the Association for Information Systems, 21*(6), 1622–1652. https://doi.org/10.17705/1jais.00649

Hernández-Orallo, J. (2017). Evaluation in artificial intelligence: From task-oriented to ability-oriented measurement. *Artificial Intelligence Review, 48*(3), 397–447. https://doi.org/10.1007/s10462-016-9505-7

Hill, K. (2020). Wrongfully accused by an algorithm. In *Ethics of Data and Analytics* (pp. 138–142). Auerbach Publications.

Jussupow, E., Spohrer, K., Heinzl, A., and Gawlitza, J. (2021). Augmenting medical diagnosis decisions? An investigation into physicians' decision-making process with artificial intelligence. *Information Systems Research, 32*(3), 713–735.

Kirsch, L. J. (1996). The management of complex tasks in organizations: Controlling the systems development process. *Organization Science, 7*(1), 1–21.

Kirsch, L. J. (2004). Deploying common systems globally: The dynamics of control. *Information Systems Research, 15*(4), 374–395.

Krancher, O., Oshri, I., Kotlarsky, J., and Dibbern, J. (2022). Bilateral, collective, or both? Formal governance and performance in multisourcing. *Journal of the Association for Information Systems, 23*(5), 1211–1234.

Lebovitz, S., Levina, N., and Lifshitz-Assaf, H. (2021). Is AI ground truth really 'true'? The dangers of training and evaluating AI tools based on experts' know-what. *Management Information Systems Quarterly, 45*(3b), 1501–1525.

Lehrig, T., and Krancher, O. (2018). *Change of Organizational Routines under Malleable Information Technology: Explaining Variations in Momentum.* Proceedings of the Thirty Ninth International Conference of Information System.

Li, J., Li, M., Wang, X., and Thatcher, J. B. (2021). Strategic directions for AI: The role of CIOS and boards of directors. *MIS Quarterly*, *45*(3).

Lipton, Z. C. (2018). The mythos of model interpretability: In machine learning, the concept of interpretability is both important and slippery. *Queue*, *16*(3), 31–57.

Lou, B., and Wu, L. (2021). AI on drugs: Can artificial intelligence accelerate drug development? Evidence from a large-scale examination of bio-pharma firms. *MIS Quarterly*, *45*(3).

Luccioni, A. S., Corry, F., Sridharan, H., Ananny, M., Schultz, J., and Crawford, K. (2022). A framework for deprecating datasets: Standardizing documentation, identification, and communication. *2022 ACM Conference on Fairness, Accountability, and Transparency*, 199–212. https://doi.org/10.1145/3531146.3533086

Mayer, A.-S., Strich, F., and Fiedler, M. (2020). Unintended consequences of introducing AI systems for decision making. *MIS Quarterly Executive*, *19*(4).

Nagbøl, P. R., and Müller, O. (2020). X-RAI: A framework for the transparent, responsible, and accurate use of machine learning in the public sector. *Proceedings of Ongoing Research, Practitioners, Workshops, Posters, and Projects of the International Conference EGOV-CeDEM-EPart 2020*, 9. http://dgsociety.org/wp-content/uploads/2020/08/CEUR-WS-Proceedings-2020_Full-Manuscript.pdf#page=273

Nagbøl, P. R., Müller, O., and Krancher, O. (2021). Designing a risk assessment tool for artificial intelligence systems. In L. Chandra Kruse, S. Seidel, and G. I. Hausvik (eds), *The Next Wave of Socio-technical Design* (pp. 328–339). Springer International Publishing.

Nations, U. (2018). *United Nations E-Government Survey 2018*. United Nations. https://www.un-ilibrary.org/content/books/9789210472272

Orlikowski, W. J. (1996). Improvising organizational transformation over time: A situated change perspective. *Information Systems Research*, *7*(1), 63–92.

Recker, J., Indulska, M., Green, P., Burton-Jones, A., and Weber, R. (2019). Information systems as representations: A review of the theory and evidence. *Journal of the Association for Information Systems*, *20*(6), 5.

Repenning, N. P., and Sterman, J. D. (2002). Capability traps and self-confirming attribution errors in the dynamics of process improvement. *Administrative Science Quarterly*, *47*(2), 265–295.

Robey, D., Ross, J., and Boudreau, M.-C. (2002). Learning to implement enterprise systems: An exploratory study of the dialectics of change. *Journal of Management Information Systems*, *19*(1), 17–46.

Russell, S., and Norvig, P. (2002). *Artificial Intelligence: A Modern Approach*. Prentice Hall.

Ryan, R. M., and Deci, E. L. (2000). Self-determination theory and the facilitation of intrinsic motivation, social development, and well-being. *American Psychologist*, *55*(1), 68.

Secretariat, Treasury Board of Canada. (2020). Algorithmic Impact Assessment (AIA). In *Aem*. Secretariat, Treasury Board of Canada. https://www.canada.ca/en/government/system/digital-government/digital-government-innovations/responsible-use-ai/algorithmic-impact-assessment.html

Sein, M., Henfridsson, O., Purao, S., Rossi, M., and Lindgren, R. (2011). Action design research. *Management Information Systems Quarterly*, *35*(1), 37–56.

Selbst, A. D., Boyd, D., Friedler, S. A., Venkatasubramanian, S., and Vertesi, J. (2019). Fairness and abstraction in sociotechnical systems. *Proceedings of the Conference on Fairness, Accountability, and Transparency*, 59–68. https://doi.org/10.1145/3287560.3287598

Strich, F., Mayer, A.-S., and Fiedler, M. (2021). What do I do in a world of artificial intelligence? Investigating the impact of substitutive decision-making AI systems on employees' professional role identity. *Journal of the Association for Information Systems*, *22*(2), 9.

Sun, T. Q., and Medaglia, R. (2019). Mapping the challenges of artificial intelligence in the public sector: Evidence from public healthcare. *Government Information Quarterly*, *36*(2), 368–383.

Tangi, L., Van Noordt, C., Combetto, M., Gattwinkel, D., and Pignatelli, F. (2022). *AI Watch. European Landscape on the Use of Artificial Intelligence by the Public Sector* (ISBN 978-92-76-53058-9). Publications Office of the European Union. doi:10.2760/39336

Teodorescu, M. H., Morse, L., Awwad, Y., and Kane, G. C. (2021). Failures of fairness in automation require a deeper understanding of human-ML augmentation. *MIS Quarterly*, *45*(3).

United Nations and Department of Economic and Social Affairs. (2020). *United Nations e-Government Survey 2020: Digital Government in the Decade of Action for Sustainable Development*. United Nations, Department of Economic and Social Affairs.

Van den Broek, E., Sergeeva, A., and Huysman, M. (2021). When the machine meets the expert: An ethnography of developing AI for hiring. *MIS Quarterly*, *45*(3).

Wallace, L., Keil, M., and Rai, A. (2004). How software project risk affects project performance: An investigation of the dimensions of risk and an exploratory model. *Decision Sciences*, *35*(2), 289–321.

Yin, R. K. (2009). *Case Study Research: Design and Methods*. Sage.

15. Trustworthy public sector AI: research progress and future agendas

Naomi Aoki, Melvin Tay and Masaru Yarime

INTRODUCTION

Many governments and public service agencies worldwide are already leveraging artificial intelligence (AI) technologies. A continuing shift toward the use of AI in public sector operations and services (hereafter referred to as 'AI-PS') is expected globally, with at least 49 countries that have either already launched, or are planning to launch, national AI strategies, many of which have laid out approaches for the public sector (Berryhill, 2019; Berryhill et al., 2019). This transition towards AI-PS requires overcoming a range of challenges, including the challenges of securing the financial and human resources needed for the implementation of AI technology, regulating the use of autonomous intelligent systems with laws and regulations, resolving ethical issues concerning machine judgement and moral dilemmas, and achieving social acceptance and trust in AI-PS (Wirtz et al., 2019).

Our chapter sheds light on one of the challenges involved in the transition towards AI-PS: building societal trust in AI-PS. We contribute to the scholarship on this topic, by first offering reasons for why promoting human trust in AI or building trustworthy AI is particularly important in the public sector. We then look into the question of how far scientific research has progressed toward generating insights that can help with this effort. We address this question based on a systematic literature review (SLR) of journal articles retrieved from leading bibliographic databases, namely, Scopus and the Web of Science (WoS), work that, to the best of our knowledge, has not been done before on this specific topic. The findings from the SLR led us to identify what needs to be done to advance research on this topic, and consequently, we propose propositions for future research to investigate.

Before we proceed, some key terms call for definition. By trust, we mean one's confidence in an AI-driven system, 'based on the perceived probability of its performing the work expected of it and displaying favorable behaviour' (Aoki, 2020, para. 1). We are concerned with the public sector, defined as the entity entrusted with core government functions such as law-making and enforcement and the delivery of public services exclusively by itself or jointly with other stakeholders. Next, by societal trust in AI-PS, we mean the trust of a broad range of stakeholders in society. These stakeholders include citizens who consume public services provided through AI and whose welfare is affected by algorithm-assisted decisions. They also include front-line service providers who use AI systems in the delivery of public services, and policymakers and administrators who have to decide whether or not to deploy AI.

DISTINCTIVE PUBLIC SECTOR REASONS FOR WHY AI-PS NEEDS TO BE TRUSTWORTHY

Before we discuss reasons unique to the public sector for why AI needs to be trustworthy, it is worth noting two general reasons, regardless of sectoral context. Studies of human-machine interaction point to a positive linkage between humans' trust in machines and their intention to use them (de Vries et al., 2003; Lewandowsky et al., 2000; Moray et al., 2000; Muir and Moray, 1989). Studies have also found trust to be a predictor of the use of automated services such as mobile commerce payment services (Gao and Waechter, 2017) and e-government platforms (Alzahrani et al., 2017). Although the technological artifacts under investigation are not necessarily AI-driven, these studies suggest that promoting societal trust in AI is essential for a pragmatic reason: so AI will be widely accepted and utilised in society.

Another critical reason is ethical and pertains to the fact that algorithm-assisted decision-making is not free from bias and flaws. When AI decision-aid systems are fed data that embody narrow human values and prejudices, they generate biased output, which leads to systematic and inadvertent discrimination against certain people who are affected by the decisions (Weyerer and Langer, 2019). Furthermore, AI can make misguided decisions because machine learning is based on correlation, not causation (Hao, 2019). Consequently, AI systems must be trustworthy in respect to not causing harm to human welfare and individual rights through biased or fraudulent output – a requirement stipulated in the European Commission's Ethics Guidelines for Trustworthy AI (Directorate-General for Communications Networks, Content and Technology, European Commission, 2019). Algorithm-assisted decisions should also be made accountable, possibly with 'explainable AI' (XAI) – a technology that 'makes its behavior more intelligible to humans by providing explanations' (Gunning et al., 2019).

While the abovementioned pragmatic and normative reasons apply to general AI use regardless of sectoral context, we now offer a twofold argument specific to the public sector for why AI has to be trustworthy if it is to be integrated into the public sector and if AI-PS is going to be embraced by society at large. Our twofold argument pertains to (1) the coercive nature of what the public sector does or seeks to achieve, and (2) concerns over the legitimacy of the sources of discretion and authority exercised by the public sector, especially in a democratic context.

The Coercive Nature of Public Sector Activities

Rainey et al. (1976) indicate points of consensus in the literature regarding characteristics that distinguish the public sector from the private sector; one of them is the 'coercive,' 'monopolistic,' and 'unavoidable' nature of many government activities (p. 236). Unlike commercial services and products offered by the private sector, individuals 'cannot avoid participation in the financing of most government activities, and in the consumption of many of the outputs of governments' (Rainey et al., 1976, p. 238). This unavoidable and hence coercise aspect of government activities applies as well to activities undertaken with AI.

Examples of AI use having a coercive impact on citizens can be found in core government functions, such as justice and law enforcement, and policymaking. In some US state courts, AI is used to generate recidivism scores that reflect the estimated likelihood of a defendant or convicted criminal re-offending, and judges can take this score into account to decide the severity of penalties or sentences (Hao, 2019). In the same vein, police departments around the world, from New York (New York City Police Department [NYPD], n.d.) to Abu Dhabi

(Abu Dhabi Digital Authority, 2020), are adopting AI-enabled facial recognition technology for law enforcement. In Belgium, CitizenLab – a civic-tech company – has developed a system aided by machine learning that helps civil servants to analyse citizens' views and opinions for data-driven policymaking (Berryhill et al., 2019). When AI is used in core government functions such as these, taxpayers and residents in the jurisdictions where this is being done inescapably have a stake in the outcomes.

The public sector use of AI-driven chatbots and virtual assistants is another example that can have coercive and broad impacts on citizens. In the future, the option to speak with a human agent may become limited, or even disappear, as governments seek to further digitise public administration. Estonia is spearheading this idea with its intention to launch *Bürokratt*, 'a voice-mediated virtual assistant that can answer any query' related to public services, and 'an interoperable network of AI applications accessible via voice' (Petrone, 2022).

The coercive nature of public sector operations and services, combined with the scale of their impacts, should evoke a pronounced and distinct sense of moral obligation on the part of policymakers and service providers to ensure that AI-PS is trustworthy. This obligation should be guided by a sense of responsibility to the public or at least by a desire to avoid blame should a public AI system harm or mistreat citizens or service users. Empirical studies reveal that this is a possibility. For example, regarding the use of COMPAS – a widely used AI-driven software system for predicting recidivism, Larson et al. (2016) found racial disparity in the likelihood of being incorrectly judged to be at a higher risk of recidivism, while Dressel and Farid (2018) found the software to be no more accurate than human predictions. Moreover, Petrović et al. (2020) observed that AVs are not free from accidents, although AV accidents differ from those of conventional vehicles. Citizens, too, might be more cautious about trusting AI-PS than trusting the AI used in commercial products or services, precisely because there is limited or no escape from the impact of AI-PS, which is not the case with commercial products or services, which they can simply choose not to purchase.

The Discretion Argument

Another normative reason why AI-PS needs to be trustworthy concerns the legitimacy of AI discretion in the context of democracy. Because of their non-elected status, to be legitimate, administrators have to be trustworthy agents in the eyes of citizens, and they have to exercise their discretion in a democratically conscientious manner. With the rise of advanced AI that can exercise discretion, we argue that it should be trusted for the same normative reason.

As asserted by Thompson (1985), at the root of the administrative discretion argument is the ideal of an ethics of neutrality, which is expected of non-elected administrative officers in a democratic state. If administrative officers adhere to such ethics, they act neutrally without being driven by their own moral principles and without regard for their own political ideology or position; that is, they use their discretion to serve as reliable executors of the objectives of their political and organisational masters. However, Thompson (1985) points out that an ethics of neutrality is an illusion and mis-instructive because it ignores a political reality – administrators regularly initiate and formulate policies. In this process, they 'may put forward their own views, argue with their superiors, and contest proposals' (p. 556), and thus, their discretion goes beyond executing the intentions of legislators. Other scholars accept that this level of administrative discretion is inevitable because 'reality is shown to be far more complex and varied than legislators had ever dreamed' (Bovens and Zouridis, 2002, p. 175) and '[n]o law can be written to cover all situations' (Barth and Arnold, 1999, p. 338).

In light of this political reality, scholars in public administration have called for the democratic control and accountability of non-elected administrators who exercise discretion behind closed doors. A classic essay by Levitan (1946) warns that administrators fail to use their discretion in a democratically conscientious way when their expertise narrows their vision; when they are 'removed from the local currents of thoughts, the desires and prejudices of the people'; and when they are inclined to 'lose sight of the true master-servant relationship and to develop an attitude of condescension toward the citizen' (pp. 577–578). As a solution to this problem, Levitan (1946) calls for the promotion of administrative responsibility – 'ability and courage' – on the part of administrators and for them to use their discretion wisely for democratically conscientious ends (p. 580). Scholars have shed light on the issue of unfair treatment of citizens subject to the discretion of administrators, due in part to administrators' inclination to promote the interests of the social groups they represent (Mosher, 1968). This concern has prompted the empirical testing of the effects of such active representation at the street level (Andrews and Miller, 2013; Gilad and Dahan, 2021).

Integrating AI technology into the public sector constitutes a revolutionary shift in the locus of administrative discretion from humans to AI. Although the discretionary power of narrow AI in use today is limited, the rise of more advanced AI may mean that systems with machine-learning capabilities will wield more discretion in lieu of humans. This scenario is plausible in light of the controversial prospect of artificial general intelligence and the ongoing transition from public bureaucracies to algocracies – governance systems that are 'organized and structured on the basis of computer-programmed algorithms' (Danaher, 2016, p. 247). The same concerns about the democratic legitimacy of human discretion should apply to the discretion of AI, which is neither elected nor human. Accordingly, the same questions should arise about making AI discretion democratically conscientious and about whether AI can be a trustworthy agent empowered to exercise discretion on behalf of citizens, and if so, to what degree. These questions are not applicable to the private sector because there is no need to contest the democratic legitimacy of discretion in producing commercial goods and services.

A SYSTEMATIC REVIEW OF RESEARCH ON SOCIAL TRUST IN AI-PS

Based on the two major lines of reasoning explained above, we argue that issues of trust in AI-PS should receive attention in the context of public administration and the public sector. However, studies on this topic remain limited and nascent. We demonstrate this deficiency based on the results of the SLR described below. We asked, 'How far has research progressed towards generating evidence and insights, in particular, ones that can help to promote trust in AI-PS or build trustworthy AI-PS?' and 'What are the gaps that need to be filled to advance our knowledge of this topic?'

Search Strategy

We examined the literature indexed on two leading bibliographic databases – Scopus and the Web of Science (WoS) – as of December 28, 2021, and shortlisted relevant research for review.

To ensure analytical rigour and replicability, the process was based on the Preferred Reporting Items for Systematic Reviews and Meta-Analyses (PRISMA) method, developed 'primarily for systematic reviews of studies that evaluate the effects of health interventions' (Page et al., 2021, p. 2). We followed the PRISMA guidelines to the extent that they conformed to the literature on our subjects of interest. Figure 15.1 shows a modified PRISMA flow diagram detailing the process of identifying, screening, and selecting the studies for review.[1]

For both the Scopus and WoS databases, we first retrieved articles whose titles, abstracts, and keywords contained one or more terms in all of the following three categories: (1) terms relating to AI, namely, 'artificial intelligence,' 'AI,' 'machine learning,' and 'deep learning,' (2) terms relating to the public sector, namely, 'public sector,' 'public administration,' 'public management,' 'public service,' and 'government,' and (3) terms relating to trust, namely, 'trust' or 'trustworthy.' The initial search yielded 309 articles from Scopus and 101 from WoS. Thereafter, we dropped duplicates and retained only English journal articles marked 'final' for the publication stage in Scopus and articles whose database source was the Web of Science Core Collection in WoS.

We further excluded any article that did not address both the concepts of trust and AI. The public sector was central to some of the articles, but less so in others. However, we adopted a lenient approach to include both cases, retaining (1) articles with a broader scope that covered both public and private sector cases; (2) articles that explicitly mentioned AI-PS (at least once); (3) articles on AI use in hybrid governance involving both public and private sectors; and (4) articles on smart cities, because we assumed a smart city would involve various stakeholders, including governments. We excluded articles that treated the government as a regulator of AI use in the market. The final sample contained 32 articles for review.[2]

Descriptive Characteristics of the Literature

Summarised below are the key characteristics of the articles we reviewed:

- The articles are relatively recent and have strong currency; the earliest study was published in 2018, and the majority ($n = 26$) were published in 2020 or later.
- No single journal has a monopoly on the subjects of interest; 32 articles were published across 29 journals (listed in Box X.1), and each journal published no more than two relevant articles.
- Attesting to the interdisciplinary nature of trust in AI-PS, the journals that published the relevant articles span multi-disciplinary fields, as shown in Figure 15.2.
- No article was published in a mainstream public administration journal or a journal with an explicit public sector theme, except one article published in *Government Information Quarterly*.
- The largest cluster of sector-specific articles ($n = 4$) concerns AI use in health care, while the rest are dispersed in their topical focus. The issue of trust may be most significant in

---

[1]   The PRISMA checklist is available on the Harvard Dataverse site as part of the supplementary material for this chapter: https://doi.org/10.7910/DVN/HHKQCR

[2]   A full list of the 32 articles is available on the Harvard Dataverse site as part of the supplementary material for this chapter: https://doi.org/10.7910/DVN/HHKQCR.

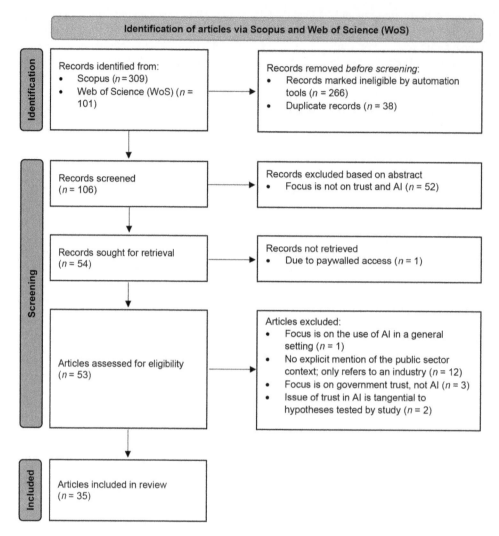

Source: Adapted from the framework in Page et al. (2021).

Figure 15.1   Modified PRISMA 2020 flow diagram

health care because this area involves the use of substantial amounts of personal data and has implications for a patient's welfare.

- Articles where the types of AI are specified most often concern 'predictive analytics and data visualisation,' and 'cognitive robotics, identity analytics, and autonomous systems,' as shown in Figure 15.3.
- The geographical scope of the articles is global; aside from those with a transnational focus, other economies covered include Australia, Belgium, Mainland China, Croatia, India, Japan, Malaysia, the Netherlands, Saudi Arabia, Switzerland, the UK, and the US.

- Of the 32 articles, only 12 involve an empirical approach, and among them, hypothesis testing is rare.

In sum, the 32 articles are thinly scattered across a range of disciplines, journals, geographic regions, areas of public service, and the types of AI studied. In general, there is a dearth of empirical studies addressing trust in AI-PS.

BOX 15.1 JOURNALS THAT PUBLISHED THE ARTICLES REVIEWED

ACM Transactions on Interactive Intelligent Systems

Artificial Intelligence

BMC Medical Ethics Association

Business Information Review

Communication Studies

Computers in Human Behavior

Energy Reports

Environment and Urbanization ASIA

Government Information Quarterly

IEEE Access

IEEE Intelligent Systems

IEEE Technology and Society Magazine

International Journal of Advanced Computer Science and Applications

International Journal of Information Management

International Journal of Recent Technology and Engineering

International Journal on Emerging Technologies

Journal of Medical Ethics

Journal of the American Medical Informatics

Medijska Istrazivanja

Monitoring Obshchestvennogo Mneniya: Ekonomicheskie i Sotsial'nye Peremeny

Moral Philosophy and Politics

Nature Machine Intelligence

Philosophical Transactions of the Royal Society A: Mathematical, Physical and Engineering Sciences

Policy and Internet

Small Wars and Insurgencies

Social Science Computer Review

Technology in Society

Telecommunications Policy

Transforming Government: People, Process and Policy

Predictors of Trust in AI-PS Mentioned in the Literature

Research can help with the effort to build trustworthy AI-PS by identifying the predictors of societal trust in AI-PS. The articles we reviewed propose candidates for potential predictors or sources of trust. Several refer to the three sources of human trust in machines proposed in ergonomics research; these are the designers' benevolent intention or purpose for inventing the machine, the process by which the machine works, and the machine's performance (Lee and Moray, 1992; Lee and See, 2004). Inspired by this framework, Aoki (2020) hypothesised that citizens trust AI chatbots used in the public sector (1) when they recognise the government's good intentions to use the technology to benefit its citizens (purpose); (2) when they understand how the chatbots work (process); and (3) when they perceive that the chatbots can provide adequate responses to their inquiries (performance).

We found further arguments in line with the purpose-process-performance framework. In tandem with the purpose source of trust, Lee (2021) argues that the values of AI system developers and decision makers are more important for warranting lay users' trust than users'

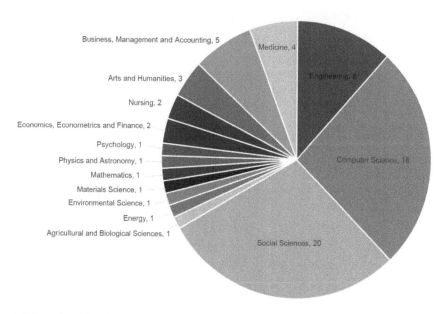

Note: Articles retrieved from Scopus were automatically tagged by Scopus with a subject area (or subject areas) from a full category list. For consistency, articles available only from the Web of Science were manually classified based on the Scopus list of subject areas. The total number of articles is 32, and a given article may be assigned to more than one subject area.

Figure 15.2   Subject areas assigned to the reviewed articles

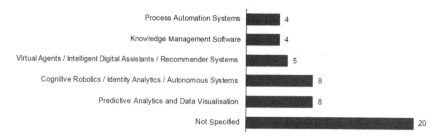

Note: The total number of articles is 32, and some articles discuss more than one type of AI.

Figure 15.3   Types of AI discussed in the literature

'epistemological understanding of [the] function and competence' (p. 5) of AI, which is hard for them to achieve. While Lee's (2021) argument suggests that the purpose source of trust is more important than the process source of trust in AI, other scholars highlight the importance of making the process accountable via XAI (Dazeley et al., 2021) and algorithmic transparency and accountability (Harrison and Luna-Reyes, 2020; Shah, 2018). Also, in regard to the process basis of trust, Aoki (2021) proposed that the 'humans-are-in-the-decision-loop (HDL) hypothesis' (i.e., communicating the assurance that humans are still involved in the decision-making process) makes a difference in the level of trust citizens place in AI-PS. As for factors related to the performance source of trust, Al-Mushayt (2019) highlights the importance of the quality of AI-enabled services.

The literature also mentions trust predictors related to the nature of the data upon which AI is built, such as credibility, integrity, interoperability, security and privacy, fairness, and unbiasedness (Anawar et al., 2019; Harrison and Luna-Reyes, 2020; Kundu, 2019; Shah, 2018; Thapa and Camtepe, 2021). Others also mention factors related to the broad institutional and regulatory environments in which AI is deployed, such as the level of trust in government itself (Al-Mushayt, 2019) and the existence of credible hard laws (Carter, 2020; Shneiderman, 2020), as well as soft laws encompassing 'the array of multi-stakeholder initiatives, standards, codes of conduct and the like' that are not enforceable by government authorities (Shank, 2021, p. 25). At the stage of system development, additional checks on AI algorithms and systems that can be run through auditing, independent oversight (Falco et al., 2021; Harrison and Luna-Reyes, 2020; Shneiderman, 2020), and multi-stakeholder participation (Harrison and Luna-Reyes, 2020) might also help to build trustworthy AI-PS.

Progress in Empirical Research on Hypothesis Testing

We found only a few empirical studies involving hypothesis testing. Each of these investigated one of three types of hypotheses, concerning

- the effects of potential users' trust in AI-PS on their intention to use it,
- the effects of AI use on trust in public services or government, and
- the predictors of trust in AI-PS.

Kuberkar and Singhal (2020) tested the first proposition using an online survey targeting public transport commuters. They attempted to investigate the association between the commuters' trust in chatbot technology used for public transport and their intention to use the chatbot and recommend it to others. Ingrams et al. (2021) tested the second proposition by conducting a vignette survey experiment with US participants recruited through TurkPrime; they examined whether the use of AI in tax return inspections, in lieu of human tax inspectors, made a difference in the participants' trust in the Internal Revenue Service. Wang et al. (2021) investigated the linkage between citizens' effective use of a tax AI voice robot and their trust in government and found it to be non-significant. Aoki (2020) focused on the third type of hypothesis and found that levels of public trust in chatbots depended on the area of public service in which they were used and argued that this was related to differences in expected levels of chatbot performance. Aoki (2021) also examined the HDL hypothesis noted earlier, using a vignette survey experiment in Japan.

We also observed the inconsistent ways in which trust is operationalised for hypothesis testing. Wang et al. (2021) followed Teo et al. (2008) and measured citizens' trust in government by using their level of agreement with the following statements: 'The AI voice robot acts in citizens' best interests,' 'I feel comfortable interacting with the AI voice robot since it generally fulfills its duties efficiently,' 'I can rely on the AI voice robot to do its part when I interact with it,' and 'I am comfortable relying on the AI voice robot to meet its obligations.' The operationalisation of citizens' trust in a chatbot in Kuberkar and Singhal (2020), based on a survey, seems to have been predicated on citizens' willingness to use AI, under the assumption that the chatbot is trustworthy. This is inferred from citizens' agreement with the following statements: 'I will use a Chatbot for public transport if it is trustworthy,' 'I will use a Chatbot for public transport if it is reliable,' and 'I will use a Chatbot for public transport if it is dependable.' Aoki (2020, 2021) asked survey respondents to directly report levels of initial trust in AI-PS and their initial trust in AI-PS relative to human agents. In contrast, Ingrams et al. (2021) did not directly ask about trustworthiness; instead, their measure of perceived trustworthiness was based on a threefold scale developed by Grimmelikhuijsen and Meijer (2014) that measures a general predisposition to trust in government, based on the government's competence, honesty, and benevolence.

AGENDA FOR FUTURE RESEARCH

In light of the dearth of empirical research on the predictors of trust in AI-PS, we propose the following propositions for future empirical research. The first set is in line with the purpose-process-performance framework:

P₁   The perceived motives of the developers of AI systems (the purpose basis of trust) have an impact on societal trust in AI-PS.

P₂   The perceived motives of policymakers and administrators in using AI systems (the purpose basis of trust) have an impact on citizens'/service users' trust in AI-PS.

P₃   The explainability of AI-PS (the process basis of trust) has an impact on societal trust in AI-PS.

P₄   The data transparency of AI-PS (the process basis of trust) has an impact on societal trust in AI-PS.

P₅   The performance of AI-PS (the performance basis of trust) has an impact on societal trust in AI-PS.

P₆   The levels of societal trust in AI and humans engaged in public sector operations differ, due in part to the difference in expected levels of their performance (the performance basis of trust).

Although it was not explicitly discussed in the articles we reviewed, we present the following proposition concerning AI literacy related to the process basis of trust:

P₇   One's AI literacy affects his or her trust in AI-PS.

The effect can be positive or negative. On one hand, experts with high AI literacy understand the processes behind AI systems well, which may eliminate their fear of AI and lead them to trust the technology. On the other hand, they might not trust AI, precisely because they understand the extent of its risks and dangers and because they do not possess the same positive expert bias towards AI that lay people with less AI literacy might have.

In addition, some of the articles we reviewed assert that the nature of the data might be an essential predictor of stakeholders' trust. Therefore, we propose that future research investigate the following proposition regarding the nature of input data:

P₈   The perceived credibility, integrity, interoperability, security and privacy, fairness, and unbiased nature of the input data for AI enhance the levels of societal trust in AI-PS.

The literature we reviewed also mentions the importance of institutional settings. In light of such arguments, future research could address the following propositions:

P$_9$ The presence of independent oversight enhances societal trust in AI-PS.

P$_{10}$ Credible (a) hard and (b) soft laws for AI enhance societal trust in AI-PS.

P$_{11}$ Trust in government is positively correlated with societal trust in AI-PS.

In addition to areas of public sector operations and services, it is possible that societal trust differs based on the type of AI system, for example, between a predictive analytical system and a virtual agent. Therefore, we posit:

P$_{12}$ Levels of societal trust in AI-PS depend on the type of AI used.

Moreover, we argue that levels of societal trust in AI-PS may differ from those in AI used in industrial and commercial settings, due to the coercive nature of public sector actions. Therefore, we propose a novel proposition, as follows:

P$_{13}$ Levels of societal trust in AI-PS of a coercive nature differ from levels of trust in similar AI systems or technologies used in industrial and commercial settings for private use, which are not coercive.

The degrees of coerciveness of AI-PS also vary among areas of public sector operations and services, as do the expected scales of impact (for example, the numbers of people affected) and the severity of possible damage, and this might also be correlated with societal trust. Accordingly, we propose the following proposition:

P$_{14}$ The strength of societal trust in AI-PS depends on the area of public sector operations and services, due to differences in (a) the coercive aspects of the services, (b) the expected scales of impact, and (c) the severity of possible harm.

We argue, in addition, that AI-PS needs to be trustworthy because increasingly autonomous AI can exercise discretion, which is a source of concern in a democratic context. In light of this, we propose the following propositions for further investigation:

P$_{15}$ Levels of social trust in AI-PS depend on the degree of discretion AI is empowered to exercise; the higher the level of discretion, the more cautious stakeholders will be about trusting AI-PS.

P$_{16}$ Levels of social trust in AI-PS differ depending on the type of political regime; in democratic regimes, stakeholders may be more cautious about trusting AI-PS than in autocracies, due to concerns about the legitimacy of discretion implemented by non-elected agents in the public sector.

Finally, the nature of trust might depend on the trusters. For instance, children, the elderly and people with disabilities might have different attitudes toward virtual agents used to respond to citizen inquiries. As discussed earlier, politicians, policymakers, and street-level bureaucrats might have reasons for trusting or not trusting AI systems based on their position within the government. Accordingly, future research could explore the following proposition:

P$_{17}$ Trust in AI-PS differs among stakeholders.

CONCLUSION

AI is revolutionising the operations of public sectors around the world. Earning trust from all stakeholders – both citizens and policymakers – is key to making a successful transition to AI-PS. Public sector agencies have unique reasons for why their use of AI must be trustworthy, primarily because of the coercive nature of their operations and services, combined with the wide-scale impact of AI-PS on society. From a democratic standpoint, the transition to algocracy necessitates that AI act as a trustworthy agent that can reliably deploy its discretion to serve the populace in a democratically conscientious manner. However, despite the importance of societal trust in AI-PS, research lags behind reality. In the SLR of articles we retrieved as of December 28, 2021, we found that there is a dearth of rigorous empirical research on this topic; hence, we developed a number of propositions worth investigating to address this gap. Testing these propositions should produce valuable insights for public managers and developers to consider as they use and develop AI-PS.

REFERENCES

Abu Dhabi Digital Authority. (2020, December 7). *Abu Dhabi Police and ADDA Launch AI System for Automated Detection of Traffic Violations.* https://www.adda.gov.ae/Media-Centre/News/Abu-Dhabi -Police-and-ADDA-launch-AI-system-for-automated-detection-of-traffic-violations
Al-Mushayt, O. S. (2019). Automating e-government services with artificial intelligence. *IEEE Access*, *7*, 146821–146829. https://doi.org/10.1109/ACCESS.2019.2946204
Alzahrani, L., Al-Karaghouli, W., and Weerakkody, V. (2017). Analysing the critical factor influencing trust in e-government adoption from citizens' perspective: A systematic review and a conceptual framework. *International Business Review*, *26*(1), 164–175. https://doi.org/10.1016/j.ibusrev.2016 .06.004
Anawar, S., Zakaria, N., Masud, Z., Zulkiflee, M., Harum, N., and Ahmad, R. (2019). IoT technological development: Prospect and implication for cyberstability. *International Journal of Advanced Computer Science and Applications*, *10*(2), 428–437. https://doi.org/10.14569/ijacsa.2019.0100256
Andrews, R., and Miller, K. J. (2013). Representative bureaucracy, gender, and policing: The case of domestic violence arrests in England. *Public Administration*, *91*(4), 998–1014. https://doi.org/10 .1111/padm.12002
Aoki, N. (2020). An experimental study of public trust in AI chatbots in the public sector. *Government Information Quarterly*, *37*(4), 101490. https://doi.org/10.1016/j.giq.2020.101490
Aoki, N. (2021). The importance of the assurance that 'humans are still in the decision loop' for public trust in artificial intelligence: Evidence from an online experiment. *Computers in Human Behavior*, *114*, 106572. https://doi.org/10.1016/j.chb.2020.106572
Barth, T. J., and Arnold, E. (1999). Artificial intelligence and administrative discretion: Implications for public administration. *The American Review of Public Administration*, *29*(4), 332–351. https://doi .org/10.1177/02750749922064463
Berryhill, J. (2019). *Report Launch – OPSI Primer on AI for the Public Sector.* Paris, France: Observatory of Public Sector Innovation. https://oecd-opsi.org/blog/ai-primer-blog/
Berryhill, J., Heang, K. K., Clogher, R., and McBride, K. (2019). *Hello, World: Artificial Intelligence and Its Use in the Public Sector.* Paris, France: Organisation for Economic Co-operation and Development. https://doi.org/10.1787/726fd39d-en
Bovens, M., and Zouridis, S. (2002). From street-level to system-level bureaucracies: How information and communication technology is transforming administrative discretion and constitutional control. *Public Administration Review*, *62*(2), 174–184. https://doi.org/10.1111/0033-3352.00168
Carter, D. (2020). Regulation and ethics in artificial intelligence and machine learning technologies: Where are we now? Who is responsible? Can the information professional play a role? *Business Information Review*, *37*(2), 60–68. https://doi.org/10.1177/0266382120923962

Danaher, J. (2016). The threat of algocracy: Reality, resistance and accommodation. *Philosophy & Technology, 29*, 245–268. https://doi.org/10.1007/s13347-015-0211-1

Dazeley, R., Vamplew, P., Foale, C., Young, C., Aryal, S., and Cruz, F. (2021). Levels of explainable artificial intelligence for human-aligned conversational explanations. *Artificial Intelligence, 299*, 103525. https://doi.org/10.1016/j.artint.2021.103525

de Vries, P., Midden, C., and Bouwhuis, D. (2003). The effects of errors on system trust, self-confidence, and the allocation of control in route planning. *International Journal of Human-Computer Studies, 58*(6), 719–735. https://doi.org/10.1016/S1071-5819(03)00039-9

Directorate-General for Communications Networks, Content and Technology (European Commission). (2019). *Ethics Guidelines for Trustworthy AI*. Brussels, Belgium: European Commission. https://data .europa.eu/doi/10.2759/177365

Dressel, J., and Farid, H. (2018). The accuracy, fairness, and limits of predicting recidivism. *Science Advances, 4*(1), 1–5. https://doi.org/10.1126/sciadv.aao5580

Falco, G., Shneiderman, B., Badger, J., Carrier, R., Dahbura, A., Danks, D., … Hart, C. (2021). Governing AI safety through independent audits. *Nature Machine Intelligence, 3*(7), 566–571. https:// doi.org/10.1038/s42256-021-00370-7

Gao, L., and Waechter, K. A. (2017). Examining the role of initial trust in user adoption of mobile payment services: An empirical investigation. *Information Systems Frontiers, 19*(3), 525–548. https:// doi.org/10.1007/s10796-015-9611-0

Gilad, S., and Dahan, M. (2021). Representative bureaucracy and impartial policing. *Public Administration, 99*(1), 137–155. https://doi.org/10.1111/padm.12681

Grimmelikhuijsen, S. G., and Meijer, A. J. (2014). Effects of transparency on the perceived trustworthiness of a government organization: Evidence from an online experiment. *Journal of Public Administration Research and Theory, 24*(1), 137–157. https://doi.org/10.1093/jopart/mus048

Gunning, D., Steflk, M., Choi, J., Miller, T., Stumpf, S., and Yang, G-Z. (2019). XAI – Explainable artificial intelligence. *Science Robotics, 4*(37). https://doi.org/10.1126/scirobotics.aay7120

Hao, K. (2019, January 21). *AI is Sending People to Jail – And Getting It Wrong*. Cambridge, MA: MIT Technology Review.

Harrison, T. M., and Luna-Reyes, L. F. (2020). Cultivating trustworthy artificial intelligence in digital government. *Social Science Computer Review, 40*(2), 494–511. https://doi.org/10.1177/ 0894439320980122

https://www.technologyreview.com/2019/01/21/137783/algorithms-criminal-justice-ai/

Ingrams, A., Kaufmann, W., and Jacobs, D. (2021). In AI we trust? Citizen perceptions of AI in government decision making. *Policy & Internet, 14*(2), 390–409. https://doi.org/10.1002/poi3.276

Kuberkar, S., and Singhal, T. K. (2020). Factors influencing adoption intention of AI powered chatbot for public transport services within a smart city. *International Journal of Emerging Technologies in Learning, 11*(3), 948–958.

Kundu, D. (2019). Blockchain and trust in a smart city. *Environment and Urbanization ASIA, 10*(1), 31-43. https://doi.org/10.1177/0975425319832392

Larson, J., Mattu, S., Kirchner, L., and Angwin, J. (2016, May 23). *How We Analyzed the COMPAS Recidivism Algorithm*. NY: ProPublica. https://www.propublica.org/article/how-we-analyzed-the -compas-recidivism-algorithm

Lee, J., and Moray, N. (1992). Trust, control strategies and allocation of function in human-machine systems. *Ergonomics, 35*(10), 1243–1270. https://doi.org/10.1080/00140139208967392

Lee, J. D., and See, K. A. (2004). Trust in automation: Designing for appropriate reliance. *Human Factors, 46*(1), 50–80. https://doi.org/10.1518/hfes.46.1.50_30392

Lee, S. S. (2021). Philosophical evaluation of the conceptualisation of trust in the NHS' Code of Conduct for artificial intelligence-driven technology. *Journal of Medical Ethics, 48*(4), 272–277. https://doi .org/10.1136/medethics-2020-106905

Levitan, D. M. (1946). The responsibility of administrative officials in a democratic society. *Political Science Quarterly, 61*(4), 562–598. https://doi.org/10.2307/2144373

Lewandowsky, S., Mundy, M., and Tan, G. (2000). The dynamics of trust: Comparing humans to automation. *Journal of Experimental Psychology: Applied, 6*(2), 104–123. https://doi.org/10.1037/1076 -898X.6.2.104

Miner, A. S., Laranjo, L., and Kocaballi, A. B. (2020). Chatbots in the fight against the COVID-19 pandemic. *NPJ Digital Medicine, 3*(65), 1–4. https://doi.org/10.1038/s41746-020-0280-0

Moray, N., Inagaki, T., and Itoh, M. (2000). Adaptive automation, trust, and self-confidence in fault management of time-critical tasks. *Journal of Experimental Psychology: Applied, 6*(1), 44–58. https://doi.org/10.1037/1076-898X.6.1.44

Muir, B., and Moray, N. (1989). Operators' trust in and use of automatic controllers. In *Proceedings of the 22nd Annual Conference of the Human Factors Association of Canada* (163–166).

New York City Police Department (NYPD). (n.d.). NYPD questions and answers: Facial recognition. NY: NYPD. https://www1.nyc.gov/site/nypd/about/about-nypd/equipment-tech/facial-recognition.page

Page, M. J., McKenzie, J. E., Bossuyt, P. M., Boutron, I., Hoffmann, T. C., Mulrow, C. D., … Brennan, S. E. (2021). The PRISMA 2020 statement: An updated guideline for reporting systematic reviews. *International Journal of Surgery, 88*, 105906. https://doi.org/10.1016/j.ijsu.2021.105906

Petrone, J. (2022, January 26). *Estonia's New Virtual Assistant Aims to Rewrite the Way People Interact with Public Services*. Estonia: E-Estonia. https://e-estonia.com/estonias-new-virtual-assistant-aims-to-rewrite-the-way-people-interact-with-public-services/

Petrović, D., Mijailović, R., and Pešić, D. (2020). Traffic accident with autonomous vehicles: Type of collisions, manoeuvres and errors of conventional vehicles' drivers. *Transportation Research Procedia, 45*, 161–168. https://doi.org/10.1016/j.trpro.2020.03.003

Rainey, H. G., Backoff, R. W., and Levine, C. H. (1976). Comparing public and private organizations. *Public Administration Review, 36*(2), 233–244. https://doi.org/10.2307/975145

Shah, H. (2018). Algorithmic accountability. *Philosophical Transactions of the Royal Society A: Mathematical, Physical and Engineering Sciences, 376*(2128), 20170362. https://doi.org/10.1098/rsta.2017.0362

Shank, C. E. (2021). Credibility of soft law for artificial intelligence – planning and stakeholder considerations. *IEEE Technology and Society Magazine, 40*(4), 25–36. https://doi.org/10.1109/MTS.2021.3123737

Shneiderman, B. (2020). Bridging the gap between ethics and practice: Guidelines for reliable, safe, and trustworthy human-centered AI systems. *ACM Transactions on Interactive Intelligent Systems (TiiS), 10*(4), 1–31. https://doi.org/10.1145/3419764

Teo, T. S. H., Srivastava, S. C., and Jiang, L. (2008). Trust and electronic government success: An empirical study. *Journal of Management Information Systems, 25*(3), 99–132. https://doi.org/10.2753/MIS0742-1222250303

Thapa, C., and Camtepe, S. (2021). Precision health data: Requirements, challenges and existing techniques for data security and privacy. *Computers in Biology and Medicine, 129*, 104130. https://doi.org/10.1016/j.compbiomed.2020.104130

Thompson, D. F. (1985). The possibility of administrative ethics. *Public Administration Review, 45*(5), 555–561. https://doi.org/10.2307/3109930

Wang, C., Teo, T. S., and Janssen, M. (2021). Public and private value creation using artificial intelligence: An empirical study of AI voice robot users in Chinese public sector. *International Journal of Information Management, 61*, 102401. https://doi.org/10.1016/j.ijinfomgt.2021.102401

Weyerer, J. C., and Langer, P. F. (2019). Garbage in, garbage out: The vicious cycle of AI-based discrimination in the public sector. In *Proceedings of the 20th Annual International Conference on Digital Government Research*. https://doi.org/10.1145/3325112.3328220

Wirtz, B. W., Weyerer, J. C., and Geyer, C. (2019). Artificial intelligence and the public sector – applications and challenges. *International Journal of Public Administration, 42*(7), 596–615. https://doi.org/10.1080/01900692.2018.1498103

Index